Beta Sigma Phi

Cook Quick
COOKBOOK

Fillet of Sole with Dill Sauce

Marinated Chicken Wings; Shrimp and Cheese Canapes; and Wrapped Chicken Livers

Beta Sigma Phi

Cook Quick COOKBOOK

Cover photograph, Strawberry-Rhubarb Souffle, recipe on page 149.

EDITORIAL STAFF

Managing Editor	Mary Jane Blount
Cookbook Editors	Georgia Brazil
	Mary Cummings
	Jane Hinshaw
	LaNita Stout
Book Design, Typography	Shirley Edmondson

© Favorite Recipes Press, A Division of Heritage House, Inc. MCMLXXXV
P. O. Box 1408, Nashville, Tennessee 37202
Library of Congress Cataloging-in-Publication Data
Main entry under title:
The Beta Sigma Phi cook quick cookbook.

Includes index.
1. Cookery, American. I. Beta Sigma Phi.
TX715.N5126 1985   641.5   85-15860
ISBN 0-87197-200-X

Contents

Meals in Minutes

Today's busy lifestyles mean that homemakers must make every minute count. We are concerned with providing our families with the best in nutrition and taste but find our time limited because of activities outside the home — careers, community work, sports, etc. But even on tight schedules, the homemaker can master the art of cooking quick and maintain the quality of "homemade."

Homemakers are continually challenged today to plan nutritious meals in minutes — the key is "flexible organization." This need to be prepared for last minute entertaining, change in family schedules, or even delays in shopping, has created a growing demand for convenience foods and quick-cooking ideas. And thanks to the generosity of Beta Sigma Phi sisters, this *Cook Quick Cookbook* will provide many proven recipes for those meals in minutes.

The best way to cook quick is to adjust your total cooking environment and schedule. Organize your time, as well as your kitchen, with precision. Keep your kitchen uncluttered, so everything will be ready for quick meal preparation. Invest in time-saving appliances — microwave ovens, blenders, food processors. All of these can save valuable time and money.

Although the need is for organization, be careful not to limit your creativity. The goal should be "flexible organization" — structured, yet viable enough for *your* lifestyle.

Organize Your Kitchen

Take an inventory of your kitchen equipment — including all utensils. Get rid of the items that you never use, and store or give away duplicate items. Now, think about where you use certain items and plan their storage accordingly. Dishes should be near the eating area and/or dishwasher, pots and pans near the stove and food staples near your work area. The time you spend rearranging your kitchen will be saved over and over as you prepare meals for your family.

One of the essentials of a totally organized kitchen is the "emergency shelf." The emergency may be unexpected dinner guests, a sudden change in plans that leaves even less time than usual, or you may have simply not had time to plan ahead. Every homemaker needs to be prepared for these occasions. The emergency shelf will be a shining example of your flexible organization — and everyone will marvel at how efficient you are, even in emergencies!

Plan several meals that can be prepared from canned goods and other convenience foods. (Remember, with thoughtful planning these can be nutritious meals too.) Add these items to your grocery list, in addition to your normal week's groceries. Store the emergency items together and DO NOT use them unless an emergency arises. When you do need them, be sure to make a note to replenish the supply on your next shopping trip. This way, you'll always be ready for any occasion.

When planning these menus, some of the items you might consider include:

CANNED GOODS: Ham, tuna, an assortment of vegetables, cream soups, fruit, pie fillings, tomato paste, pickles, jelly, brown bread, bouillon cubes.

DRY GOODS: Pasta, rice, dry soup and sauce mixes, dry milk, instant tea and coffee, non-dairy creamer, cake and frosting mixes, pancake mix, dried fruits.

Organize Your Time

Your most effective cook-quick resource is your ability to plan ahead. Start by planning menus for the whole week. Follow this menu plan closely as you make your shopping list. Be sure to add staples that are running low. This preparation for shopping may seem time-consuming at first, but will save time and eliminate the need for return trips to the supermarket. In addition to time, you'll save money if you:

1. Shop only once a week.
2. Take your shopping list and stick to it.

As you plan your shopping day, always allow extra time *after* shopping for advance preparations that will ease your workload at mealtime.

1. Divide large quantity packages and store in meal-sized portions.
2. Cook meat before storage whenever possible: brown ground beef, then store in packages for chili, meat sauces and casseroles; cook chicken and package for casseroles and salads.
3. Shape ground beef into patties, or mix and shape for meat loaves or meatballs before freezing.
4. Grate cheese and store tightly covered to use as needed.
5. Chop onions, green peppers and celery and freeze so they're ready when you need them.
6. Squeeze citrus fruit and freeze the juice in ice trays. Store in plastic bags in the freezer until needed. The rind may be grated and stored in small plastic bags in the freezer, too.

These ideas for advance preparation will take extra time on shopping day, but will save you double the time when you are preparing a meal in a hurry at the end of a busy day. And, as you use these, creative ideas of your own will continue to increase the time you save.

Menu Planning

As you look through the *Cook Quick Cookbook*, you'll find recipes that will combine to make impressive menus. This, along with your family favorites adapted for cooking quick, will enable you to plan meals that will be a pleasure to prepare and sheer delight to serve.

The main dish section in this cookbook will give you a collection of recipes that are destined to become favorites. For entertaining unexpected guests try *Drop-In Company Chicken Casserole* (page 107). With a package of the chicken that you cooked, chopped and froze on shopping day, and the addition of convenience foods from the emergency shelf, dinner will be instant delight! There are recipes to please everyone. *Quick Hawaiian Fish Fillets* (page 155) is perfect for the seafood lover, and the meat and potatoes enthusiasts will love *Beef and Potato*

Bake (page 125). Serve your family *Mushroom Tetrazzini* (page 114), a nutritious, meatless main dish that will be sure to please!

When you think cooking quick, most people think of purchased breads, muffins, and biscuits. Check through this bread section for quick tricks to make refrigerated biscuits into homemade goodies to fill your home with the delightful aroma of home-baked bread — without the long hours you'd expect!

Every meal has its crowning glory — and in the *Cook Quick* dessert section, you can find the grand finale for any meal — in minutes! Time and effort have always seemed synonymous with pie and pastry making. Convenience foods have changed that. With ready-made pie shells, pudding and pie filling mixes, fresh fruit and garnishes, you'll be serving freshly made pies year-round. Your family will also love these new twists with cake mixes. A German chocolate cake mix becomes a nutritious delight when you bake *Peanut Butter Cake* (page 58). Spread protein-rich peanut butter over the cake and then top with frosting. Guaranteed success!

Probably the quickest cooking done today is in the microwave oven. With the *Microwave Magic* section, you'll truly work magic with meals. From appetizers like *Crab Supremes* (page 144) right up to a fabulous dessert like *Strawberry-Rhubarb Souffle* (page 149), the microwave oven will help you cook quick and memorable meals.

Be sure to consider today's fabulous variety of convenience foods when planning meals. Most are of superior quality with real taste appeal — oftentimes comparable to homemade. With your ingenuity, convenience foods can become the basis for a wonderfully attractive, nutritious meal. While you have invested the very minimum time in actual preparation, your meals will have the appearance of a meal that took hours in the kitchen.

Plan your meals with an eye for color contrast, as well as taste contrast. Although you're cutting corners on the preparation time, presentation can transform simple to marvelous. Learning a few tricks for garnishes adds appeal. Most fresh vegetables can be adapted to add interest to meats and cooked vegetables. Scoop out the center of an eggplant, squash, or even a round loaf of bread — and you have a very unusual container that will be a conversation piece.

Quick Breakfast Ideas-in just minutes!

For the most important meal of the day, try these tasty breakfast ideas.

In a jiffy:
- Orange juice, oatmeal cookies spread with peanut butter, milk.

In 5 minutes:
- Tomato juice, cereal with milk, graham crackers.
- Yogurt topped with fresh strawberries, bran muffin.
- Tangerine, frozen French toast with confectioners' sugar or ground cinnamon.

In 10 minutes:
- Honeydew-melon wedge, instant hot oatmeal with milk, raisin toast with apple butter.
- Mixed fruits in quick-thaw pouch, toasted frozen waffles with syrup, ham slices.
- Two different ready-to-eat cereals mixed and topped with strawberries, milk; toast with cinnamon sugar.

In 15 minutes:

- Apricot nectar, pancakes and sausages with syrup.
- Grapefruit juice, eggs poached in milk and served on toast.

In 20 minutes:

- Cranberry juice, Canadian bacon with buttermilk biscuits, cafe au lait.
- Grapefruit sections, corned beef hash with pan-fried pineapple slices, raisin-bran toaster cakes.
- Frozen red raspberries in quick-thaw pouch, cheese omelet, crescent rolls.

Extra nice for extra special breakfasts:

- Glasses of fruit juice topped with scoops of sherbet.
- Hot gingerbread with whipped cream cheese.
- Dip tomato slices in flour to coat. Brown both sides. Great with ham and eggs!
- Corn fritters served with syrup and pork sausage links.
- Breakfast parfait: layer cereal, fruit, and ice cream!
- Heat equal parts of butter or margarine and maple-flavor syrup until butter melts. Serve on waffles or pancakes.

Mastering the art of simple sauces and toppings is another idea for pepping up quick meals. There is such a variety of tastes and textures that you'll be able to change any meal to suit your family's preferences. The following chart will introduce you to a new cooking experience!

Simple Sauces

Transform a meat, fish or poultry dish into a masterpiece just by adding a simple sauce! Basic savory sauces are few in number, but their variations are almost limitless when spices, herbs or seasonings are added. Here are some quick sauces using creamed soups as a base — so easy for today's busy cooks. Also, see Sauces on page 142.

JIFFY SAUCE	SOUP BASE	HOW TO MAKE IT
Cheese	Cream of celery, chicken or mushroom	Mix 3 tablespoons milk with ½ cup Cheddar cheese; season to taste.
Mock Hollandaise	Cream of celery, chicken or mushroom	Mix ¼ cup mayonnaise with 3 tablespoons water and 1 tablespoon lemon juice; season to taste.
Mushroom	Cream of mushroom	Mix with chopped, fresh mushrooms; season to taste.
Peppery Cheese	Cheddar cheese	Mix with cayenne pepper and Tabasco sauce to taste.
Sour Cream	Cream of celery, chicken or mushroom	Mix with ½ cup sour cream. Add milk, if needed; season to taste.
Tomato	Tomato	Saute onions and green peppers. Add a dash of Worcestershire sauce for extra flavor; season to taste.

Tip Top Toppings

Garnishing your casserole gives it a special "company" look that somehow makes it taste even better! But don't think you have to be traditional. Try these tasty toppings on your next casserole and create a brand new recipe!

Corn Bread
Mashed Potatoes
Toasted Wheat Germ
Pretzel Crumbs
Dry Stuffing Mix
Pastry Cutouts

Chow Mein Noodles
French-Fried Onion Rings
Corn or Potato Chips,
   Crushed
Sesame Seed
   or Toasted Nuts

Green Pepper Rings,
   Snipped Parsley
For a different twist,
   after baking, top
   with lemon
   or avocado slices

Making Your Own Bread Crumb Topping

Here's a great casserole topper that's easy and economical to prepare:

Toast stale bread in a 300-degree oven until crisp. Crush toasted bread in a blender or with a rolling pin. Toss with seasonings such as Parmesan cheese, oregano, curry, lemon peel, sage or thyme. One slice of bread = approximately ¼ cup crumbs.

Shortcuts to Meals in Minutes

- When missing an important ingredient, use these substitutions without altering the recipe:

    1/8 teaspoon garlic powder = 1 small pressed clove

    1/2 cup tomato sauce and 1/2 cup water = 1 cup tomato juice

    1 tablespoon prepared mustard = 1 teaspoon dry mustard

    2 tablespoons flour = 1 tablespoon cornstarch (as a thickening agent)

    3 tablespoons dry cocoa and 1 tablespoon butter = 1 square (1 ounce)
                                                   unsweetened chocolate

    1 tablespoon instant minced onion = 1 small fresh onion

- As you prepare a casserole, double the recipe. Place half in a foil-lined baking dish, and cover tightly with foil. Place in the freezer. When it's frozen solid, lift out of the baking dish. When you need a fantastic meal in a hurry, remove from freezer and place in the same baking dish for baking.

- Plan a meal with several dishes that may be baked at the same time to save both time and energy.

- Freeze chili in ice cube trays, then transfer to plastic bags for storage. Thaw and heat as needed.

- Use leftover gravy instead of cream soup in casserole dishes.

- Use your double boiler for maximum effectiveness by cooking vegetables in the bottom while you prepare white sauce or cheese sauce in the top.

- Shorten baking time for potatoes by cutting a thin slice from each end and slashing down the length of the potato.

- Use aluminum foil whenever possible to save clean-up time, as well as to seal in flavor and moistness.

- Butter French bread slices and season with garlic. Freeze slices on cookie sheet, then store in a plastic bag. Remove from freezer and heat in the oven as needed.

- Make a quick and delicious fruit compote for unexpected guests. Mix a variety of leftover fruit pieces and canned fruit, being careful not to bruise them. Serve with a mixture of the combined fruit juices and a touch of your favorite liqueur.

- Make a double batch of cookie dough and place it in frozen fruit juice concentrate cans. Refrigerate or freeze until needed. Remove the bottom of the can and push the dough out, slicing as desired. Bake according to your recipe and you'll have quick homemade cookies on the busiest day!

- When preparing a main dish casserole that is mixed in one bowl, mix it in the baking dish instead — saves clean-up time.

- Place stale bread or crackers in blender container. Process until reduced to crumbs. Store in a covered container to use as needed.

- For a quick cake "frosting," place chocolate candy bars on top of hot cake. Let stand for several seconds, then spread evenly with a knife. Another easy topping is a sprinkling of confectioners' sugar.

- Eliminate extra trips to the pantry during meal preparation by assembling all ingredients before starting.

- If your recipe calls for buttered crumbs, save time by shaking crushed wheat germ on the food instead. Gives a great flavor and is super-nutritious!

- Plan your meal preparation according to length of time each dish requires. Start with the dish that takes the longest, working the others in during cooking time. This will save time, and all the foods will be served at their best.

- When you make waffles, prepare an extra recipe and freeze the extras. Place frozen waffles (unthawed) in a hot oven for a few minutes and you'll have delicious fresh-tasting waffles any time you want them.

- When a recipe for sauces or custards calls for scalded milk, use cold milk instead. It blends just as well with less danger of curdling. A smoother product is the result, and you save the time you'd spend scalding milk and cleaning up the pan.

- Combine 1 cup confectioners' sugar and 2 tablespoons frozen lemonade and mix until smooth. Use as dessert topping on cakes, puddings or custards. Topping may be stored in refrigerator or freezer.

- Place 2 tablespoons cornstarch in 1-cup measuring cup. Fill cup with all-purpose flour and sift 3 times. Mixture is equal to 1 cup of sifted cake flour.

- To cook frozen vegetables in the oven, remove the frozen block from its package and place it on a square of foil. Put two pats butter on top; season with salt, pepper and herbs as desired. Fold foil over and tightly seal, leaving room inside the package for steam expansion. Bake at 425 degrees for 30 to 40 minutes — no messy pans and so easy.

- Always label packages and containers for the freezer. Include the name of the item and the date frozen. This will save time in finding what you want and also eliminate waste.

- When your recipe calls for sour milk, use buttermilk, or pour 1 tablespoon lemon juice or vinegar into a measuring cup. Add enough milk to equal 1 cup. Let stand for 5 minutes before using.
- Dip kitchen shears in cold water before using to chop dates, raisins, marshmallows and other sticky foods.

Microwave

- Always choose the minimum cooking time. Remember, food continues to cook after it is removed from the microwave.
- Keep your microwave clean. Built-up grease or spatters can slow cooking times.
- When poaching or frying an egg in a browning dish, always prick the center of the yolk with fork to keep the egg from exploding.
- Do not try to hard-cook eggs in the shell in a microwave. They will build up pressure and burst.
- To prevent soggy rolls, elevate rolls on roasting rack or place on paper towels while heating.
- Do not use metal dishes or aluminum foil except as specifically recommended by the manufacturer of your microwave.
- Be sure to prick potatoes before baking to allow steam to escape.
- Cut a small slit in pouch-packed frozen foods before heating to allow steam to escape.
- When placing more than one food item in microwave, arrange foods in a circle near edges of oven.
- Cover foods that need to be steamed or tenderized.
- Do not try to pop popcorn unless you have a microwave-approved corn popper.
- Use your microwave oven to melt chocolate, soften cream cheese and butter.
- Roast shelled nuts on High for 6 to 10 minutes, stirring frequently.
- Peel fruit. Place in 1 cup hot water. Microwave on High for 30 to 45 seconds; remove skins easily.
- Plump dried fruit by placing in a dish with 1 to 2 teaspoons water. Cover tightly with plastic wrap. Heat on High for ½ to 1½ minutes.
- Precook barbecued ribs or chicken until almost done, then place on the grill to sear and add a charcoal flavor.
- Soften brown sugar by placing in a dish with a slice of bread or apple. Heat on High for 30 to 45 seconds, stirring once.
- Dry bread for crumbs or croutons. Place cubed or crumbled bread on paper towels. Heat on High for 6 to 7 minutes, stirring occasionally.
- Warm baby food or bottles by removing metal lid and heating on High for 10 to 20 seconds.
- Freshen chips and crackers by heating on High for 15 to 30 seconds. Let stand for 2 to 3 minutes.
- Dry herbs by placing on paper towels and heating on High for 2 to 3 minutes or until dry.
- Ripen an avocado by heating on Low for 2 to 4 minutes.

Appetizers

Easy Avocado Appetizers, recipe on page 19.

Appetizers

Carole's Cheese Ball

1   8-ounce package cream cheese, softened
1 to 1 1/2 cups grated sharp Cheddar cheese
1 teaspoon grated onion
Garlic powder to taste
1 teaspoon Worcestershire sauce
1/2 cup chopped walnuts

Combine cheeses in bowl; mix well. Add onion, garlic powder and Worcestershire sauce. Shape into ball. Press walnuts evenly over ball. Chill, wrapped in plastic wrap, in refrigerator. Place on serving plate with crackers for spreading.

Carole Gaulden
Xi Kappa, West Palm Beach, Florida

Three-Cheese Ball

3   3-ounce packages cream cheese, softened
2   4-ounce jars Old English cheese spread
2   4-ounce jars blue cheese spread
1/2 onion, grated
1 tablespoon Worcestershire sauce
Salt and pepper to taste
1 1/2 cups chopped pecans
Chopped parsley
Paprika

Combine cheeses, onion, Worcestershire sauce, salt and pepper in bowl; mix well. Roll in mixture of pecans and parsley. Sprinkle with paprika. Chill, covered, for 3 to 5 days to improve flavor. Place on serving plate with crackers for spreading. Yield: 20-25 servings.

Minna Gross
Preceptor Kappa Kappa, Fairfield, California

Crunchy Cheese Ball

1   8-ounce package cream cheese, softened
2 cups ground ham
1/4 cup mayonnaise
1 tablespoon minced onion
2 tablespoons chopped parsley
1/4 teaspoon dry mustard
Chopped nuts

Combine all ingredients except nuts in bowl; mix well. Shape into ball. Roll in nuts, coating evenly. Chill in refrigerator. Place on serving plate.

Judith Deir
Kappa Kappa, Newcastle, Ontario, Canada

Ole Cheese Ball

2   8-ounce packages cream cheese, softened
1 cup grated sharp Cheddar cheese
1 medium avocado, mashed
1 small onion, minced
1 can chopped green chilies, drained
1 teaspoon garlic powder
Salt to taste
1/2 cup chopped pecans

Combine cheeses with next 5 ingredients; mix well. Shape into ball. Chill in refrigerator. Roll in pecans, coating evenly. Place on serving plate with crackers for spreading.

Donna Emerson
Omega, Whitefish, Montana

Bonnie's Pineapple-Cheese Ball

1   8-ounce package cream cheese, softened
1/2 cup crushed pineapple, well drained
1 teaspoon seasoned salt
1 tablespoon chopped green pepper
1 tablespoon chopped green onion
1 cup chopped nuts

Combine first 5 ingredients and half the nuts in bowl; mix well. Shape into ball. Chill in refrigerator. Roll in remaining nuts, coating evenly. Place on serving plate with crackers for spreading.

Bonnie A. Schnoor
Beta, Abqaiq, Saudi Arabia

Salmon Cheese Ball

1   16-ounce can salmon, drained
2   8-ounce packages cream cheese, softened
1 tablespoon grated onion
1 teaspoon Worcestershire sauce
Dash of Tabasco sauce
Chopped parsley

Combine salmon and next 4 ingredients in bowl; mix well. Shape into ball. Roll in parsley, coating evenly. Place on serving plate with red onion rings and crackers for spreading.

Linda Fisher
Preceptor Epsilon Epsilon, Hollywood, Florida

Black Bread Cheese Dip

1 1/2 pounds Old English cheese, grated
1/4 pound Roquefort cheese, crumbled
2 tablespoons butter, softened
2 tablespoons grated onion
1 tablespoon Worcestershire sauce
1/4 teaspoon dry mustard
1 small bottle of beer
2 loaves dark rye bread

Combine cheeses, butter, onion, Worcestershire sauce, mustard and beer in blender container. Process until smooth. Scoop out center of 1 loaf bread to form shell; cut center and remaining loaf bread into bite-sized pieces. Pour cheese mixture into bread shell. Place on serving plate. Arrange bread pieces around shell for dipping.

Mary Ann Madar
Preceptor Beta Alpha, Elizabeth, Pennsylvania

Appetizers

Victoria's Broccoli Dip

- 1 10-ounce package frozen chopped broccoli
- 1/2 bunch green onions, chopped
- 1 teaspoon garlic salt
- 1/2 teaspoon lemon juice
- 1/2 teaspoon Worcestershire sauce
- 2 cups mayonnaise
- Salt to taste
- 1 round loaf bread

Cook broccoli using package directions; drain. Combine broccoli, green onions, garlic salt, lemon juice, Worcestershire sauce, mayonnaise and salt in bowl; mix well. Scoop out center of loaf to form shell; cut center into bite-sized pieces. Place loaf on serving plate. Spoon dip into bread shell. Arrange bread pieces and assorted vegetables around bread shell for dipping.

Victoria Shepley
Xi Epsilon Mu, Harrow, Ontario, Canada

Hot Cheese-Broccoli-Mushroom Dip

- 1 can golden mushroom soup
- 2 cans mushrooms
- 1 10-ounce package frozen chopped broccoli, cooked
- Salt to taste
- Garlic powder to taste
- 1 8-ounce package Velveeta cheese, softened, chopped

Combine soup, mushrooms, broccoli and seasonings in blender container. Process until well mixed. Pour into saucepan. Add cheese. Cook until cheese is melted, stirring frequently. Pour into serving dish. Serve with assorted chips and crackers.

Jane Brown
Xi, Honolulu, Hawaii

Spicy Chicken Dip

- 1 can cream of mushroom soup
- 1 8-ounce package cream cheese
- 1 5-ounce can chunk chicken
- 1/8 teaspoon garlic powder
- 1/8 teaspoon pepper
- 1 3-ounce package slivered almonds
- 1 2-ounce can sliced mushrooms, drained
- 1/2 teaspoon Worcestershire sauce

Combine all ingredients in saucepan. Cook over medium heat until heated through, stirring frequently. Serve hot with chips. Yield: 3 cups.

Beckey Epley
Xi Omicron Gamma, Dallas, Texas

Chili Chip Dip

- 1 8-ounce package cream cheese, softened
- 1 15-ounce can chili without beans
- 1 medium green pepper, finely chopped
- 1 medium onion, finely chopped
- 2 cups Monterey Jack cheese
- 1 cup chopped black olives (opt.)

Spread cream cheese on 12-inch serving platter. Heat chili in saucepan. Spread over cream cheese. Layer green pepper, onion, cheese and black olives on chili. Chill in refrigerator. Serve with tortilla chips or crackers.

Susan Schwan
Alpha Sigma, Devils Lake, North Dakota

Tangy Cottage Cheese-Tomato Juice Dip

- 1/2 cup tomato juice
- 1 medium onion, chopped
- 1 tablespoon finely chopped green pepper
- 1 cup tomato juice
- 1 24-ounce carton low-fat cottage cheese
- 1 teaspoon Beau Monde seasoning
- 1 tablespoon hot horseradish
- 1/4 teaspoon garlic salt
- 1/8 teaspoon pepper
- 2 teaspoons oregano
- Several drops of red or yellow food coloring
- 1/4 cup Parmesan cheese

Combine 1/2 cup tomato juice, onion and green pepper in blender container. Process for 30 seconds. Add 1 cup tomato juice, half the cottage cheese and seasonings. Process for 1 minute. Add remaining cottage cheese and food coloring. Process for 30 seconds. Stir in Parmesan cheese with wooden spoon. Spoon into serving dish. Chill for several hours. Serve with assorted vegetables, fruits and crackers for dipping. Yield: 25-30 servings.
Note: May store this low-calorie dip in refrigerator for several days to use as needed for parties or weight-conscious family snacks.

Norma Grace Bauer
Laureate Alpha Epsilon, Altamont, Illinois

Nadine's Dip

- 2 cups mayonnaise
- 2 cups small curd cottage cheese
- 1 cup sour cream
- 1 package ranch-style dressing mix

Combine mayonnaise, cottage cheese and sour cream in bowl; mix well. Stir in dressing mix. Store in refrigerator. Serve with potato chips and vegetables for dipping.
Note: May serve as salad dressing or with baked potatoes.

Mary Coulter
Preceptor Laureate Eta, Moberly, Missouri

Appetizers

Hot Crab Dip

2   7-ounce cans crab meat
3   3-ounce packages cream
    cheese with chives

Dash of Worcestershire
    sauce
Dash of Tabasco sauce

Combine all ingredients in bowl; mix well. Spoon into small baking dish. Bake at 350 degrees for 20 to 30 minutes. Place baking dish and dish of wheat crackers for dipping on warming tray to serve.

Marlene McDougall
Beta Theta, Goderich, Ontario, Canada

Quick Cucumber Dip

1 medium cucumber,
    peeled, grated
1/2 small onion, grated

1/4 cup salt
2 cups sour cream

Combine cucumber and onion in colander. Sprinkle with salt. Let stand for 1 hour. Rinse well; drain. Mix with sour cream in bowl. Spoon into serving dish. Serve with potato chips.

Eleanor S. Mackey
Preceptor Omega, Waynesboro, Virginia

Dill Dip

2 cups sour cream
2 cups mayonnaise
5 tablespoons parsley
    flakes
5 tablespoons onion flakes

5 teaspoons Beau
    Monde seasoning
5 teaspoons dillweed
1 round loaf
    pumpernickel

Mix sour cream, mayonnaise, parsley and onion flakes, seasoning and dillweed in bowl. Chill for several hours or overnight. Scoop out center of loaf to form shell; cut center into bite-sized pieces. Spoon dip into bread shell. Place on serving platter with bread pieces and assorted vegetables for dipping.

Connie Beuoy
Preceptor Beta Mu, Carmel, Indiana

Hot Mustard Dip

1   4-ounce can
    dry mustard
1 cup white vinegar

1 cup sugar
1 teaspoon salt
2 eggs, beaten

Mix dry mustard and vinegar in top of double boiler. Let stand overnight. Add sugar, salt and eggs. Boil for 10 minutes; cool. Pour into glass jar. Store in refrigerator. Serve with pretzels, deep-fried vegetables or Chinese food for dipping. Yield: 3 cups.

Susan Thomason
Xi Alpha Rho, Danville, Kentucky

Joan's Fruit Dip

1   8-ounce package cream
    cheese, softened
1   8-ounce jar
    marshmallow creme
Fresh pineapple chunks

Bananas, sliced
Strawberries
Orange wedges
Banana, sliced

Combine cream cheese and marshmallow creme in bowl; mix well. Chill in refrigerator. Arrange fruit around edge of serving platter. Place bowl of dip in center. Yield: 2 cups.

Joan Gilman
Xi Alpha Beta, Council Bluffs, Iowa

Garlene's Fruit Dip

3/4 cup packed
    brown sugar
1/4 cup confectioners'
    sugar

1   8-ounce package cream
    cheese, softened
1 teaspoon vanilla extract
3 tablespoons milk

Cream brown sugar, confectioners' sugar and cream cheese in bowl until light and fluffy. Blend in vanilla. Stir in milk 1 tablespoon at a time until of desired consistency. Spoon into serving bowl. Serve with strawberries, apples, bananas and other fruits for dipping. Yield: 2 cups.

Garlene Knight
Preceptor Beta Epsilon, Cedar Rapids, Iowa

Kahlua Fruit Dip

1 cup sour cream
1 cup whipped topping
3/4 cup packed brown sugar

1/3 cup Kahlua
1   6-ounce package
    chopped peanuts

Combine sour cream and whipped topping in bowl; mix well. Blend brown sugar and Kahlua in bowl. Add sour cream mixture and peanuts; mix well. Spoon into serving bowl. Serve with cherries, bananas and other summer fruits for dipping.

Suzanne Mantooth
Iota Chi, Chesterfield, Missouri

16

Appetizers

Chipped Beef Double-Do

4 3-ounce packages cream
   cheese, softened
1/4 cup sour cream
1 3-ounce package thinly
   sliced beef, chopped

1 small green pepper,
   finely chopped
2 scallions, chopped
Garlic powder to taste
Seasoned salt to taste

Combine cream cheese and sour cream in mixer bowl; beat until smooth. Add remaining ingredients; mix well. Spoon into serving dish. Serve with chips for dipping.
Note: May reduce sour cream to 2 tablespoons and shape into ball. Chill, wrapped in plastic wrap. Roll in 1/2 cup chopped pecans. Serve with crackers for spreading.

Cecelia A. Perez
Xi Mu Xi, Spring, Texas

Beef Taco Dip

1 pound ground beef
1/4 cup chopped onion
1 3-ounce package cream
   cheese, softened
1 6-ounce can
   tomato paste

1 8-ounce can
   tomato sauce
1 package chili
   seasoning mix
1/2 teaspoon salt
1/2 teaspoon pepper

Brown ground beef with onion in skillet, stirring frequently; drain. Combine cream cheese, tomato paste, tomato sauce and seasonings in Crock·Pot; mix well. Stir in ground beef. Cook until heated through. Serve with nacho-flavored tortilla chips. Yield: 20 servings.

Marilyn Schoneman
Theta Rho, New Hampton, Iowa

Chili Con Queso

1 pound ground beef
2 pounds Velveeta
   cheese, chopped

1 12-ounce can
   picante sauce

Brown ground beef in skillet, stirring until crumbly; drain. Add cheese; stir until cheese melts. Stir in picante sauce. Cook until heated through. Spoon into chafing dish. Serve with chips for dipping.
Note: Add a small amount of milk if necessary to make of desired consistency.

Judy Bard
Alpha Omega Phi, New Boston, Texas

Guacamole

2 medium avocados, mashed
1 teaspoon lemon juice
1 3-ounce package cream
   cheese, softened
1/2 teaspoon chili powder

1/2 teaspoon onion salt
1/2 teaspoon garlic powder
Hot pepper sauce to taste
1 tomato, peeled, seeded,
   chopped (opt.)

Combine avocados, lemon juice and next 4 ingredients in bowl; mix well. Stir in hot pepper sauce and tomato. Serve with nacho-flavored tortilla chips.

Edwina L. Cage
Preceptor Gamma Omega, Amarillo, Texas

Chili Dip

1 4-ounce can
   diced chilies
2 4-ounce cans
   chopped olives
3 medium tomatoes, chopped

4 to 6 green
   onions, chopped
2 tablespoons vinegar
1 tablespoon oil

Combine all ingredients in serving bowl; mix well. Chill overnight to blend flavors. Serve with corn chips.

Bee Grimm
Preceptor Gamma Kappa, Stockton, California

Layered Taco Dip

1 can bean dip
1 can refried beans
1 cup hot guacamole
1 cup mild guacamole
2 tablespoons
   mayonnaise
2 tablespoons
   sour cream

1 package taco
   seasoning mix
Cheddar cheese, grated
Monterey Jack
   cheese, grated
Chopped tomatoes
Sliced black olives
Chopped green onions

Mix bean dip and beans in bowl. Spread in 9 x 13-inch dish. Combine guacamoles, mayonnaise, sour cream and taco seasoning mix in bowl; mix well. Spread over bean mixture. Layer cheeses, tomatoes, olives and green onions over guacamole mixture. Serve with chips.

Lea Ann Lord
Alpha Epsilon Epsilon, Seminole, Texas

Appetizers

Pam's Taco Dip

2 medium avocados,
   mashed
1 tablespoon
   lemon juice
Salt and pepper
   to taste
3/4 cup sour cream
3/4 package taco
   seasoning mix

1/4 cup mayonnaise
1 can bean dip
Grated cheese
1 small onion, chopped
1 medium tomato,
   chopped
1 8-ounce can black
   olives, chopped

Mix avocados, lemon juice, salt and pepper in small bowl; set aside. Combine sour cream, taco seasoning mix and mayonnaise in bowl; mix well. Layer bean dip, avocado mixture and sour cream mixture on serving dish. Sprinkle with cheese. Top with onion, tomato and olives. Serve with corn chips or tortilla chips.

Pam Nesius
Xi Alpha Zeta, Glenrock, Wyoming

Tex-Mex Dip

2 cans bean dip
3 medium avocados,
   mashed
2 tablespoons
   lemon juice
1/2 teaspoon salt
1/4 teaspoon pepper
1 cup sour cream
1 package taco
   seasoning mix

1/2 cup mayonnaise
1 large bunch green
   onions, chopped
3 medium tomatoes,
   chopped
1 6-ounce can pitted
   black olives, sliced
1/2 pound sharp Cheddar
   cheese, grated

Spread bean dip on large serving platter. Spoon mixture of avocados, lemon juice, salt and pepper over bean dip. Spread mixture of sour cream, taco seasoning mix and mayonnaise over top. Layer green onions, tomatoes and olives over sour cream mixture. Sprinkle with cheese. Serve with tortilla chips.

Loretta S. Armstrong
Alpha Beta Phi, APO New York
Carol Zysset
Delta Beta, Williamsport, Pennsylvania

Peanut Butter Dip

1 cup sour cream
1 cup peanut butter

3 ounces frozen orange
   juice concentrate

Combine sour cream, peanut butter and juice concentrate in bowl; mix well. Chill, covered, for several hours or overnight. Serve with celery sticks, carrot strips, apple wedges or pretzels for dipping. Yield: 2 cups.

Grace M. Baylor
Preceptor Alpha, Waynesboro, Pennsylvania

Jan's Spinach Dip

1 10-ounce package
   frozen chopped
   spinach, thawed
1/2 cup sour cream
1/2 cup mayonnaise
1/4 cup chopped
   green onions
1/2 teaspoon dillweed

1 1/2 teaspoons fresh
   lemon juice
1/2 teaspoon
   seasoned salt
1/4 cup chopped parsley
Several drops of
   Tabasco sauce
1 head red cabbage

Press spinach in sieve to drain well. Mix with remaining ingredients except cabbage in large bowl. Chill, covered, for 24 hours. Scoop out center of cabbage to form bowl. Reserve center of cabbage for other use. Spoon dip into cabbage bowl to serve. Place on serving platter. Arrange assorted crackers around edge for dipping.

Jan Johnson
Nu Delta, Burlington, Kansas

Quick and Easy Spinach Dip

2 10-ounce packages
   frozen chopped
   spinach
1 cup mayonnaise
1 cup sour cream

1 can water
   chestnuts, chopped
1 small onion, chopped
1 package dry vegetable
   soup mix

Cook spinach according to package directions; drain well. Combine spinach, mayonnaise, sour cream, water chestnuts, onion and soup mix in serving bowl; mix well. Chill for several hours. Serve with corn chips, assorted crackers or party-sized dark bread.

Wanda McGough
Delta Pi, Montgomery, Alabama

Spinach Dip a la Jana

1 10-ounce package
   frozen chopped
   spinach
2 cups mayonnaise

1/4 cup chopped parsley
1/4 cup finely chopped
   green onions

Cook spinach according to package directions; drain well. Mix with remaining ingredients in serving bowl. Chill overnight. Serve with assorted crackers and fresh vegetables for dipping.

Jana Mabry
Alpha Omega Phi, New Boston, Texas

Appetizers

Sue's Cheese-Shrimp Fondue

2 rolls garlic cheese
1 can cream of
   shrimp soup

2 4-ounce cans shrimp
1 2-ounce can
   sliced mushrooms

Melt cheese with soup in double boiler, stirring to blend well. Add drained shrimp and mushrooms. Cook just until heated through. Pour into fondue pot. Serve with toasted cubes of French bread or crackers.

Rita Eichelzer
Xi Eta Zeta, Emmetsburg, Iowa

Marlene's Shrimp Dip

1 8-ounce package
   cream cheese,
   softened
1/2 cup mayonnaise
1/4 cup milk
1 tablespoon Accent

1/2 tablespoon dillweed
1/8 teaspoon
   Tabasco sauce
1 teaspoon minced onion
1 7-ounce can shrimp,
   drained, rinsed

Combine cream cheese, mayonnaise and milk in bowl; mix until smooth. Add seasonings and onion; mix well. Stir in shrimp. Spoon into serving bowl. Chill for 2 hours. Yield: 6 servings.

Marlene J. Baucum
Xi Xi, Phoenix, Arizona

Nancy's Shrimp Dip

1 1/2 cups chopped
   shrimp
1 8-ounce package
   cream cheese
1/2 cup mayonnaise

1 green onion,
   finely chopped
1 teaspoon
   Worcestershire sauce
Garlic salt to taste

Place all ingredients in blender container. Process until smooth. Pour into serving bowl. Chill for several hours. Serve with assorted fresh vegetables for dipping. Yield: 2 cups.

Nancy Watson
Xi Gamma, El Cajon, California

Dianne's Shrimp Dip

1 8-ounce package
   cream cheese,
   softened
1/4 cup salad dressing
1 teaspoon lemon juice

Dash of Tabasco sauce
1 stalk celery, chopped
2 green onions, chopped
1 7-ounce can
   shrimp, drained

Combine cream cheese and salad dressing in bowl; mix until smooth. Stir in lemon juice and Tabasco sauce. Add celery, green onions and shrimp; stir gently. Spoon into serving bowl. Serve with assorted crackers for dipping.

Dianne Wilson
Zeta Epsilon, Orangeville, Ontario, Canada

Easy Avocado Appetizers

2 California avocados,
   peeled, seeded
1/2 cup red chili salsa

3/4 cup mild Cheddar
   cheese, grated

Slice each avocado into 8 wedges; arrange on baking sheet. Spoon salsa into center of each wedge. Sprinkle cheese over top. Broil until cheese melts. Remove to serving plate. Serve with flour tortilla squares or crisp corn chips.

Photograph for this recipe on page 13.

Cassinedas

1 package 8-inch
   flour tortillas
1/2 pound Monterey
   Jack cheese, shredded

1/2 pound Colby
   cheese, shredded
Chopped green onions

Heat oiled griddle to 350 to 375 degrees. Place tortilla on griddle. Sprinkle with cheese and onions. Cook until cheese begins to melt. Fold tortilla in half to enclose filling. Cook until cheese is melted. Cool on paper towels. Repeat for all tortillas. Cut each tortilla into 4 pieces. Arrange on serving plate. Serve with sour cream, taco sauce or guacamole.

Sonie Durbin
Alpha Sigma, Devil's Lake, North Dakota

Hot Cheese Puffs

2 cups shredded
   sharp cheese
1/2 cup butter,
   softened
1 cup flour

1 teaspoon freeze-
   dried chives
1/2 teaspoon
   seasoned salt

Combine cheese and butter in bowl; mix well. Add remaining ingredients; mix well. Shape into 1-inch balls. Place on ungreased baking sheet. Chill, covered, for up to 48 hours. Bake at 400 degrees for 15 to 20 minutes or until golden brown. Arrange on serving dish. Yield: 3 dozen.

Phyllis B. Painter
Preceptor Omega, Staunton, Virginia

Appetizers

Cheese Wafers

1 stick margarine,
   softened
1 cup grated
   sharp cheese
1 cup flour

1 teaspoon salt
1/4 teaspoon red pepper
1 cup crisp
   rice cereal

Combine margarine and cheese in bowl. Mix in flour, salt and red pepper with hands. Add rice cereal; mix well. Shape into small balls. Place on baking sheet. Press with fork to flatten. Bake at 350 degrees for 20 minutes or until brown. Yield: 6 dozen.

Buena Snellgrove
Xi Alpha Psi, New Brockton, Alabama

Little Burritos

1 8-ounce package
   cream cheese,
   softened
1 8-ounce carton
   sour cream
1 to 2 4-ounce cans
   chopped green chilies

3/4 cup shredded
   Cheddar cheese
1/4 cup hot salsa
1 1/4 teaspoons
   garlic salt
10 to 12 corn tortillas

Combine first 6 ingredients in bowl; mix well. Spread on tortillas. Roll gently to enclose filling. Chill for 3 hours to overnight. Slice into bite-sized pieces. Arrange on serving plate.

Dorothy Bodenstab
Pi Chi, Alma, Missouri

Olive-Cheese Balls

1 4-ounce jar cheese
   spread with bacon
1/4 cup butter,
   softened
3/4 cup flour

Dash of Tabasco sauce
Dash of Worcestershire
   sauce
36 olives

Combine first 5 ingredients in bowl; mix well. Shape into balls around olives. Place on baking sheet. Bake at 400 degrees for 15 minutes. Arrange on serving dish. Yield: 3 dozen.

Chris Kebert
Laureate Beta Omicron, Harlingen, Texas

Parmesan Bows

3 8-count cans
   refrigerator
   buttermilk biscuits
1 1/2 cups oil
2 1/2 teaspoons
   garlic powder

1 tablespoon
   parsley flakes
1 tablespoon oregano
1/4 teaspoon pepper
1/2 cup Parmesan cheese

Cut each biscuit into 3 pieces. Roll each piece into rope and tie in knot. Place on baking sheet. Bake using package directions. Combine remaining ingredients in shallow dish; mix well. Add hot bows. Let stand for 2 to 3 hours or until liquid is absorbed, stirring every 15 minutes. Store, covered, in aluminum foil pans for short periods; place in freezer for longer periods. Bake at 350 degrees until heated through to serve. Yield: 6 dozen.

Donna Roth
Preceptor Beta Epsilon, Marion, Iowa

Tomato-Cheese Rounds

1/2 cup grated
   Cheddar cheese
1/2 cup mayonnaise
3 tablespoons minced
   green pepper
1/4 cup minced onion
1/2 teaspoon
   garlic powder

1/2 teaspoon
   cayenne pepper
1/2 teaspoon salt
1 loaf party
   rye bread
Tomatoes, thinly sliced
Bacon bits
Paprika

Combine first 7 ingredients in bowl; mix well. Place bread slices on baking sheet. Broil until toasted on one side. Turn bread over. Top each slice with tomato slice, dollop of cheese mixture, bacon bits and sprinkle of paprika. Broil for 3 to 5 minutes or until bubbly. Yield: 8-10 servings.

Nancy Watson
Xi Gamma, El Cajon, California

Date with a Ritz

1 15-ounce can
   sweetened
   condensed milk
1 cup chopped dates
1 cup chopped nuts
1 box Ritz crackers

1 cup confectioners'
   sugar
1 to 2 teaspoons milk
1 teaspoon vanilla
   extract

Combine sweetened condensed milk, dates and nuts in saucepan. Simmer for 4 minutes, stirring constantly; cool. Place 1 teaspoon mixture on each cracker. Arrange on baking sheet. Bake for 6 minutes. Drizzle with mixture of remaining ingredients. Yield: 8 dozen.

Gaye Tow
Xi Beta Nu, Oklahoma City, Oklahoma

Appetizers

Ripe Olive Quiche, recipe below.

Cheese Tarts

1 onion, chopped
8 to 10 slices
    crisp-fried
    bacon, crumbled

2 cups grated
    mozzarella cheese
24 baked tartlet shells
24 mushroom slices

Saute onion in skillet until tender. Layer bacon, onion and cheese in tartlet shells. Top with mushroom slice. Place on baking sheet. Bake at 400 degrees until heated through and cheese melts. Yield: 2 dozen.

Bev Delucry
Delta Kappa, Mississauga, Ontario, Canada

Grape Appetizers

Green seedless grapes
1 3-ounce package
    cream cheese,
    softened

1 3-ounce
    package slivered
    almonds

Make lengthwise cut halfway through grapes from stem end. Stuff with a small amount of cream cheese. Place 1 or 2 slivered almonds in cream cheese. Arrange on serving dish.

Joan Stockman
Laureate Omega, Arvada, Colorado

Ripe Olive Quiche

1 10-ounce package
    frozen patty
    shells, thawed
2 eggs, beaten
1 8-ounce package
    cream cheese,
    softened

2 cups chopped
    ripe olives
1 2-ounce can rolled
    anchovies with capers
1/2 cup grated
    Fontina cheese
1/2 cup Parmesan cheese

Knead patty shells together. Roll out on lightly floured surface. Press into 10-inch fluted tart pan. Beat eggs with cream cheese until light and fluffy. Pour into pastry shell. Layer olives, anchovies, Fontina and Parmesan cheeses over cream cheese mixture. Bake at 400 degrees for 40 minutes or until brown. Cut into thin wedges. Serve hot or cold.

Photograph for this recipe above.

Appetizers

Mexican Quiche Appetizers

1 cup grated
  Swiss cheese
1 cup grated
  Cheddar cheese
5 eggs, beaten
1 4-ounce can
  chopped green chilies

Mix cheeses in greased 9 x 13-inch baking dish. Pour eggs over cheese. Sprinkle with chilies. Bake at 350 degrees for 20 to 30 minutes or until set. Cool for 5 minutes before cutting into squares.

Lynn Olive
Preceptor Delta Alpha, Lee's Summit, Missouri

Mini Quiches

1 recipe 4-crust
  pie pastry
12 slices crisp-fried
  bacon, crumbled
3/4 cup shredded
  Swiss cheese
1/4 cup finely
  chopped scallions
4 eggs
1 1/2 cups light cream
1/2 teaspoon salt
1/4 teaspoon
  white pepper
1/4 teaspoon nutmeg
Paprika

Roll out pastry 1/4 at a time on floured surface. Cut into 2 1/2 to 3 1/2-inch circles. Fit into tartlet cups. Sprinkle bacon, cheese and scallions into tartlets. Combine eggs, cream, salt, pepper and nutmeg in bowl; mix well. Spoon into shells. Sprinkle with paprika. Bake at 350 degrees for 20 to 25 minutes or until centers are set. Yield: 40 servings.

Rita Eichelzer
Xi Eta Zeta, Emmetsburg, Iowa

Ground Beef Hors d'Oeuvres

1 pound ground beef
1/2 teaspoon
  garlic salt
1 teaspoon oregano
1 pound hot sausage
1/2 teaspoon
  Worcestershire sauce
1/2 teaspoon
  fennel seed
1 pound Velveeta
  cheese, chopped
1 1/2 loaves party
  rye bread

Brown ground beef with garlic salt and oregano in skillet, stirring until crumbly; drain well. Brown sausage with Worcestershire sauce and fennel seed in skillet, stirring until crumbly; drain. Add ground beef mixture and cheese; stir until well mixed. Place 1 tablespoon on each slice rye bread. Place on baking sheet. Bake at 400 degrees for 10 to 12 minutes or until bubbly. Serve warm.

Mary Dunworth
Xi Alpha Beta, Coldwater, Michigan

Appetizer Meatballs

1 pound ground beef
1/4 cup minced onion
1/4 cup cornflake
  crumbs
1/2 cup milk
1/4 cup chili sauce
1 teaspoon salt
1/4 teaspoon pepper
2 tablespoons flour
2 tablespoons instant
  coffee powder

Combine ground beef with next 6 ingredients in bowl; mix well. Shape into 36 tiny meatballs. Place in 9 x 13-inch baking dish. Bake at 400 degrees for 12 to 15 minutes or until brown. Drain, reserving 1/4 cup pan juices. Blend flour into 1/4 cup cold water in saucepan. Stir in coffee powder and reserved drippings. Cook until thick, stirring constantly. Combine flour mixture and meatballs in chafing dish. Serve with toothpicks.

Susan Aldrich
Gamma Omega, McCall, Idaho

Cocktail Meatballs

1 1/2 pounds
  ground beef
1/4 cup (about)
  bread crumbs
1 teaspoon each Accent,
  garlic powder
1 teaspoon each salt
  and pepper
1 1/2 teaspoons
  mustard
1 egg
1 12-ounce bottle
  of chili sauce
1/2 cup grape jelly
1 medium onion, sliced

Combine ground beef with next 7 ingredients in bowl; mix well. Shape into 36 small meatballs. Brown in a small amount of oil in skillet; drain. Mix chili sauce, jelly and onion in saucepan. Add meatballs. Simmer for 1 1/2 hours. Serve in chafing dish. Yield: 3 dozen.

Melodee Thompson
Alpha Sigma, Devil's Lake, North Dakota

Linda's Cocktail Meatballs

2 pounds ground beef
1 envelope dry onion
  soup mix
1 cup dry bread crumbs
2 eggs
2 tablespoons Accent
1 24-ounce bottle
  of catsup
1 8-ounce jar
  apple jelly

Combine ground beef with next 4 ingredients in bowl; mix well. Shape into small balls. Fry in small amount of oil in skillet, browning evenly on all sides; drain. Mix catsup and jelly in saucepan. Add meatballs. Simmer for 1 1/2 hours. Spoon into chafing dish. Serve with toothpicks.

Linda Stull
Delta Kappa, Parkersburg, West Virginia

22

Appetizers

Pizza Meatballs

1 pound ground beef
1 cup Italian-style
   dry bread crumbs
2 tablespoons
   minced onion
1 teaspoon garlic salt

1/8 teaspoon pepper
4 ounces mozzarella
   cheese
1 24-ounce jar
   pizza sauce
Parmesan cheese

Combine ground beef with next 4 ingredients in bowl; mix well. Cut mozzarella cheese into 24 cubes. Shape ground beef mixture into balls around cheese cubes, enclosing cheese completely. Place in lightly greased 9 x 13-inch baking dish. Bake at 350 degrees for 20 to 25 minutes or until brown. Bring pizza sauce to a simmer in saucepan. Combine with meatballs in chafing dish. Sprinkle with Parmesan cheese. Serve with toothpicks.

Marla Thomas
Delta Beta, Montoursville, Pennsylvania

Reuben Sandwich Hors d'Oeuvre

12 ounces Swiss cheese
1 10-ounce can
   sauerkraut
4 4-ounce packages
   sliced corned beef

1/4 cup Thousand Island
   salad dressing
1 loaf party
   rye bread

Melt cheese over low heat in saucepan. Add sauerkraut, corned beef and salad dressing; mix well. Cook until heated through. Spoon into chafing dish. Serve with rye bread. Yield: 12-20 servings.

Sharon E. Denil
Xi Beta Alpha, Appleton, Wisconsin

Barbecued Chicken Wings

Chicken wings

Barbecue sauce

Cut wings into 3 pieces, discarding tip portions. Cook in water to cover in saucepan for 20 minutes; drain. Place on baking sheet with shallow sides. Bake at 350 degrees for 30 minutes. Brush with barbecue sauce. Arrange on serving plate.
Note: May cook on grill instead of in oven.

Melanie Kaminski
Gamma Kappa, Rockledge, Florida

Deviled Ham Balls

1 7-ounce can
   deviled ham
2 tablespoons
   minced onion

1 8-ounce package
   cream cheese,
   softened
1 cup chopped pecans

Combine deviled ham, onion and cream cheese in bowl; mix well. Shape into small balls. Roll in pecans, coating evenly. Arrange on serving plate; place toothpick in each ball. Yield: 2 dozen.

Joyce Moore
Xi Zeta, Charleston, South Carolina

Pinwheels

1 3-ounce package
   cream cheese,
   softened
1/2 teaspoon
   prepared mustard
1/2 teaspoon
   horseradish

1/2 teaspoon
   parsley flakes
1 8-count can
   refrigerator crescent
   dinner rolls
4 slices boiled ham

Combine first 4 ingredients in bowl; mix well. Separate roll dough into 4 rectangles, pressing perforations to seal. Spread with cream cheese mixture. Top with ham slice. Roll from narrow side as for jelly roll. Cut each roll into 8 slices. Place on baking sheet. Bake at 375 degrees for 12 minutes. Yield: 32 servings.

Nancy Ingman
Preceptor Iota Kappa, Corona del Mar, California

Dragon Puffs

1/2 pound hot sausage
2 teaspoons
   hoisin sauce
2 scallions,
   finely chopped

Salt to taste
2 10-count cans
   refrigerator rolls
2 cups (or more) oil
   for deep frying

Brown sausage in skillet, stirring until crumbly; drain. Add hoisin sauce, scallions and salt; mix well. Roll out rolls into thin circles on floured surface. Place about 1 teaspoon sausage mixture on each roll. Pull edges up to enclose filling; seal well. Deep-fry in hot oil until golden brown; drain. Yield: 20 servings.

Frieda Y. Ross
Preceptor Alpha Zeta, Pleasant Garden, North Carolina

Appetizers

Goobies

1 pound hot sausage
1 poung ground beef
1 onion, finely
  chopped
2 pounds Velveeta
  cheese, cubed

2 tablespoons
  Worcestershire sauce
Salt and pepper
  to taste
3 to 4 loaves party
  rye bread

Brown sausage, ground beef and onion in skillet, stirring frequently; drain. Add cheese and seasonings, stirring to melt cheese. Spread on rye bread. Place on baking sheet. Broil until bubbly.

Nora Conyers
Preceptor Epsilon, Fairbury, Nebraska

Anita's Hot Sausage Appetizers

1 pound hot sausage
3 cups baking mix

1 small jar Cheez Whiz
1/2 cup milk

Combine all ingredients in bowl; mix well. Shape into 1-inch balls. Place on ungreased baking sheet. Bake at 400 degrees for 15 to 20 minutes or until brown.

Anita M. Wilson
Laureate Alpha Mu, Mansfield, Ohio

Hot Sausage Squares

1 1/2 pounds hot sausage
1 onion, chopped
2 eggs, beaten
1/2 cup grated
  Swiss cheese

1/2 cup Parmesan cheese
3 cups baking mix
1 cup milk
1/3 cup mayonnaise
1 egg yolk, beaten

Brown sausage and onion in skillet, stirring frequently. Drain mixture and cool. Stir in eggs and cheeses. Combine baking mix, milk and mayonnaise in bowl; mix well. Pat half the dough into ungreased 10 x 15-inch baking pan. Top with sausage and remaining dough. Brush with egg yolk. Bake at 375 degrees for 30 minutes. Cut into squares; serve hot.

Laura R. Babcock
Exemplar Preceptor, Athens, Pennsylvania

Sausage Balls

3 cups baking mix
1 pound sausage

12 ounces Cheddar
  cheese, grated

Combine all ingredients in bowl; mix well. Shape into balls. Place on baking sheet. Bake at 350 degrees for 15 minutes. Yield: 20 servings.

Theresa A. Wise
Beta, Abqaiq, Saudi Arabia

Sausage Croissants

1 8-count can
    refrigerator
    crescent rolls
1/2 pound sausage
1 8-ounce can sliced
    mushrooms, drained

3 tablespoons
    Parmesan cheese
2 tablespoons
    melted butter
3 tablespoons
    Parmesan cheese

Separate rolls on waxed paper. Mix sausage, mushrooms and 3 tablespoons Parmesan cheese in bowl. Place spoonful of sausage mixture on each roll. Roll from large end to enclose filling. Fit into paper-lined muffin cups. Bake at 325 degrees for 35 minutes. Brush with melted butter. Sprinkle with additional Parmesan cheese. Yield: 8 croissants.

Pamela Majoras
Omicron Pi, Vermilion, Ohio

Barbecued Wieners with Mystery Sauce

1 24-ounce jar
    grape jelly

1 6-ounce jar mustard
2 to 4 pounds wieners

Mix jelly and mustard in saucepan. Heat until jelly melts, stirring constantly. Cut wieners into bite-sized pieces. Add to sauce. Simmer for 5 minutes. Spoon into chafing dish. Serve with toothpicks.

Margaret Bell
Theta, Oklahoma City, Oklahoma

Bonelos Uhang (Shrimp Fritters from Guam)

1 cup baking mix
Salt and pepper
  to taste
1/4 teaspoon
  garlic powder
1/4 cup milk
2 eggs, beaten

1 pound chopped shrimp
1/2 10-ounce package
  frozen baby peas
1 4-ounce can
  chopped mushrooms,
  drained
Oil for deep frying

Combine dry ingredients in bowl. Add milk and eggs; mix well. Stir in shrimp, peas and mushrooms. Drop by teaspoonfuls into hot oil. Deep-fry until golden brown; drain. Yield: 3 dozen.
Note: May thin batter with additional milk if necessary.

Gillian Peitzmeyer
Zeta Phi, St. Mary's, Georgia

Appetizers

Crab Meat Appetizers on English Muffins

6 English muffins
1 6-ounce jar
   Cheez Whiz
1 6-ounce can
   crab meat
1 stick butter,
   softened

1 1/2 teaspoons
   mayonnaise
1/4 teaspoon
   garlic powder
1/2 teaspoon
   seasoned salt

Split English muffins in half; place on baking sheets. Combine remaining ingredients in bowl; mix well. Spread on muffins. Cut each muffin into quarters. Freeze until firm. Store in freezer bags. Place on baking sheet. Broil for 10 minutes or until golden brown. Serve warm. Yield: 4 dozen.

Sally A. Luman
Pi Beta, Aurora, Illinois

Gulf Coast Appetizer

1/4 cup margarine,
   softened
1 3-ounce package
   cream cheese,
   softened
1 4-ounce can chopped
   green chilies
1 6-ounce can shrimp
1 6-ounce can
   crab meat

5 or 6 dashes of
   Tabasco sauce
1 cup grated
   Cheddar cheese
24 Melba rounds
2/3 cup sour cream
1/4 teaspoon salt
1/2 cup grated
   Cheddar cheese
Paprika

Cream margarine and cream cheese in bowl until fluffy. Add next 5 ingredients; mix well. Spread 1 teaspoonful on each Melba round. Combine sour cream, salt and 1/2 cup Cheddar cheese in small bowl. Spread small dollop on each round. Sprinkle with paprika. Place on baking sheet. Bake at 325 degrees for 15 minutes. Yield: 2 dozen.

Mary Lou Szymanski
Xi Pi Psi, Eagle Lake, Texas

Artichokes in Sauce

1 10-ounce package
   frozen artichokes
1/4 cup melted butter
2 tablespoons
   lemon juice

2/3 cup mayonnaise
1/2 tablespoon
   celery salt
1/4 cup Parmesan cheese

Cook artichokes in saucepan using package directions. Drain and chop artichokes. Add butter, lemon juice, mayonnaise and celery salt; mix well. Spoon into greased ovenproof serving dish. Sprinkle with cheese. Bake at 450 degrees for 10 minutes. Serve with crackers. Yield: 6-8 servings.

Betty Bower
Preceptor Delta, Pompano Beach, Florida

Hungarian Mushrooms

1 large onion, chopped
6 tablespoons butter
2 tablespoons flour
2 tablespoons milk
3/4 cup sour cream
3/4 teaspoon salt

1/4 teaspoon each
   pepper, paprika
1 1/4 pounds fresh
   mushrooms, sliced
3/4 cup sour cream

Saute onion in butter in skillet. Sprinkle flour over onion. Stir in milk and 3/4 cup sour cream. Bring to a simmer, stirring constantly. Add seasonings and mushrooms. Simmer, covered, for 5 minutes, stirring occasionally. Stir in remaining 3/4 cup sour cream. Cook just until heated through. Pour into chafing dish. Serve with crackers or small pastry shells.

Mary Ann Madar
Preceptor Beta Alpha, Elizabeth, Pennsylvania

Donna's Marinated Mushrooms

3/4 cup oil
1/3 cup wine vinegar
2 tablespoons
   lemon juice
1 tablespoon
   chopped chives

1 small clove of
   garlic, chopped
1 teaspoon each
   salt, tarragon
1/2 teaspoon sugar
1 pound mushrooms

Combine all ingredients except mushrooms in bowl; mix well. Add mushrooms, tossing to coat well. Chill, covered, for 2 hours to 2 weeks. Place in serving dish; serve with toothpicks.

Donna Bennett
Xi Zeta Zeta, Colby, Kansas

Mushroom Party Snacks

1 pound fresh mushrooms
3/4 cup mashed potato
1/4 cup cottage cheese

2 tablespoons dry onion
   soup mix
2 teaspoons milk

Wash mushrooms and pat dry. Remove stems and chop. Combine chopped stems with remaining ingredients in bowl; mix well. Spoon mixture into mushroom caps. Place on baking sheet. Bake at 375 degrees for 15 minutes. Arrange on serving dish. Yield: 12 servings.

Pat M. Henry
Xi Alpha Kappa, Clyde, North Carolina

Appetizers

Hazel's Spinach Balls

3 eggs
1 10-ounce package
    frozen chopped
    spinach
1 cup herb-flavored
    stuffing mix
1 onion, grated

1/2 cup Parmesan cheese
1/2 stick butter,
    melted
1/2 teaspoon
    poultry seasoning
1/2 teaspoon each
    salt and pepper

Beat eggs in bowl until foamy. Add well-drained spinach and remaining ingredients; mix well. Shape into 18 balls. Place on baking sheet. Bake at 325 degrees for 15 minutes or until golden brown. Serve hot or cold. Yield: 1 1/2 dozen.

Hazel Minerich
Laureate Alpha Nu, Sedro-Woolley, Washington

Spinach Hors d'Oeuvres

3 eggs
1 cup flour
1 teaspoon each
    baking powder,
    salt
1 cup milk

1 pound Monterey Jack
    cheese, grated
2 10-ounce packages
    frozen chopped
    spinach
1 stick butter

Beat eggs in bowl. Add flour, baking powder, salt and milk; mix well. Stir in cheese and well-drained spinach. Melt butter in 9 x 13-inch baking dish. Pour spinach mixture into dish. Bake at 350 degrees for 35 minutes. Cut into squares when cool. Yield: 40 servings.

Marjorie Anderson Dakin
Laureate Xi, Spokane, Washington

Spinach Squares

1 cup flour
1 teaspoon salt
1 teaspoon
    baking powder
2 eggs, beaten
1 stick margarine,
    melted

1 cup milk
1/2 cup chopped onion
1 10-ounce package
    frozen spinach,
    cooked
1 pound Cheddar
    cheese, grated

Combine first 6 ingredients in bowl; mix well. Add onion, spinach and cheese; mix well. Spoon into greased 9 x 13-inch baking pan. Bake at 350 degrees for 30 to 35 minutes or until set. Cut into bite-sized squares when cool.
Note: May freeze squares and reheat at 350 degrees for 10 minutes to serve.

Linda A. Tondryk
Alpha Theta, Holcomb, New York

Corrine's Breadsticks

1 package pita-
    bread rounds

Margarine, softened
Krazy salt

Split pita-bread rounds open. Spread inside of each round with margarine. Sprinkle with salt. Cut each round into 1/2-inch strips. Place on baking sheet. Bake at 350 degrees for 15 minutes.

Corrine Soper
Preceptor Theta, Selinsgrove, Pennsylvania

Herbed Breadsticks

1/2 pound margarine,
    softened
2 teaspoons
    chopped parsley
1 teaspoon chives
1 teaspoon marjoram

1 teaspoon garlic salt
1 teaspoon tarragon
3 tablespoons toasted
    sesame seed
24 very thin bread
    slices, trimmed

Combine margarine with seasonings in bowl; mix well. Spread on bread slices. Cut each slice into 4 strips. Place on baking sheet. Bake at 250 degrees for 30 minutes. Turn oven off. Let stand in closed oven for 30 minutes. Cool. Store in airtight container for several weeks. Yield: 8 dozen.

JoAnn J. Kresky
Preceptor Chi, Lansing, Michigan

Cracker Snacks

2 11-ounce packages
    oyster crackers
1 1/2 cups oil
1/4 teaspoon
    lemon pepper

1/4 teaspoon
    garlic powder
1/4 teaspoon dillweed
1 envelope ranch-style
    salad dressing mix

Place crackers in large bowl. Combine remaining ingredients in small bowl; mix well. Pour over crackers; toss to coat well. Let stand in covered container for 8 hours to overnight, stirring occasionally.

LaVerne Dees
Xi Gamma, APO, New York

Dilled Crackers

1 cup oil
1 envelope ranch-style
    salad dressing mix
2 tablespoons dillweed

1/4 teaspoon
    garlic powder
1 12-ounce package
    oyster crackers

Heat oil in saucepan. Blend in salad dressing mix and seasonings. Pour over crackers in bowl; toss to coat well. Let stand for 3 hours, stirring frequently.

Agnes Weibel
Theta Eta, Rochester, Michigan

Appetizers

Seasoned Crackers

2 teaspoons dillweed
2 teaspoons garlic salt
1 envelope ranch-style
   salad dressing mix

3/4 cup oil
2 12-ounce packages
   oyster crackers

Combine first 4 ingredients in small bowl; mix well. Pour over crackers in bowl; toss to coat well. Place in airtight container. Let stand for 2 hours or longer before serving.

Cynthia Holtmeyer
Pi, Brunswick, Missouri

Cracker-Butter Crunch

12 ounces salted gold
   fish crackers
1 1/2 cups seedless
   raisins
1 1/2 cups peanuts
1 cup margarine,
   melted

1/2 cup sugar
1/2 cup packed light
   brown sugar
2 tablespoons light
   corn syrup
2 teaspoons
   vanilla extract

Mix crackers, raisins and peanuts in 10 x 15-inch baking pan. Bake at 250 degrees for several minutes. Combine margarine, sugars, corn syrup and 2 tablespoons water in saucepan; mix well. Cook to 270 degrees on candy thermometer, stirring constantly. Stir in vanilla. Remove cracker mixture from oven. Pour syrup over cracker mixture, tossing to coat well. Spread on baking sheets to cool; break into pieces. Yield: 6 cups.

Grace M. Baylor
Preceptor Alpha, Waynesboro, Pennsylvania

Cheerios Nuggets

6 cups Cheerios
1 cup salted peanuts
1 cup raisins
4 cups pretzel sticks
1 cup packed
   brown sugar

1/2 cup margarine
1/4 cup light
   corn syrup
1/2 teaspoon salt
1/2 teaspoon soda

Mix first 4 ingredients in bowl. Combine brown sugar, margarine, corn syrup and salt in saucepan. Bring to a simmer. Cook for 2 minutes, stirring constantly; remove from heat. Stir in soda. Pour over cereal mixture; toss to coat well. Spread on 10 x 15-inch baking pan. Bake at 250 degrees for 15 minutes; stir. Let stand for 30 minutes before breaking into pieces. Yield: 12 cups.

Dee McBride
Nu Delta, Burlington, Kansas

Onion Toasties

1 envelope dry
   onion soup
   mix

2 sticks butter,
   softened
1 loaf bread, trimmed

Mix soup mix and butter in bowl. Spread on bread slices. Cut each slice into 3 strips. Place on baking sheet. Bake at 400 degrees for 7 minutes or until crisp. Yield: 15-20 servings.

Dianne Wilson
Zeta Epsilon, Orangeville, Ontario, Canada

Harvest Popcorn

4 quarts popped popcorn
Salt to taste
3 tablespoons
   melted butter
2 cups salted peanuts
1 teaspoon onion powder

1/2 teaspoon
   garlic powder
1 teaspoon
   lemon pepper
1 teaspoon dillweed

Season popcorn with salt and butter in bowl. Stir in peanuts. Sprinkle with mixture of remaining seasonings. Spread in two 9 x 13-inch baking pans. Bake at 350 degrees for 6 minutes. Store in airtight container. Yield: 4 1/2 quarts.

Shirley Fryatt
Laureate Alpha Sigma, Federal Way, Washington

Sugared Nuts

1 egg white
1/2 cup sugar
1/2 teaspoon nutmeg
1/2 teaspoon cinnamon

1 cup walnuts
1 cup pecans
1 cup cashews

Beat egg white with 1 teaspoon water in mixer bowl until stiff. Beat in sugar and spices. Fold in nuts. Spread on ungreased baking sheet. Bake at 250 degrees for 1 hour, stirring every 15 minutes.

Gloria Hillegass
Xi Alpha Rho, Danville, Kentucky

Ham and Dillwiches

6 slices Swiss cheese
6 slices boiled ham
1/4 cup mayonnaise
1/2 teaspoon
   minced onion

1 teaspoon steak sauce
1 large dill pickle,
   cut into 6 strips
6 club rolls, split

Place cheese slices on ham slices. Mix mayonnaise, onion and steak sauce in bowl. Spread over cheese. Top with pickle strip. Roll up ham to enclose pickle. Place in rolls on baking sheet. Bake at 400 degrees for 8 to 10 minutes or until heated through. Yield: 6 servings.

Judy Smallstey
Preceptor Beta Zeta, Mansfield, Ohio

Appetizers

Broiled Ham Sandwiches

8 ounces Velveeta
  cheese, cubed
1 pound bacon,
  crisp-fried,
  crumbled

1 pound ham, ground
Mayonnaise
10 English
  muffins, split

Combine cheese, bacon and ham in bowl. Add enough mayonnaise to moisten; mix well. Spread on muffin halves. Place on baking sheet. Broil until bubbly. Yield: 20 servings.

Lois Lawler
Preceptor Beta Epsilon, Cedar Rapids, Iowa

Pizzawiches

1 1/2 pounds
  ground beef
1/2 cup grated
  Cheddar cheese
1 tablespoon
  chopped onion
1 3-ounce can black
  olives, sliced

1 can tomato soup
1/2 teaspoon oregano
3/4 teaspoon
  garlic salt
1 12-count package
  hamburger buns
Grated mozzarella
  cheese

Brown ground beef in skillet, stirring until crumbly; drain. Combine next 6 ingredients in bowl. Add ground beef; mix well. Spread mixture on hamburger bun halves. Place on baking sheet. Bake at 250 degrees for 5 minutes. Sprinkle with mozzarella cheese. Broil until cheese melts.
Yield: 24 servings.

Diann L. Fowlkes
Delta Upsilon, Newman Grove, Nebraska

Stuffed Roll Snack

1 pound ground beef
1/2 onion, chopped
1 can cream of
  mushroom soup

1/2 teaspoon salt
1/2 teaspoon pepper
10 sourdough rolls

Brown ground beef with onion in skillet, stirring frequently. Add soup and seasonings; mix well. Simmer for 5 minutes. Cut rolls in half crosswise. Scoop out inside of rolls, reserving shells. Crumble half the scooped-out bread into ground beef mixture. Spoon mixture into reserved bread shells. Place on baking sheet. Bake at 350 degrees for 15 to 20 minutes or until heated through.

Jane Smith
Xi Sigma, Lakeland, Florida

Upside-Down Sandwiches

1/2 cup bread crumbs
1 tablespoon
  chopped onion
1/2 cup milk

1 pound ground beef
1 egg, beaten
6 slices bread
1/4 cup butter

Combine bread crumbs, onion and milk in bowl. Let stand for 15 minutes or until liquid is absorbed. Add ground beef and egg; mix well. Saute one side of each bread slice in butter in skillet until golden brown. Spread beef mixture on other side. Place beef side down in skillet. Cook until beef is browned. Serve hot. Yield: 6 servings.

Lila Warrell
Preceptor Upsilon, Muncie, Indiana

Avocado Soup

4 ripe avocados
3 cups cold
  chicken broth
2 teaspoons
  lime juice

1/2 teaspoon salt
1/8 teaspoon
  garlic powder
2 cups cream, chilled

Place avocados, broth, lime juice, salt and garlic powder in blender container. Process until smooth. Stir in the cream. Chill in refrigerator. Pour into soup bowls. Garnish with lemon slices. Yield: 6 servings.

Zunny McLellan
Alpha Phi, Fort McMurray, Alberta, Canada

Chilled Carrot Soup

1 cup chopped onion
1 1/2 teaspoons
  curry powder
2 tablespoons oil
3 1/2 cups
  chicken broth
4 cups sliced carrots
1 cup sliced celery

1 bay leaf
1/2 teaspoon cumin
1/2 teaspoon
  Tabasco sauce
1 cup low-fat milk
1 cup low-fat
  cottage cheese

Saute onion and curry powder in oil in large saucepan for 3 to 5 minutes. Add chicken broth, carrots, celery, bay leaf, cumin and Tabasco sauce; mix well. Simmer for 25 minutes or until vegetables are tender. Remove bay leaf. Spoon into blender container 1/4 at a time. Process until smooth. Process milk and cottage cheese in blender container until smooth. Stir into carrot mixture. Chill until serving time. Serve with additional Tabasco sauce. Yield: 7 cups.

Photograph for this recipe on opposite page.

Appetizers

Chilled Carrot Soup, recipe on page 28. Chilled Zucchini Soup, recipe below.

Delicious Cold Soup

1 can chicken and
   rice soup
1 teaspoon curry powder

1 small can
   evaporated milk
Juice of 1/2 lemon

Combine all ingredients in blender container. Process until smooth. Chill in refrigerator. Pour into soup bowls.

Erma M. Bischoff
Laureate Delta, Louisville, Kentucky

Danish-Style Cucumber Soup

2 medium cucumbers,
   peeled, sliced
1 medium leek, sliced
2 bay leaves
2 tablespoons butter
1 tablespoon flour
1 teaspoon salt
3 cups chicken broth

1 medium cucumber,
   peeled, seeded,
   grated
1 cup light
   cream, chilled
Juice of 1/2 lemon
Fresh chopped dill

Saute sliced cucumbers with leek and bay leaves in butter in skillet until tender. Stir in flour and salt. Cook until bubbly. Add broth gradually, stirring constantly. Simmer for 20 to 30 minutes. Press through sieve into bowl. Chill. Add grated cucumber, cream, lemon juice and a small amount of dill. Season to taste. Spoon into chilled cups. Top with dollop of sour cream. Yield: 6 servings.

Zunny McLellan
Alpha Phi, Fort McMurray, Alberta, Canada

Chilled Zucchini Soup

3 1/2 cups chicken
   broth
8 cups sliced zucchini
1 cup chopped onion
1 clove of garlic,
   chopped
1 teaspoon basil

1/2 teaspoon salt
1/2 teaspoon
   Tabasco sauce
1/2 cup low-fat milk
1/2 cup low-fat
   cottage cheese

Combine chicken broth, zucchini, onion, garlic, basil, salt and Tabasco sauce in large saucepan. Simmer for 15 minutes or until vegetables are tender. Spoon into blender container 1/4 at a time. Process until smooth. Process milk and cottage cheese in blender until smooth. Stir milk mixture into zucchini mixture. Chill until serving time. Yield: 7 cups.

Photograph for this recipe above.

Appetizers

Shelly's Cheese Spread

1 8-ounce package
cream cheese,
softened
1/2 cup mayonnaise
5 slices crisp-fried
bacon, crumbled

1 tablespoon chopped
green onion
1/4 teaspoon dillweed
1/8 teaspoon pepper
1 1/4 cups whole
almonds

Combine all ingredients except almonds in bowl; mix well. Chill in refrigerator. Shape into ball or log. Cover with almonds. Place on serving plate.

Shelly Magneson
Xi Beta Nu, Des Moines, Iowa

Crab Delight

Shredded lettuce
1 cup chopped
cooked shrimp
2 8-ounce packages
cream cheese,
softened
2 8-ounce packages
frozen crab
meat, thawed

1 12-ounce bottle
of seafood
cocktail sauce
Triscuit crackers

Arrange lettuce on 7 x 12-inch serving platter. Combine shrimp and cream cheese in bowl; mix well. Shape into 2 rolls. Place on lettuce. Flake crab meat and pat dry. Sprinkle around shrimp rolls. Drizzle seafood sauce over all. Serve with Triscuit crackers. Yield: 20 servings.

Paulette Klaja
Xi Delta Lambda, Pittsburgh, Pennsylvania

Crab Meat Spread

4 3-ounce packages
cream cheese,
softened
2 tablespoons
mayonnaise
1 tablespoon
chopped onion
1 teaspoon lemon juice

1 teaspoon
Worcestershire sauce
Garlic salt to taste
1/2 14-ounce bottle
of chili sauce
1 6-ounce can crab
meat, drained
Chopped parsley

Combine cream cheese with next 5 ingredients in bowl; mix well. Place in serving dish. Top with chili sauce, flaked crab meat and parsley. Serve with crackers for spreading.

Joyce Moore
Xi Zeta, Charleston, South Carolina

Crab Pate

1 1/2 envelopes
unflavored gelatin
1 can cream of
mushroom soup
1 6-ounce can crab
meat, drained

1 8-ounce package
cream cheese,
softened
3/4 cup mayonnaise
1 small onion, grated
1 cup chopped celery

Soften gelatin in 3 tablespoons cold water. Bring soup to a simmer in saucepan. Add gelatin, stirring to dissolve well. Add remaining ingredients; mix well. Pour into oiled 4-cup mold. Chill until firm. Unmold on serving plate; garnish with parsley. Serve with crackers. Yield: 4 cups.

Mary Lee Bowman
Laureate Eta, Warner Robins, Georgia

Quick-as-a-Wink Spread

1 8-ounce package
cream cheese
1 2-ounce
jar horseradish

1 6-ounce jar
seafood sauce

Place cream cheese on serving plate. Spread horseradish over top. Drizzle seafood sauce over top and edges of cream cheese. Serve with crackers.

Cindy Nicol
Xi Alpha Chi, Peterborough, Ontario, Canada

Salmon Spread

1 16-ounce can salmon
1 8-ounce package
cream cheese,
softened

1 teaspoon liquid smoke
1 teaspoon lemon juice
Onion flakes to taste

Combine all ingredients in bowl; mix well. Spoon into serving bowl. Serve with crackers for spreading.

Lois Lawler
Preceptor Beta Epsilon, Cedar Rapids, Iowa

Sandwich Spread

1 pound pressed ham
2 large onions
6 hard-boiled eggs

4 large pickles
Salad dressing

Combine ham, onions, eggs and pickles in food processor. Process with chopping blade until chopped. Mix with enough salad dressing in bowl to make of spreading consistency. Spread on sandwiches.

Suzie Walden
Alpha Chi, Pope Air Force Base, North Carolina

Apple-Apricot Cooler, Frothy Apple Juice Cooler, Surprise Spicy Refresher, recipes on pages 32 and 33.

Beverages

Apple-Apricot Cooler

2 quarts apple
  juice, chilled
1 quart apricot
  nectar, chilled
1/4 cup lime juice
1 quart club
  soda, chilled
1/2 teaspoon
  peppermint extract

Combine all ingredients in pitcher; mix well. Pour over crushed ice in chilled glasses. Garnish with strips of lemon rind. Yield: 4 quarts.

Photograph for this recipe on page 31.

Frothy Apple Juice Cooler

1 quart chilled
  apple juice
1 pint vanilla ice
  cream, softened
1 8-ounce can crushed
  pineapple, drained
1/2 teaspoon cinnamon

Combine all ingredients in blender container. Process until frothy. Pour into glasses. Garnish with pineapple cubes on skewers and mint sprigs. Yield: 2 quarts.

Photograph for this recipe on page 31.

Apricot Brandy Punch

5 cups orange juice
3 cups lemon juice
1 cup gin
2 fifths apricot Brandy
2 quarts tonic water
1/2 cup sugar

Chill all liquid ingredients in refrigerator. Combine with sugar in punch bowl; mix well. Add ice ring. Yield: 6 quarts.

Sonia Redfield
Beta Theta, Laurel, Maryland

Diana's Banana Punch

4 cups sugar
1 32-ounce can
  pineapple juice
1 6-ounce can frozen
  orange juice
  concentrate
1 6-ounce can frozen
  lemonade concentrate
6 bananas
2 to 3 quarts
  ginger ale

Bring sugar and 6 cups water to a boil in saucepan; mix well. Chill in refrigerator. Combine with juices in large freezer container. Mix bananas with a small amount of juice mixture in blender container. Process until smooth. Add to juice mixture. Freeze until slushy. Thaw for 1 hour before serving. Combine with chilled ginger ale in punch bowl; mix gently. Yield: 2 gallons.

Diana Allen
Preceptor Alpha Zeta, Grand Prairie, Texas

Cold Quack

1 10-ounce can Fresca
1 10-ounce can
  sugar-free black
  cherry cola
1 tablespoon
  apple cider
1 tablespoon
  cider vinegar

Combine all ingredients in pitcher; mix well. Chill in refrigerator. Serve over ice in glasses. Yield: 4 servings.

Prexy Pegram
Preceptor Eta Beta, Boerne, Texas

Cranapple Punch

3/4 cup sugar
1 teaspoon whole cloves
6 1-inch
  cinnamon sticks
2 cups Burgundy (opt.)
2 quarts cranapple
  juice cocktail

Combine sugar and spices with 3/4 cup water in saucepan. Simmer for 10 minutes; strain. Mix with remaining ingredients in pitcher. Chill in refrigerator. Pour into punch bowl; garnish with thinly sliced orange.

Jo Anne Robinson
Preceptor Gamma Nu, Cincinnati, Ohio

Deep Freeze Daiquiris

2 6-ounce cans
  frozen pink
  lemonade concentrate
1 6-ounce can frozen
  limeade concentrate
2 10-ounce packages
  frozen strawberries,
  thawed
1 fifth light rum

Combine all ingredients with 4 1/2 cups water in large pitcher. Process 1/2 at a time in blender until smooth. Freeze for 12 hours. Thaw for 30 minutes before serving; stir to mix well. Yield: 2 quarts.

Sandra Hackney
Delta Omega, Shawnee, Oklahoma

Delicious Punch

3 bananas
Juice of 3 lemons
1 46-ounce can
  pineapple juice
2 cups sugar
1 2-liter bottle
  of 7-Up
3 small packages
  lemon-lime drink mix

Mash bananas with lemon juice. Combine with remaining ingredients and 2 quarts water in large freezer container. Freeze until slushy. Serve in punch bowl. Yield: 20 servings.

Marie Farmer
Xi Zeta Epsilon, Noblesville, Indiana

Beverages

Frozen Bacardis

1   6-ounce can frozen
       limeade concentrate
6 ounces rum
1 jigger grenadine

2 tablespoons
    confectioners' sugar
1 limeade can rum

Combine all ingredients and 1 cup ice in blender container. Process until smooth. Add ice to fill container, processing until mixture is smooth after each addition. Serve immediately or store in freezer, allowing several minutes to thaw slightly before serving. Yield: 5 cups.

Dianne Strand
Alpha Sigma, Devil's Lake, North Dakota

Fruit Punch

2   3-ounce packages
       apricot gelatin
2 cups sugar
1   46-ounce can
       pineapple juice

1 1/2 cups orange juice
1 cup lemon juice
3 to 4 large bottles
    of ginger ale

Dissolve gelatin in 1 cup hot water in punch bowl. Add sugar; stir until well mixed. Stir in 7 cups cold water and remaining ingredients. Yield: 40 servings.

Mary Allen
Chi Gamma Rho, Columbus, Georgia

Lou's Luau Punch

2   48-ounce cans
       unsweetened
       pineapple juice
1   16-ounce can cream
       of coconut

1 quart light rum
1 ounce almond extract
1   6-ounce can frozen
       lemonade concentrate
1 quart club soda

Combine pineapple juice, coconut cream, rum and almond flavoring in 8-quart punch bowl; mix well. Add lemonade concentrate and 3 lemonade cans water. Stir in club soda gently at serving time. Garnish with thinly sliced lemon and pineapple juice and fruit ice rings. Yield: 7-8 quarts.

Mary Louise Graham
Xi Zeta Lambda, Titusville, Florida

Party Punch

1   46-ounce can
       pineapple juice
1   12-ounce can
       frozen orange
       juice concentrate

1   12-ounce can frozen
       lemonade concentrate
1   26-ounce bottle
       of ginger ale

Combine juices with 1 to 1 1/2 quarts water in large container. Freeze 1 portion in ring mold if desired. Combine remaining punch with ginger ale in punch bowl. Add ice ring. Yield: 50 servings.

Dee McBride
Nu Delta, Burlington, Kansas

Strawberry Tea Punch

16 teaspoons
       instant tea
1   12-ounce can frozen
       lemonade concentrate

2   10-ounce packages
       frozen strawberries,
       thawed
1 cup sugar

Dissolve tea in 1 gallon water in large container. Combine remaining ingredients in mixer bowl; mix well. Add to tea. Serve over cracked ice in punch bowl. Yield: 20 servings.

Janielle Riley
Xi Zeta Epsilon, Westfield, Indiana

Summertime Slush

4 tea bags
1 1/2 cups sugar
2   6-ounce cans
       frozen orange
       juice concentrate

2   6-ounce cans frozen
       lemonade concentrate
2 cups whiskey
7-Up

Bring 2 cups water to a boil in saucepan. Add tea bags; steep until tea is very strong. Combine with sugar, juices, whiskey and 5 to 7 1/2 cups boiling water in large freezer container. Freeze for 24 hours or longer. Place 1 scoop mixture in glass; fill with 7-Up.

Pat Livingston
Gamma Kappa, Cocoa, Florida

Surprise Spicy Refresher

1 cup sugar
1 cup apple juice
1 1/2 teaspoons
    cinnamon
1/2 teaspoon cloves

1/4 teaspoon ginger
10 cups apple juice
1 quart chilled
    pineapple juice
1/4 cup lemon juice

Combine sugar, 1 cup apple juice and spices in saucepan. Boil for 3 minutes. Cool. Combine with 10 cups apple juice and remaining ingredients in punch bowl. Add ice cubes. Garnish with lemon slices. Serve in chilled mugs with cinnamon stick stirrers. Yield: 4 quarts.

Photograph for this recipe on page 31.

Beverages

Winning Tea Punch

1 cup instant tea
1 6-ounce can frozen limeade concentrate
1 6-ounce can frozen lemonade concentrate
1 6-ounce can frozen pineapple juice concentrate
1 pint cranberry juice cocktail

Combine all ingredients and 2 quarts water in punch bowl; mix well. Add ice at serving time. Yield: Twenty-five 5-ounce servings.

Dorothy Droste
Laureate Alpha Kappa, Alton, Illinois

Tom and Jerry Mix

12 eggs, separated
1 16-ounce box brown sugar
1 16-ounce box confectioners' sugar
1 teaspoon cream of tartar
1/4 teaspoon salt
1 teaspoon vanilla extract

Beat egg yolks in bowl until thick and lemon colored. Mix in brown sugar. Blend confectioners' sugar into stiffly beaten egg whites. Fold egg whites and remaining ingredients gently into egg yolks. Store in refrigerator for up to 2 weeks. Stir before using. Mix 2 tablespoons mix with one jigger of whiskey in mug. Fill with hot water. Sprinkle with nutmeg. Yield: 32 servings.

Maxine Olson
Alpha Iota, American Falls, Idaho

Tequila Punch

6 to 12 ounces Tequila
1 12-ounce can frozen lemonade concentrate
Lemon juice
Salt

Combine Tequila, lemonade concentrate and 3 lemonade cans water in pitcher; mix well. Fill blender container 1/2 full of mixture. Add cracked ice to fill. Process until smooth. Pour into punch bowl. Repeat with remaining Tequila mixture. Serve in glasses with rims dipped in lemon juice and salt.

Bee Grimm
Preceptor Gamma Kappa, Stockton, California

Tutti-Frutti Ade

1 1-ounce package orange drink mix
2/3 cup sugar
1 1-ounce package lime drink mix
2/3 cup sugar
1 1-ounce package cherry drink mix
2/3 cup sugar
Lemon-lime soda

Combine each package of drink mix with 2/3 cup sugar and 1 quart water in separate bowls; stir to dissolve well. Pour each into ice cube tray. Freeze until firm. Place 1 cube of each flavor in tall glass. Fill glass with soda.

Kathleen Richardson
Alpha, Springfield, Missouri

Gina's Wine Punch

2 quarts Burgundy
2 tablespoons lemon juice
1 quart apple juice
1 cup sugar
1 quart ginger ale

Combine wine, juices and sugar in punch bowl; mix well. Stir in ginger ale gently at serving time. Yield: 1 gallon.

Gina Zerella
Sigma, Vineland, New Jersey

Holiday Wine Punch

1 6-ounce can frozen orange juice concentrate
1 6-ounce can frozen lemonade concentrate
2 1/2 quarts cranberry juice cocktail
1/2 cup sugar
1 quart ginger ale
3 cups Cold Duck

Combine juices with sugar and 3 cups water in punch bowl; mix well. Stir in ginger ale and Cold Duck at serving time. Yield: 36 servings.

Rose Long
Preceptor Theta, Eagle Grove, Iowa

Baby Doll

3 tablespoons chocolate syrup
1 cup milk
2 scoops vanilla ice cream

Combine all ingredients in tall glass. Stir vigorously to mix well. Serve with straw. Yield: 1 serving.

Arlene Brooks
Xi Beta Alpha, Jupiter, Florida

Low-Cal Milk Shake

1/2 banana
1/3 cup nonfat dry milk powder
1 envelope sugar substitute

Combine all ingredients and 1 glass of ice cubes in blender container. Process until smooth. Pour into tall serving glass. Yield: 1 serving.

Connie Zehr
Xi Beta Beta, Lincoln, Nebraska

Creamy Tuna Potato Topper; Ratatouille Topping; and Sausage Special

Basque Tuna Casserole

Beverages

Holiday Dairy Punch

1 12-ounce can frozen lemonade concentrate
1 6-ounce can frozen limeade concentrate
1/2 gallon vanilla ice cream
1/2 gallon lime sherbet
1/2 gallon milk
2 quarts ginger ale

Combine juice concentrates and 1 quart water in pitcher; mix well. Scoop ice cream and sherbet into large punch bowl. Stir in milk. Add the juice mixture and ginger ale, mixing gently. Yield: 50 servings.

Shirley Ringdahl
Decorah, Iowa

Frosted Orange Creme

1/4 cup instant orange breakfast drink mix
2 tablespoons sugar
1/2 cup milk
1/2 teaspoon vanilla extract

Combine all ingredients with 1 cup water and 2 cups crushed ice in blender container. Process until smooth. Pour into serving glasses. Garnish with fresh fruit. Yield: 3 cups.

Angie Cyr
Xi Delta Tau, Stillwater, Oklahoma

Janice Kay's Orange Drink

1 6-ounce can orange juice concentrate
1 cup milk
1 teaspoon vanilla extract
1/2 cup sugar

Combine all ingredients with 1 cup water in blender container. Process until blended. Add 9 ice cubes 1 at a time, processing constantly. Pour into glasses.

Janice Kay Heider
Mu Sigma, Williams, Iowa

Orange Julius

1 6-ounce can frozen orange juice concentrate
1 cup milk
1/2 cup sugar
1 teaspoon vanilla extract

Combine all ingredients and 1 cup water in blender container. Add 10 to 12 ice cubes 1 at a time, processing until smooth after each addition. Pour into serving glasses. Yield: 6 cups.

Alice L. Duba
Alpha Gamma, Fresno, California

Kahlua

3 1/2 cups sugar
1 2-ounce jar instant coffee granules
1 quart vodka
1 vanilla bean, broken

Dissolve sugar and coffee in 2 cups boiling water in 1/2-gallon container. Add vodka and vanilla bean. Store, covered, in dark place for 30 days. Strain into decanter.

Melanie Kaminski
Gamma Kappa, Rockledge, Florida

Camper's Hot Cocoa Mix

1 25-ounce box nonfat dry milk powder
1 6-ounce jar nondairy coffee creamer
1 16-ounce can instant chocolate drink mix
1/4 cup cocoa
2 cups confectioners' sugar

Combine all ingredients in large bowl; mix well. Store in airtight container. Combine 3 tablespoons mix and 1 cup hot water in mug for each serving. Yield: 17 cups.

Susan Aldrich
Psi, Jerome, Idaho

Angie's Hot Cocoa Mix

1 11-ounce jar nondairy coffee creamer
1 8-quart box nonfat dry milk powder
1 1 1/2-pound can instant chocolate drink mix
1 cup confectioners' sugar

Combine all ingredients in bowl; mix well. Store in airtight container. Combine 1/3 cup mix with 1 cup hot water in mug for each serving.

Angie Cyr
Xi Delta Tau, Stillwater, Oklahoma

Harvest Fruit Punch

8 tea bags
1 1/2 cups sugar
3 cups orange juice
1/4 cup lemon juice

Bring 2 cups water to a boil in large saucepan. Add tea bags. Steep for 5 minutes. Remove tea bags. Stir in sugar until dissolved. Add remaining ingredients and 2 quarts boiling water. Heat until steaming. Serve hot. Yield: 1 gallon.

Alexa Parris
Xi Alpha Kappa, LaFayette, Georgia

Beverages

Hot Buttered Rum Mix

1   16-ounce box
    brown sugar
1/2 pound butter

1 teaspoon each
    allspice, cinnamon
    and nutmeg

Combine all ingredients in bowl; mix well. Store, covered, in refrigerator for up to 1 week. Combine 2 teaspoons mix and 1 ounce rum with 1 cup boiling water for each serving. Yield: 25 servings.

Patricia Marie Dingmon
Theta, Albany, Oregon

Bridgton Beta Hot Buttered Rum

1/2 cup butter
1   16-ounce box
    brown sugar
6 tablespoons honey

2 tablespoons cinnamon
4 teaspoons nutmeg
Rum

Combine butter, brown sugar, honey and spices in saucepan. Simmer for 5 minutes, stirring to mix well. Place 1 spoonful mixture and 1 jigger rum in each mug. Fill with hot water; mix well. Garnish with whipped cream or ice cream and drizzle of Drambuie. Yield: 10-12 servings.

Vivian Howard
Xi Alpha Xi, Bridgton, Massachusetts

Hot Spiced Wine

2 quarts Burgundy
1 cup sugar
1 teaspoon cinnamon

1 teaspoon cloves
1/2 teaspoon allspice
1/8 teaspoon nutmeg

Combine all ingredients and 1 quart water in large saucepan; mix well. Simmer for 1 hour. Yield: 12 servings.
Note: May mix sugar and spices in larger quantities for spicing wine and store in airtight container. Use 1 cup mix to 1/2 gallon wine.

Jan Johnson
Nu Delta, Burlington, Kansas

Friendship Tea Mix

1   18-ounce jar
    instant orange
    breakfast drink mix
1 cup sugar
1/2 cup sweetened
    lemonade mix
1/2 cup instant tea

1   3-ounce package
    apricot gelatin
1 cup sugar
2 1/2 teaspoons
    cinnamon
1 teaspoon cloves

Combine all ingredients in large bowl; mix well. Store in airtight container. Combine 1 1/2 tablespoons mix and 1 cup hot water in mug for each serving. Yield: 50 servings.

Carla Stark
Alpha Chi, Ft. Bragg, North Carolina

Hot Tea Mix

1 cup instant tea
2 cups orange breakfast
    drink mix
1 1/2 cups sugar

1   3-ounce package
    lemonade mix
1 teaspoon each
    cloves, cinnamon

Mix all ingredients in large bowl. Combine 1 heaping teaspoon with 1 cup hot water for each serving. Yield: 5 cups.

Jacki Woods
Xi Iota Mu, Crescent City, California

Orange Summer Tea

8 tea bags
2 cups sugar

2 cups orange juice
3/4 cup lemon juice

Bring 1 quart water to a boil in saucepan. Add tea bags. Steep for 5 minutes. Bring 2 cups water and sugar to a boil in small saucepan, stirring to dissolve sugar. Combine tea, sugar mixture, juices and 2 quarts cold water in large pitcher. Serve over ice in glasses. Yield: 20 servings.

Jenny Hungerbuhler
Epsilon Zeta, Corbin, Kentucky

Russian Tea

3 tea bags
Juice and rind of
    2 oranges
Juice and rind of
    3 lemons

1 slice (or more)
    pineapple
1 cup sugar
4 whole cloves

Combine all ingredients with 2 quarts boiling water in saucepan. Let stand, covered, for 1 hour. Strain tea into refrigerator container. Store in refrigerator for up to 5 days. Serve hot. Yield: 2 1/2 quarts.

Johnnie Templeton
Alpha Chi, Pope Air Force Base, North Carolina

Breads

Pumpkin-Walnut Loaf, recipe on page 47.

Breads

Angel Biscuits

5 cups flour
1 teaspoon soda
1 teaspoon salt
1 tablespoon
    baking powder

3 tablespoons sugar
3/4 cup shortening
1 cake yeast
2 cups buttermilk

Sift all dry ingredients into bowl. Cut in shortening until crumbly. Dissolve yeast in 1/2 cup lukewarm water. Add buttermilk and yeast to flour mixture; stir until just moistened. Store, covered, in refrigerator. Roll desired amount of dough 1/2 inch thick on lightly floured surface; cut as desired. Place on greased baking sheet. Bake at 400 degrees for 12 minutes.

Marguerite Rinella
Laureate Delta, Louisville, Kentucky

Goody Biscuits

3/4 cup margarine
2 cups buttermilk
    biscuit mix

1 8-ounce can
    cream-style corn

Melt margarine in 9 x 13-inch baking dish in 350-degree oven. Combine biscuit mix and corn in bowl; mix well. Roll on floured surface; cut into squares. Dip in butter. Place in baking pan with sides touching. Bake for 20 to 25 minutes or until brown. Yield: 1-1 1/2 dozen.

Betty Sue Stuart
Brunswick, Missouri

Mayonnaise Biscuits

1 cup self-rising flour
1/2 cup milk
1 tablespoon sugar

2 tablespoons
    mayonnaise

Combine all ingredients in bowl; mix well. Fill greased muffin cups 1/2 full. Bake at 400 degrees for 10 to 15 minutes or until light brown. Yield: 1 dozen.

Nancy Hunt
Xi Delta Sigma, Charlottesville, Virginia

No-Knead Biscuits

1 package dry yeast
1 1/2 sticks
    margarine, melted

1/4 cup sugar
1 egg, beaten
4 cups self-rising flour

Dissolve yeast in 2 cups very warm water. Cream margarine, sugar and egg in bowl until light and fluffy. Stir in yeast and flour. Spoon into greased muffin cups. Bake at 350 degrees for 20 minutes. Yield: 2 dozen.

Vera Foster
Alpha Upsilon, Osage Beach, Missouri

Snow Biscuits

1 package dry yeast
2 tablespoons oil
2 cups flour

1/2 teaspoon salt
3 tablespoons sugar

Dissolve yeast in 3/4 cup warm water. Add oil; mix well. Sift dry ingredients together. Add to yeast mixture; mix well. Knead on floured surface for 5 minutes or until smooth and elastic. Shape into balls. Place in greased 9-inch baking dish. Let rise for 45 to 60 minutes or until doubled in bulk. Bake at 425 degrees for 10 to 12 minutes or until golden brown. Remove from pan. Cool slightly before serving. Yield: 9 servings.

Sue Moorman
Omega, Whitefish, Montana

Joyce's Breadsticks

1 loaf frozen
    bread dough
A small amount of milk

Onion salt or garlic
    salt to taste

Wrap bread dough in foil; thaw. Cut into 20 pieces. Roll each into 12-inch rope; place on greased baking sheet. Brush with milk; sprinkle with salt. Bake at 375 degrees for 20 minutes or until golden for soft breadsticks or darker for hard breadsticks. Store in uncovered container. Yield: 1 2/3 dozen.

Joyce Burke
Xi Eta Zeta, Emmetsburg, Iowa

Mexican Corn Bread

2 cups coarse cornmeal
1 teaspoon salt
1 teaspoon soda
1 egg, beaten
2 cups buttermilk

1 cup grated mild
    Cheddar cheese
5 or 6 jalapeno
    peppers, chopped
1 medium onion, chopped

Combine cornmeal, salt and soda in bowl. Stir in egg and buttermilk. Add cheese, jalapeno peppers and onion. Pour into greased 9 x 13-inch baking dish. Bake at 400 degrees for 25 minutes. Yield: 12 servings.
Note: Serve with black-eyed peas on New Year's Day!

Sammye Speegle
Beta Nu, Duncan, Oklahoma

Breads

Stella's Mexican Corn Bread

1/2 cup flour
1/2 cup yellow cornmeal
1 1/2 teaspoons baking powder
1/2 teaspoon salt
2 tablespoons brown sugar
1/4 cup margarine
1 egg, separated
1/2 cup evaporated milk
1/2 8-ounce can cream-style corn
1 small can chopped green chilies
1 cup grated longhorn cheese

Sift dry ingredients into bowl. Cut in margarine until crumbly. Fold beaten egg yolk, evaporated milk and corn into stiffly beaten egg white. Add to dry ingredients; mix lightly. Pour half the batter into greased 9-inch square baking pan. Sprinkle with chilies and cheese. Pour remaining batter over top. Bake at 375 degrees for 35 to 40 minutes or until corn bread tests done. Yield: 9 servings.

Stella I. Furr
Xi Psi, Douglas, Arizona

Southern Corn Bread

1/2 cup cornmeal
1 teaspoon salt
1 tablespoon sugar
1 egg, well beaten
1/2 cup flour
1/2 cup milk
1 tablespoon baking powder
2 tablespoons shortening

Combine cornmeal, salt, sugar and 1/2 cup boiling water in bowl. Cool. Add remaining ingredients in order listed, mixing well after each addition. Pour into greased 8-inch iron skillet. Bake at 425 degrees for 20 minutes. Yield: 4 servings.

Jean M. DeLane
Preceptor Delta Beta, Decatur, Illinois

Best Beer Bread

3 cups self-rising flour
3 tablespoons sugar
1 12-ounce can beer
1 stick margarine, melted

Combine flour and sugar in glass bowl. Add beer; mix well with nonmetal spoon. Pour into greased 9-inch glass pie plate. Bake at 350 degrees for 1 hour. Drizzle with butter. Bake for 10 minutes longer. Cut into wedges.

Ireene C. Fournier
Preceptor Theta Beta, Dallas, Texas

Connie's Beer Bread

3 tablespoons sugar
1 12-ounce can beer, at room temperature
3 cups self-rising flour
1/4 cup melted margarine

Combine first 3 ingredients in bowl; mix well. Pour into greased loaf pan. Drizzle margarine over batter. Bake at 350 degrees for 45 minutes. Turn onto wire rack to cool.

Connie Beuoy
Preceptor Beta Mu, Carmel, Indiana

Cheese-Corn-Olive Bread

2 1/2 cups flour
2 tablespoons sugar
2 teaspoons baking powder
1/2 teaspoon soda
1/2 teaspoon salt
1 teaspoon dry mustard
Pinch of cayenne pepper
1/4 cup butter
1 cup grated cheese
1 egg
1 cup buttermilk
1 teaspoon Worcestershire sauce
3/4 cup drained canned corn
1 cup chopped olives

Sift dry ingredients together into large mixing bowl. Cut in butter until crumbly. Add cheese; mix well. Combine egg, buttermilk and Worcestershire sauce in bowl; mix well. Make well in dry ingredients. Add buttermilk mixture. Mix with wooden spoon until just moistened. Stir in corn and olives. Pour into greased loaf pan. Bake at 375 degrees for 45 minutes or until bread tests done.

Cheryl Hassett
Alpha Gamma, Lara, Victoria, Australia

Parmesan Cheese Bread

2 cups buttermilk baking mix
1 cup sugar
1 stick butter, softened
2 eggs, well beaten
1 cup milk
3/4 cup Parmesan cheese

Combine baking mix and sugar in bowl; mix well. Cut in butter until crumbly. Stir in eggs and milk. Add cheese; mix well. Pour into greased 9 x 13-inch baking pan. Bake at 350 degrees for 45 minutes. Cut into squares. Yield: 12 servings.

Janet K. Wallace
Preceptor Alpha Gamma, Everett, Washington

Quick Cheese Bread

2 eggs, beaten
2 5 1/2-ounce packages biscuit mix
2 teaspoons dry mustard
1 1/2 cups grated sharp Cheddar cheese
2 tablespoons butter

Combine eggs and 3/4 cup water in bowl. Add biscuit mix; mix well. Stir in mustard and cheese. Pour into buttered loaf pan. Bake at 350 degrees for 45 minutes. Cool in pan for 15 minutes. Remove to wire rack to cool completely.

Virginia Thomas
Laureate Beta, Nashville, Tennessee

41

Breads

One-Hour Bread

1 package dry yeast
1 egg
2 tablespoons sugar

2 tablespoons oil
3 cups flour

Dissolve yeast in 1 cup warm water. Add egg, sugar and oil; mix well. Stir in flour. Let rise in warm place for 30 minutes. Knead on floured surface until smooth and elastic. Shape into loaves or rolls. Place in greased baking pan. Let rise for 30 minutes. Bake at 350 degrees for 12 to 15 minutes or until brown.

Elaine Sills
Preceptor Alpha Nu, El Paso, Texas

Master Mix

9 cups flour
1 cup dry milk powder
1/3 cup baking powder
1 tablespoon salt

2 teaspoons cream
    of tartar
1/4 cup sugar
2 cups shortening

Sift dry ingredients together 3 times into large mixing bowl. Cut in shortening until crumbly. Store in airtight container. **Biscuits:** Combine 1 cup Master Mix and 1/4 cup milk in bowl; mix well. Knead 15 times on floured surface. Roll 1/2 inch thick. Cut with biscuit cutter. Place on baking sheet. Bake at 450 degrees for 10 minutes.
Nut Bread: Combine 2 cups Master Mix, 1/3 cup sugar and 1/3 cup nuts in bowl. Add 2/3 cup milk and 1 egg; mix well. Bake in greased loaf pan at 350 degrees for 1 hour.

Sarah Williams
Xi Iota Gamma, Lufkin, Texas

Pizza Dough Crusts

1 package dry yeast
1 tablespoon sugar
1 1/2 teaspoons salt

2 tablespoons oil
3 cups flour

Dissolve yeast in 1 cup warm water in bowl. Add sugar, salt, oil and half the flour; mix well. Add remaining flour; mix well. Knead on floured surface until smooth and elastic. Place in greased bowl, turning to grease surface. Let rise until doubled in bulk. Divide into 2 portions. Roll to fit pizza pan. Yield: 2 pizza crusts.

Brenda Moody
Xi Omega, Bowling Green, Kentucky

No-Knead Crescent Rolls

1 cup hot milk
1/2 cup sugar
1/2 cup oil
1 teaspoon salt

3 eggs, well beaten
1 1/2 packages
    dry yeast
5 cups flour

Combine first 4 ingredients and 1/2 cup cold water in bowl. Add eggs and yeast; mix well. Add flour gradually, mixing well after each addition. Cover with waxed paper and towel. Let rise until doubled in bulk. Divide into 3 portions. Roll each portion into circle on floured surface. Cut into crescents. Place on baking sheet. Let rise until doubled in bulk. Bake at 375 degrees for 13 minutes or until brown. Brush warm rolls with butter. Yield: 4 dozen.

Kitty M. Taylor
Preceptor Delta Alpha, Lee's Summit, Missouri

Quickie Yeast Rolls

1 package dry yeast
2 tablespoons sugar
2 tablespoons oil
1/2 teaspoon salt

1 egg
2 1/2 to 2 3/4
    cups flour
Butter, softened

Dissolve yeast in 3/4 cup warm water in 2 1/2-quart bowl. Add sugar, oil, salt and egg. Stir until sugar and salt dissolve. Add 1 cup flour; mix well. Cover. Place on rack over bowl of hot water. Let rise for 15 minutes. Stir batter. Add 1 1/2 cups flour; mix well. Knead in remaining flour if necessary on floured cloth. Knead for 3 minutes. Shape into balls. Arrange in baking pan. Brush with butter. Let rise, covered, over hot water for 25 minutes. Bake at 425 degrees for 12 to 15 minutes or until light brown. Remove from pan to wire rack. Brush with butter. Yield: 1 1/3 dozen.

Bette L. Carraher
Preceptor Beta Upsilon, Ashtabula, Ohio

Breads

Apple Kuchen

1/2 cup butter
1 2-layer package
    yellow cake mix
1 20-ounce can
    sliced pie apples
1/2 cup sugar
1 teaspoon cinnamon
1 cup sour cream
1 egg

Cut butter into cake mix until crumbly. Pat into 9 x 13-inch baking pan, shaping rim. Bake at 350 degrees for 10 minutes. Arrange apple slices on warm crust. Sprinkle mixture of sugar and cinnamon on apples. Blend sour cream and egg in bowl. Drizzle over apples. Topping will not completely cover apples. Bake for 20 to 25 minutes longer or until edges are light brown.

Virginia Rankin
Preceptor Beta Epsilon, Florence, Colorado

Breakfast Coffee Cake

1/2 cup packed
    brown sugar
1/2 cup chopped pecans
1 1/2 loaves frozen
    bread dough, thawed
Cinnamon to taste
1 small package
    vanilla pudding
    and pie filling mix
1/2 cup melted butter

Sprinkle brown sugar and pecans in greased bundt pan. Shape bread dough into 1-inch balls. Place on top of sugar and nuts. Sprinkle with cinnamon and pudding mix. Pour butter over top. Let rise at room temperature overnight. Bake at 325 degrees for 25 minutes. Invert on serving plate. Serve warm.

Sharon Kenitzer
Preceptor Pi, Polson, Montana

Cream Cheese Coffee Cake

2 cans 8-count
    refrigerator crescent
    dinner rolls
2 8-ounce packages
    cream cheese,
    softened
1 cup sugar
1 1/2 teaspoons
    vanilla extract
1 egg, separated
1/3 cup sugar
Chopped nuts to taste
Cinnamon to taste

Roll out half the rolls on floured surface. Fit into 9 x 13-inch baking pan. Beat cream cheese, 1 cup sugar, vanilla and egg yolk in mixer bowl until smooth. Beat egg white in small bowl until frothy. Blend into cream cheese mixture. Pour into prepared pan. Roll out remaining rolls on floured surface. Place over filling. Sprinkle with remaining ingredients. Bake at 350 degrees for 35 minutes or until brown.
Yield: 8 servings.

Shirley James
Preceptor Iota, Albuquerque, New Mexico

Easy Cinnamon Coffee Cake

1/2 stick butter,
    softened
1 12 to 18-count
    package frozen rolls
1 stick butter, melted
2 tablespoons cinnamon
1 small package
    vanilla pudding and
    pie filling mix
1/2 cup packed
    brown sugar

Butter bundt pan generously with softened butter. Arrange rolls in pan. Pour melted butter over rolls. Sprinkle with mixture of cinnamon, dry pudding mix and brown sugar. Let stand at room temperature overnight. Bake at 350 degrees for 20 minutes. Cool in pan for 3 to 4 minutes. Invert on serving plate.

Ireene C. Fournier
Preceptor Theta Beta, Dallas, Texas

Easy Coffee Cake

1 2-layer package
    yellow cake mix
1 package dry yeast
1 cup flour
2 eggs
1 can cherry pie filling
5 tablespoons
    butter, melted
1 cup confectioners'
    sugar
1 tablespoon corn syrup

Combine 1 1/2 cups cake mix, yeast, flour, eggs and 2/3 cup water in mixer bowl. Beat for 2 minutes. Spread in greased 9 x 13-inch cake pan. Spoon pie filling over dough. Mix remaining cake mix and butter in bowl until crumbly. Sprinkle over pie filling. Bake at 375 degrees for 30 minutes. Cool. Combine confectioners' sugar, corn syrup and 1 tablespoon water in small bowl; mix well. Drizzle over coffee cake.

Deanna Rowe
Xi Epsilon Sigma, Lawrenceburg, Indiana

Easy Yogurt Coffee Cake

1/2 2-layer package
    yellow cake mix
1 egg
1/2 cup raisins (opt.)
1 carton fruit-
    flavored yogurt
3 tablespoons sugar
1/2 teaspoon cinnamon

Combine first 4 ingredients in bowl; mix well with wooden spoon. Pour into greased and floured 8-inch square cake pan. Sprinkle mixture of sugar and cinnamon over batter. Bake at 350 degrees for 25 minutes. Cool.
Note: May use strawberry cake mix with strawberry yogurt or lemon cake mix with lemon yogurt.

Colleen Slaughter
Xi Beta, Las Vegas, Nevada

Breads

Monkey Bread

4 10-count cans refrigerator biscuits	1 cup packed brown sugar
2/3 cup sugar	1 teaspoon cinnamon
1 teaspoon cinnamon	2 tablespoons corn syrup
1 stick butter	

Cut each biscuit into quarters. Mix sugar and 1 teaspoon cinnamon in bag. Add biscuits; shake until coated. Arrange in greased bundt pan. Combine remaining ingredients in saucepan. Bring to a boil, stirring constantly. Pour over biscuits. Bake at 350 degrees for 40 to 50 minutes or until brown. Invert on serving plate. Yield: 12 servings.

Carla Stark
Alpha Chi, Ft. Bragg, North Carolina

Quick Cheese Coffee Cake

1 10-count package flaky refrigerator biscuits	1/2 cup sugar
	1 tablespoon flour
	1 egg
1 8-ounce package cream cheese, softened	1/4 teaspoon cinnamon
	2 tablespoons sugar

Place biscuits in 9 x 9-inch baking pan. Pat to cover bottom and sides. Combine cream cheese, 1/2 cup sugar, flour and egg in bowl; mix well. Pour into prepared pan. Sprinkle with mixture of cinnamon and 2 tablespoons sugar. Bake at 350 degrees for 25 minutes or until set. Yield: 9 servings.

Dorothy Gilley
Alpha Omega Omicron, Azle, Texas

Quick Pecan Breakfast Ring

1/2 cup melted margarine	2 tablespoons milk
1 cup packed brown sugar	3 10-count cans refrigerator biscuits
	1 cup pecans

Blend margarine, brown sugar and milk in bowl. Pour half the mixture into greased tube pan. Arrange biscuits on edge in pan. Pour remaining brown sugar over top; sprinkle with pecans. Bake at 350 degrees for 35 minutes. Invert on serving plate.

Suzanne Mantooth
Iota Chi, Chesterfield, Missouri

One-Two-Three-Four Coffee Cake

1 cup sugar	1 tablespoon baking powder
2 cups flour	Raisins
3 eggs	Chopped nuts
1/2 cup oil	Cinnamon-sugar
3/4 cup milk	

Combine first 6 ingredients in bowl; mix well. Pour into 2 greased 9-inch cake pans. Sprinkle with raisins, nuts and cinnamon-sugar. Bake at 350 degrees for 20 to 25 minutes or until brown. Yield: 10 servings.

Ruth Fischer
Preceptor Zeta Lambda, Santa Rosa, California

Sour Cream Coffee Cake

1/2 cup chopped nuts	2 eggs, well beaten
1/4 cup sugar	1 tablespoon vanilla extract
1/4 cup packed brown sugar	1 1/2 cups flour
1 teaspoon cinnamon	1 teaspoon baking powder
1 teaspoon nutmeg	1/2 teaspoon soda
1/2 cup butter, softened	1 cup sour cream
1 cup sugar	

Combine first 5 ingredients in small bowl; set aside. Cream butter with 1 cup sugar in bowl until light and fluffy. Add eggs and vanilla; beat well. Add remaining dry ingredients and sour cream; beat until well blended. Do not overbeat. Pour half the batter into greased and lightly floured 9-inch square baking pan. Top with half the nut mixture. Repeat layers. Bake at 375 degrees for 30 to 35 minutes or until brown.

Karen Bauer
Beta Tau, Stevensville, Montana

Sunday Morning Coffee Cake

2 1/2 cups flour	1/2 teaspoon soda
1/2 teaspoon salt	1/2 teaspoon cinnamon
2 cups packed brown sugar	1/2 teaspoon nutmeg
	1 cup milk
2/3 cup margarine	2 eggs, well beaten
2 teaspoons baking powder	1/2 cup chopped nuts

Combine flour, salt, brown sugar and margarine in bowl; mix until crumbly. Reserve 1/2 cup mixture for topping. Add baking powder, soda, cinnamon and nutmeg to remaining mixture; mix well. Add milk and eggs; mix well. Pour into greased 9 x 13-inch baking pan. Sprinkle with reserved crumbs and nuts. Bake at 375 degrees for 25 to 30 minutes or until brown.

Faye L. Kean
Xi Theta Delta, Ashtabula, Ohio

Breads

Hawaiian Toast with Custard Sauce, recipe below.

Hawaiian Toast with Custard Sauce

2 eggs	6 slices bread
1/2 cup milk	3/4 cup fine
1 tablespoon honey	cornflake crumbs
1/2 teaspoon salt	3 oranges,
1/4 teaspoon	peeled, sliced
vanilla extract	Custard Sauce

CUSTARD SAUCE

1/3 cup honey	3 eggs
2 tablespoons flour	1 teaspoon grated
1/2 teaspoon salt	orange rind
2 cups milk	

Combine eggs, milk, honey, salt and vanilla in bowl; beat lightly. Dip bread slices in egg mixture; coat on both sides with crumbs. Place in well-buttered 10 x 15-inch baking pan. Bake at 400 degrees for 5 minutes. Turn slices over. Bake for 5 to 7 minutes or until crisp. Top each slice with orange slices and 1/2 cup Custard Sauce. Yield: 6 servings.

Combine honey, flour and salt in saucepan; mix well. Stir in milk gradually. Cook over low heat until thickened, stirring constantly. Combine eggs and orange rind in mixing bowl; beat lightly. Stir a small amount of hot mixture into eggs; stir eggs into hot mixture. Cook for 2 minutes, stirring constantly. Yield: 3 cups.

Photograph for this recipe above.

Nanny's Doughnuts

1 egg, beaten	1 teaspoon salt
1 cup sugar	1/2 teaspoon nutmeg
2 1/2 teaspoons	3 1/2 cups flour
melted butter	1 cup milk
3 1/2 teaspoons	Oil for deep frying
baking powder	

Combine egg, sugar and butter; beat well. Mix baking powder, salt, nutmeg and flour. Add flour mixture alternately with milk to creamed mixture, beating well after each addition. Pat dough to 1/2-inch thickness on floured surface; cut with well-floured doughnut cutter. Deep-fry until brown on both sides. Yield: 3 dozen.

Vera Jennings
Xi Zeta, Sparta, New Jersey

Breads

Funnel Cakes

2 eggs, beaten
2 cups milk
1/2 teaspoon
  vanilla extract
1/4 teaspoon salt
1/2 teaspoon
  baking powder
3 cups flour
2 cups corn oil
Confectioners' sugar

Beat eggs, milk and vanilla in bowl. Sift in dry ingredients; mix until smooth. Beat until light. Pour into stoppered funnel. Swirl batter in circular motion into hot oil in skillet. Fry for 1/2 to 1 minute on each side until golden. Drain on paper towel. Sift confectioners' sugar over top. Yield: 10 servings.

Connie Wade
Xi Theta Nu, Jefferson City, Missouri

Banana Tea Bread

1/3 cup butter
2/3 cup sugar
1 3/4 cups sifted flour
2 teaspoons
  baking powder
1/4 teaspoon soda
1/2 teaspoon salt
2 eggs, well beaten
1 cup ripe
  mashed bananas
1/2 cup coarsely
  chopped nuts

Cream butter and sugar in bowl until light and fluffy. Sift in flour, baking powder, soda and salt; mix well. Add eggs, bananas and nuts; mix well. Pour into greased small loaf pan. Bake at 350 degrees for 1 hour and 10 minutes. Turn onto wire rack to cool. Yield: 10-12 servings.

Mary Ford
Nu Gamma, Crescent City, California

Easy Banana Bread

3 bananas
1 cup sugar
1/4 cup butter,
  softened
1/4 teaspoon
  baking powder
1 egg
1 3/4 cups flour
1 teaspoon soda
1 teaspoon
  vanilla extract

Rinse bananas; drain. Mash in mixer bowl. Add remaining ingredients. Beat until blended. Pour into greased 5 x 7-inch loaf pan. Bake at 325 degrees for 30 to 45 minutes or until bread tests done. Turn onto wire rack to cool.

Vivian Howard
Xi Alpha Xi, Bridgton, Maine

Cheddar-Apple Bread

1/2 cup shortening
1/2 cup sugar
1 egg
1 can apple pie filling
2 1/2 cups sifted flour
1 teaspoon salt
1 teaspoon soda
1 teaspoon
  baking powder
1 cup shredded
  Cheddar cheese
1/2 cup chopped walnuts

Cream shortening, sugar and egg in bowl until light and fluffy. Add pie filling; beat well. Sift dry ingredients together. Add to creamed mixture with cheese and walnuts; mix until just moistened. Pour into greased 5 x 9-inch loaf pan. Bake at 350 degrees for 1 1/2 hours.

Photograph for this recipe on opposite page.

Fresh Cranberry-Nut Bread

2 cups sifted flour
1 cup sugar
1 1/2 teaspoons
  baking powder
1/2 teaspoon soda
1 teaspoon salt
1/4 cup shortening
3/4 cup orange juice
1 tablespoon grated
  orange rind
1 egg, well beaten
1/2 cup chopped
  nuts (opt.)
1 cup coarsely chopped
  fresh cranberries

Sift dry ingredients into bowl. Cut in shortening until crumbly. Combine orange juice, orange rind and egg; mix well. Add to dry ingredients; mix just until moistened. Fold in nuts and cranberries. Pour into greased and floured loaf pan. Bake at 350 degrees for 1 hour.

Sandra Thexton
Xi Delta Eta, Richmond, British Columbia, Canada

Lemon Bread

1 2-layer package
  lemon cake mix
3/4 cup oil
4 eggs
1 small package lemon
  instant pudding mix
1 teaspoon
  vanilla extract
1 teaspoon
  margarine
1 teaspoon cinnamon
1/2 cup sugar

Combine first 7 ingredients in mixer bowl. Beat for 8 minutes. Spoon half the batter into 2 greased loaf pans. Sprinkle with 1/4 cup mixture of cinnamon and sugar. Repeat with remaining batter and cinnamon-sugar. Bake at 350 degrees for 40 minutes. Turn onto wire rack to cool. Yield: 2 loaves.

Shirley Fryatt
Laureate Alpha Sigma, Federal Way, Washington

Breads

Cheddar-Apple Bread, recipe on page 46.

Grape Nuts Bread

1 cup Grape Nuts
2 cups sour milk
1 cup sugar
1 egg
1 teaspoon salt

1 teaspoon soda
4 cups flour
4 teaspoons
    baking powder

Soak Grape Nuts in sour milk in bowl for 10 minutes. Stir in remaining ingredients. Spoon into greased muffin cups. Let stand for 30 minutes. Bake at 350 degrees for 45 minutes. Turn onto wire rack to cool. Yield: 2 dozen.

Betty A. Carragher
Preceptor Laureate, Waukegan, Illinois

Pumpkin-Nut Bread

3 cups sugar
1 cup oil
4 eggs
1 1/2 teaspoons salt
1 teaspoon cinnamon
1 teaspoon nutmeg

2 cups pumpkin
3 1/3 cups flour
2 teaspoons soda
1 teaspoon
    vanilla extract
1 cup chopped nuts

Combine all ingredients in large mixing bowl; mix well. Line greased loaf pans with waxed paper. Pour in batter. Bake at 350 degrees for 1 hour or until bread tests done. Turn onto wire rack to cool. Yield: 3 small or 2 large loaves.

Marjorie Ann Seals
Gamma Omicron, Canal Fulton, Ohio

Pumpkin-Walnut Loaf

2 cups flour
2 teaspoons pumpkin
    pie spice
1 1/2 teaspoons
    baking powder
1/2 teaspoon soda
1/4 teaspoon salt
1/4 cup milk

1/2 cup canned pumpkin
3/4 cup butter,
    softened
3/4 cup sugar
1 egg
1/2 cup chopped
    walnuts

Combine flour, pumpkin pie spice, baking powder, soda and salt. Combine milk and pumpkin in bowl; blend well. Cream butter and sugar in bowl until light and fluffy. Beat in egg. Add flour mixture alternately with pumpkin mixture, mixing well after each addition. Stir in walnuts. Spoon into greased and floured loaf pan. Bake at 350 degrees for 45 minutes or until loaf tests done. Cool in pan for 10 minutes. Turn onto wire rack to cool completely.

Photograph for this recipe on page 39.

Breads

All-Bran Refrigerator Muffins

2 cups All-Bran	5 teaspoons soda
1 cup shortening	1 teaspoon salt
2 1/2 cups sugar	2 cups All-Bran
4 eggs	1 quart buttermilk
5 cups flour	

Pour 2 cups boiling water over 2 cups All-Bran in bowl; cool. Combine remaining ingredients in bowl; mix well. Add softened All-Bran; stir until just mixed. Fill greased muffin cups 1/2 full. Bake at 400 degrees for 25 minutes. Yield: 4 dozen. Note: May add dates, raisins or fruit as desired. Batter may be stored in refrigerator for 6 weeks.

Verna M. Cox
Preceptor Alpha Chi, San Francisco, California

Margaret's Banana-Bran Muffins

1 1/4 cups flour	1/2 cup packed
1/2 cup natural bran	brown sugar
1/3 cup wheat germ	1 egg, beaten
1 teaspoon	2/3 cup mashed banana
baking powder	1/2 cup yogurt
1 teaspoon soda	1 tablespoon
Pinch of salt	molasses
1/2 cup butter,	3/4 cup raisins
softened	

Combine first 6 ingredients in bowl; mix well. Cream butter, brown sugar and egg in bowl until light and fluffy. Add banana, yogurt and molasses; mix well. Add to dry ingredients; stir until just mixed. Stir in raisins. Spoon into paper-lined muffin cups. Bake at 375 degrees for 20 to 25 minutes or until brown. Yield: 1 dozen.

Margaret R. Rose
Sigma, Lewisporte, Newfoundland, Canada

Donna's Banana-Bran Muffins

2 eggs	4 bananas, mashed
1 cup honey	2 teaspoons soda
1 1/2 cups milk	2 cups whole
1/4 cup butter,	wheat flour
softened	3 cups bran

Cream eggs, honey, milk, butter and bananas in bowl until fluffy. Add soda; mix well. Mix flour and bran. Add to creamed mixture 1 cup at a time, mixing well after each addition. Fill each lined muffin cup with 1/4 cup batter. Bake at 400 degrees for 20 to 30 minutes or until muffins test done.

Donna Goeringer
Beta Theta, Rapid City, South Dakota

Mincemeat-Bran Muffins

2 eggs, beaten	2 teaspoons soda
1 cup sugar	2 teaspoons
3/4 cup oil	baking powder
2 cups milk	1 teaspoon salt
1 cup All-Bran	1 cup mincemeat
2 cups flour	

Beat eggs with sugar and oil. Add milk and All-Bran; beat well. Sift in dry ingredients; mix well. Add mincemeat; mix well. Store in refrigerator for 2 weeks or less. Fill greased muffin cups 2/3 full. Bake at 375 degrees for 20 minutes. Yield: 2 dozen.

Shirley Duffus
Preceptor Iota, Rosetown, Saskatchewan, Canada

Pam's Six-Week Bran Muffins

1 1/2 cups	1 quart buttermilk
chopped dates	5 cups flour
5 teaspoons soda	1 teaspoon salt
1 cup shortening	2 cups 40% bran flakes
2 cups sugar	4 cups All-Bran
4 eggs	1 cup nuts

Mix dates with soda in bowl. Add 2 cups boiling water; cool. Cream shortening and sugar in bowl until light and fluffy. Add eggs 1 at a time, beating well after each addition. Add buttermilk alternately with flour and salt, mixing well after each addition. Combine cereals and nuts in large bowl. Add buttermilk mixture and dates; mix well. Store in tightly covered 1-gallon container in refrigerator. Do not stir. Spoon into greased muffin cups. Bake at 400 degrees for 20 minutes.

Pam Nesius
Xi Alpha Zeta, Glenrock, Wyoming

Six-Week Bran Muffins

1 15-ounce package	1 teaspoon salt
Raisin Bran	4 eggs, beaten
3 cups sugar	1 cup oil
5 cups flour	1 quart buttermilk
5 teaspoons soda	

Mix cereal, sugar, flour, soda and salt in large bowl. Add eggs, oil and buttermilk; mix well. Store in covered container in refrigerator for 6 weeks or less. Stir batter. Spoon into greased muffin cups. Bake at 400 degrees for 15 to 20 minutes or until brown. Yield: 6 dozen.

Ruth A. Crank
Xi Alpha Kappa, Hermitage, Tennessee
Kathleen J. Shafer
Theta Epsilon, Julesburg, Colorado

Breads

Chocolate Muffins

1 1/2 cups flour
1/2 cup cocoa
1 tablespoon
    baking powder
1/4 teaspoon salt
1/3 cup sugar

1/2 cup chopped pecans
2 eggs, beaten
3/4 cup milk
1 teaspoon
    vanilla extract
1/4 cup melted butter

Combine dry ingredients and pecans in bowl. Beat eggs with remaining ingredients. Add to flour mixture; stir until just mixed. Fill lightly greased muffin cups 2/3 full. Bake at 400 degrees for 15 to 20 minutes or until muffins test done. Yield: 1 dozen.

Dorine Jones
Xi Upsilon Theta, Gustine, California

Ice Cream Muffins

2 cups self-rising
    flour

2 cups vanilla ice
    cream, softened

Combine flour and ice cream in bowl; beat until smooth. Fill well-greased muffin cups 3/4 full. Bake at 425 degrees for 20 to 25 minutes or until brown.
Note: May add 1 egg and 2 tablespoons oil for richer muffins. Substitute 1 1/2 cups flour, 1 tablespoon baking powder and 1 teaspoon salt for self-rising flour.

Mary Gamble
Xi Beta Alpha, Huntsville, Alabama

Peanut Butter Muffins

2 cups sifted flour
1 tablespoon
    baking powder
1 teaspoon salt
1/4 cup sugar

1/2 cup peanut butter
1 egg, beaten
1 cup milk
1/4 cup oil

Mix dry ingredients in bowl. Add peanut butter; mix until crumbly. Add mixture of egg, milk and oil; stir until just mixed. Fill greased muffin cups 1/2 full. Bake at 400 degrees for 20 to 25 minutes or until golden brown. Yield: 1 dozen.

Norma Kapis
Xi Pi, Fresno, California

Pumpkin Muffins

4 eggs, beaten
2 cups sugar
1 1/2 cups oil
1 3/4 cups pumpkin
3 cups sifted flour
1 tablespoon cinnamon
1 teaspoon nutmeg

2 teaspoons
    baking powder
2 teaspoons soda
1 teaspoon salt
2 cups raisins
1/2 cup (about) packed
    brown sugar (opt.)

Combine eggs, sugar, oil and pumpkin in large bowl; beat well. Add next 6 dry ingredients; mix well. Stir in raisins. Fill greased muffin cups 2/3 full. Sprinkle with brown sugar. Bake at 375 degrees for 15 to 20 minutes or until brown. Yield: 4 dozen.

Janet Gekill
Eta Kappa, Chatham, Ontario, Canada

Birthday Breakfast Buns

1/3 cup butter
3/4 cup packed
    brown sugar
1/2 cup chopped
    pecans

1 or 2   10-count
    packages refrigerator
    biscuits
2 tablespoons sugar
1 teaspoon cinnamon

Combine butter, brown sugar, pecans and 1/4 cup water in saucepan. Simmer for 10 minutes. Pour into 9-inch round cake pan. Roll biscuits into 10 x 12-inch rectangle on floured surface. Sprinkle with mixture of sugar and cinnamon. Roll as for jelly roll from long side. Cut into 1-inch slices. Place in prepared pan. Bake at 400 degrees for 20 minutes or until brown. Yield: 1 dozen.

Dawn Moudy
Beta Iota, McCall, Idaho

Cinnamon Rolls

3 cups self-rising
    flour
4 1/2 tablespoons
    shortening
1 cup milk
1/2 cup margarine,
    softened
1/4 cup sugar

1/4 cup packed
    brown sugar
1/2 cup pecans
1 tablespoon cinnamon
1 1/4 cups
    confectioners' sugar
3 tablespoons milk

Combine first 3 ingredients in bowl; mix well. Roll into 14 x 20-inch rectangle on floured surface. Spread with margarine; sprinkle with mixture of 1/4 cup sugar, brown sugar, pecans and cinnamon. Roll as for jelly roll; cut into 1-inch slices. Arrange in greased 9 x 13-inch baking dish. Bake at 350 degrees for 20 to 25 minutes or until brown. Blend confectioners' sugar and 3 tablespoons milk in small bowl. Drizzle over warm rolls. Yield: 1 dozen.

Millissa Duffey
Theta, Vincennes, Indiana

Breads

Easy Sweet Rolls

1   36-count package
    frozen rolls
1 small package
    butterscotch pudding
    and pie filling mix
1/2 teaspoon cinnamon
3/4 cup packed
    brown sugar
1/2 cup nuts
1 stick margarine,
    chopped

Arrange frozen rolls in buttered bundt pan. Mix pudding mix, cinnamon, brown sugar and nuts in small bowl; sprinkle over rolls. Arrange margarine slices over top. Place in cold oven. Let rise overnight for 8 to 9 hours. Bake at 350 degrees for 30 minutes. Turn onto foil-covered baking sheet. Pull apart gently; serve immediately.

Note: May bake 12 rolls at a time but use entire amount of topping ingredients for each batch.

Reva J. Falk
Preceptor Theta, Tucson, Arizona

Molasses Buns

1/4 cup sugar
1 cup molasses
1 cup margarine
1 cup raisins
2 to 3 cups flour
1 teaspoon soda
2 teaspoons allspice
1 egg
2 teaspoons
    baking powder

Combine all ingredients and 1/2 cup hot water in bowl; mix well. Roll on floured surface. Cut with biscuit cutter. Place on baking sheet. Bake at 350 degrees for 20 minutes.

Beverley Lundrigan
Corner Brook, Newfoundland, Canada

Quick Breakfast Rolls

8 marshmallows
1/4 cup melted
    margarine
Cinnamon-sugar
1   8-count can
    refrigerator
    crescent dinner
    rolls

Dip each marshmallow in margarine; roll in cinnamon-sugar to coat. Place on rolls; roll from wide end to enclose marshmallow. Dip in margarine; coat with cinnamon-sugar. Place on baking sheet. Bake according to package directions.

Flo Leetch
Preceptor Delta Alpha, Lee's Summit, Missouri

Sticky Buns

24 frozen dinner rolls
1 small package
    butterscotch pudding
    and pie filling mix
1 cup packed
    brown sugar
1/4 cup sugar
1 teaspoon cinnamon
1/2 cup chopped pecans
1/2 cup melted
    margarine

Arrange rolls in greased and floured bundt pan. Sprinkle mixture of pudding mix, sugars, cinnamon and pecans over rolls. Drizzle margarine over top. Let stand, uncovered, at room temperature overnight. Bake at 350 degrees for 30 minutes. Invert onto serving plate.

Mary Ann Hamm
Beta Omicron, Castle Rock, Colorado

Dorothy's Crepes

3 eggs
1/4 teaspoon salt
2 cups flour
2 cups milk
1/4 cup melted butter

Beat eggs with salt in mixer bowl. Add flour alternately with milk, beating well after each addition. Chill for 1 hour or longer. Cook a small amount of batter at a time in lightly buttered crepe pan.

Note: This batter makes thick crepes. Add 1 to 2 tablespoons milk if thinner crepes are desired.

Dorothy Bodenstab
Pi Chi, Alma, Missouri

German Pancake

1/2 cup flour
1/2 cup evaporated
    milk
1/4 teaspoon salt
4 eggs
1/4 cup butter

Combine flour, evaporated milk and salt in bowl; mix well. Add eggs 1 at a time, beating well with wire whisk after each addition. Melt butter in ovenproof skillet, coating side. Cook batter in prepared skillet over medium heat until firm enough to loosen from side with spatula. Slash cross through pancake. Bake at 425 degrees for 15 minutes or until puffed and golden. Garnish with confectioners' sugar. Serve with syrup or lemon juice. Yield: 4 servings.

Jouett Smith
Epsilon Kappa, Hachita, New Mexico

Desserts

Cherry Angel Torte, recipe on page 52.

Desserts

Tangerine Sunshine Cake, recipe on page 61.

Cherry Angel Torte

1/2 cup sugar
3 tablespoons flour
2 tablespoons
   cornstarch
1/2 teaspoon salt
1 3/4 cups milk
2 egg yolks, beaten
1 teaspoon
   vanilla extract

1/2 cup whipping
   cream, whipped
4 cups Northwest fresh
   cherries, pitted
1 10-inch angel
   food cake
1 cup sweetened
   whipped cream

Combine 1/2 cup sugar, flour, cornstarch and salt in sauce-pan. Stir in milk gradually. Cook over medium heat until mixture is thickened, stirring constantly. Stir a small amount of hot mixture into egg yolks; stir egg yolks into hot mixture. Bring just to a boil, stirring constantly. Cool. Blend in vanilla. Chill in refrigerator. Beat until smooth; fold in whipped cream. Cut 2 cups cherries into halves; chop 2 cups cherries. Split cake into 3 layers. Fold chopped cherries into whipped cream mixture. Spread between cake layers. Spread sweeten-ed whipped cream over top. Arrange cherry halves cut side down over top.

Photograph for this recipe on page 51.

Apple Cake

3 eggs, beaten
1 2-layer package
   yellow cake mix
1 can apple pie filling
3 tablespoons flour

2 cup packed
   brown sugar
1 teaspoon cinnamon
1/4 cup butter,
   softened

Combine eggs and cake mix in bowl; mix well. Fold in pie filling. Pour into greased and floured 9 x 13-inch cake pan. Combine flour, brown sugar and cinnamon in bowl. Cut in butter until crumbly. Sprinkle over cake. Bake at 350 degrees for 35 to 40 minutes or until brown.

Stacy Zuger
Theta Delta, Endicott, Washington

Spiced Apple Cake

1 2-layer package
   spice cake mix
2 cans apple
   pie filling

1 tablespoon
   lemon juice

Sprinkle half the dry cake mix over bottom of 9 x 13-inch cake pan. Spoon pie filling over cake mix. Sprinkle remaining cake mix over apples. Pour mixture of 1 cup water and lemon juice over top. Bake at 350 degrees for 1 hour. Serve warm with ice cream.

Bobbie Williams
Xi Chi, Sophia, West Virginia

Desserts

Fresh Apple Cake with Caramel Sauce

3 eggs	1 teaspoon salt
1 3/4 cups sugar	1 teaspoon cinnamon
1 cup oil	2 cups diced apples
2 cups flour	2 cups chopped nuts
1 teaspoon soda	Caramel Sauce

Caramel Sauce

2 tablespoons	1/2 cup sugar
(rounded) flour	1/4 cup margarine
1/2 cup packed	1 teaspoon
brown sugar	vanilla extract

Mix eggs and sugar in bowl. Add oil; mix well. Sift in flour, soda, salt and cinnamon; mix well. Fold in apples and nuts. Pour into prepared 9 x 13-inch baking pan. Bake at 350 degrees for 40 minutes. Cool slightly. Pour Caramel Sauce over cake.

Combine flour, sugars and 1 cup water in saucepan. Cook until sugars are dissolved and mixture is thickened, stirring constantly. Stir in margarine and vanilla.

Jean A. Wiyatt
Epsilon Tau, Stafford, Virginia

Applesauce Cake

1/2 cup butter,	1 teaspoon cinnamon
softened	1/2 teaspoon salt
1 cup sugar	1/4 teaspoon cloves
1 egg	3/4 cup raisins
1 1/4 cups less 1	3/4 cup nuts
tablespoon flour	1 tablespoon flour
1 teaspoon soda	1 cup applesauce

Cream butter and sugar in bowl until light and fluffy. Add egg; mix well. Add next 5 dry ingredients to creamed mixture; mix well. Coat raisins and nuts with 1 tablespoon flour. Fold into batter with applesauce. Pour into greased 9 x 13-inch cake pan. Bake at 350 degrees for 30 minutes. Yield: 24 servings.

Phyllis Truax
Xi Eta Iota, Big Cove Tannery, Pennsylvania

Easy Method Carrot Cake

3 cups flour	4 eggs
2 teaspoons soda	2 jars junior baby
2 teaspoons	food carrots
baking powder	1 1/2 cups oil
2 teaspoons cinnamon	3/4 cup nuts (opt.)
2 cups sugar	

Combine first 5 ingredients in bowl. Add eggs, carrots and oil; mix well. Stir in nuts. Pour into greased and floured bundt pan. Bake at 350 degrees for 40 to 45 minutes. Cool in pan for 10 minutes. Turn onto wire rack to cool completely. Spread glaze or cream cheese frosting over cake.

Lorraine Fenton
Xi Omicron, Milford, Massachusetts

Rose's Carrot Cake

2 cups sugar	2 cups flour
4 eggs	2 teaspoons soda
1 cup oil	2 teaspoons cinnamon
3 small jars strained	1 teaspoon
baby food carrots	vanilla extract
1 cup drained	1 cup chopped walnuts
crushed pineapple	1 cup boiled raisins

Combine first 5 ingredients in bowl; mix well. Add flour, soda and cinnamon; mix well. Add vanilla. Fold in walnuts and raisins. Pour into greased and floured 9 x 13-inch cake pan. Bake at 375 degrees for 40 to 45 minutes or until cake tests done. Cool.

Rose Noviello
Delta Beta, South Williamsport, Pennsylvania

Chess Cake

1 2-layer package	1 16-ounce package
butter-recipe	confectioners' sugar
yellow cake mix	1 stick margarine,
2 eggs	softened
1 stick margarine,	1 8-ounce package
softened	cream cheese,
2 eggs	softened

Combine cake mix, 2 eggs and 1 stick margarine in bowl; mix well. Spread in 9 x 13-inch cake pan. Batter will be very thick. Combine 2 eggs, confectioners' sugar, 1 stick margarine and cream cheese in bowl; blend well. Spread over cake mix layer. Bake at 350 degrees for 50 to 60 minutes. Yield: 30 servings.
Note: Cake will rise and then fall. People have commented that the cake tastes like ice cream.

Paula C. Middleton
Xi Mu Eta, Houston, Texas

Fast Fixing Chocolate Chip Cake

1/4 cup oil	1 6-ounce package
1 2-layer package	chocolate chips
devil's food	1 small package
cake mix	chocolate instant
2 eggs	pudding mix

Pour oil into 9 x 13-inch cake pan. Add remaining ingredients and 1 1/4 cups water to pan; mix with fork until blended. Bake at 350 degrees for 35 to 45 minutes or until cake tests done. Cool. Sprinkle with confectioners' sugar.

Sharon Vollmer
Zeta Zeta, Lafayette, Indiana

Desserts

Chocolate Fudge Cake

1/3 cup oil
2 2-ounce envelopes premelted baking chocolate
1 egg
1 1/4 cups instant flour
1 cup sugar
1/2 teaspoon soda
1/2 teaspoon salt
1/2 teaspoon vanilla extract
1/2 cup chocolate chips
1 cup chopped nuts

Combine oil, chocolate, egg, flour, sugar, soda, salt and vanilla in 9-inch square pan. Beat with fork until blended. Sprinkle chocolate chips and nuts over batter. Bake at 350 degrees for 30 minutes. Cut into squares when cool. Garnish with whipped topping and maraschino cherries.
Yield: 9-12 servings.

Diane Nelms
Alpha Sigma, Mobile, Alabama

Sour Cream-Chocolate Chip Cake

6 tablespoons butter, softened
1 cup sugar
2 eggs
1 1/3 cups flour
1 1/2 teaspoons baking powder
1 teaspoon soda
1 teaspoon cinnamon
1 cup sour cream
1 6-ounce package semisweet chocolate chips
1 tablespoon sugar

Cream butter and 1 cup sugar in bowl until light and fluffy. Add eggs 1 at a time, beating well after each addition. Add dry ingredients; mix well. Stir in sour cream. Pour into greased and floured 9 x 13-inch baking pan. Sprinkle with chocolate chips and 1 tablespoon sugar. Bake at 350 degrees for 35 minutes. Cool.

Deborah Sterling
Lambda, Boise, Idaho

Triple-Threat Chocolate Cake

1 2-layer package sour cream chocolate cake mix
1 small package chocolate instant pudding mix
4 eggs
1 cup sour cream
1/2 cup oil
1 teaspoon vanilla extract
1 12-ounce package chocolate chips

Combine 1/2 cup water and all ingredients except chocolate chips in large mixer bowl. Beat for 4 minutes or until smooth. Stir in chocolate chips. Pour into greased and floured bundt pan. Bake at 350 degrees for 50 to 60 minutes. Cool for 15 minutes. Turn onto serving platter. Garnish with sprinkle of confectioners' sugar and strawberries.
Yield: 12 servings.

Cyndy Talmant
Xi Alpha Mu, Sparks, Nevada

Coca-Cola Cake

2 cups flour
2 cups sugar
2 sticks margarine
3 tablespoons cocoa
1 cup Coca-Cola
1/2 cup buttermilk
1 teaspoon soda
1 teaspoon vanilla extract
2 eggs, beaten
2 cups miniature marshmallows
1 stick margarine
3 tablespoons cocoa
6 tablespoons Coca-Cola
1 16-ounce package confectioners' sugar
1 cup chopped nuts (opt.)

Combine flour and sugar in large bowl. Combine 2 sticks margarine, 3 tablespoons cocoa and 1 cup cola in saucepan. Bring to a boil. Pour over flour mixture; mix well. Add buttermilk, soda, vanilla and eggs; mix well. Stir in marshmallows. Batter will be thin. Pour into greased and floured 9 x 13-inch baking pan. Marshmallows will float to top. Bake at 350 degrees for 30 to 35 minutes or until cake tests done. Cool for 5 minutes. Combine 1 stick margarine, 3 tablespoons cocoa and 6 tablespoons cola in saucepan; heat until margarine melts. Add to confectioners' sugar in bowl; mix until smooth. Stir in nuts. Spread over warm cake.

Kaye Henderson
Xi Beta Zeta, Challis, Idaho

Mississippi Mud Cake

2 cups sugar
4 eggs
1 1/2 cups cake flour
Pinch of salt
1 1/2 cups pecans
2 sticks margarine, melted
1/2 cup cocoa
1 package miniature marshmallows
1 16-ounce package confectioners' sugar
1 teaspoon vanilla extract
1/2 cup milk
1/2 stick margarine, softened
1/3 cup cocoa

Beat sugar and eggs in bowl until fluffy. Add flour, salt, pecans and mixture of melted margarine and 1/2 cup cocoa; mix well. Pour into greased and floured 9 x 13-inch cake pan. Bake at 350 degrees for 25 minutes. Sprinkle marshmallows over cake. Bake for 2 minutes longer. Cool. Combine remaining ingredients in bowl; mix well. Spread over cake.

Renee Nichols
Gamma Kappa, Cape Canaveral, Florida

Desserts

Polka Dot Cake

1 1/4 cups chopped dates
3/4 cup butter, softened
1 cup sugar
2 eggs
2 cups sifted flour
1 teaspoon soda

1/2 teaspoon salt
1 teaspoon vanilla extract
1 6-ounce package chocolate chips
1/2 cup chopped nuts

Combine dates and 1 cup hot water in bowl; cool. Cream butter and sugar in bowl until light and fluffy. Add eggs. Beat until fluffy. Sift flour, soda and salt together. Add to creamed mixture alternately with dates, mixing well after each addition. Fold in vanilla and half the chocolate chips. Pour into greased and floured 9 x 13-inch cake pan. Sprinkle remaining chocolate chips and nuts over batter. Bake at 350 degrees for 35 minutes. Yield: 15 servings.

Betty Hahn
Alpha Theta, Brookings, South Dakota

Sour Cream Texas Sheet Cake

2 sticks butter
1/4 cup cocoa
2 cups sugar
1 cup sour cream
1 teaspoon soda
2 eggs
2 cups flour
Dash of salt

6 tablespoons milk
1/4 cup cocoa
1 stick butter
1 16-ounce package confectioners' sugar
1/2 teaspoon vanilla extract

Combine 1 cup water, 2 sticks butter and 1/4 cup cocoa in saucepan. Boil for 3 minutes, stirring constantly. Add sugar and next 5 ingredients; mix well. Pour into greased and floured 9 x 13-inch baking pan. Bake at 325 degrees for 20 minutes. Combine milk, 1/4 cup cocoa and 1 stick butter in saucepan. Boil for 1 minute, stirring constantly. Add confectioners' sugar and vanilla; mix well. Pour over hot cake.

Jana Weigle
Xi Alpha Rho, Danville, Kentucky

Texas Sheet Cake

1/2 cup shortening
3 tablespoons cocoa
2 cups flour
2 cups sugar
1/2 teaspoon salt
1 teaspoon soda
1 teaspoon vanilla extract
1 teaspoon cinnamon
2 eggs, beaten

1/2 cup milk
1 stick margarine
3 tablespoons cocoa
1/2 cup milk
1 16-ounce package confectioners' sugar
1 teaspoon vanilla extract
1/2 cup chopped pecans

Combine shortening, cocoa and 1 cup water in saucepan. Bring to a boil. Add mixture of flour, sugar and salt; mix well. Add soda, vanilla, cinnamon, eggs and milk; mix well. Pour into greased and floured 10 x 15-inch baking pan. Bake at 350 degrees for 20 minutes. Combine margarine, 3 tablespoons cocoa and 1/2 cup milk in saucepan. Bring to a boil. Add remaining ingredients. Pour over warm cake. Cool.

Dawn Fox
Alpha Gamma, APO New York

Grace's Turtle Cake

1 14-ounce package caramels
1/3 cup evaporated milk
1 2-layer package German chocolate cake mix

3/4 cup evaporated milk
3/4 cup margarine
1 cup pecans
1 cup chocolate chips

Melt caramels with 1/3 cup evaporated milk in saucepan; cool. Combine cake mix, 3/4 cup evaporated milk and margarine in bowl; mix well. Spread half the batter in greased and floured 9 x 13-inch cake pan. Bake at 350 degrees for 15 minutes. Spoon caramel mixture over baked layer. Sprinkle with pecans and chocolate chips. Spread remaining cake batter over top. Bake for 15 to 20 minutes longer or until cake tests done. Cut into squares when cool.

Grace McIntyre
Xi Beta Rho, Norman, Oklahoma

Turtle Cake

1 2-layer package German chocolate cake mix
1 14-ounce package caramels

3/4 cup butter
1/2 can evaporated milk
1 cup chocolate chips
1 cup chopped pecans

Prepare cake mix according to package directions. Pour half the batter into prepared 9 x 13-inch baking pan. Bake at 350 degrees for 15 minutes. Melt caramels and butter with evaporated milk in saucepan over low heat, stirring constantly. Pour over baked layer. Add layers of chocolate chips, pecans and remaining cake batter. Bake for 20 minutes longer. Yield: 15 servings.

Beth Jensen
Preceptor Alpha Upsilon, Clear Lake, Iowa

Desserts

Wacky Cake

3 cups flour
2 cups sugar
2 teaspoons soda
10 tablespoons cocoa
2 tablespoons vinegar

2 teaspoons
   vanilla extract
10 tablespoons
   melted margarine

Sift first 4 ingredients together into ungreased 9 x 13-inch cake pan. Make 3 wells in dry ingredients. Pour each liquid ingredient into 1 well. Pour 2 cups cold water over all. Beat with spoon. Bake at 350 degrees for 30 minutes.

Jan Crissup
Preceptor Delta Alpha, Lee's Summit, Missouri

Chocolate Oil Cake

3 cups flour
2 cups sugar
1 teaspoon soda
1 teaspoon salt
1/2 cup cocoa

2 tablespoons vinegar
3/4 cup oil
2 teaspoons
   vanilla extract

Combine all ingredients in mixer bowl. Beat for 2 minutes. Pour into greased and floured 9 x 13-inch cake pan. Bake at 350 degrees for 30 minutes or until cake tests done. Frost cooled cake as desired.

Toni Harvey
Iota Omega, Meadville, Pennsylvania

Chop Suey Cake

2 cups flour
2 cups sugar
2 eggs
2 teaspoons soda
1/2 teaspoon salt
1 cup chopped nuts
1 20-ounce can
   crushed pineapple
1 stick margarine,
   softened

1 8-ounce package
   cream cheese,
   softened
2 cups confectioners'
   sugar
2 tablespoons
   milk
1 teaspoon
   vanilla extract

Combine flour, sugar, eggs, soda, salt, nuts and pineapple in bowl; mix well. Pour into greased and floured 9 x 13-inch cake pan. Bake at 350 degrees for 35 minutes or until cake tests done. Cream margarine and cream cheese in bowl until light and fluffy. Add remaining ingredients; mix well. Spread over hot cake.

Tommie Holcomb
Eta Iota, Moore, Oklahoma

Cream of Coconut Cake

1 2-layer package
   white cake mix
1 15-ounce can
   cream of coconut
1 15-ounce can
   sweetened condensed
   milk

1 8-ounce carton
   whipped topping
1 cup toasted
   coconut
1/2 cup nuts (opt.)

Prepare and bake cake mix according to package directions using 9 x 13-inch baking pan. Cool for 15 minutes. Punch holes in cake using knife handle. Drizzle cream of coconut and condensed milk over cake. Cool for 15 minutes longer. Spread whipped topping over top. Sprinkle with coconut and nuts.

Betty F. Wiley
Delta Omega, Shawnee, Oklahoma

Coconut Creme Cake

2 2/3 cups flour
1 1/2 cups sugar
1 1/2 teaspoons salt
4 teaspoons
   baking powder
2 teaspoons
   orange extract
1 teaspoon
   vanilla extract

2/3 cup oil
4 eggs, separated
1/4 teaspoon cream
   of tartar
1 15-ounce can cream
   of coconut
1 9-ounce carton
   whipped topping

Combine flour, sugar, salt and baking powder in mixer bowl. Add flavorings, oil, egg yolks and 3/4 cup water; beat until smooth. Beat egg whites with cream of tartar until stiff peaks form. Fold into batter. Pour into greased and floured 9 x 13-inch baking pan. Bake at 350 degrees for 30 to 40 minutes or until cake tests done. Pierce cake at 1-inch intervals with toothpick. Pour cream of coconut over cake; cool. Top with whipped topping. Garnish with coconut. Yield: 12 servings.

Edyth M. Schuyler
Preceptor Rho, Lakewood, Colorado

Fast and Fabulous Fruitcake

2 eggs, slightly beaten
3 cups mincemeat
1 15-ounce can
   sweetened
   condensed milk
1 3/4 cups mixed
   candied fruit

1 cup chopped walnuts
2 1/2 cups flour
1 teaspoon soda
2 cups sifted
   confectioners' sugar
1/4 cup mixed
   candied fruit

Line greased 9-inch tube pan with greased waxed paper. Combine first 5 ingredients in bowl; mix well. Sift in flour and soda; mix well. Spoon into prepared pan. Bake at 300 degrees for 1 hour and 50 minutes. Cool in pan for 15 minutes. Invert on cake plate; remove waxed paper. Cool completely. Combine confectioners' sugar and enough boiling water in bowl to make thick glaze. Spread over fruitcake. Garnish with 1/4 cup candied fruit.

Joan Webster
Preceptor Gamma Iota, Ottawa, Ontario, Canada

Desserts

No-Bake Fruitcake

1 16-ounce box
    vanilla wafers,
    crushed
1/2 pound candied red
    cherries, chopped
1/2 pound candied
    green pineapple,
    chopped
1 cup seedless raisins

4 cups chopped pecans
1 16-ounce package
    miniature
    marshmallows
1 stick margarine
1 15-ounce can
    sweetened
    condensed milk

Mix vanilla wafer crumbs, fruit and pecans in bowl. Melt marshmallows and margarine with sweetened condensed milk in double boiler. Pour over fruit mixture; mix well. Pack into waxed paper-lined tube pan. Chill for 48 hours. Invert on serving plate; remove waxed paper.

Susan Duett
Delta Theta, Columbus, Mississippi

Fresh Fruit Cake

1 1/2 cups orange
    juice
3/4 cup sugar
2 tablespoons
    cornstarch
1/4 teaspoon salt
1 teaspoon grated
    orange rind

1 teaspoon grated
    lemon rind
1 package angel
    food cake mix
3 medium
    peaches, sliced
1 pint strawberries
1 cup blueberries

Combine first 6 ingredients in glass measure. Microwave, covered, on High for 6 to 7 minutes or until thickened, stirring every 2 minutes. Chill for 1 hour. Prepare cake mix according to package directions. Spread in 10 x 15-inch baking pan lined with greased waxed paper. Bake at 375 degrees for 20 minutes. Loosen from pan sides and invert on waxed paper-lined wire rack; peel off waxed paper. Cool completely. Place on large tray. Brush with half the sauce. Arrange fruit over cake. Brush with remaining sauce. Yield: 12 servings.

Adeline Hoffman
Xi Zeta, West Orange, New Jersey

Fruit Cocktail Cake

1 1/2 cups sugar
2 cups flour
1/2 teaspoon soda
1/2 teaspoon salt
1 16-ounce can fruit
    cocktail, drained,
    mashed
1 teaspoon
    vanilla extract

2 eggs, beaten
1/2 cup packed
    brown sugar
1/2 cup chopped nuts
1/2 cup shredded
    coconut
3/4 cup sugar
1/2 cup milk
1/4 cup butter

Combine first 4 ingredients in bowl. Add fruit cocktail, vanilla and eggs; mix well. Pour into greased and floured 9 x 13-inch cake pan. Combine brown sugar, nuts and coconut in bowl. Sprinkle over batter. Bake at 350 degrees for 40 minutes. Combine 3/4 cup sugar, milk and butter in saucepan. Bring to a boil. Cook for 2 minutes, stirring constantly. Pour hot glaze over hot cake. Cool.

Cindy Lee Crawford
Xi Pi, Fresno, California

Hawaiian Fruit Cake

2 cups flour
2 cups sugar
2 teaspoons soda
2 cups crushed
    pineapple with juice

2 eggs
1 teaspoon
    vanilla extract
1 cup chopped nuts

Combine all ingredients in bowl; mix well. Pour into ungreased 9 x 13-inch cake pan. Bake at 350 degrees for 40 minutes. Cool.

Edith Durbin
Laureate Alpha Epsilon, Effingham, Illinois

Frosted Hummingbird Cake

3 cups flour
2 cups sugar
1 teaspoon salt
1 teaspoon soda
1 teaspoon cinnamon
3 eggs, beaten
1 1/2 cups oil
1 1/2 teaspoons
    vanilla extract
1 8-ounce can
    crushed pineapple

2 cups chopped pecans
2 cups chopped bananas
1/2 cup butter,
    softened
1 8-ounce package
    cream cheese,
    softened
1 16-ounce
    package
    confectioners' sugar

Combine first 5 ingredients in large bowl. Add eggs and oil; stir until just blended. Do not beat. Add vanilla, pineapple, pecans and bananas. Pour into 3 greased and floured 9-inch cake pans. Bake at 350 degrees for 25 minutes or until cake tests done. Cool in pans for 10 minutes. Remove layers to wire rack to cool completely. Cream butter, cream cheese and confectioners' sugar in bowl until light and fluffy. Spread between layers and over top and side of cake.

Thelma Knipmeyer
Alma, Missouri

Desserts

Lemon Meringue Cake

2 eggs, separated
1/2 cup sugar
1 1-layer package
   yellow cake mix
1 teaspoon
   lemon extract
1/4 cup sliced almonds

Beat egg whites until soft peaks form. Add sugar gradually, beating until stiff and glossy. Combine cake mix, 1/2 cup water, egg yolks and flavoring in mixer bowl. Beat at low speed for 2 minutes. Pour into greased and floured 8-inch round cake pan. Spoon meringue over batter to within 1 inch of side; smooth with spatula. Sprinkle with almonds. Bake at 350 degrees for 30 minutes or until cake pulls from side of pan. Cool on wire rack before serving. Yield: 6 servings.

Helen Heath
Preceptor Upsilon, Muncie, Indiana

Swedish Nut Cake

2 cups sugar
2 cups flour
1/2 cup nuts
2 teaspoons soda
1 teaspoon
   vanilla extract
1 20-ounce can
   crushed pineapple
1 stick margarine,
   softened
1 8-ounce package
   cream cheese,
   softened
1/2 cup nuts
1 3/4 cups
   confectioners'
   sugar
1 teaspoon
   vanilla extract

Combine sugar, flour, nuts, soda, 1 teaspoon vanilla and pineapple with juice in greased 9 x 13-inch cake pan; mix well. Bake at 350 degrees for 40 minutes or until cake tests done. Cream remaining ingredients in bowl until light and fluffy. Spread on hot cake. Cool before serving. Yield: 16 servings.

Mary A. Roell
Mu Iota, Lawrenceburg, Indiana

Easy as One-Two-Three Cake

1 cup shortening
2 cups sugar
3 cups flour
4 eggs
1 cup milk
1 tablespoon
   baking powder
1/2 teaspoon salt
2 teaspoons vanilla
   extract (opt.)

Combine all ingredients in large mixer bowl. Beat at medium speed for 2 minutes. Pour into greased and floured bundt pan. Bake at 350 degrees for 40 to 50 minutes or until cake tests done. Cool. Frost if desired or use for shortcake.

Nancy Morgan
Xi Zeta, APO New York

Peanut Butter Cake

1 2-layer package
   German chocolate
   cake mix
1 cup peanut butter
1 can ready-to-spread
   chocolate frosting

Prepare and bake cake mix according to package directions using 9 x 13-inch baking pan. Spread peanut butter over hot cake. Cool completely. Frost with chocolate frosting.

Ann Kline
Preceptor Delta, Sulphur, Louisiana

Joyce's Pineapple Cake

2 cups sugar
1 20-ounce can
   crushed pineapple
1 teaspoon soda
1 teaspoon
   vanilla extract
2 cups flour
1 cup chopped pecans
1 8-ounce package
   cream cheese,
   softened
1 stick butter, melted
3/4 cup sugar
1 cup chopped pecans

Combine first 6 ingredients in order listed, mixing well by hand after each addition. Pour into ungreased 9 x 13-inch baking pan. Bake at 350 degrees for 30 to 35 minutes. Blend cream cheese and butter in bowl. Add sugar and pecans; mix well. Pour over hot cake.

Joyce Rader
Chi Alpha, Bedford, Texas

Layered Pineapple Cake

1 1-layer package
   yellow cake mix
1 small package vanilla
   instant pudding mix
1 8-ounce package
   cream cheese,
   softened
2 cups milk
1 12-ounce can
   crushed pineapple,
   drained
1 12-ounce carton
   whipped topping

Prepare and bake cake mix using package directions for 8 x 12-inch cake pan. Cool. Combine pudding mix, cream cheese and milk in bowl; mix well. Spread over cake. Top with pineapple and whipped topping. Chill in refrigerator. Cut into squares to serve.

Shirley Corder
Pi Chi, Corder, Missouri

Desserts

Claire's Pineapple Cake

2 cups flour
2 cups sugar
2 eggs
2 teaspoons soda
1/2 teaspoon salt
1 20-ounce can
  crushed pineapple
1/2 cup broken walnuts

Combine all ingredients in bowl; mix well. Pour into greased and floured 9 x 11-inch cake pan. Bake at 350 degrees for 35 minutes. Cool. Yield: 10-12 servings.

Claire Carson
Laureate Rho, Norristown, Pennsylvania

Evelyn's Pineapple Cake

1 2-layer package
  yellow cake mix
1 cup oil
4 eggs, lightly beaten
2 16-ounce cans
  crushed juice-pack
  pineapple
1 large package
  vanilla instant
  pudding mix
1 8-ounce
  carton whipped
  topping

Combine cake mix, oil, eggs and 1 can pineapple in large bowl; mix with fork. Do not use mixer. Pour into greased and floured 9 x 13-inch baking pan. Bake at 350 degrees for 30 minutes. Cool completely. Combine 1 can pineapple and pudding mix in bowl; mix until thickened. Fold in whipped topping. Spread over cake. Chill, covered, in refrigerator.

Evelyn Knight
Alpha Omega Omicron, Azle, Texas

Pineapple-Lemon Surprise

1 2-layer package
  lemon cake mix
2 egg whites
1 small package
  lemon pudding mix
1 7-Up
1 16-ounce can
  crushed pineapple
3/4 cup sugar
2 teaspoons cornstarch
2 egg yolks
1 cup coconut

Prepare cake mix according to package directions with 2 egg whites, pudding mix and substituting 7-Up for water. Pour into prepared 9 x 13-inch baking pan. Bake using package directions. Combine pineapple, sugar, cornstarch and egg yolks in saucepan. Cook until thickened, stirring constantly. Stir in coconut. Spread warm pineapple mixture over cake. Let stand overnight before serving.

Billie K. Adams
Iota Eta, Marrero, Louisiana

Essex Poppy Seed Cake

3 cups flour
1 1/2 teaspoons
  baking powder
1 1/2 teaspoons salt
2 1/2 cups sugar
1 1/2 cups milk
1 cup plus 2
  tablespoons oil
3 tablespoons
  poppy seed
3 eggs
1 1/2 teaspoons
  vanilla extract
1 teaspoon
  almond flavoring
3/4 cup confectioners'
  sugar
2 tablespoons fresh
  orange juice
2 tablespoons
  melted butter
1/2 teaspoon
  vanilla extract
1/2 teaspoon
  almond flavoring

Combine first 10 ingredients in mixer bowl. Beat for 3 minutes. Pour into greased and floured 12-cup bundt pan. Bake at 350 degrees for 1 hour. Cool in pan for 15 minutes. Turn onto cake plate. Combine confectioners' sugar, orange juice, butter and flavorings in bowl; mix well. Pour over warm cake. Cool.

Beverly Benson
Delta Upsilon, Newman Grove, Nebraska

Pumpkin Roll

3 eggs
1 cup sugar
2/3 cup pumpkin
1 teaspoon lemon juice
3/4 cup flour
2 teaspoons cinnamon
1/2 teaspoon nutmeg
1 teaspoon ginger
1 teaspoon
  baking powder
1/2 teaspoon salt
1 cup chopped nuts
1 cup (about)
  confectioners' sugar
1/4 cup butter,
  softened
2 3-ounce packages
  cream cheese,
  softened
1 cup confectioners'
  sugar
1/2 teaspoon
  vanilla extract

Beat eggs for 5 minutes. Add sugar gradually, beating constantly. Add pumpkin and lemon juice; mix well. Sift next 6 dry ingredients together into bowl. Fold in pumpkin mixture. Spread in greased and floured 10 x 15-inch baking sheet. Sprinkle nuts over batter, pressing lightly. Bake at 375 degrees for 12 to 15 minutes or until cake tests done. Turn onto towel sprinkled with 1 cup confectioners' sugar. Roll cake and towel from narrow end as for jelly roll. Chill for 1 hour. Cream butter, cream cheese, 1 cup confectioners' sugar and vanilla in bowl until light and fluffy. Unroll cake. Spread with cream cheese mixture. Reroll. Freeze for 2 hours to 2 weeks. Thaw for several minutes before serving.

Maxine Olson
Alpha Iota Preceptor, American Falls, Idaho

Desserts

Easy Pound Cake

2/3 cup margarine, softened
3 eggs
1 1/3 cups sugar
2 teaspoons vanilla extract
2 1/3 cups cake flour
1 teaspoon baking powder
1/2 teaspoon salt
3/4 cup milk

Combine margarine and eggs in mixer bowl; beat well. Add sugar and vanilla; beat until smooth. Sift dry ingredients together. Add to creamed mixture alternately with milk, mixing well after each addition. Pour into buttered tube pan. Bake at 350 degrees for 50 to 60 minutes or until cake tests done. Cool in pan for 10 minutes. Invert onto cake plate to cool completely. Spread with favorite glaze.

Jane Kelley
Xi Kappa Nu, Silsbee, Texas

Pound Cake Surprise

1 loaf-style pound cake
1 tablespoon grated lemon rind
1 10-ounce jar currant jelly
2 tablespoons lemon juice
1 snack-sized can prepared lemon pudding
Slivered almonds

Cut cake into 4 layers. Mix lemon rind and jelly in bowl. Spread between cake layers. Frost with mixture of lemon juice and lemon pudding. Sprinkle with slivered almonds. Yield: 8 servings.

Dorinne Rosson
Alpha Omega Omicron, Azle, Texas

Rum Cream Cake

6 tablespoons (scant) butter
1 cup flour
6 egg yolks
1 cup minus 1 tablespoon sugar
1 tablespoon unflavored gelatin
1 pint whipping cream, whipped
1/2 cup rum

Cut butter into flour in bowl until crumbly. Add 3 tablespoons ice water; mix well. Roll on floured surface. Fit into 9-inch pie plate. Bake at 350 degrees for 15 minutes or until golden brown. Cool. Beat egg yolks until light. Add sugar. Beat until light and fluffy. Soften gelatin in 1/2 cup cold water in saucepan. Bring to a boil over low heat, stirring constantly. Add to egg mixture, stirring briskly. Fold in whipped cream gently. Blend in rum gradually. Chill until thick. Pour chilled mixture into crust. Chill until firm. Garnish with grated chocolate or chopped pistachio nuts.

Marjorie M. Lancaster
Preceptor Xi, Seal Beach, California

Sharlene's Seven-Up Cake

1/2 pound margarine, softened
1/2 cup shortening
3 cups sugar
5 eggs
3 cups flour
1 teaspoon vanilla extract
1 teaspoon lemon extract
1 cup 7-Up

Combine all ingredients in mixer bowl. Beat with electric mixer until blended. Pour into greased and floured bundt pan. Bake at 325 degrees for 1 hour and 10 minutes or until cake tests done. Cool. Drizzle confectioners' sugar icing over cake.

Sharlene Exline
Xi Epsilon Epsilon, Forest, Ohio

Sherry Cake

1 2-layer package yellow cake mix
1 small package vanilla pudding mix
2/3 cup Sherry
3/4 cup oil
4 eggs
2 tablespoons cinnamon
Pinch of salt

Combine all ingredients in mixer bowl. Beat for 2 minutes. Pour into greased and floured bundt pan. Bake at 350 degrees for 40 minutes. Cool in pan for 10 minutes. Turn onto cake plate. Drizzle with Sherry-flavored confectioners' sugar glaze.

Glenda Stanley
Sherwood Park, Alberta, Canada

Sorry Cake

1 16-ounce package brown sugar
2 cups buttermilk baking mix
3 eggs
1 teaspoon vanilla extract
1 cup nuts

Combine all ingredients in bowl; mix well. Spread in greased and floured 9 x 13-inch baking pan. Bake at 350 degrees for 30 minutes.
Note: This cake is flat and chewy like a brownie and looks "sorry."

Marguerite Rinella
Laureate Delta, Louisville, Kentucky

Desserts

Coffee Cloud Sponge Cake

1 tablespoon instant coffee powder	1/2 cup sugar
2 cups sifted flour	1 1/2 cups sugar
1 tablespoon baking powder	1 teaspoon vanilla extract
1/2 teaspoon salt	6 egg yolks, beaten
6 egg whites	1 cup pecans
1/2 teaspoon cream of tartar	

Dissolve coffee in 1 cup boiling water; cool. Sift flour, baking powder and salt together. Beat egg whites with cream of tartar in mixer bowl until soft peaks form. Add 1/2 cup sugar, 2 tablespoons at a time, beating constantly until stiff peaks form. Add 1 1/2 cups sugar and vanilla to beaten egg yolks. Add sifted dry ingredients alternately with coffee to egg yolk mixture, beginning and ending with dry ingredients and beating constantly at low speed. Fold in 1 cup nuts gently. Fold egg yolk mixture 1/4 at a time gently into stiffly beaten egg whites until just blended. Pour into ungreased tube pan. Bake at 350 degrees for 60 to 70 minutes or until cake tests done. Invert cake in pan. Cool completely. Loosen from side of pan; remove to cake plate.

Hanni C. Collyer
Xi Gamma Rho, Columbus, Georgia

Frances' Sponge Cake

1/2 cup egg whites	3 tablespoons lemon juice
1/2 teaspoon salt	1 cup cake flour, sifted
1/2 cup sugar	
1/2 cup egg yolks	
1/2 cup sugar	

Beat egg whites with salt until stiff peaks form. Add 1/2 cup sugar gradually, beating until stiff and glossy. Beat egg yolks until thick. Add 1/2 cup sugar gradually; beat well. Stir in lemon juice. Fold flour gently into egg yolks. Fold egg yolks gently into egg whites. Pour into ungreased tube pan. Bake at 325 degrees for 1 hour. Invert pan on funnel. Cool completely before removing from pan.

Frances Lueck
Pi Chi, Alma, Missouri

Tangerine Sunshine Cake

1 2-layer package yellow cake mix	4 eggs
1 small package vanilla instant pudding mix	1/3 cup oil
	1 envelope whipped topping mix
4 teaspoons freshly grated tangerine rind	1/2 cup milk
	2 teaspoons freshly ground tangerine rind
3 tablespoons freshly squeezed tangerine juice	2 California-Arizona tangerines, peeled, sectioned

Combine first 6 ingredients and 1 cup water in large mixer bowl. Beat at medium speed for 4 minutes. Pour into well-greased 10-inch bundt pan. Bake at 350 degrees for 50 minutes or until cake tests done. Cool for 10 minutes. Invert onto serving plate. Cool completely. Garnish with sprinkle of confectioners' sugar. Prepare topping mix with milk according to package directions, omitting vanilla. Stir in tangerine rind and segments. Serve with cake.

Photograph for this recipe on page 52.

John's Mom's Old-Fashioned Shortcake

1/3 cup butter, softened	2 eggs, beaten
1 cup sugar	1 cup milk
2 cups self-rising flour	1 teaspoon vanilla extract

Combine all ingredients in bowl; mix well. Pat into greased and floured 10-inch iron skillet. Bake at 350 degrees for 30 minutes. Cut into wedges; split. Serve with strawberries or other fresh fruit.

Sarah M. Singleton
Xi Omega, Bowling Green, Kentucky

Fast Frosting

1 stick margarine	1/4 cup milk
1 cup sugar	1/2 cup chocolate chips

Combine margarine, sugar and milk in saucepan. Boil for 1 minute; remove from heat. Add chocolate chips. Beat until smooth. Spread over cooled cake.
Yield: Enough for 9 x 13-inch cake.
Note: May substitute butterscotch chips for chocolate chips.

Elaine Rowett
Preceptor Pi, Sturgis, South Dakota

Desserts

Mint-Puff Candy Squares, recipe on page 63.

Butterscotch Quickies

1　6-ounce package
　　butterscotch chips

1/3 cup peanut butter
3 cups cornflakes

Melt butterscotch chips and peanut butter in double boiler; stir to blend well. Stir in cornflakes; mix well. Drop by teaspoonfuls onto waxed paper. Chill until firn.

Eve Robinson
Beta Alpha, Kelvington, Saskatchewan, Canada

Kathy's Peanut Brittle

1 cup sugar
1/2 cup light
　　corn syrup
1 stick butter

1 1/3 cups raw Spanish
　　peanuts with hulls
1 teaspoon soda

Bring sugar, corn syrup, butter and 1/4 cup water to a boil in saucepan. Stir in peanuts. Cook to hard-crack stage or 305 degrees on candy thermometer; remove from heat. Stir in soda. Pour onto buttered baking sheet. Break into pieces when cool. Yield: 10 servings.

Jeanie Lombardi
Xi Nu Iota, Santa Rosa, California

Easy Pralines

1 cup sugar
1/2 cup packed
　　brown sugar
1/2 cup evaporated
　　milk
1 tablespoon margarine

1　3-ounce package
　　butterscotch
　　pudding and pie
　　filling mix
1 cup chopped pecans

Bring all ingredients except pecans to a boil in saucepan over low heat; stir to blend well. Cook for 5 minutes, stirring constantly. Stir in pecans. Beat until thick. Drop by teaspoonfuls onto waxed paper. Cool until firm. Yield: 2 dozen.

Jolene Broussard
Preceptor Delta, Sulphur, Louisiana

Mock Toffee

Graham crackers
1/2 cup butter
1/2 cup sugar

1　4 1/2-ounce
　　package sliced
　　almonds

Arrange graham crackers slightly overlapping in single layer on heavily buttered cookie sheet. Bring butter and sugar to a boil in saucepan. Cool for 2 minutes, stirring constantly. Pour over graham crackers. Sprinkle with almonds. Bake at 325 degrees for 15 minutes; cool. Break into pieces. Yield: 4 dozen.

Lou Matthews
Preceptor Beta Mu, Pueblo, Colorado

Desserts

Just Like Almond Roca

1 pound butter
2 1/3 cups sugar
1 1/2 cups almonds

1 6-ounce package
 chocolate chips
1/4 cup ground walnuts

Mix butter and sugar in heavy skillet. Cook for 8 minutes on medium-high heat, stirring frequently. Add almonds. Cook for 8 minutes longer, stirring constantly. Pour into 9 x 13-inch pan lined with buttered foil. Sprinkle chocolate chips over top. Spread evenly when melted. Top with walnuts. Break into pieces when cool. Yield: 3 pounds.

Dawn Moudy
Beta Iota, McCall, Idaho

Chow Candy Clusters

1 12-ounce package
 semisweet
 chocolate chips
1 12-ounce package
 butterscotch chips

1/2 cup salted cashews
1 5-ounce can chow
 mein noodles

Melt chocolate and butterscotch chips in saucepan over low heat; stir to blend well. Stir in cashews and noodles; mix well. Drop by tablespoonfuls onto waxed paper. Chill until firm. Yield: 3 dozen.

Shirley Fryatt
Laureate Alpha Sigma, Federal Way, West Virginia

No-Cook Fudge

1 16-ounce package
 confectioners' sugar
6 tablespoons cocoa
1/4 cup evaporated
 milk
1 teaspoon
 vanilla extract

1 stick margarine,
 melted
1/2 cup chopped
 nuts (opt.)

Sift confectioners' sugar and cocoa twice into bowl. Stir in evaporated milk and vanilla. Add margarine and nuts; mix well. Spread in buttered 9 x 13-inch dish. Chill until firm. Cut into squares.

Bee Grimm
Preceptor Gamma Kappa, Stockton, California

Velvety Cheese Fudge

4 pounds confectioners'
 sugar, sifted
1 cup cocoa, sifted
1 pound margarine

1 pound Velveeta
 cheese, cubed
1 teaspoon
 vanilla extract

Sift confectioners' sugar and cocoa together into bowl. Melt margarine and cheese in double boiler; stir to blend well. Stir into dry ingredients; mix well. Add vanilla. Pour into greased 9 x 13-inch pan. Let stand until firm. Cut into squares. Yield: 6 1/2 pounds.

Constance M. Orell
Xi Eta Eta, North Huntingdon, Pennsylvania

Mint-Puff Candy Squares

5 cups puffed rice
1/2 cup crushed hard
 mint candy
3 cups miniature
 marshmallows

2 tablespoons butter
1 6-ounce package
 semisweet
 chocolate chips

Heat puffed rice in shallow baking pan in preheated 350-degree oven for 10 minutes. Pour into large well-greased bowl. Add candy; mix well. Combine marshmallows and butter in saucepan. Cook over low heat until melted, stirring occasionally. Pour over puffed rice and candy; stir until evenly coated. Press into well-greased 9 x 13-inch baking pan. Melt chocolate chips in double boiler over hot water, stirring occasionally. Spread over puffed rice. Chill. Cut into squares. Yield: 2 dozen.

Photograph for this recipe on opposite page.

Kaye's Peanut Clusters

1 12-ounce package
 milk chocolate chips
1 12-ounce package
 butterscotch chips

1/4 cup peanut butter
4 cups unsalted dry
 roasted peanuts

Melt chocolate chips, butterscotch chips and peanut butter in double boiler; stir to blend well. Add peanuts; mix well. Drop by spoonfuls onto lightly greased baking sheet. Chill until firm. Yield: 5 dozen.

Kaye Dame
Xi Phi, Gainesville, Florida

Salted Peanut Clusters

1 pound
 chocolate-almond
 bark

1 12-ounce package
 chocolate chips
1 pound salted peanuts

Melt almond bark and chocolate chips in saucepan over low heat; stir to blend well. Stir in peanuts. Drop by teaspoonfuls onto waxed paper. Cool until set.

Marjorie K. Lessman
Xi Alpha Kappa, Dalton, Nebraska

Desserts

Scotcheroos

1 cup sugar
1 cup light corn syrup
1 cup peanut butter
6 cups crisp
   rice cereal
1 6-ounce package
   semisweet
   chocolate chips
1 6-ounce package
   butterscotch chips

Bring sugar and corn syrup to a boil in saucepan. Blend in peanut butter. Add cereal; mix well. Press into buttered 9 x 13-inch pan. Let stand for several minutes. Melt chocolate and butterscotch chips in saucepan over low heat; blend well. Spread over cereal mixture. Chill until firm. Cut into bars. Yield: 4 dozen.

Shirley Fryatt
Laureate Alpha Sigma, Federal Way, West Virginia

Praline Nuggets

1 cup finely crushed
   vanilla wafers
1 cup finely
   chopped pecans
1 cup confectioners'
   sugar
2 tablespoons cocoa
4 1/2 teaspoons light
   corn syrup
1/4 cup praline
   liqueur
Confectioners' sugar

Combine first 4 ingredients in bowl; mix well. Stir in mixture of corn syrup and liqueur. Shape by teaspoonfuls into balls. Roll in confectioners' sugar. Yield: 4 dozen.

Donna Wilhelm
Xi Rho, Brownwood, Texas

Fresh Fruit Cheesecake, recipe below.

Fresh Fruit Cheesecake

1 1/4 cups graham
   cracker crumbs
1/4 cup finely
   chopped pecans
1/2 teaspoon cinnamon
3 tablespoons
   butter, melted
2 tablespoons honey
3/4 cup ricotta cheese
1/2 cup yogurt
2 eggs
2 tablespoons freshly
   squeezed lemon juice
1 teaspoon
   vanilla extract
2 ripe bananas, sliced
1/4 cup flour
2 tablespoons honey
2 kiwifruit,
   peeled, sliced
1/2 pint fresh
   strawberries

Combine graham cracker crumbs, pecans and cinnamon in bowl. Add butter and 2 tablespoons honey; mix well. Press into buttered pie plate. Bake at 350 degrees for 10 minutes. Cool completely. Combine ricotta cheese, yogurt, eggs, lemon juice and vanilla in blender container. Process until smooth. Add bananas, flour and 2 tablespoons honey. Process until smooth. Pour into prepared crust. Bake at 350 degrees for 30 minutes or until set. Chill in refrigerator. Arrange kiwifruit and strawberries over top. Yield: 6-8 servings.

Photograph for this recipe above.

Desserts

Blender Cheesecake

1 21-ounce can
  pie filling
1 3-ounce package
  lemon gelatin
2 cups cottage cheese

2 tablespoons
  lemon juice
1 8-ounce carton
  whipped topping

Spread pie filling in 8 x 8-inch pan. Combine next 3 ingredients and 1/2 cup boiling water in blender container. Process until smooth. Combine with whipped topping in bowl; mix well. Spoon over pie filling. Chill until firm. Cut into squares. Invert squares on serving plates. Yield: 12-16 servings.

Maryann Cotterill
Theta Iota, Hendersonville, North Carolina

Lemon Cheesecake

1/4 cup melted butter
3 cups graham
  cracker crumbs
1 small package
  lemon gelatin
1 cup sugar

1 8-ounce package
  cream cheese,
  softened
1 teaspoon vanilla extract
1 pint whipping
  cream, whipped

Mix butter and crumbs in bowl. Press into 9 x 13-inch baking dish, reserving small amount for topping. Bake at 400 degrees for 5 minutes. Dissolve gelatin in 1 cup boiling water in bowl; cool. Cream sugar and cream cheese in mixer bowl until light and fluffy. Beat in vanilla. Add gelatin; mix well. Fold whipped cream gently into creamed mixture. Spoon into prepared dish. Chill in refrigerator. Yield: 20 servings.

Hilda Foster
Gamma Sigma, Fernie, British Columbia, Canada

Frozen Mocha Cheesecake

1 1/4 cups chocolate
  wafer crumbs
1/4 cup sugar
1/4 cup melted butter
1 8-ounce package
  cream cheese,
  softened
2/3 cup chocolate
  syrup

1 14-ounce can
  sweetened
  condensed milk
2 tablespoons
  instant coffee
  granules
1 cup whipping
  cream, whipped

Combine cookie crumbs, sugar and butter in bowl. Press over bottom and side of 9-inch springform pan. Chill in refrigerator. Beat cream cheese in mixer bowl until fluffy. Add chocolate syrup and condensed milk; mix well. Stir in coffee dissolved in 1 teaspoon hot water. Fold in whipped cream. Pour into prepared crust. Freeze, covered, for 6 hours or until firm. Place on serving dish; remove side of pan. Garnish with additional cookie crumbs. Yield: 12-15 servings.

Jeannie Cox
Preceptor Upsilon, Muncie, Indiana

Grandma's Pineapple Cheesecake

1 16-ounce can
  crushed pineapple
1 1/2 cups graham
  cracker crumbs
1/2 cup melted
  margarine
1/2 cup sugar
4 3-ounce packages
  cream cheese,
  softened

1/2 cup sugar
3 eggs
1 teaspoon
  vanilla extract
1/8 teaspoon salt
1 8-ounce carton
  sour cream
1/4 cup sugar

Drain pineapple, reserving 2 tablespoons juice. Combine cracker crumbs, margarine and 1/2 cup sugar in bowl; mix well. Press into 10-inch pie plate to form crust. Beat cream cheese and 1/2 cup sugar in mixer bowl until light and fluffy. Add eggs 1 at a time, mixing well after each addition. Beat in vanilla and salt. Mix in pineapple. Pour into crust. Bake at 350 degrees for 30 minutes. Combine remaining ingredients with reserved pineapple juice. Spead on cheesecake. Bake for 10 minutes longer. Chill in refrigerator. Yield: 8 servings.

Joyce Walsworth
Nu Gamma, Crescent City, California

Frozen Raspberry Cheesecake

1 cup chocolate
  wafer crumbs
1/2 cup melted butter
2/3 cup confectioners'
  sugar
3 3-ounce packages
  cream cheese,
  softened

1 egg, separated
2/3 cup raspberry
  juice
1 teaspoon lemon
  juice
1 cup whipping
  cream, whipped

Mix cookie crumbs and butter in bowl. Press over bottom and side of 8 or 9-inch springform pan. Freeze for several minutes. Cream confectioners' sugar and cream cheese in mixer bowl until light and fluffy. Beat in egg yolk and juices. Fold stiffly beaten egg white and whipped cream gently into cheese mixture. Pour into prepared crust. Freeze for 4 hours or until firm. Place on serving dish; remove side of pan. Garnish with raspberries or additional cookie crumbs. Yield: 8 servings.

Doris Decker
Laureate Alpha Alpha, Kingston, Ontario, Canada

Desserts

Amaretto Cheesecake

1 cup flour	1/4 cup flour
1/4 cup sugar	1 1/2 cups sugar
2 teaspoons grated	1/4 teaspoon salt
lemon rind	6 eggs
1 egg yolk	1/3 cup Amaretto
1/2 cup butter,	1 cup whipping cream
softened	1/4 cup confectioners'
5 8-ounce packages	sugar
cream cheese,	1 teaspoon
softened	almond extract

Combine 1 cup flour, 1/4 cup sugar and lemon rind in bowl. Mix in egg yolk and butter to make dough. Chill, wrapped in waxed paper, for 1 hour. Press over bottom and halfway up side of 9-inch springform pan with floured fingers. Beat cream cheese in mixer bowl until fluffy. Add 1/4 cup flour, 1 1/2 cups sugar and salt gradually, beating until light. Add eggs 1 at a time, mixing well after each addition. Add Amaretto. Beat for 3 minutes. Pour into prepared crust. Bake at 275 degrees for 2 hours or until set. Chill in refrigerator. Beat remaining ingredients in bowl until stiff. Place cheesecake on serving plate; remove side of pan. Spread whipped cream over top. Garnish with sliced almonds.
Yield: 20 servings.

Cindee Shinn
Xi, Waipahu, Hawaii

Blueberry Cheesecake Snacks

1 3-ounce package	2 tablespoons milk
cream cheese,	24 Triscuits
softened	1/4 cup melted butter
1 8-ounce package	Cinnamon and sugar
cream cheese,	to taste
softened	1 can blueberry
2 16-ounce cartons	pie filling
whipped topping	

Beat cream cheese in mixer bowl until light and fluffy. Add whipped topping and milk; beat until smooth. Pour into 9 x 13-inch dish. Chill for 2 hours. Place Triscuits on baking sheet. Brush with butter. Sprinkle with cinnamon and sugar. Broil for 1 minute; cool. Cut cream cheese mixture into 24 squares. Place 1 square on each Triscuit. Top with dollop of pie filling. Yield: 2 dozen.

Mary Scherbarth
Xi Alpha Theta, Fairbury, Nebraska

Cheesecake Miniatures

24 vanilla wafers	1 teaspoon
2 8-ounce packages	vanilla extract
cream cheese,	1 teaspoon
softened	lemon juice
2 eggs	1/4 teaspoon salt
1 14-ounce can	1 can cherry
sweetened	pie filling
condensed milk	

Place 1 vanilla wafer flat side down in 24 paper-lined muffin cups. Beat cream cheese in mixer bowl until fluffy. Add eggs, condensed milk, vanilla, lemon juice and salt; mix well. Fill prepared muffin cups 2/3 full. Bake at 350 degrees for 12 to 15 minutes or until filling is puffed; cool. Spoon pie filling over top. Store in refrigerator. Yield: 2 dozen.

Sharon E. Race
Xi Beta Tau, Little Valley, New York

Cherry Blossoms

16 vanilla wafers	2 teaspoons
2 eggs	vanilla extract
3/4 cup sugar	1 can cherry
2 8-ounce packages	pie filling
cream cheese,	
cubed	

Place each vanilla wafer in paper-lined muffin cup. Beat eggs with sugar in mixer bowl until foamy and thick. Beat in cream cheese until smooth. Add vanilla. Spoon into prepared muffin cups. Bake at 375 degrees for 10 to 12 minutes or until set. Remove paper liners. Top with pie filling.
Yield: 16 servings.

Donna Roth
Preceptor Beta Epsilon, Marion, Iowa

Cheesecake Fruit Tarts

24 vanilla wafers	2 eggs
3/4 cup sugar	1 teaspoon
2 8-ounce packages	vanilla extract
cream cheese,	2 cans fruit
softened	pie filling

Place each vanilla wafer in paper-lined muffin cup. Cream sugar and cream cheese in mixer bowl until light and fluffy. Beat in eggs and vanilla. Spoon into muffin cups. Bake at 375 degrees for 10 minutes; cool. Top with pie filling. Chill thoroughly. Yield: 2 dozen.

Shirley Ellen
Laureate Alpha Tau, National City, California
Susan Halfmann
Lamesa, Texas

Desserts

Cookies

Butterscotch Shortbread, recipe on page 71.

Applesauce Brownies

1/2 cup shortening
1 1/2 cups sugar
2 cups sweetened
    applesauce
2 eggs, beaten
2 cups flour
2 tablespoons cocoa

1/2 teaspoon each salt,
    soda and cinnamon
2 tablespoons sugar
1/2 cup chopped pecans
1 6-ounce package
    chocolate chips

Combine first 9 ingredients in mixer bowl; beat until well blended. Pour into greased and floured 10 x 15-inch baking pan. Sprinkle with 2 tablespoons sugar, pecans and chocolate chips. Bake at 350 degrees for 25 minutes. Cut into bars when cool. Yield: 3 dozen.

Carolyn A. Brenneis
Epsilon Nu, Blair, Nebraska

Blonde Brownies

3/4 cup melted butter
2 cups packed
    brown sugar
2 eggs
2 teaspoons
    vanilla extract
2 1/4 cups flour

1 teaspoon
    baking powder
1 teaspoon salt
1/4 teaspoon soda
1 cup chopped walnuts
1 cup chocolate chips

Blend butter and brown sugar in bowl. Mix in eggs and vanilla. Add mixture of dry ingredients; mix well. Stir in walnuts. Spoon into greased and floured 9 x 13-inch baking pan. Sprinkle with chocolate chips. Bake at 350 degrees for 20 minutes or until still moist and chewy. Do not overbake. Cut into bars when cool. Yield: 2 dozen.

Doreen Skippen
Gamma Sigma, Fernie, British Columbia, Canada

Saucepan Brownies

1 stick margarine
2 1-ounce squares
    unsweetened
    chocolate
1 cup sugar
1/2 cup flour

1 teaspoon
    baking powder
1 teaspoon
    vanilla extract
1 cup chopped pecans
2 eggs

Melt margarine and chocolate in saucepan; blend well. Add sugar, flour, baking powder, vanilla and pecans; mix well. Beat in eggs. Pour into buttered 9 x 9-inch baking pan. Bake at 350 degrees for 30 minutes. Cut into bars when cool. Yield: 1 1/2 dozen.

Sandra Hackney
Delta Omega, Shawnee, Oklahoma

Desserts

Super Brownies

1   16-ounce can
      chocolate syrup
1 syrup can oil
1 syrup can sugar

1 syrup can flour
6 eggs
1 teaspoon
      vanilla extract

Combine all ingredients in mixer bowl; mix well. Pour into waxed paper-lined 9 x 13-inch baking pan. Bake at 350 degrees for 30 minutes. Cool in pan. Sprinkle with confectioners' sugar or frost as desired. Cut into large squares. Yield: 15 servings.

Shirley Davis
Xi Alpha Zeta, Glenrock, Wyoming

Swedish Brownies

1 cup sugar
2 tablespoons cocoa
1/2 cup melted butter
2 eggs

3/4 cup flour
1 teaspoon
      vanilla extract
1 cup chopped nuts

Blend sugar, cocoa and butter in bowl. Add eggs, flour and vanilla; mix well. Stir in nuts. Pour into greased and floured 8 x 8-inch baking pan. Bake at 350 degrees for 25 minutes. Cool in pan. Cut into squares.

Beckey Epley
Xi Omicron Gamma, Dallas, Texas

Flash-in-the-Pan

1/3 cup oil
2   1-ounce envelopes
      liquid chocolate
1 egg
1 cup sugar
1 1/4 cups flour
1/2 teaspoon each
      soda, salt

1/2 teaspoon
      vanilla extract
1/2 cup semisweet
      chocolate chips
9 to 12 walnut
      halves

Combine first 8 ingredients and 3/4 cup water in order given in ungreased 9 x 9-inch baking pan. Beat with fork for 1 minute; scrape pan with rubber spatula. Beat for 1 minute longer; spread batter evenly. Sprinkle with chocolate chips. Arrange walnuts on top. Bake at 350 degrees for 30 minutes or until cake tests done. Cut into squares when cool. Sprinkle with confectioners' sugar if desired. Yield: 8-12 servings.
Note: May substitute peanut butter chips for chocolate chips.

Bette L. Carraher
Preceptor Beta Upsilon, Ashtabula, Ohio

Easy Mock Heath Bars

12 whole graham crackers
1/2 cup margarine
1/2 cup butter

1/2 cup sugar
Chopped nuts (opt.)
Chocolate chips (opt.)

Arrange single layer graham crackers in foil-lined 10 x 15-inch baking pan. Bring margarine, butter and sugar to a boil in saucepan. Cook for 3 minutes, stirring constantly. Pour evenly over graham crackers. Sprinkle with nuts and chocolate chips. Bake at 350 degrees for 10 minutes. Cool in pan. Yield: 4 dozen.

Joyce Cummins
Preceptor Mu, Bay City, Michigan

D'Ann's Heath Bars

12 whole graham crackers
2 sticks margarine
1 1/4 cups packed
      brown sugar

1 1/4 cups chopped
      pecans
8 milk chocolate bars

Arrange single layer of graham crackers in greased 10 x 15-inch baking sheet. Bring margarine, brown sugar and pecans to a boil in saucepan. Cook for 2 minutes, stirring constantly. Pour over graham crackers. Bake at 350 degrees for 9 minutes. Place chocolate bars on top. Spread evenly when melted. Cool in freezer until set. Cut into bars.

D'Ann Spinics
Xi Rho, Brownwood, Texas

Magic Cookie Bars

1/2 cup melted
      margarine
1 1/2 cups graham
      cracker crumbs
1   15-ounce can
      sweetened
      condensed milk

1   12-ounce package
      semisweet
      chocolate chips
1   3-ounce package
      flaked coconut
1 cup chopped nuts

Combine margarine and cracker crumbs in 9 x 13-inch baking pan. Press over bottom to form crust. Layer remaining ingredients in order listed over crumbs; press down firmly. Bake at 350 degrees for 25 to 30 minutes or until lightly browned. Cool in pan. Cut into squares. Yield: 2 dozen.

Valerie Wartman
Xi Chi, Ridgedale, Saskatchewan, Canada

Praline Butter Pecan Pie; French Cherry Pudding Pie; and Almond-Chocolate Pudding Pie

Stir-Fry Beef and Vegetables

Desserts

Toffee Bars

40 saltine crackers
1 cup margarine
1 cup packed
   brown sugar

1 12-ounce package
   semisweet
   chocolate chips
1/2 cup chopped walnuts

Arrange crackers in single layer in greased 12 x 18-inch baking sheet. Bring margarine and brown sugar to a boil in saucepan. Cook for 3 minutes, stirring constantly. Pour evenly over crackers. Bake at 350 degrees for 10 minutes. Melt chocolate chips in double boiler. Spread over crackers. Top with walnuts. Chill until set. Cut into bars to serve. Yield: 3 1/3 dozen.

Dorothy Peterson
Xi Alpha Upsilon, Whitewood, South Dakota

Turtle Bars

1 2-layer package
   German chocolate
   cake mix
1/3 cup evaporated
   milk
3/4 cup melted
   margarine

1 cup chocolate chips
1 cup chopped nuts
1 16-ounce package
   light caramels
1/3 cup evaporated
   milk

Combine cake mix, 1/3 cup evaporated milk and margarine in bowl; mix well. Pat 2/3 of the mixture into greased and floured 9 x 13-inch baking pan. Bake at 350 degrees for 6 minutes. Sprinkle with chocolate chips and nuts. Melt caramels with 1/3 cup evaporated milk in saucepan. Pour over baked layer. Top with remaining batter. Bake at 350 degrees for 15 minutes. Chill until firm. Cut into small bars. Yield: 2 1/2 dozen.

Joyce Barbach
Xi Alpha Tau, Tonawanda, New York

Banana Bars

2 cups flour
1 1/4 cups sugar
2 teaspoons soda
1/2 teaspoon salt
1 cup mashed bananas

3/4 cup oil
4 eggs
1 1/2 teaspoons
   vanilla extract
Confectioners' sugar

Mix flour, sugar, soda and salt in bowl. Add bananas, oil, eggs and vanilla, mixing until just moistened. Pour into greased and floured 10 x 15-inch baking pan. Bake at 350 degrees for 20 to 25 minutes or until done. Sprinkle with confectioners' sugar. Cut into bars when cool. Yield: 4 dozen.

Janet Phillips
Eta Nu, Mississauga, Ontario, Canada

Butterscotch Shortbread

1/2 cup butter,
   softened
1 teaspoon
   vanilla extract
1/2 cup packed
   brown sugar
1 1/4 cups sifted flour
1/4 teaspoon
   baking powder
1/8 teaspoon salt

1 6-ounce package
   Nestle's
   butterscotch chips
1/2 cup finely chopped
   toasted almonds
1 teaspoon grated
   orange rind
16 whole blanched
   almonds

Cream butter and vanilla in bowl. Beat in brown sugar gradually. Sift flour, baking powder and salt into creamed mixture; mix well. Reserve 16 butterscotch chips for decoration; add remaining chips, chopped almonds and orange rind to dough; mix well. Spread in ungreased 8-inch square pan. Mark lightly into 1 x 2-inch rectangles. Center whole blanched almonds in half the rectangles; center reserved butterscotch chips in remaining rectangles. Bake at 350 degrees for 30 minutes. Cut into bars while warm. Yield: 32 bars.

Photograph for this recipe on page 67.

Coconut-Apricot Bars with Lemon Glaze

1 2-layer package
   lemon cake mix
2 eggs
1/4 cup packed
   brown sugar
1 cup chopped
   dried apricots

1 cup flaked coconut
1 cup confectioners'
   sugar
1 teaspoon lemon juice
1/2 teaspoon grated
   lemon rind
2 tablespoons milk

Combine cake mix, eggs, brown sugar and 1/4 cup water in mixer bowl; mix well. Stir in apricots and coconut. Spoon into greased and floured 10 x 15-inch baking pan. Bake at 375 degrees for 20 to 25 minutes or until lightly browned. Beat remaining ingredients in bowl until smooth. Drizzle over warm cake. Cut into bars when cool.
Note: May omit lemon rind and increase lemon juice to 1 1/2 teaspoons.

Lois Woodward
Beta Iota, Rawlins, Wyoming

Desserts

Easy Fruit Squares

1 1/2 cups flour
1 1/4 cups sugar
1 1/2 teaspoons soda
1/4 teaspoon salt
2 eggs

1 15-ounce can
   fruit cocktail
1/2 cup packed
   brown sugar
1/2 cup chopped nuts

Combine flour, sugar, soda, salt and eggs in mixer bowl; mix well. Stir in fruit cocktail. Pour into greased and floured 9 x 13-inch baking pan. Sprinkle with mixture of brown sugar and nuts. Bake at 350 degrees for 40 minutes. Cut into squares when cool. Yield: 2 dozen.

Margaret Gliddon
Eta Nu, Mississauga, Ontario, Canada

Tangy Lemon Bars

1 2-layer package
   lemon pudding
   cake mix
1 can lemon pie filling
4 eggs

6 tablespoons
   margarine, softened
6 tablespoons
   lemon juice
Confectioners' sugar

Combine cake mix, pie filling and eggs in mixer bowl; mix well. Pour into greased and floured 11 x 13-inch baking pan. Bake at 350 degrees for 25 to 30 minutes or until lightly browned. Combine margarine and lemon juice with enough confectioners' sugar to make frosting of desired consistency. Spread on cooled cake. Cut into bars. Yield: 3-3 1/2 dozen.

Luan Montag
Iota Phi, West Bend, Iowa

Pecan Bars

1 cup butter, softened
2 cups flour
1 cup packed
   brown sugar
1 cup light corn syrup
3/4 cup sugar
4 eggs

2 tablespoons butter
2 tablespoons flour
1 teaspoon
   vanilla extract
1/4 teaspoon salt
1 cup chopped pecans

Combine 1 cup butter, 2 cups flour and brown sugar in bowl. Mix with fork. Press over bottom of 9 x 13-inch baking pan. Bake at 350 degrees for 10 minutes. Combine next 7 ingredients in mixer bowl; beat until well blended. Stir in pecans. Pour over baked layer. Bake at 350 degrees for 50 minutes. Cut into bars when cool. Yield: 3-4 dozen.

Linda Stull
Delta Kappa, Parkersburg, West Virginia

Pineapple Bars

1 cup margarine,
   softened
1/2 cup confectioners'
   sugar
2 cups flour
1 8-ounce can
   crushed pineapple
2 cups sugar

2 tablespoons
   lemon juice
4 eggs, beaten
1/4 cup flour
1 teaspoon
   baking powder
1/4 teaspoon salt

Mix margarine, confectioners' sugar and 2 cups flour in bowl until crumbly. Press into 9 x 13-inch baking dish. Bake at 350 degrees for 12 to 15 minutes or until lightly browned. Combine remaining ingredients in bowl; mix well. Pour over baked layer. Bake at 350 degrees for 20 minutes. Cut into bars when cool. Yield: 2 dozen.

Sharlotte E. Terry
Alpha Beta, APO, New York

Pumpkin Squares

4 large eggs
1 cup oil
2 cups sugar
1 16-ounce can
   pumpkin
2 cups flour
2 teaspoons each
   baking powder,
   cinnamon
1/2 teaspoon each salt,
   ginger, cloves
   and nutmeg

1 teaspoon soda
6 tablespoons
   margarine, softened
1 3-ounce package
   cream cheese,
   softened
1 tablespoon milk
1 3/4 cups
   confectioners'
   sugar, sifted
1 teaspoon
   vanilla extract

Beat eggs, oil and sugar at medium speed in mixer bowl until well blended. Add pumpkin; mix well. Sift in mixture of next 8 dry ingredients; mix well. Pour into greased and floured 11 x 17-inch baking pan. Bake at 375 degrees for 20 minutes or until cake tests done. Cream margarine and cream cheese in mixer bowl until light. Add remaining ingredients; mix well. Spread on cooled cake. Cut into squares. Yield: 4 dozen.

Kim L. Tapscott
Preceptor Beta Mu, Telford, Pennsylvania

Butter Balls

1 cup butter, softened
1/4 cup confectioners'
   sugar
2 cups flour

1 teaspoon
   vanilla extract
1 cup chopped nuts

Combine first 4 ingredients in bowl; mix well. Mix in nuts. Shape into small balls. Place on ungreased cookie sheet. Bake at 350 degrees for 12 to 15 minutes or until lightly browned. Roll in additional confectioners' sugar. Cool on wire rack.

Lavedia J. Huggins
Chi Theta, Henderson, Texas

72

Desserts

Almond Phyllo Rolls

10 sheets phyllo
  dough
1 cup melted butter

1 12-ounce can
  almond filling
Confectioners' sugar

Wrap phyllo sheets in slightly damp cloth until used. Fold 1 sheet phyllo in half on work surface. Brush top with butter. Add a second phyllo sheet; brush top with butter. Spread 1/5 of the almond filling 1/2 inch thick on narrow end of dough. Roll from filling end as for jelly roll. Place seam side down on baking sheet. Brush with butter. Repeat process with remaining ingredients. Bake at 325 degrees for 10 to 12 minutes or until golden brown and crisp. Cut into 1-inch pieces. Roll in confectioners' sugar. Yield: 3 1/2 dozen.
Note: Do not use almond paste for almond filling.

Connie Wade
Xi Theta Nu, Jefferson City, Missouri

Cake Mix Cookies

1 2-layer
  package
  cake mix
1 egg

1 1/2 cups partially
  thawed frozen
  whipped topping
Confectioners' sugar

Combine cake mix, egg and whipped topping in bowl; mix well. Shape into balls. Roll in confectioners' sugar; place on greased cookie sheet. Bake at 350 degrees for 10 minutes. Cool on wire rack. Yield: 4 dozen.

Dorothy Summers
Pi Chi, Alma, Missouri

Chocolate Cake Mix Cookies

1 2-layer package
  yellow cake mix
1/2 cup oil
2 eggs

1 6-ounce package
  chocolate chips
1/2 cup chopped nuts

Combine all ingredients and 2 tablespoons water in bowl; mix well. Drop by rounded teaspoonfuls onto cookie sheet. Bake at 350 degrees for 9 to 11 minutes or until lightly browned. Cool on wire rack. Yield: 4 dozen.
Note: May substitute chocolate cake mix for yellow and peanut butter chips for chocolate chips.

Patricia McInerney
Xi Beta Zeta, Decatur, Alabama

Chris' Chocolate Chip Cookies

1/2 cup margarine,
  softened
1/2 cup shortening
1 teaspoon
  vanilla extract
1/2 cup sugar
1 cup packed
  brown sugar

2 eggs
2 1/4 to 2 3/4
  cups flour
1 1/2 teaspoons soda
1/2 teaspoon salt
1 12-ounce package
  chocolate chips

Cream margarine, shortening and vanilla in mixer bowl until light. Add sugar and brown sugar. Cream until fluffy. Mix in eggs. Add dry ingredients; mix well. Stir in chocolate chips. Drop by spoonfuls onto greased cookie sheet. Bake at 375 degrees for 8 minutes.

Chris Archer
Gamma Omega, McCall, Idaho

Old-Fashioned Chocolate Chip Cookies

1 cup shortening
1/2 cup sugar
1 cup packed
  brown sugar
2 eggs
2 1/4 cups flour
1 teaspoon soda

1/2 teaspoon salt
1 teaspoon
  vanilla extract
1/2 cup chopped walnuts
1 6-ounce package
  chocolate chips

Cream shortening, sugar and brown sugar in mixer bowl until light and fluffy. Beat in eggs and 2 tablespoons hot water. Sift in dry ingredients; mix well. Stir in vanilla, walnuts and chocolate chips. Drop by teaspoonfuls 1 inch apart on lightly greased cookie sheet. Bake at 375 degrees for 10 to 12 minutes or until light brown. Cool on wire racks. Yield: 4 dozen.

Beatrice F. Newton
Preceptor Tau, Tigard, Oregon

Chocolate Macaroons

2 egg whites
1/2 cup sugar
1/2 teaspoon
  vanilla extract

1 6-ounce package
  chocolate chips,
  melted, cooled
3/4 cup chopped pecans

Beat egg whites in mixer bowl until soft peaks form. Add sugar gradually, beating until stiff peaks form. Fold vanilla, chocolate and pecans gently into egg whites. Drop by teaspoonfuls onto greased and lightly floured cookie sheet. Bake at 350 degrees for 10 to 12 minutes or until lightly browned. Yield: 3 dozen.

Elizabeth H. Morfitt
Preceptor Eta, Idaho Falls, Idaho

Desserts

Cocoa-Nut Balls

1 cup butter, softened
1/3 cup sugar
1 cup instant cocoa mix
2 cups flour
1/2 teaspoon salt
1 teaspoon
   vanilla extract
1 cup chopped nuts
Confectioners' sugar

Cream butter, sugar and cocoa mix in mixer bowl until light and fluffy. Add flour, salt, vanilla and nuts; mix well. Shape into 1-inch balls. Place on greased cookie sheet. Bake at 325 degrees for 15 minutes. Sprinkle with confectioners' sugar. Cool on wire rack.

Jo Anne Robinson
Preceptor Gamma Nu Cincinnati, Ohio

Super Duper Chocolate Cookies

1/2 cup shortening
3 ounces unsweetened
   chocolate
2 cups sugar
2 teaspoons
   vanilla extract
4 eggs
2 cups flour
2 teaspoons
   baking powder
1/2 cup chopped nuts
Confectioners' sugar

Melt shortening and chocolate in saucepan; blend well. Combine with sugar and vanilla in mixer bowl; mix well. Add eggs 1 at a time, mixing well after each addition. Sift in flour and baking powder. Stir in nuts. Chill for several hours. Shape into small balls; roll in confectioners' sugar. Place on cookie sheet. Bake at 350 degrees for 12 to 15 minutes or until cookies test done.

Shari Means
Zeta Pi, Fulton, Missouri

Frosted Waffle Cookies

3 squares unsweetened
   chocolate
1 cup margarine
4 eggs
1 1/2 cups sugar
2 cups flour
1/2 teaspoon
   vanilla extract
Chopped nuts to taste
1 square unsweetened
   chocolate
5 tablespoons butter
1/4 cup milk
1/2 cup sugar
1 1/2 to 2 cups
   confectioners' sugar

Melt 3 squares chocolate with margarine in saucepan; blend well. Cool slightly. Beat eggs with 1 1/2 cups sugar in bowl. Add chocolate mixture; mix well. Mix in flour, vanilla and nuts. Drop by scant tablespoonfuls onto each section of medium-hot waffle iron. Bake for 1 minute. Cool on wire rack. Melt 1 square chocolate with butter in saucepan. Add milk and 1/2 cup sugar. Cook until sugar dissolves, stirring constantly. Stir in confectioners' sugar. Spread on cooled cookies. Yield: 2 dozen.

Kay DeFrancesco
Gamma Omega, McCall, Idaho

Crackles

1 2-layer package
   cake mix
2 eggs, lightly beaten
1/2 cup shortening
3/4 cup confectioners'
   sugar

Combine cake mix, eggs, shortening and 1 tablespoon water in bowl; mix with spoon. Chill for 1 hour or longer. Shape into walnut-sized balls; roll in confectioners' sugar. Place on greased cookie sheet. Bake at 375 degrees for 8 to 10 minutes or until browned. Yield: 4 dozen.

Dorothy P. Ferrell
Preceptor Omega, Staunton, Virginia

Angel Date Cookies

1 stick margarine
3/4 cup sugar
1 8-ounce package
   dates, chopped
1 cup chopped pecans
1 teaspoon
   vanilla extract
1 cup crisp rice cereal
Flaked coconut

Combine margarine, sugar and dates in saucepan. Simmer for 3 minutes, stirring frequently; cool. Add pecans, vanilla and cereal; mix well. Shape into crescents. Roll in coconut. Let set on waxed paper until firm. Yield: 1 1/2 dozen.

Sandra Odom
Xi Psi Beta, Beeville, Texas

Date Balls

1 stick margarine
1 cup sugar
1 8-ounce package
   dates, chopped
2 cups crisp rice cereal
1/2 cup chopped pecans
2 teaspoons
   vanilla extract
1 3-ounce can
   flaked coconut

Combine margarine, sugar and dates in saucepan. Simmer until creamy, stirring constantly; remove from heat. Stir in cereal, pecans and vanilla. Shape into small balls. Roll in coconut. Chill in refrigerator. Yield: 2 dozen.

Dorinne Rosson
Alpha Omega Omicron, Azle, Texas

Desserts

Date-Nut Balls

2 sticks margarine
1 16-ounce box
    light brown sugar
1 3-ounce can
    flaked coconut

1 pound dates, chopped
3 cups crisp rice cereal
2 cups chopped nuts
1/2 16-ounce package
    confectioners' sugar

Melt margarine and brown sugar in saucepan, stirring until well blended. Add coconut and dates; mix well. Remove from heat. Stir in cereal and nuts. Shape into balls. Roll in confectioners' sugar. Yield: 8 dozen.

Norma Dagas
Xi Tau, Lafayette, Louisiana

Golden Buns

1/2 cup margarine
1 teaspoon sugar
1/4 teaspoon salt
1 cup flour
4 eggs
1 tablespoon melted
    margarine
1 1/2 tablespoons
    milk

1 cup confectioners'
    sugar
1/2 teaspoon
    lemon juice
1/2 teaspoon
    vanilla extract

Bring 1/2 cup margarine, sugar, salt and 1 cup water to a boil in saucepan. Add flour all at one time. Beat with spoon for 1 minute or until mixture forms ball. Remove from heat. Cool for 2 minutes, beating constantly. Add eggs 1 at a time, mixing well after each addition. Drop by heaping tablespoonfuls 2 inches apart on greased baking sheet. Bake at 375 degrees for 30 to 35 minutes or until golden brown. Cool slightly on wire rack. Drizzle with mixture of remaining ingredients. Yield: 2 dozen.

Jane O'Mara
Nu Delta, Burlington, Kansas

Miracle Cookies

1 cup peanut butter
1 cup sugar
1 egg, beaten

1 teaspoon
    vanilla extract

Blend peanut butter and sugar in bowl. Add egg and vanilla; mix well. Shape into 3/4-inch balls. Place on ungreased cookie sheet; flatten with floured fork. Bake at 350 degrees for 10 minutes. Cool in pan. Yield: 4 dozen.

Jane Koehn
Laureate Alpha Zeta, Jacksonville, Florida

Peanut Butter-Cornflake Cookies

3/4 cup sugar
3/4 cup light
    corn syrup

1 1/2 cups
    peanut butter
5 cups cornflakes

Bring sugar and corn syrup to a boil in saucepan, stirring to dissolve sugar; remove from heat. Blend in peanut butter. Pour over cornflakes in bowl; toss gently to mix well. Drop by teaspoonfuls onto waxed paper; cool. Yield: 3-4 dozen.

Natalie Schnakenberg
Kappa Delta, Emporia, Kansas

Praline Cookies

Waverly wafers
1 cup packed
    brown sugar

1 cup margarine
1 cup chopped pecans

Arrange single layer of wafers on foil-lined cookie sheet. Bring remaining ingredients to a boil in saucepan. Boil for 30 seconds. Pour evenly over wafers. Bake at 350 degrees for 15 minutes. Cool in pan.

Reve' Beattie
Alpha Omega Omicron, Azle, Texas

Saltine Cracker Cookies

24 to 26 saltine
    crackers
1 cup butter
1 cup sugar

1 12-ounce package
    chocolate chips
3/4 cup chopped nuts

Arrange crackers in single layer in foil-lined 10 x 15-inch baking pan. Bring butter and sugar to a boil in saucepan. Cook for 3 minutes, stirring constantly. Pour evenly over crackers. Bake at 400 degrees for 5 minutes. Sprinkle chocolate chips over top, spreading evenly when melted. Sprinkle with nuts. Cut into cookies before completely cooled.

Rose Hayes
Pi, Brunswick, Missouri

Sinful Sesames

Graham crackers
1/2 cup margarine
1/2 cup butter

1/2 cup sugar
1/2 cup chopped nuts
1/4 cup sesame seed

Arrange single layer of crackers on baking sheet. Bring margarine, butter and sugar to a boil in saucepan. Pour over crackers. Sprinkle with nuts and sesame seed. Bake at 350 degrees for 10 minutes. Cool on waxed paper. Break cookies apart before completely cooled.

Jo Anne Robinson
Preceptor Gamma Nu, Cincinnati, Ohio

Desserts

Apricot Bowling Balls

3/4 cup graham
   cracker crumbs
1/2 cup sifted
   confectioners' sugar
3/4 cup chopped
   dried apricots
1/2 cup finely
   chopped pecans

3/4 cup Grape Nuts
1/4 cup light
   corn syrup
1 tablespoon
   orange juice
1/4 cup sifted
   confectioners' sugar

Mix first 5 ingredients in bowl. Add corn syrup and orange juice; mix well. Shape into 3/4-inch balls with buttered hands. Roll in 1/4 cup confectioners' sugar. Let stand on waxed paper until firm. Store in airtight container. Yield: 3 dozen.

Carolyn Schmitt
Xi Alpha Kappa, Dalton, Nebraska

Bourbon Balls

3 cups vanilla
   wafer crumbs
1 cup confectioners'
   sugar
2 tablespoons cocoa

1 cup chopped nuts
2 tablespoons
   corn syrup
1/2 cup Bourbon
Confectioners' sugar

Mix vanilla wafer crumbs, 1 cup confectioners' sugar, cocoa and nuts in bowl. Stir in corn syrup and Bourbon. Shape into small balls. Roll in additional confectioners' sugar. Let dry on waxed paper for 24 hours. Store in airtight container. Yield: 3 1/2 dozen.
Note: May substitute rum for Bourbon.

Connie Ann Emerson
Psi Omicron, Lakeside, California

Brandy Balls

2 5-ounce packages
   vanilla wafers,
   crushed
1 pound walnuts, ground

1/4 cup each
   Brandy, rum
1/2 cup honey
Confectioners' sugar

Combine vanilla wafer crumbs and walnuts in bowl. Stir in Brandy, rum and honey; mix well. Shape into small balls. Roll in confectioners' sugar. Store in airtight container. Yield: 5 dozen.

Susan Bergstrom Tate
Omega, Whitefish, Montana

Chocolate Haystacks

1/2 cup milk
1/2 cup butter
2 cups sugar
1/3 cup cocoa
3 1/2 cups quick-
   cooking oats

1 cup flaked coconut
1/2 cup chopped
   walnuts (opt.)
1/2 teaspoon
   vanilla extract

Bring milk, butter, sugar and cocoa to a boil in saucepan; remove from heat. Add remaining ingredients; mix well. Drop by teaspoonfuls onto waxed paper; cool. Yield: 4 dozen.

Patricia Marie Dingmon
Theta, Albany, Oregon

Chocolate Oatmeal Cookies

1/2 cup milk
2 cups sugar
1/2 cup margarine

6 tablespoons cocoa
2 1/2 cups oats
1/2 cup peanut butter

Bring milk, sugar, margarine and cocoa to a boil in saucepan over medium heat. Cook for 1 minute, stirring constantly; remove from heat. Stir in oats and peanut butter. Drop by spoonfuls onto waxed paper; cool. Yield: 3-4 dozen.

Wanda McGough
Delta Pi, Montgomery, Alabama

Smore Bars

3 cups graham
   cracker crumbs
2 1/2 cups miniature
   marshmallows
1 cup chopped nuts
1 cup confectioners'
   sugar

1 teaspoon
   vanilla extract
1/2 teaspoon salt
1 12-ounce package
   chocolate chips
1 cup evaporated milk

Combine first 6 ingredients in bowl. Melt chocolate chips with evaporated milk in saucepan over low heat; blend well. Reserve 1/2 cup mixture. Pour remaining chocolate mixture into crumb mixture; mix well. Press into greased 9 x 9-inch pan. Stir 2 teaspoons water into reserved chocolate. Spread over layer in pan. Chill in refrigerator. Cut into squares. Yield: 3 dozen.

Lela Green
Preceptor Chi, Tacoma, Washington

Coconut-Orange Balls

1 12-ounce package
   vanilla wafers
1 cup confectioners'
   sugar
1/4 cup melted butter

3/4 cup chopped nuts
1 6-ounce can frozen
   orange juice
   concentrate
Flaked coconut

Crush vanilla wafers. Combine with next 4 ingredients in bowl; mix well. Shape into 1-inch balls. Roll in coconut. Chill in refrigerator.

Karla Albert
Zeta Pi, Fulton, Missouri

Desserts

Autumn Bavarian Pie, recipe on page 78.

Hot Buttered Rum-Apple Pie

1/4 cup margarine	8 cups sliced
1/2 cup packed	peeled apples
brown sugar	1 unbaked 9-inch
1/4 cup light rum	pie shell
1 teaspoon grated	1/2 cup flour
lemon rind	1/2 cup sugar
1 tablespoon	1/4 cup margarine
lemon juice	1/4 cup sliced almonds
1 teaspoon nutmeg	

Melt 1/4 cup margarine and brown sugar in large skillet. Stir in rum, lemon rind and juice and nutmeg. Add apples; mix well. Simmer, covered, for 10 minutes or until apples are tender. Cool slightly. Spoon into pie shell. Mix flour and sugar in bowl; cut in 1/4 cup margarine until crumbly. Mix in almonds. Sprinkle over apples. Bake at 375 degrees for 35 minutes.

Kathy Lindsey
Nu Gamma, Crescent City, California

Applesauce Pie

2 eggs	1/2 teaspoon nutmeg
1 cup sugar	1/2 teaspoon
1/4 teaspoon salt	lemon extract
1/2 stick butter,	1 unbaked 9-inch
softened	pie shell
1 cup applesauce	

Beat eggs in bowl until light and fluffy. Add sugar and salt gradually. Beat for 1 minute longer. Add butter, applesauce, nutmeg and lemon flavoring; mix well. Pour into pie shell. Bake at 350 degrees for 30 minutes. Cool. Garnish with mint leaves.

Betty Clark
Alpha Rho Beta, Pasadena, Texas

Magic Banana-Marshmallow Pie

1 large package	1 1/2 cups miniature
vanilla instant	colored marshmallows
pudding mix	4 bananas, sliced
1 1/2 cups whipped	1 baked chocolate
topping	pie shell

Prepare pudding mix according to package directions. Fold in whipped topping, marshmallows and bananas. Pour into cooled pie shell. Chill until set.

Janet Greenwald
Tau, Klamath Falls, Oregon

Desserts

Blueberry Pie

2 cups blueberries
3 tablespoons cornstarch
1 tablespoon lemon juice
1 cup sugar
2 cups blueberries
1 baked 9-inch pie shell

Combine 2 cups blueberries with 1/2 cup water in saucepan. Bring to a boil. Combine cornstarch, 1/2 cup water, lemon juice and sugar in bowl; mix well. Stir into saucepan. Cook until thickened, stirring constantly. Place remaining 2 cups blueberries in pie shell. Pour cooked mixture into pie shell. Chill until serving time. Garnish with whipped cream.

Nancy Edwards
Preceptor Laureate Alpha, Agawam, Massachusetts

Buttermilk Pie

3 eggs
1 1/2 cups sugar
1 cup buttermilk
1/2 cup buttermilk baking mix
1/3 cup melted margarine
1 teaspoon vanilla extract

Combine all ingredients in bowl; beat until smooth. Pour into greased pie plate. Bake at 350 degrees for 30 minutes or until knife inserted in center comes out clean. Serve with fresh mixed fruit spooned over top.

Linda Dorsch
Delta Eta, Wellington, Missouri

French Cherry Pudding Pie

1 1/4 cups fine vanilla wafer crumbs
4 teaspoons sugar
1/4 cup melted butter
2 cups milk
1/4 teaspoon almond extract
1 cup sour cream
1 large package French vanilla instant pudding mix
1 21-ounce can cherry pie filling

Combine first 3 ingredients in bowl; mix well. Press over bottom and side of 9-inch pie plate. Bake at 375 degrees for 8 minutes. Cool. Blend cold milk, flavoring and sour cream in mixer bowl. Add pudding mix. Beat at low speed for 1 minute. Pour into pie shell. Chill for 2 hours. Spoon pie filling around edge.

Photograph for this recipe on page 69.

Martha Washington's Cherry-Cream Cheese Pie

1 8-ounce package cream cheese, softened
1 15-ounce can sweetened condensed milk
1/3 cup lemon juice
1 teaspoon vanilla extract
1 graham cracker pie shell, chilled
1 can cherry pie filling

Beat cream cheese in mixer bowl until fluffy. Add condensed milk gradually; mix well. Stir in lemon juice and vanilla. Pour mixture into pie shell. Chill for 1 hour. Spread pie filling over top. Chill for 1 hour longer.

Bonita A. Palka
Alpha Theta Kappa, Houston, Texas
Murlynn Williams
Preceptor Lambda, McGill, Nevada

Almond-Chocolate Pudding Pie

1/4 cup melted butter
2 cups flaked coconut
2/3 cup slivered blanched almonds, toasted
1 large package chocolate instant pudding mix
2 3/4 cups cold milk
1/4 teaspoon almond extract
1 cup whipped topping

Mix butter and coconut in bowl. Press over bottom and side of 9-inch pie plate. Bake at 300 degrees for 20 to 30 minutes or until golden. Cool. Chop 1/2 cup almonds. Prepare pudding mix according to package directions for pie using 2 3/4 cups milk. Stir in chopped almonds and flavoring. Pour into pie shell. Chill for 4 hours or longer. Top with whipped topping and remaining slivered almonds.

Photograph for this recipe on page 69.

Autumn Bavarian Pie

1 envelope unflavored gelatin
1 cup milk
2/3 cup sugar
1/3 cup cocoa
2 tablespoons butter
2/3 cup milk
3/4 teaspoon vanilla extract
1/2 cup whipping cream, whipped
1 baked 9-inch pie shell
1/2 cup whipping cream
1 tablespoon sugar
1/4 teaspoon vanilla extract
1/4 teaspoon cinnamon
Dash of nutmeg
Chocolate leaves (opt.)

Soften gelatin in 1 cup milk in medium saucepan. Add mixture of 2/3 cup sugar and cocoa. Bring to a boil over medium heat, stirring constantly; remove from heat. Add butter; stir until melted. Blend in 2/3 cup milk and 3/4 teaspoon vanilla. Chill until thick, stirring occasionally. Fold in whipped cream gently. Pour into pie shell. Chill until firm. Combine remaining ingredients except chocolate leaves in bowl; beat until stiff. Decorate pie with spiced whipped cream and chocolate leaves.

Photograph for this recipe on page 77.

Desserts

Almond Silk Pie

1/3 cup butter,
  softened
1/2 cup sugar
1 teaspoon
  vanilla extract
3 tablespoons cocoa
2 eggs

2/3 cup chopped
  toasted almonds
1 baked 9-inch
  pie shell
2 cups (or more)
  whipped cream

Cream butter and sugar in mixer bowl. Add vanilla and cocoa powder; mix well. Add eggs 1 at a time. Beat for 5 minutes after each addition. Reserve several almonds for topping. Fold remaining almonds gently into chocolate mixture. Pour into pie shell. Top with generous layer of whipped cream and reserved almonds. Chill until serving time.

Rebecca Olson
Gamma Omega, McCall, Idaho

Chocolate Chip Pie

1 stick margarine,
  softened
1/2 cup flour
1 cup sugar
2 eggs, slightly beaten
1 cup chopped pecans

1 teaspoon
  vanilla extract
1 cup semisweet
  chocolate chips
1 unbaked 9-inch
  pie shell

Combine margarine, flour and sugar in bowl; mix well. Combine eggs, pecans, vanilla and chocolate chips; mix well. Stir in flour mixture. Pour into pie shell. Bake at 350 degrees for 30 minutes.

Evelyn Yates
Epsilon Chi, Apollo Beach, Florida

Derby Pie

1/2 cup packed
  brown sugar
1/2 cup sugar
1 stick margarine,
  melted
2 eggs, slightly beaten
1/2 cup flour

1 6-ounce package
  chocolate chips
1 cup nuts
1 teaspoon
  vanilla extract
1 unbaked 9-inch
  pie shell

Combine first 8 ingredients in bowl; mix well by hand. Pour into pie shell. Bake at 325 degrees for 1 hour.

Frances S. Wright
Xi Delta Sigma, Charlottesville, Virginia

Cheryle's Fudge Nut Pie

1/4 cup butter,
  softened
3/4 cup packed
  brown sugar
3 eggs
2 cups semisweet chocolate
  chips, melted
2 teaspoons instant
  coffee powder

1 teaspoon rum extract
1/4 cup flour
1 cup chopped nuts
1 unbaked 9-inch
  pie shell
2 1/2 tablespoons
  chopped cherries
1 cup whipped topping

Cream butter and brown sugar in bowl until light and fluffy. Add eggs; beat well. Add chocolate, coffee and rum flavoring; mix well. Stir in flour and nuts. Pour into pie shell. Bake at 375 degrees for 25 minutes. Cool. Fold cherries into whipped topping. Spread over top.

Cheryle J. McKeever
Sigma, Lansing, Michigan

Fudge Sundae Pie

1 cup evaporated milk
1 cup semisweet
  chocolate chips
1 cup miniature
  marshmallows
1/4 teaspoon salt

Vanilla wafers
1 pint (or more)
  vanilla ice cream,
  softened
1 cup slivered
  toasted almonds

Combine first 4 ingredients in double boiler. Cook until well blended and thickened, stirring constantly. Cool to room temperature. Layer vanilla wafers, ice cream and chocolate mixture alternately in 9-inch pie plate. Sprinkle almonds over top. Freeze until firm.

Dottie Cote
Preceptor Beta, Honolulu, Hawaii

Pecan Fudge Pie

1 4-ounce package sweet
  cooking chocolate
1/4 cup butter
1 15-ounce can sweetened
  condensed milk
2 eggs, well beaten

1 teaspoon
  vanilla extract
1/8 teaspoon salt
1 1/4 cups pecan halves
1 unbaked 9-inch
  pie shell

Melt chocolate and butter in medium saucepan over low heat. Add condensed milk, 1/2 cup hot water and eggs; mix well. Remove from heat. Stir in vanilla, salt and pecans. Pour into pie shell. Bake at 350 degrees for 50 to 60 minutes or until center is set. Chill for 3 hours.

Zonell Cook
Xi Iota Delta, Denver City, Texas

Desserts

Texas Cream Pie

3/4 cup sugar
1/8 teaspoon salt
1/3 cup flour
3 tablespoons cocoa
1 3/4 cups milk
2 eggs, separated

1 tablespoon margarine
1 teaspoon
   vanilla extract
1 baked 9-inch
   pie shell
1 cup whipped cream

Mix sugar, salt, flour and cocoa in saucepan. Add milk, beaten egg yolks and margarine. Cook over medium heat until thickened, stirring constantly. Add vanilla. Beat egg whites until stiff peaks form. Fold gently into custard mixture. Pour into pie shell. Top with whipped cream. Decorate with grated chocolate.

Mary Lou Szymanski
Xi Pi Psi, Eagle Lake, Texas

Blender Coconut Pie

2 cups milk
4 eggs
1/3 cup margarine
1/2 cup flour
3/4 cup sugar

1 cup coconut
1 1/2 teaspoons
   vanilla extract
Dash of nutmeg

Combine all ingredients in blender container. Process for 1 minute. Pour into well-greased and floured 10-inch pie pan. Bake at 350 degrees for 10 minutes or until custard is set.

Arlene Keast
Xi Delta Omicron, Brampton, Ontario, Canada

Cranberry-Yogurt Pie

1 3-ounce package
   orange gelatin
1 8-ounce carton
   vanilla yogurt
1 cup whole
   cranberry sauce

1 cup whipped
   topping
1 butter-flavored
   pie shell

Dissolve gelatin in 3/4 cup boiling water in medium bowl. Stir in yogurt and cranberry sauce. Chill for 45 to 60 minutes or until mixture mounds when dropped from spoon, stirring occasionally. Fold in whipped topping. Pour into pie shell. Chill for 4 hours or longer.

Anita M. Wilson
Laureate Alpha Mu, Mansfield, Ohio

Fruit Cocktail Pies

1 15-ounce can
   sweetened
   condensed milk
1/3 cup lemon juice
1 16-ounce carton
   whipped topping
1 16-ounce can fruit
   cocktail, drained

1 16-ounce can
   crushed pineapple,
   drained
1 cup chopped pecans
2 graham cracker
   pie shells
1 cup flaked coconut

Blend condensed milk and lemon juice in bowl. Fold in whipped topping, fruit and pecans. Pour into pie shells. Top with coconut. Refrigerate or freeze until serving time. Yield: 2 pies.

Arbutus Prunesti
Xi Chi, Sophia, West Virginia

Icebox Fruit Pies

2 15-ounce cans
   sweetened
   condensed milk
1 16-ounce carton
   whipped topping

2 6-ounce cans
   frozen fruit juice
   concentrate, thawed
3 graham cracker
   pie shells

Combine condensed milk, whipped topping and concentrate in bowl; blend well. Pour into pie shells. Chill overnight. Yield: 3 pies.
Note: Use 1 flavor fruit juice or mix 2 flavors together. Combinations of pineapple and fruit punch; lime and pink lemonade; orange and pink lemonade; grape and pineapple; fruit punch and pink lemonade; apple and pineapple are excellent.

Frankie Wooster
Preceptor Zeta Sigma, Wichita Falls, Texas

Ice Cream Pie

1/4 cup light
   corn syrup
1/4 cup peanut butter
2 1/4 cups coarsely
   crushed honey-nut
   cereal

1 quart vanilla
   ice cream, softened
1/4 cup chocolate syrup
2 tablespoons
   ground nuts

Blend corn syrup and peanut butter in bowl. Add cereal; mix well. Pat into 9-inch pie plate. Chill until firm. Spread ice cream in prepared pie plate. Drizzle chocolate over top; sprinkle with nuts. Serve immediately or freeze until firm.

Joyce Brown
Xi Zeta Nu, Stockton, California

Desserts

Grasshopper Pie

20 Oreo cookies, crushed
2 tablespoons margarine, melted
1 15-ounce can sweetened condensed milk
3 tablespoons green Creme de Menthe
2 tablespoons white Creme de Cacao
1 cup whipping cream, whipped

Reserve 2 tablespoons cookie crumbs for topping. Add margarine to remaining crumbs; mix well. Pat over bottom and side of buttered 9-inch pie plate. Bake at 360 degrees for 8 minutes. Cool. Blend condensed milk, Creme de Menthe and Creme de Cacao in bowl. Fold in whipped cream. Pour into cooled crust. Top with reserved crumbs. Freeze for 4 to 6 hours or until firm. Pie will not freeze solid.

Doris Gray
Preceptor Delta Eta, Arlington, Texas

Kahlua Pie

18 chocolate sandwich cookies
1/2 cup melted margarine
2 tablespoons confectioners' sugar
1 7-ounce jar marshmallow creme
1/4 cup Kahlua
1 12-ounce carton whipped topping

Remove and discard cookie centers; crush cookies. Mix with margarine and confectioners' sugar in bowl. Press over bottom and side of 10-inch pie plate. Bake at 350 degrees for 10 minutes. Cool. Blend marshmallow creme with Kahlua in bowl. Fold in whipped topping. Pour into pie shell. Garnish with almonds and grated milk chocolate. Freeze until firm.

Connie Wade
Xi Theta Nu, Jefferson City, Missouri

Lemonade Pie

1 15-ounce can sweetened condensed milk
1 6-ounce can frozen pink lemonade concentrate
1 8-ounce carton whipped topping
1 graham cracker pie shell

Combine condensed milk and slightly thawed lemonade in mixer bowl; beat until light and fluffy. Fold in whipped topping. Pour into pie shell. Chill for 2 hours or longer.
Note: Double recipe of filling will make 3 pies.

Kim L. Tapscott
Preceptor Beta Mu, Telford, Pennsylvania

Lemon Ice Cream Pies

1 6-ounce can frozen lemonade concentrate, partially thawed
1/2 gallon vanilla ice cream, softened
2 8-inch graham cracker pie shells

Combine lemonade and ice cream in mixer bowl; beat until creamy. Pour into pie shells. Freeze until firm. Garnish with graham cracker crumbs. Yield: 2 pies.

Phyllis McDuffie
Xi Omicron Gamma, Mesquite, Texas

Key Lime Pie

1 15-ounce can sweetened condensed milk
1 tablespoon grated lemon rind
1/2 teaspoon grated lime rind
1/4 cup fresh lime juice
3 or 4 drops of green food coloring
3 eggs, separated
1/4 teaspoon cream of tartar
1 baked 9-inch pie shell
1/4 cup shredded coconut, toasted

Combine condensed milk, rinds, juice, food coloring and beaten egg yolks in bowl; blend well. Beat egg whites with cream of tartar until stiff and glossy. Fold gently into lime mixture. Spoon into pie shell. Chill for several hours. Sprinkle with coconut before serving.

Antoinette S. Leone
Preceptor Gamma Upsilon, Monessen, Pennsylvania

Lime Pie

1 stick margarine
2 tablespoons sugar
1 cup flour
1 15-ounce can sweetened condensed milk
1 6-ounce can frozen limeade concentrate
Several drops of green food coloring
1 16-ounce carton whipped topping

Melt margarine in 9-inch pie plate. Add sugar and flour; mix well. Press over bottom and side of plate; flute edge. Bake at 375 degrees for 8 to 10 minutes or until light brown; cool. Blend condensed milk, limeade concentrate and food coloring in bowl. Fold in whipped topping. Pour into pie shell. Chill until serving time.

Lorraine Patterson
Laureate Gamma, Spencer, Iowa

Desserts

Mock Key Lime Pie

1 15-ounce can
   sweetened
   condensed milk
1 8-ounce carton
   whipped topping

1 6-ounce can
   frozen limeade
   concentrate, thawed
1 graham cracker
   pie shell

Combine first 3 ingredients in bowl; blend well. Pour into pie shell. Chill for 3 hours or longer. Garnish with chopped nuts.

Cheryl Hug
Preceptor Alpha, Sarasota, Florida

Special Peach Pie

3/4 cup flour
1/2 teaspoon salt
1 teaspoon
   baking powder
1 small package
   vanilla pudding and
   pie filling mix
1/2 cup milk
1 egg

3 tablespoons butter
1 29-ounce can
   sliced peaches
1 8-ounce package
   cream cheese,
   softened
1/2 cup sugar
Cinnamon-sugar

Combine first 7 ingredients in bowl; mix well. Pour into well-buttered 9-inch pie plate. Drain peaches, reserving juice. Arrange peaches over batter. Blend cream cheese, sugar and 3 to 4 tablespoons reserved peach juice in bowl. Spoon over peaches. Sprinkle cinnamon-sugar over top. Bake at 350 degrees for 30 to 35 minutes or until center is set. Serve warm.

Twilla Kay Einig
Beta Alpha Kappa, The Colony, Texas

R. R.'s Peanut Butter Pie

1 3-ounce package
   cream cheese,
   softened
1 cup confectioners'
   sugar

1/4 cup peanut butter
1 16-ounce carton
   whipped topping
1 graham cracker
   pie shell

Combine first 3 ingredients in bowl; mix well. Fold in whipped topping. Pour into pie shell. Chill until serving time.

Kyle Stallard
Xi Gamma Xi, Bristol, Tennessee

Peanut Butter-Ice Cream Pie

1 quart vanilla
   ice cream,
   softened
1 cup peanut butter

1 cup whipping
   cream, whipped
1 8-inch graham
   cracker pie shell

Beat ice cream and peanut butter in mixer bowl until blended. Fold in whipped cream. Pour into pie shell. Freeze until firm. Thaw for 30 minutes before serving. Garnish with drizzle of chocolate sauce.

Joyce Barbach
Xi Alpha Tau, Tonawanda, New York

Jennifer Sue's Pecan Pie

3 eggs
1 cup sugar
1/2 cup corn syrup
1/4 cup melted butter

1 cup pecans
1 unbaked 9-inch
   pie shell

Beat eggs lightly in 2-quart bowl. Add sugar, corn syrup and butter; mix well. Stir in pecans. Pour into shell. Bake near center of oven at 350 degrees for 35 to 40 minutes or until filling is slightly firm.
Note: Center of pie may look soft when pie is gently shaken, but will become firm when cool.

Jennifer Sue Turnbough
Xi Delta Eta, Plainview, Texas

Pecan Torte Pie

3 egg whites
1 cup sugar
1 teaspoon
   vanilla extract

24 butter crackers,
   crushed
1 cup chopped pecans

Beat egg whites in large bowl until stiff. Fold in sugar, vanilla, crackers and pecans in order listed. Pour into buttered 9-inch pie plate. Bake at 350 degrees for 30 minutes. Garnish with whipped cream.

Vaundeleath Kotar
Alpha Nu, Baton Rouge, Louisiana

Southern Pecan Pie

1 cup sugar
1 cup corn syrup
2 eggs, slightly
   beaten
1 cup chopped pecans
1/8 teaspoon salt

1 teaspoon
   vanilla extract
1 tablespoon
   salted butter
1 unbaked 9-inch
   pie shell

Combine sugar, syrup and eggs in bowl; mix well. Add next 4 ingredients; mix well. Pour into pie shell. Bake at 400 degrees for 15 minutes. Reduce temperature to 350 degrees. Bake for 30 to 35 minutes longer or until set.

Linda Buzzini
Nu Gamma, Crescent City, California

Desserts

No-Brainer Pecan Custard Pie

1/3 cup butter
1/3 cup packed
  brown sugar
2/3 cup chopped pecans
1 baked 9-inch
  pie shell
1/4 teaspoon cinnamon

1 large package egg
  custard mix
2 3/4 cups milk
1 egg yolk
1 cup whipping
  cream, whipped

Combine butter, brown sugar and pecans in heavy saucepan. Cook until well mixed, stirring constantly. Spread in pie shell. Bake at 425 degrees for 5 minutes or until bubbly. Cool. Combine cinnamon, custard mix, milk and egg yolk in saucepan; blend well. Bring to a boil, stirring constantly. Cool for 30 minutes, stirring frequently. Pour into pie shell. Chill for 4 hours or longer. Top with whipped cream. Garnish with whole pecans.

Lauralee Wells
Preceptor Iota, Shreveport, Louisiana

Jane's Pineapple Cream Pie

1 pint sour cream
1 8-ounce can
  juice-pack
  crushed pineapple
1 tablespoon sugar

1 package vanilla
  instant pudding mix
1 8-inch graham
  cracker pie shell

Combine first 4 ingredients in bowl; mix well. Pour into pie shell. Chill for 30 minutes or longer. Garnish with mint leaves.

Jane E. Shrader
Xi Alpha Tau, Williamsville, New York

Pineapple Cream Pie

1 14-ounce can
  juice-pack
  crushed pineapple
1 small package
  vanilla instant
  pudding mix

1 cup yogurt
1/2 teaspoon
  vanilla extract
Pinch of cinnamon
1 9-inch graham
  cracker pie shell

Combine pineapple, pudding mix, yogurt, vanilla and cinnamon in bowl; mix well. Spoon into pie shell. Chill until set.

Suzanne Pizzuto
Pi, Nepean, Ontario, Canada

Pineapple Fluff Pies

1 15-ounce can
  sweetened
  condensed milk
1 16-ounce carton
  whipped topping
2 tablespoons
  lemon juice

1 20-ounce can
  crushed pineapple,
  drained
1/2 cup chopped pecans
2 baked 9-inch
  pie shells

Combine first 3 ingredients in mixer bowl; beat until blended. Stir in pineapple and pecans. Pour into pie shells. Chill for 2 hours. Yield: 2 pies.

Sheila Slaughter
Alpha Kappa Upsilon, The Colony, Texas

Easy Millionaire Pie

1 15-ounce can
  sweetened
  condensed milk
6 tablespoons
  lemon juice
1 8-ounce can
  crushed pineapple,
  well drained

1 cup chopped
  pecans
1 16-ounce carton
  whipped topping
1 10-inch baked
  pie shell

Blend condensed milk and lemon juice in bowl. Add pineapple and pecans; mix well. Fold in whipped topping. Pour into pie shell. Chill for 1 hour or longer.

Joanna Lee
Xi Epsilon Kappa, Rusk, Texas

Millionaire Pie

1 cup confectioners'
  sugar
1 8-ounce package
  cream cheese,
  softened
1/2 cup nuts

1 8-ounce can
  crushed pineapple
1 envelope whipped
  topping mix,
  prepared
1 baked pie shell

Cream confectioners' sugar with cream cheese in bowl until light and fluffy. Add nuts and pineapple; mix well. Fold in whipped topping. Pour into pie shell. Chill until serving time.

Mrs. Sharon L. Coble
Epsilon Kappa, Playas, New Mexico

Desserts

Praline Butter Pecan Pie

2 tablespoons light
  brown sugar
2 tablespoons butter
1/3 cup chopped pecans
1 9-inch pie shell,
  partially baked

1 1/2 cups cold milk
1 cup vanilla ice
  cream, softened
1 large package butter
  pecan instant
  pudding mix

Combine brown sugar, butter and pecans in saucepan. Heat until butter melts. Pour into pie shell. Bake at 450 degrees for 5 minutes. Cool. Blend milk and ice cream in mixer bowl. Add pudding mix. Beat at low speed for 1 minute or until blended. Pour into pie shell. Chill for 3 hours or until set. Garnish with whipped topping and pecan halves.

Photograph for this recipe on page 69.

Raspberry Pastel Party Pie

1 10-ounce package
  frozen red
  raspberries, thawed
1 3-ounce package
  raspberry gelatin

1 pint vanilla
  ice cream
1 baked 9-inch
  pie shell

Drain raspberries, reserving juice. Add enough water to reserved juice to measure 1 1/4 cups. Bring to a boil in saucepan. Add gelatin; stir until dissolved. Add ice cream by spoonfuls, stirring until melted. Chill until partially set. Fold in raspberries. Pour into pie shell. Chill until firm. Garnish with whipped cream.

Beverly Oldaker
Laureate Alpha Delta, Pueblo, Colorado

Strawberry Glaze Pie

2 cups flour
2 tablespoons sugar
1 1/4 teaspoons salt
2/3 cup oil
3 tablespoons milk
1 quart strawberries

1 cup sugar
2 tablespoons
  cornstarch
1 3-ounce package
  strawberry gelatin

Combine flour, 2 tablespoons sugar and salt in bowl. Whip oil and milk in small bowl. Add to dry ingredients; mix well. Press into deep pie plate. Bake at 425 degrees for 10 to 12 minutes. Cool. Arrange strawberries in pie shell. Dissolve 1 cup sugar in 1 cup boiling water in saucepan. Add cornstarch dissolved in a small amount of cold water. Cook until thickened, stirring constantly; remove from heat. Add gelatin; stir until dissolved. Pour over strawberries. Chill until firm.

Cindy Nicol
Xi Alpha Chi, Peterborough, Ontario, Canada

Strawberry Mile-High Pie

2 egg whites
1 cup sugar
1 tablespoon
  lemon juice

2 10-ounce packages
  frozen strawberries
1 graham cracker
  pie shell

Beat egg whites and sugar in mixer bowl as for meringue. Add lemon juice and frozen strawberries. Beat at high speed for 15 minutes. Pour into pie shell. Freeze until firm.

Elizabeth H. Morfitt
Preceptor Eta, Idaho Falls, Idaho

Joyce's Strawberry Pie

1 cup sugar
3 tablespoons
  cornstarch
1 small package
  strawberry
  gelatin

6 to 8 drops of red
  food coloring
3 baskets fresh
  strawberries
1 baked 9-inch
  pie shell

Combine sugar, cornstarch and 1 cup water in saucepan. Cook until thickened and clear, stirring constantly. Stir in gelatin and food coloring until dissolved. Cool. Wash and hull strawberries. Arrange strawberries in pie shell. Pour syrup over top. Chill until serving time.

Joyce Brown
Xi Zeta Nu, Stockton, California

No-Fail Pie Crusts

1 cup (heaping)
  shortening
3 cups flour

1 egg, beaten
1 teaspoon salt
1 teaspoon vinegar

Cut shortening into flour in bowl until crumbly. Mix egg, salt, vinegar and 5 tablespoons warm water in bowl. Add to flour mixture; stir until mixture forms ball.
Yield: Four 9-inch pie shells.

Marie Harris
Alpha Omicron Eta, Sherman, Texas

On-The-Shelf Pie Crust Mix

6 cups flour
1 1/2 teaspoons
  baking powder

1 1/2 teaspoons salt
2 cups shortening

Combine all ingredients in bowl; mix until crumbly. Store in covered container at room temperature. Combine 1 cup mixture with 3 tablespoons milk or half and half for each pie shell.

Joyce Horvath
Xi Iota Gamma, Wellington, Ohio

Desserts

Strawberry Cream Pie, recipe on page 94.

Angel Food Delight

1 large package
   vanilla instant
   pudding mix

1 angel food cake
Fruit (opt.)

Prepare pudding mix, using package directions. Tear cake into bite-sized pieces. Fold into pudding. Add fruit; mix gently. Spoon into serving dishes. Yield: 10 servings.

Linda Owen
Iota Eta, Marrero, Louisiana

Fruited Angel Dessert

1 large angel
   food cake
1 15-ounce can
   crushed pineapple
1 6-ounce jar
   maraschino cherries,
   drained, chopped

1 12-ounce carton
   whipped topping
1 3-ounce can
   flaked coconut,
   toasted

Tear cake into bite-sized pieces. Layer cake, pineapple, cherries, whipped topping and coconut 1/2 at a time in 9 x 13-inch dish. Chill, covered, overnight. Yield: 12 servings.

Mary Gamble
Xi Beta Alpha, Huntsville, Alabama

Apple Crisp

3 cups sliced apples
1 cup (about) sugar
Cinnamon to taste
Nutmeg to taste
1 cup plus 2
   tablespoons packed
   brown sugar
1 cup oats

1 cup plus 2
   tablespoons flour
Salt to taste
2 teaspoons
   baking powder
2 sticks margarine,
   melted
1 egg

Combine apples, sugar and spices in bowl; mix well. Spoon into greased 8 x 12-inch baking dish. Mix brown sugar, oats, flour, salt, baking powder, margarine and egg in bowl. Sprinkle over apples. Bake at 350 degrees for 30 minutes or until apples are tender. Serve warm or cool with whipped cream or ice cream. Yield: 6-8 servings.

Eleanor S. Mackey
Preceptor Omega, Waynesboro, Virginia

Desserts

Apple-Oatmeal Crisp

2 cups oats
1/2 cup butter,
   softened
1/2 cup raisins
1/2 cup chopped walnuts
Cinnamon to taste
1/4 cup packed dark
   brown sugar
1/2 teaspoon
   vanilla extract
4 cups sliced apples

Combine all ingredients except apples in bowl; mix well. Reserve 1 cup mixture. Add apples to remaining mixture; toss to coat well. Spoon into greased 10-inch pie plate. Sprinkle reserved oats mixture over top. Bake at 350 degrees for 30 minutes or until lightly browned. Yield: 6-8 servings.

Bridgett Chandler
Delta Omega, Danville, Kentucky

Little Touch of Belgium

3 pounds apples,
   peeled, sliced
1/3 cup sugar
1 teaspoon lemon juice
2 teaspoons cinnamon
2/3 cup butter
2 cups sifted flour
1 1/2 teaspoons
   baking powder
1 1/4 cups sugar
2 egg yolks
2/3 cup butter

Cook apples with 1/3 cup sugar, lemon juice, cinnamon and 1/2 cup water in saucepan until tender. Drain and cool. Cut 2/3 cup butter into mixture of flour, baking powder and 1 1/4 cups sugar in bowl until crumbly. Mix in egg yolks. Reserve 1 cup mixture for topping. Press remaining mixture into greased 9-inch springform pan. Add apples. Sprinkle with reserved flour mixture. Dot with 2/3 cup butter. Sprinkle with additional sugar. Bake at 350 degrees for 1 hour. Cool in pan. Place on serving dish; remove side.
Yield: 9-12 servings.

Nancy Sprague
Theta Iota, Hendersonville, North Carolina

Ozark Pudding

3/4 cup sugar
1 egg, beaten
2 tablespoons flour
1 1/2 teaspoons
   baking powder
1 teaspoon
   vanilla extract
1/2 cup chopped apples
1/2 cup chopped nuts

Beat sugar and egg in mixer bowl until thick. Add flour, baking powder and vanilla; mix until smooth. Stir in apples and nuts. Pour into buttered 10-inch pie plate. Bake at 350 degrees for 35 minutes or until knife inserted in center comes out clean. Serve with whipped cream or ice cream.
Yield: 6 servings.

Lula B. Shaw
Preceptor Delta Beta, Downey, California

Renee's Banana Split Cake

1 box graham
   crackers, crushed
3/4 cup melted butter
1 tablespoon
   brown sugar
1 16-ounce box
   confectioners' sugar
2 eggs, beaten
1 cup melted butter
1 20-ounce can
   crushed pineapple,
   drained
4 bananas, sliced
1 12-ounce carton
   whipped topping
Maraschino cherries
Chopped nuts

Combine cracker crumbs, 3/4 cup butter and brown sugar in bowl; mix well. Press into 9 x 13-inch dish. Mix confectioners' sugar, eggs and 1 cup butter in bowl until smooth. Spread over crumbs. Layer pineapple, bananas, whipped topping, cherries and nuts over creamed mixture. Chill in refrigerator. Yield: 12-15 servings.

Renee Nichols
Gamma Kappa, Cape Canaveral, Florida

Banana Split Delight

2 cups graham
   cracker crumbs
1/4 cup melted butter
2 eggs
2 cups confectioners'
   sugar
1/4 cup butter,
   softened
5 or 6 bananas,
   quartered lengthwise
1 20-ounce can
   crushed pineapple,
   drained
1 16-ounce carton
   whipped topping
Chopped walnuts
Maraschino cherries

Combine cracker crumbs and 1/4 cup melted butter in 9 x 13-inch dish; press evenly over bottom. Combine eggs, confectioners' sugar and 1/4 cup butter in mixer bowl. Beat at high speed for 12 minutes. Spread over crumbs. Layer bananas, pineapple, whipped topping, walnuts and maraschino cherries over creamed mixture. Chill for 4 hours or longer.

Diann Kellestine
Beta Theta, Goderich, Ontario, Canada

Desserts

Maisie's Banana Split Cake

2 cups Cookie Crumb Crust Mix	4 or 5 bananas, sliced
1/4 cup melted butter	2 10-ounce packages frozen strawberries, thawed
2 cups sifted confectioners' sugar	1 16-ounce carton whipped topping
1/2 cup butter, softened	1/2 cup chopped nuts
1 20-ounce can crushed pineapple, drained	

Combine Cookie Crumb Crust Mix with 1/4 cup melted butter in bowl. Press into ungreased 9 x 13-inch dish. Cream confectioners' sugar and 1/2 cup butter in mixer bowl for 15 minutes. Spread over crust. Layer pineapple, bananas and strawberries with juice over creamed mixture. Top with whipped topping and nuts. Chill or freeze until serving time. Yield: 12 servings.

COOKIE CRUMB CRUST MIX

1 pound butter, softened	1 1/2 cups packed brown sugar
6 cups flour	1 1/2 cups chopped nuts

Cut butter into mixture of remaining ingredients in bowl until crumbly. Press into 2 ungreased baking sheets. Bake at 375 degrees for 15 minutes. Crumble when cool. Store in airtight container. Use for any crumb crust within 6 weeks. Yield: 10 1/2 cups.

Maisie Wallace
Laureate Iota, Nelson, British Columbia, Canada

Alice's Banana Pudding

Vanilla wafers	5 cups milk
Sliced bananas	1 8-ounce carton sour cream
3 3-ounce packages vanilla instant pudding mix	1 8-ounce carton whipped topping

Layer vanilla wafers and bananas in 9 x 13-inch dish. Mix pudding mix and milk in bowl, using package directions. Blend sour cream and whipped topping in bowl. Fold gently into pudding. Spoon over bananas. Chill for 4 hours.
Note: May substitute banana pudding for any or all of vanilla.

Alice B. Cox
Sigma Iota, Angleton, Texas

Quick Banana Pudding

1 small package vanilla instant pudding mix	1 cup half and half
1 cup milk	3 bananas, sliced
1 teaspoon vanilla extract	1 12-ounce carton whipped topping
	1 medium box vanilla wafers, crushed

Combine pudding mix, milk, vanilla and half and half in bowl; mix until smooth. Fold in remaining ingredients. Spoon into serving bowl. Chill in refrigerator.
Yield: 8-10 servings.

Mary Lou Szymanski
Xi Pi Psi, Eagle Lake, Texas

Blueberry Surprise

1 package graham crackers, crushed	1/2 cup sugar
1/4 cup butter, melted	1 16-ounce carton whipped topping
2 to 3 teaspoons sugar	1 20-ounce can blueberry pie filling
2 to 3 bananas, sliced	
1 8-ounce package cream cheese, softened	

Combine cracker crumbs, butter and 2 to 3 teaspoons sugar in bowl; mix well. Press in 9 x 13-inch dish. Arrange bananas over crust. Beat cream cheese and 1/2 cup sugar in bowl until fluffy. Add whipped topping; mix well. Spread over bananas. Top with pie filling. Chill in refrigerator. Yield: 15 servings.

Jeanne Rasmussen
Omicron, Missoula, Montana

Blueberry Refrigerator Dessert

2 cups graham cracker crumbs	1 1/4 cups milk
1 stick margarine, melted	1 teaspoon vanilla extract
1/4 cup confectioners' sugar	1 8-ounce carton whipped topping
1 10-ounce package miniature marshmallows	1 20-ounce can blueberry pie filling
	Graham cracker crumbs

Combine cracker crumbs, margarine and confectioners' sugar in bowl; mix well. Press into 9 x 13-inch dish. Chill in refrigerator. Melt marshmallows with milk and vanilla in saucepan; cool. Fold in whipped topping. Spread over crumbs. Spread pie filling over marshmallow layer. Swirl with knife to marbleize. Sprinkle with additional cracker crumbs. Chill until set. Yield : 15-18 servings.

Judy Dehne
Preceptor Beta, Bismarck, North Dakota

Desserts

Blueberry Cobbler

1 20-ounce can
    apple pie filling
Blueberries
1/2 cup sugar

1 teaspoon cinnamon
1/2 teaspoon allspice
3/4 cup baking mix
Milk

Layer pie filling and blueberries in buttered 8 x 8-inch baking pan. Sprinkle with mixture of sugar, cinnamon and allspice. Combine baking mix with enough milk in bowl to make a medium batter. Pour over blueberries. Bake at 375 degrees for 20 minutes. Yield: 8 servings.

Bonnie Webster
Preceptor Alpha, Fairbanks, Alaska

Blueberry Delight

14 graham crackers
1 small package
    vanilla instant
    pudding mix
2 cups cold milk

1 cup whipped topping
1 20-ounce can
    blueberry pie
    filling

Arrange single layer of graham crackers in 9 x 9-inch pan. Prepare pudding mix with milk, using package directions. Let stand for 5 minutes. Fold in whipped topping. Spread half the pudding over crackers. Add second layer of crackers and remaining pudding. Top with remaining crackers. Spread pie filling over top. Chill for 3 hours. Yield: 9 servings.

Glenda Blackburn
Upsilon Nu, Versailles, Missouri

Butter Brickle Dessert

Graham cracker crumbs
2 small packages
    vanilla instant
    pudding mix
1 1/2 cups milk
1 quart butter brickle
    ice cream, softened

1 8-ounce carton
    whipped topping
4 or 5 Heath
    bars, crushed

Prepare graham cracker crust, using package directions. Press into 9 x 13-inch dish. Chill in refrigerator. Combine pudding mix, milk and ice cream in bowl; mix well. Spread over crumbs. Top with whipped topping and crushed candy. Chill until firm. Yield: 12 servings.

Lynda N. Keller
Xi Beta Nu, Des Moines, Iowa

Butter Pecan Four-Layer Delight

1/2 cup margarine,
    softened
1/4 cup sugar
3/4 cup flour
1/2 cup chopped pecans
1 cup confectioners'
    sugar
1 8-ounce package
    cream cheese,
    softened

1 8-ounce carton
    whipped topping
2 small packages
    butter pecan instant
    pudding mix
2 1/2 cups milk
1 teaspoon
    vanilla extract
1/8 cup chopped pecans

Combine first 4 ingredients in bowl; mix well. Press into 9 x 13-inch baking pan. Bake at 300 degrees for 10 minutes. Cool. Cream confectioners' sugar and cream cheese in bowl until fluffy. Add 1 cup whipped topping; mix well. Spread over crust. Combine pudding with milk and vanilla in bowl. Beat for 2 minutes. Spread over creamed mixture. Spread remaining whipped topping over layers. Sprinkle with 1/8 cup pecans. Chill for 2 hours or longer. Yield: 12-15 servings.

Beverly Van Dyk
Alpha Beta, Rocky Ford, Colorado

Cherry Delight

1 15-ounce can
    sweetened
    condensed milk
1 20-ounce can
    crushed pineapple,
    drained

1 can cherry
    pie filling
1 8-ounce carton
    whipped topping
1/2 cup chopped walnuts

Combine sweetened condensed milk with pineapple and pie filling in bowl; mix well. Fold in whipped topping and walnuts gently. Chill for 30 minutes. Yield: 8 servings.

Jeannette Johnston
Xi Zeta Epsilon, Noblesville, Indiana

French Cherry Dessert

1 8-ounce package
    vanilla wafers,
    crushed
1 tablespoon sugar
6 tablespoons melted
    margarine
3/4 cup sifted
    confectioners' sugar

4 ounces cream
    cheese, softened
1 envelope whipped
    topping, prepared
1 can cherry
    pie filling
1 tablespoon sugar

Mix vanilla wafer crumbs, 1 tablespoon sugar and margarine in bowl. Press into 8 x 12-inch dish. Cream confectioners' sugar and cream cheese in bowl until fluffy. Fold in whipped topping. Spread over crumb layer. Mix pie filling and 1 tablespoon sugar in bowl. Spread over top. Chill in refrigerator. Yield: 12 servings.

Priscilla Robinson
Zeta Phi, Bryan, Ohio

Desserts

Pie Perfect Cherry Cobbler

1 cup oil
4 eggs, beaten
1 cup sugar
1 teaspoon
    vanilla extract
2 cups flour
1/2 teaspoon salt
1 teaspoon
    baking powder
2 tablespoons sugar
2 teaspoons cinnamon
1 21-ounce can
    cherry pie filling

Beat oil and eggs in mixer bowl until thick. Add sugar gradually; beat well. Mix in vanilla. Sift flour, salt and baking powder together 3 times. Add to egg mixture; mix well. Pour half the batter into greased and floured 9 x 13-inch baking pan. Combine 2 tablespoons sugar and cinnamon. Sprinkle 4 teaspoons over batter. Spread pie filling over top. Drizzle remaining batter over pie filling. Sprinkle remaining cinnamon and sugar mixture over top. Bake at 350 degrees for 25 to 35 minutes or until brown. Yield: 15 servings.

Evelyn I. Mason
Xi Theta, Lead, South Dakota

Almond Torte

1 package Stella Dora
    Almond Toast
1 cup milk
1 large package
    chocolate pudding
    and pie
    filling mix
3 cups milk
1 teaspoon rum
    flavoring
1 large package vanilla
    pudding and pie
    filling mix
3 cups milk
1 teaspoon rum
    flavoring
1 16-ounce carton
    whipped topping
Chopped almonds
Cherries

Dip toast in 1 cup milk. Arrange in 9 x 13-inch baking dish. Prepare chocolate pudding according to package directions, using 3 cups milk and 1 teaspoon rum flavoring. Pour over toast; cool. Prepare vanilla pudding according to package directions, using remaining milk and flavoring. Pour over chocolate pudding. Chill overnight. Top with whipped topping, almonds and cherries. Yield: 12-16 servings.

Marjorie A. Bailey
Preceptor Delta, Kittery Point, Maine

Leslie's Chocolate Eclair Cake

1 16-ounce box
    graham crackers
2 small packages
    vanilla instant
    pudding mix
3 1/2 cups milk
1 8-ounce carton
    whipped topping
2 1-ounce squares
    unsweetened
    chocolate, melted
2 tablespoons light
    corn syrup
2 teaspoons
    vanilla extract
3 tablespoons milk
3 tablespoons butter,
    melted
1 1/2 cups
    confectioners' sugar

Arrange 1 layer graham crackers in 9 x 13-inch dish. Combine pudding mix and 3 1/2 cups milk in bowl. Beat at medium speed for 2 minutes. Fold in whipped topping. Spread half the mixture over crackers. Repeat layers and top with third layer of crackers. Mix remaining ingredients in bowl until smooth. Spread over crackers. Chill, covered, for 24 hours. Yield: 18 servings.

Leslie Peacock
Xi Upsilon Rho, Oxnard, California

Chocolate Eclair Dessert

1 16-ounce box
    graham crackers
2 small packages
    vanilla instant
    pudding mix
1 8-ounce carton
    whipped topping
1 2-layer can
    chocolate icing

Line 9 x 13-inch dish with graham crackers. Prepare pudding mix using package directions. Mix in whipped topping. Spread half the mixture over crackers. Add second layer of crackers and remaining pudding. Top with third layer of crackers. Spread icing over top. Chill for 2 hours or longer. Yield: 15 servings.

Estelle D. Seachrist
Preceptor Alpha Kappa, Fishersville, Virginia

Chocolate Almond Mousse

1/2 envelope
    unflavored gelatin
4 1/2 teaspoons sugar
1 tablespoon cocoa
3/4 cup milk
1 tablespoon
    almond liqueur
1/4 cup whipping
    cream, whipped

Combine first 3 ingredients in saucepan; blend in milk. Let stand for 1 minute. Cook over low heat for 5 minutes or until gelatin is dissolved, stirring constantly. Stir in liqueur. Chill until partially set. Fold in whipped cream. Spoon into dessert dishes. Chill until set. Garnish with additional whipped cream and slivered almonds.

Photograph for this recipe on page 104.

Desserts

Easy Chocolate Mousse

2 teaspoons
   unflavored gelatin
1 cup sugar
1/2 cup cocoa

2 teaspoons
   vanilla extract
1 pint whipping cream

Soften gelatin for 1 minute in 2 tablespoons cold water in small bowl. Add 1/4 cup boiling water; stir to dissolve. Combine remaining ingredients in mixer bowl. Beat at medium speed until stiff peaks form. Blend in gelatin. Pour into serving dishes. Chill for 30 minutes or longer. Yield: 4 servings.

Donna Jean Trusler
Preceptor Pi, Polson, Montana

Quick Chocolate Mousse

1 cup half and half,
   scalded
1 6-ounce package
   semisweet
   chocolate chips
1 egg

Pinch of salt
1 tablespoon Creme
   de Menthe
1 cup whipping
   cream, whipped

Combine first 5 ingredients in blender container. Process on High for 1 minute. Pour into serving dishes. Chill until set. Top with whipped cream to serve. Yield: 4-6 servings.

Sharon E. Reimer
Zeta Epsilon, Shelburne, Ontario, Canada

Punch Bowl Cake

1 2-layer package
   chocolate cake mix
3 small packages
   chocolate instant
   pudding mix

3 8-ounce cartons
   whipped topping

Prepare and bake cake mix in ungreased 9 x 13-inch cake pan using package directions. Crumble cooled cake. Prepare pudding mix, using package directions. Layer cake crumbs, pudding and whipped topping 1/3 at a time in punch bowl. Chill in refrigerator.

Joyce Rader
Chi Alpha, Bedford, Texas

Hot Fudge Sauce

1 1-ounce square
   unsweetened chocolate
1 cup sugar
3 tablespoons
   cornstarch

1 teaspoon butter
Pinch of salt
1 teaspoon
   vanilla extract

Combine all ingredients with 1 cup water in saucepan. Cook until melted and well blended, stirring frequently; cool slightly. Serve over ice cream. Yield: 6 servings.

Lillian Hibbard
Xi Zeta Theta, Rural Waverly, Missouri

Quick Cobbler

2 16-ounce cans
   fruit, drained
1 cup flour
1 cup sugar
Pinch of salt

1 teaspoon
   baking powder
1 egg, beaten
6 tablespoons butter,
   melted

Spread fruit in buttered 9 x 13-inch baking dish. Combine dry ingredients in bowl. Add egg; mix until crumbly. Sprinkle over fruit. Drizzle with butter. Bake at 375 degrees for 35 minutes.
Note: May use fresh fruit.

Jean Howard
Preceptor Gamma Kappa, Stockton, California

Fresh Fruit Dumplings

8 cups fresh fruit
1 cup (about) sugar
1/3 cup shortening

2/3 cup flour
1/2 cup milk

Bring fruit and sugar to a boil in heavy saucepan. Cut shortening into flour in bowl until crumbly. Stir in milk. Drop by spoonfuls into fruit; reduce heat. Simmer until cooked through, turning as needed. Serve hot with butter or cream. Yield: 8 servings.

Wanda Arnold
Xi Alpha Delta, Louisville, Tennessee

Fruit Pudding Dessert

1 20-ounce can
   fruit cocktail
1 20-ounce can
   pineapple
   tidbits
1 10-ounce can
   mandarin oranges

1 3-ounce package
   vanilla instant
   pudding mix
1 3-ounce package
   lemon instant
   pudding mix
2 bananas, sliced

Drain fruit, reserving 2 cups mixed juice. Combine canned fruit in serving bowl. Sprinkle pudding mixes over top. Add reserved juice; mix well. Chill in refrigerator. Stir in bananas at serving time.

Mary Carabin
Preceptor Tau, Norwalk, Ohio

Desserts

Graham Cracker Pudding Bars

24 graham crackers
1 stick butter, melted
1 6-ounce can
   evaporated milk
1 tablespoon flour
1 egg
1 cup sugar

1 cup chopped nuts
1 cup coconut
1 cup graham
   cracker crumbs
2 teaspoons
   vanilla extract

Arrange half the graham crackers in 10 x 15-inch pan. Combine next 5 ingredients in saucepan. Cook until thick, stirring constantly. Stir in nuts, coconut, cracker crumbs and vanilla; mix well. Spread over crackers. Top with layer of remaining crackers. Frost as desired. Chill in refrigerator. Cut into bars. Yield: 3-4 dozen.

Agnes C. Tracy
Laureate Nu, Flint, Michigan

Lemon Fruit Parfaits

1 small
   package lemon
   instant
   pudding mix
1 3/4 cups milk
1/4 cup Sherry

1 16-ounce can
   tropical fruit
   salad, chilled,
   drained
Whipped topping
Sliced almonds

Prepare pudding mix according to package directions, using milk and Sherry for liquid. Chill in freezer for 10 minutes. Spoon into 6 parfait glasses. Add fruit and whipped topping to each glass. Chill until serving time. Garnish with sliced almonds. Yield: 6 servings.

Estelle D. Seachrist
Preceptor Alpha Kappa, Fishersville, Virginia

Lemon Layer Dessert

1 cup flour
1/2 cup margarine,
   melted
1/2 cup chopped nuts
1 8-ounce package
   cream cheese,
   softened

1 16-ounce carton
   whipped topping
1 1/2 cups
   confectioners' sugar
2 small packages
   lemon instant
   pudding mix

Mix flour, margarine and nuts in bowl. Press into 9 x 13-inch baking dish. Bake at 350 degrees for 15 minutes. Cool. Combine cream cheese and half the whipped topping in mixer bowl. Add confectioners' sugar; mix well. Spread over prepared crust. Prepare pudding mix using package directions. Pour over cream cheese layer. Chill in refrigerator. Top with remaining whipped topping.

Anna L. Yetter
Xi Gamma Omega, Beavertown, Pennsylvania

Lemon Souffle

2 tablespoons butter,
   softened
1 cup sugar
2 tablespoons flour

2 eggs, separated
1 cup milk
Juice and grated rind
   of 1 lemon

Cream butter and sugar in mixer bowl until fluffy. Mix in flour. Add beaten egg yolks, milk, lemon juice and lemon rind; mix well. Fold in stiffly beaten egg whites. Pour into greased baking dish. Place in pan of boiling water. Bake at 350 degrees for 45 minutes or until set. Yield: 6 servings.

Vivian D. Myers
Preceptor Delta Beta, Norwalk, California

Poached Peaches and Rum Custard

1 1/4 cups sugar
2 teaspoons rum extract
8 medium peaches,
   peeled
1/4 cup sugar
1/4 teaspoon salt

1 tablespoon
   cornstarch
2 cups milk
2 egg yolks
1 teaspoon rum extract

Bring 1 1/4 cups sugar, 2 teaspoons rum flavoring and 6 cups water to a boil in saucepan. Add peaches. Simmer, covered, for 10 minutes, basting occasionally; drain. Place in serving dishes. Chill in refrigerator. Blend next 5 ingredients in saucepan. Cook over medium heat until mixture thickens, stirring constantly. Stir in 1 teaspoon rum flavoring. Cover custard with waxed paper. Cool to room temperature. Spoon over peaches. Yield: 8 servings.

Joan Stockman
Laureate Omega, Arvada, Colorado

Fruit Pizza

1 package sugar
   cookie mix
1 8-ounce package
   cream cheese,
   softened

1 cup confectioners'
   sugar
1 29-ounce can
   sliced peaches
2 teaspoons cornstarch

Prepare cookie mix using package directions. Press onto greased pizza pan. Bake at 350 degrees until lightly browned. Cool. Beat cream cheese and confectioners' sugar in mixer bowl until fluffy. Spread on crust. Drain peaches, reserving juice. Arrange peaches in pinwheel design on creamed layer. Combine reserved juice with cornstarch in saucepan. Cook until thickened, stirring constantly. Spoon over peaches. Chill in refrigerator. Cut into wedges to serve.

Diana Heames
Xi Delta Psi, Canton, Michigan

Desserts

Grand Marnier Souffle

3 egg yolks
1/4 cup sugar
1 cup whipping
   cream, whipped
1 ounce Grand
   Marnier
Shaved chocolate

Beat egg yolks and sugar in mixer bowl for 2 minutes or until thick. Reserve 1/3 cup whipped cream for topping. Fold remaining whipped cream gently into egg mixture. Blend in Grand Marnier. Spoon into parfait glasses. Freeze for 2 hours or longer. Top with reserved whipped cream and chocolate to serve. Yield: 4-6 servings.

Louella Skogberg
Psi, Regina, Saskatchewan, Canada

Kaye's Pineapple Dessert

Graham crackers
1 20-ounce can
   crushed pineapple
1 cup sugar
3 tablespoons
   cornstarch
3 eggs, beaten
1 teaspoon
   vanilla extract
1 cup chopped nuts
Whipped cream

Line 9 x 9-inch pan with graham crackers. Bring pineapple, sugar and cornstarch to a boil in saucepan. Cook until thick, stirring constantly. Add a small amount of hot mixture to eggs; stir eggs into hot mixture. Cook for 1 minute longer. Stir in vanilla and nuts. Pour over graham crackers. Top with layer of crackers. Chill in refrigerator. Serve with whipped cream. Yield: 6-8 servings.

Kaye McIntosh
Xi Iota Eta, Andrews, Texas

Pistachio Dessert

16 graham crackers,
   crushed
1/4 cup packed
   brown sugar
1 stick butter, melted
1 quart vanilla ice
   cream, softened
1 1/2 cups milk
2 small packages
   pistachio instant
   pudding mix
1 16-ounce carton
   whipped topping
4 Heath bars, crushed

Combine cracker crumbs, brown sugar and butter in bowl; mix well. Press into 9 x 13-inch baking dish. Bake at 350 degrees for 10 minutes. Cool. Mix ice cream, milk and pudding mix in bowl until smooth. Pour over crumb layer. Freeze until firm. Top with whipped topping and crushed candy. Freeze until serving time. Yield: 20 servings.
Note: May store in refrigerator instead of freezer for softer consistency.

Mardele Toth
Xi Tau, Havre, Montana

Four-Layer Dessert

1 cup flour
1/2 cup butter
1/2 cup finely
   chopped pecans
1 8-ounce package
   cream cheese,
   softened
1 cup confectioners'
   sugar
1 cup whipped
   topping
2 small packages
   pistachio
   pudding mix
3 cups milk
1 cup whipped
   topping

Combine flour, butter and pecans in bowl; mix well. Press into 9 x 13-inch baking pan. Bake at 375 degrees for 15 minutes. Cool. Blend cream cheese, confectioners' sugar and 1 cup whipped topping in bowl until smooth. Spoon over crust; spread gently. Combine pudding mix and milk in bowl; mix well. Pour over creamed layer. Top with remaining whipped topping. Chill in refrigerator. Yield: 12 servings.

Shirley James
Preceptor Iota, Albuquerque, New Mexico

Green Stuff

1 small package
   pistachio instant
   pudding mix
1 16-ounce carton
   whipped topping
1 15-ounce can
   crushed pineapple
1 16-ounce can fruit
   cocktail, drained
1 11-ounce can
   mandarin oranges,
   drained
1/2 cup chopped nuts

Combine pudding mix and whipped topping in bowl; mix well. Stir in fruit and nuts. Spoon into serving bowl. Chill in refrigerator. Yield: 8 servings.

Adeline Smith
Iota Eta, Harvey, Louisiana

Rice Chantilly

1/2 cup minute rice
1/2 cup raisins
1/4 teaspoon salt
2 cups milk
1 small package
   vanilla pudding and
   pie filling mix
1 cup whipped topping

Combine rice, raisins and 1/2 cup hot water in saucepan. Let stand, covered, for 10 minutes. Add salt, milk and pudding mix. Cook according to pudding package directions; cool. Fold in whipped topping. Spoon into individual serving dishes. Chill in refrigerator. Garnish with nutmeg. Yield: 6-8 servings.

Jean Zeller
Laureate Theta, New Albany, Indiana

Desserts

Prism Cake

1   3-ounce package
    orange gelatin
1   3-ounce package
    cherry gelatin
1   3-ounce package
    lime gelatin
1   3-ounce package
    lemon gelatin

1 cup pineapple juice
1/4 cup sugar
2 cups graham
    cracker crumbs
1/2 cup melted butter
2 cups whipped topping
1 cup finely
    chopped nuts

Dissolve orange gelatin in 1/2 cup hot water in 9 x 13-inch dish. Stir in 1/2 cup cold water. Repeat process with cherry and lime gelatins. Chill each mixture until set. Dissolve lemon gelatin in hot pineapple juice in bowl. Stir in sugar and 1/2 cup cold water. Chill until partially set. Combine cracker crumbs and butter in bowl. Press into 9 x 13-inch dish. Dice 3 congealed flavors of gelatin. Stir into lemon gelatin with whipped topping; mix gently. Pour into prepared crust. Top with nuts. Chill until set. Yield: 9-12 servings.

Virginia P. Cook
Preceptor Gamma Sigma, Sarasota, Florida

No-Bake Rum Cake

2 packages Stella Dora
    anise biscuits
2 ounces dark rum
1 small package
    chocolate instant
    pudding mix

2 ounces dark rum
1 small package
    vanilla instant
    pudding mix
1   16-ounce carton
    whipped topping

Arrange half the biscuits in bottom of 9-inch springform pan. Pour 2 ounces rum over biscuits. Prepare chocolate pudding mix, using package directions. Spread over biscuits. Repeat layers, using vanilla pudding mix. Chill overnight. Place on serving plate; remove side of pan. Frost with whipped topping. Yield: 8-10 servings.

Margaret M. Gossman
Xi Eta, Pukalani, Hawaii

Snowballs

1/2 pound margarine,
    softened
1/2 cup sugar
2/3 cup crushed
    pineapple
1 cup chopped pecans

2 eggs, separated
36 brown-edged cookies
1   16-ounce carton
    whipped topping
1 cup coconut

Cream margarine and sugar in mixer bowl until fluffy. Add pineapple, pecans and egg yolks; mix well. Fold in stiffly beaten egg whites. Spread 12 cookies with half the mixture. Top with 12 cookies. Repeat layers. Frost each stack with whipped topping. Sprinkle with coconut. Place on serving plate. Chill for 12 to 24 hours. Yield: 12 servings.

Brenda Moody
Xi Omega, Bowling Green, Kentucky

Almond Creme Strawberries

2 pints large
    strawberries
1 small package vanilla
    instant pudding mix
1 cup milk

1 cup whipping
    cream, whipped
1 teaspoon
    almond extract

Stem strawberries. Cut deep X in stem end of each berry; spread apart to make petals. Prepare pudding mix according to package directions using 1 cup milk. Fold in whipped cream and flavoring gently. Pipe pudding mixture into strawberries using large writing tip. Arrange in serving dishes. Yield: 8-10 servings.

Debbi Smith
Xi Gamma Sigma, Elma, Washington

Strawberry Crunch

1 cup flour
1/3 cup packed
    brown sugar
1/2 cup melted butter
1/2 cup chopped nuts
2 egg whites

2/3 cup sugar
1   10-ounce package
    frozen strawberries,
    partially thawed
1   16-ounce carton
    whipped topping

Combine first 4 ingredients in bowl; mix well. Spread on baking sheet. Bake at 350 degrees for 20 minutes, stirring occasionally. Cool. Place half the crumbs in 9 x 13-inch dish. Beat egg whites in mixer bowl until frothy. Add sugar gradually, beating until stiff. Beat in strawberries until well blended. Fold in whipped topping gently. Pour over crumbs. Top with remaining crumbs. Freeze, covered, until firm. Yield: 12-15 servings.

Juanita Lunn
Alpha Kappa, Mt. Vernon, Ohio

Strawberry Tango

1 1/2 cups sour cream
1 cup packed
    brown sugar

1/2 cup Amaretto
2 pints fresh
    strawberries

Combine sour cream, brown sugar and Amaretto in bowl; mix well. Fold in strawberries. Spoon into serving dishes. Garnish with whole strawberry. Yield: 4 servings.

Marilyn Wilkinson
Zeta Epsilon, Orangeville, Ontario, Canada

Desserts

Strawberry Cream Pie

20 ladyfingers,
  separated
1 1/2 tablespoons
  cream Sherry
1 small package
  vanilla instant
  pudding mix

1 1/2 cups milk
1 pint fresh
  California
  strawberries
6 tablespoons
  currant jelly

Arrange enough ladyfinger halves, filling side up, over bottom of 9-inch pie plate to cover. Cut remaining ladyfingers in half crosswise; arrange to form side of pie shell. Sprinkle with Sherry. Prepare pudding mix according to package directions, using 1 1/2 cups milk. Spoon pudding over ladyfingers. Arrange strawberries in 2 rings around edge of pie. Melt jelly in saucepan over low heat, stirring constantly; spoon over strawberries. Serve immediately or chill until serving time.

Photograph for this recipe on page 85.

Leslie's Dump Cake

1 16-ounce can
  crushed pineapple,
  drained
1/2 pound brown sugar
1 can apple pie filling

1 2-layer package
  yellow cake mix
2 sticks butter,
  melted
1 cup nuts (opt.)

Layer all ingredients in order listed in 9 x 13-inch cake pan. Bake at 350 degrees for 40 minutes or until cake tests done. Yield: 12 servings.

Leslie Williams
Xi Alpha Rho, Danville, Kentucky

Pecan-Apple Fantasy

2 16-ounce cans
  apple pie filling
1 2-layer package
  yellow cake mix

1 1/2 cups melted
  margarine
1 1/4 cups chopped
  pecans

Layer pie filling and dry cake mix in 9 x 13-inch baking dish; press to smooth. Drizzle margarine over top; sprinkle with pecans. Bake at 325 degrees for 1 1/2 hours. Serve warm with whipped topping or ice cream. Yield: 12 servings.
Note: Do not use pudding-recipe cake mix.

Pat M. Henry
Xi Alpha Kappa, Clyde, North Carolina

Cherry-Pineapple Dessert

1 can cherry
  pie filling
1 16-ounce can
  pineapple chunks,
  drained
1 2-layer package
  yellow cake mix

1 1/2 cups chopped nuts
1 8-ounce can coconut
2 sticks margarine,
  melted

Mix pie filling and pineapple in bowl; spread in 9 x 13-inch baking dish. Sift cake mix over fruit. Layer nuts, coconut and margarine over top. Bake at 350 degrees for 45 to 50 minutes.

Mary Lee Bowman
Laureate Eta, Warner Robins, Georgia

Kathryn's Dump Cake

1 16-ounce can
  crushed
  pineapple
1 16-ounce can
  pie cherries

1 2-layer package
  yellow cake mix
1 stick margarine,
  melted
1/2 cup nuts

Layer pineapple, cherries and dry cake mix in ungreased 9 x 13-inch baking pan. Drizzle margarine over layers; sprinkle with pecans. Bake at 375 degrees for 30 minutes. Serve with ice cream or whipped cream.

Kathryn Simpson
Xi Alpha Zeta, Glenrock, Wyoming

Laurie's Dump Cake

1 20-ounce can
  crushed pineapple,
  drained
1 can cherry pie filling
1 2-layer package
  yellow cake mix

1/2 cup chopped walnuts
2 sticks margarine,
  sliced

Layer all ingredients in order listed in greased 9 x 13-inch cake pan. Bake at 350 degrees for 1 hour. Cool.

Laurie Kamman
Xi Alpha Rho, Buffalo, New York

Easy Crisp Cherry Cobbler

2 20-ounce cans
  cherry pie filling
1 2-layer package
  white cake mix

2 sticks margarine,
  melted

Spread pie filling in ungreased 9 x 13-inch baking dish. Sprinkle with cake mix. Drizzle with margarine. Bake at 350 degrees for 45 minutes.

Ruth Wicks
Xi Eta Epsilon, Bernville, Pennsylvania

Desserts

Dakota Cherry Dessert

1 20-ounce can
    crushed pineapple
1 21-ounce can
    cherry pie filling

1 2-layer package
    white cake mix
1/2 cup chopped walnuts
2 sticks margarine

Layer pineapple with juice, pie filling and cake mix in 9 x 13-inch baking dish. Sprinkle walnuts over top. Dot with margarine. Bake at 350 degrees for 40 to 45 minutes or until brown. Serve warm or cool with ice cream or whipped topping. Yield: 24 servings.

Dorothy Peterson
Xi Alpha Upsilon, Whitewood, South Dakota

Easy Peach Cobbler

2 29-ounce cans
    sliced peaches
1 teaspoon nutmeg
1 tablespoon cinnamon

1 2-layer package
    lemon cake mix
1 1/2 sticks butter,
    melted

Pour peaches and juice into 9 x 13-inch baking pan. Sprinkle with spices and cake mix. Dot with butter. Bake at 350 degrees for 30 to 45 minutes or until golden brown. Yield: 12 servings.

Anne Schroeder
Xi Beta Alpha, Appleton, Wisconsin

Fruit Pudding

1 2-layer package
    yellow cake mix
1 15-ounce can
    crushed pineapple
1 16-ounce can
    sliced peaches

1 20-ounce can
    cherry pie filling
1/2 cup chopped pecans
1 stick margarine

Sprinkle cake mix in greased 8 x 12-inch baking pan. Add undrained fruit and pie filling. Stir to moisten cake mix. Sprinkle with pecans; dot with margarine. Bake at 300 degrees for 45 minutes. Yield: 12-15 servings.

Frieda Y. Ross
Preceptor Alpha Zeta, Pleasant Garden, North Carolina

Pumpkin Cake

4 eggs, slightly beaten
1 20-ounce can
    pumpkin pie filling
1 2-layer package
    yellow cake mix

1 stick margarine,
    melted
Chopped nuts (opt.)

Combine eggs and pie filling in buttered 9 x 13-inch cake pan; mix well. Sprinkle with cake mix. Drizzle with margarine. Sprinkle nuts over top. Bake at 350 degrees for 45 minutes. Cool. Serve with whipped topping.

Joan Stebbins
Xi Alpha Beta, Council Bluffs, Iowa

Rhubarb Delight

4 cups chopped
    rhubarb
1 cup sugar
Pinch of salt

1 1-layer package
    cake mix
1/4 cup melted
    margarine

Combine rhubarb, sugar and salt in bowl; mix well. Spoon into greased 7 x 11-inch baking pan. Sprinkle with cake mix. Drizzle margarine over top. Bake at 350 degrees for 45 minutes. Yield: 8 servings.

Joyce Burke
Xi Eta Zeta, Emmetsburg, Iowa

The Life Saver Dessert for Company

4 cups chopped rhubarb
2 cups sugar
1 small package
    strawberry gelatin

1 2-layer package
    white cake mix
1/2 stick margarine
1 cup coconut

Combine rhubarb, sugar and gelatin in bowl; mix well. Spoon into greased 9 x 13-inch baking dish. Sprinkle cake mix over top. Dot with margarine. Top with coconut. Bake at 350 degrees for 1 hour. Serve with whipped topping. Yield: 6 servings.

Carole W. Thompson
Xi Alpha Kappa, Sidney, Nebraska

Amaretto Ice Cream

1 can sweetened
    condensed milk
2 egg yolks, beaten
1/4 teaspoon
    almond extract

1/4 cup Amaretto
2 cups whipping
    cream, whipped
1/2 cup chopped
    toasted almonds

Combine first 4 ingredients in bowl; mix well. Fold in whipped cream and almonds gently. Spoon into foil-lined loaf pan. Freeze, covered, until firm. Thaw for several minutes before serving. Serve with sweetened fresh strawberries. Yield: 6 servings.

Jane Presley
Laureate Beta Delta, Odessa, Texas

Desserts

Frozen Dessert

6 cups chocolate-
  flavored crisp
  rice cereal
1 cup light corn syrup

1 cup crunchy
  peanut butter
1/2 gallon vanilla
  ice cream

Combine cereal, corn syrup and peanut butter in bowl; mix well. Press into 9 x 13-inch dish. Slice ice cream. Place slices over cereal layer, smoothing edges together. Freeze overnight. Cut into squares to serve. Yield: 12 servings.
Note: May use plain rice cereal and chocolate ice cream if desired.

Cheryl Strouse
Xi Sigma, Lakeland, Florida

Ice Cream Delight

1/2 gallon vanilla
  ice cream, softened
22 Oreo cookies,
  crushed

1 8-ounce carton
  whipped topping

Combine all ingredients in bowl; mix well. Spoon into 9 x 13-inch dish. Freeze overnight. Yield: 15-20 servings.

Glenda C. Haas
Lambda Tau, Howard, Pennsylvania

Ice Cream Sundae Shortcake

1 20-ounce can
  pie filling
1 quart ice cream

2 4-count packages
  shortcake cups

Heat pie filling in saucepan over low heat. Spoon ice cream into shortcake cups. Spoon pie filling over top.
Yield: 8 servings.

Mary L. Beien
Xi Delta Sigma, Atchison, Kansas

Lichee Nut Dream

1/2 gallon pineapple
  sherbet, softened

1 large can lichee
  nuts, drained

Combine sherbet and lichee nuts in bowl; mix well. Spoon back into sherbet container. Freeze until firm. Serve in individual dishes with Chinese almond cookies.

Mary Lou Aberasturi
Preceptor Zeta Psi, Marysville, California

Nutty Brickle Dessert

1 cup melted margarine
2 cups flour
1/2 cup oats
1/2 cup packed
  brown sugar

1/2 cup chopped pecans
1 12-ounce jar
  caramel sauce
1/2 gallon ice
  cream, softened

Combine margarine, flour, oats, brown sugar and pecans in bowl; mix well. Press into baking sheet. Bake at 400 degrees for 10 to 12 minutes or until lightly browned. Cool. Crumble half the mixture into 9 x 13-inch dish. Drizzle half the sauce over crumbs. Spread ice cream over sauce. Layer remaining crumbs and sauce over ice cream. Freeze until firm.
Yield: 10-12 servings.

Kathie Connor
Preceptor Alpha Epsilon, St. Thomas, Ontario, Canada

Oreo Smush Dessert

1 19-ounce package
  Oreo cookies,
  crushed
1 stick margarine
1/2 gallon vanilla
  ice cream, softened

2 8-ounce jars
  fudge sauce
1 16-ounce carton
  whipped topping

Combine cookie crumbs and melted margarine in 9 x 13-inch dish, reserving a small amount for topping. Press evenly over bottom of pan. Layer ice cream, fudge sauce, whipped topping and reserved crumbs over crust. Freeze until firm.
Yield: 18 servings.

Carol Sassin
Xi Psi Beta, Beeville, Texas

Quick Ice Cream Dessert

1 11-ounce box
  vanilla wafers,
  crushed
1/2 gallon vanilla
  ice cream

1 12-ounce jar
  caramel ice cream
  topping
6 Heath bars, crushed

Sprinkle vanilla wafer crumbs in 9 x 13-inch dish. Slice ice cream. Arrange over crumbs, smoothing edges together. Pour caramel topping over ice cream. Sprinkle with crushed candy. Freeze until firm. Yield: 16 servings.

Ruby G. Hartje
Xi Gamma Nu, Anna, Illinois

Main Dishes

Country-Style Ham and Noodles, recipe on page 127.

Quick Shepherd's Pie, recipe on page 100.

Canadian Hash

3 to 4 cups ground
  roast beef
1/2 to 1 green
  pepper, ground
1/2 to 1 onion, ground
Salt and pepper
  to taste

Roast beef gravy
1 can vegetable soup
Cooked vegetables
Mashed potatoes
2 tablespoons butter

Combine roast beef, green pepper and onion in 2-quart casserole. Season with salt and pepper. Add enough gravy to moisten. Add soup and vegetables; mix well. Spread mashed potatoes over top; dot with butter. Bake at 375 degrees for 30 minutes or until bubbly. Yield: 4 servings.

Marge Mikell
Preceptor Iota, Jackson, Mississippi

No-Peek Casserole

2 8-ounce cans
  mushrooms
1 envelope dry onion
  soup mix

2 pounds stew beef
1 can cream of
  mushroom soup
1/2 cup Burgundy

Combine all ingredients in 2-quart casserole. Bake, tightly covered, at 300 degrees for 3 hours. Do not uncover during cooking. Serve with rice or noodles. Yield: 6 servings.

Mercy Siess
Preceptor Theta Psi, Stockton, California

Steak and Potato Bake

6 cube steaks
Flour
2 tablespoons
  shortening
Salt and pepper
  to taste

Onions, sliced
1 2-pound package
  frozen French-fried
  potatoes
2 cans cream of
  mushroom soup

Coat steaks with flour. Brown in shortening in skillet. Reserve drippings. Place steaks in 9 x 13-inch baking dish. Season with salt and pepper. Layer onions and potatoes over steak. Add 1/2 cup water and 2 cans soup to pan drippings; mix well. Pour over potatoes. Bake at 350 degrees for 1 hour. Yield: 6 servings.

Sharlene Exline
Xi Epsilon Epsilon, Forest, Ohio

Main Dishes

Steak and Potato Casserole

4 4-ounce pieces of
   tenderized
   round steak
4 slices bacon, cut
   into halves

1 small onion, sliced
4 to 6 medium potatoes,
   peeled, sliced
1 can cream of
   mushroom soup

Layer steak, bacon, onion and potatoes in 9 x 9-inch baking dish. Pour soup over top. Bake at 350 degrees for 1 hour or until steak and potatoes are tender. Yield: 4 servings.

Donna Nystrom
Xi Eta Kappa, Sterling, Kansas

Tenderloin and Dressing

10 tenderloin steaks
1 package stuffing
   mix, prepared
1 package pork
   gravy mix

1 package mushroom
   gravy mix
1 package onion
   gravy mix

Brown steaks in skillet. Layer stuffing and steaks in 9 x 13-inch baking pan. Prepare gravy mixes together according to package directions, using amount of liquid required for each. Pour over steaks. Bake at 350 degrees for 45 minutes or until bubbly. Yield: 10 servings.
Note: May substitute boned chicken, sliced roast beef or ham for steak.

Helen Still
Mu Alpha, Smithville, Missouri

Barbecued Beans

1 pound ground beef
1 onion, chopped
1 31-ounce can pork
   and beans
1 14-ounce bottle
   of catsup
2 tablespoons vinegar

1/2 cup packed
   brown sugar
1 clove of garlic,
   minced
1 tablespoon
   Worcestershire sauce
1 bay leaf

Brown ground beef and onion in skillet, stirring frequently; drain. Add remaining ingredients; mix well. Spoon into greased baking dish. Bake at 350 degrees for 45 minutes.

Meryde G. English
Xi Kappa, Winnemucca, Nevada

Ravioli-Broccoli Bake

1 10-ounce package
   frozen chopped
   broccoli
2 20-ounce cans
   ravioli

1 cup sour cream
1 8-ounce package
   mozzarella cheese,
   shredded

Cook broccoli using package directions; drain. Place in greased 2-quart baking dish. Mix ravioli and sour cream in bowl. Spoon over broccoli. Sprinkle with cheese. Bake at 350 degrees for 25 to 30 minutes. Yield: 4-6 servings.

Marv Mantooth
Alpha Gamma, APO, New York

No-Mess Cabbage Casserole

1 1/2 pounds
   ground beef
1 medium onion, chopped
1 teaspoon salt
1/2 teaspoon pepper

1 4-ounce can
   mushrooms, drained
1 medium head
   cabbage, chopped
1 can tomato soup

Brown ground beef with onion in skillet, stirring until crumbly; drain. Add salt, pepper and mushrooms. Layer cabbage and ground beef mixture in casserole. Spread soup over top, sealing to edges. Bake, covered, at 350 degrees for 1 hour. Yield: 4 servings.

Karen S. Eveland
Xi Alpha Nu, Pierce, Idaho

Cabbage Roll Casserole

1 pound ground beef
1 tablespoon oil
1 onion, chopped
6 tablespoons long
   grain rice
1 teaspoon salt

1/8 teaspoon pepper
1 10-ounce can
   mushrooms, drained
1 can tomato soup
6 cups coarsely
   shredded cabbage

Cook ground beef in oil in skillet for 1 to 2 minutes, stirring until crumbly. Add onion, rice and seasonings. Saute for 2 to 3 minutes. Stir in mushrooms, soup and 1 soup can water; mix well. Place cabbage in greased casserole. Pour ground beef mixture over cabbage. Do not mix. Bake at 325 degrees for 2 hours.

Karen E. Bowe
Gamma Gamma, Kitchener, Ontario, Canada

Easy Ground Beef Casserole

1 pound very lean
   ground chuck
1 can cream of
   mushroom soup

1 16-ounce package
   Tater Tots
Salt and pepper
   to taste

Layer all ingredients in order listed in 2-quart casserole. Bake at 350 degrees for 1 hour. Yield: 4 servings.

Marie Shell
Alpha Gamma, APO, New York

Main Dishes

Dinner-in-a-Dish

1 pound ground beef
1 onion, chopped
1 tablespoon margarine
1 16-ounce can
    whole kernel corn
1 16-ounce can
    green beans

1 can tomato soup
1 teaspoon
    Worcestershire sauce
1/2 teaspoon salt
Dash of pepper
1 8-ounce package
    potato chips, crushed

Brown ground beef with onion in margarine in skillet, stirring frequently. Drain vegetables, reserving 1/3 cup liquid. Add vegetables, reserved liquid, soup and seasonings to ground beef; mix well. Pour into greased 1 1/2-quart casserole. Sprinkle potato chips on top. Bake at 350 degrees for 30 to 40 minutes or until bubbly.

Joyce Cummins
Preceptor Mu, Bay City, Michigan

Easy Layered Casserole

1 1/2 pounds
    ground beef
4 cups thinly sliced
    peeled potatoes
Salt and pepper
    to taste
1 17-ounce can whole
    kernel corn, drained

1 large onion, chopped
4 carrots, peeled,
    sliced
1/2 teaspoon marjoram
1 8-ounce can
    tomato sauce
1/2 cup grated
    Cheddar cheese

Brown ground beef in skillet, stirring until crumbly; drain. Place potatoes in greased baking dish. Season with salt and pepper. Layer corn, onion, carrots and ground beef over potatoes. Season with marjoram, salt and pepper. Spread tomato sauce over top. Bake, covered, at 350 degrees for 30 minutes. Sprinkle with cheese. Bake, uncovered, for 10 minutes longer. Garnish with parsley.

Vivian J. Thompson
Nu Gamma, Crescent City, California

Ground Beef-Potato Casserole

1 pound ground chuck
1/4 teaspoon onion salt
1/2 can cream of
    celery soup

1 16-ounce
    package
    Tater Tots

Pat ground chuck into 8-inch square baking pan. Sprinkle with onion salt. Spread soup over ground chuck. Arrange potatoes on top in rows. Bake at 350 degrees for 1 hour.

Nina Rae Harris
Preceptor Delta Alpha, Ft. Myers, Florida

Cabbage-Potato Casserole

3 cups sliced potatoes
3 cups chopped cabbage
1/2 stick margarine
1 cup sour cream
1 to 1 1/2 pounds
    ground beef

1 onion, chopped
3/4 cup milk
1 can cream of
    chicken soup
Salt and pepper
    to taste

Cook potatoes in water in saucepan until nearly tender; drain. Saute cabbage in margarine in skillet until tender. Stir in sour cream. Brown ground beef with onion in skillet, stirring until crumbly; drain. Combine milk, soup, salt and pepper in bowl; mix well. Layer potatoes, cabbage, ground beef and soup mixture in greased 2-quart baking dish. Bake at 350 degrees for 30 minutes. Yield: 6 servings.

Roseleen Corder
Pi Chi, Alma, Missouri

Quick Shepherd's Pie

1/3 cup chopped onion
1 clove of garlic, crushed
1 to 2 tablespoons oil
1 1/2 pounds ground beef
1 can cream of
    mushroom soup
1 8-ounce can sliced
    carrots, drained
1/4 teaspoon salt
1/8 teaspoon pepper

1/2 cup chopped
    dill pickle
1 6-serving package
    mashed potatoes
2 tablespoons
    Parmesan cheese
2 tablespoons
    heavy cream
1 tablespoon
    chopped parsley

Saute onion and garlic in hot oil in large skillet. Add ground beef. Cook until brown and crumbly, stirring occasionally. Stir in soup, carrots, salt, pepper and pickle. Simmer for 15 to 20 minutes, stirring occasionally. Prepare mashed potatoes according to package directions, adding cheese, cream and parsley. Place ground beef mixture in a 1-quart ovenproof deep dish; spoon potatoes around edge. Broil until brown. Serve immediately. Garnish with additional pickle slices. Yield: 4-6 servings.

Photograph for this recipe on page 98.

Ground Beef-Zucchini Casserole

2 pounds zucchini,
    chopped
3/4 cup finely
    chopped onion
1 cup shredded carrots
5 tablespoons
    margarine

1 1/2 cups stuffing mix
1 can cream of
    chicken soup
1/2 cup sour cream
1 1/2 cups stuffing mix
2 tablespoons
    margarine

Cook zucchini in boiling salted water in saucepan until tender. Drain in colander, pressing out excess liquid. Saute onion and carrots in 5 tablespoons margarine in skillet until brown. Place in greased baking dish. Add 1 1/2 cups stuffing mix, soup and sour cream; mix well. Fold in zucchini. Sprinkle mixture of 1 1/2 cups stuffing mix and 2 tablespoons butter over top. Bake at 350 degrees for 30 minutes.

Marian R. Forck
Tau Mu, Russellville, Missouri

Main Dishes

Coronado Casserole

2 pounds zucchini,
    sliced
1 pound lean
    ground beef
1 teaspoon salt
1/4 teaspoon each
    pepper, garlic powder
1 cup finely
    chopped onion
3 cups cooked rice
1 4-ounce can green
    chilies, chopped
2 eggs, beaten
1 1/2 cups cottage
    cheese
2 tablespoons grated
    Parmesan cheese
2 cups grated
    Cheddar cheese

Cook zucchini in salted water in saucepan for 5 minutes; drain. Cook ground beef with seasonings and onion in skillet until ground beef is cooked through and onion is tender-crisp. Add rice, chilies and zucchini. Blend eggs, cottage cheese and Parmesan cheese. Stir into ground beef mixture. Pour into 2 greased shallow 2-quart casseroles. Top each with 1 cup Cheddar cheese. Bake 1 at 350 degrees for 30 minutes. Store remaining casserole, covered, in freezer. Yield: Two 6-serving casseroles.

Shirley B. Griffin
Preceptor Upsilon, Crowley, Louisiana

Enchilada Casserole

1 pound ground round
1 onion, chopped
Garlic to taste
1 can cream of
    mushroom soup
1 can cream of
    chicken soup
1 4-ounce can green
    chilies, chopped
1 4-ounce can
    pitted olives
1 cup milk
1 can mild
    enchilada sauce
12 corn tortillas, torn
4 ounces Cheddar
    cheese, grated

Brown ground round with onion and garlic in skillet, stirring frequently; drain. Add soups, chilies, olives and milk; mix well. Pour enchilada sauce into baking dish. Layer tortillas, ground round mixture and cheese over top. Bake, covered with foil, for 1 1/4 hours. Bake, uncovered, for 15 minutes longer.

Sally Giulieri
Preceptor Theta Psi, Stockton, California

Four-Can Mexican Casserole

1 pound ground beef
1/2 cup chopped onion
1 can ranch-style
    beans
1 can pork and beans
1 can Spanish rice
1 can Ro-Tel
1 8-ounce package
    Velveeta cheese,
    sliced
1 8-ounce package
    corn chips

Brown ground beef with onion in skillet, stirring frequently; drain. Add beans, rice and Ro-Tel. Simmer for 15 minutes. Pour into 2-quart casserole. Cover with cheese. Sprinkle enough corn chips over top to cover cheese. Bake at 350 degrees for 20 minutes. Yield: 4 servings.

Kathy Chancellor
Xi Epsilon Kappa, Rusk, Texas

Sheila's Mexican Casserole

1 pound ground beef
1 small onion, chopped
6 flour tortillas
1 16-ounce can
    chili beans
1 can cream of
    mushroom soup
1 cup picante sauce
1 pound Cheddar
    cheese, grated

Brown ground beef and onion in skillet, stirring frequently; drain. Layer tortillas, ground beef mixture, chili beans, soup, picante sauce and cheese in greased 9 x 13-inch baking dish. Bake at 350 degrees for 40 minutes or until bubbly.

Sheila Slaughter
Alpha Kappa Upsilon, The Colony, Texas

Tamale Casserole

3/4 cup chopped onion
1 tablespoon butter
1 pound lean
    ground beef
1 teaspoon salt
1/8 teaspoon pepper
1 teaspoon chili
    powder
1/2 cup sliced
    pitted olives
1 14-ounce can
    tamales with
    chili gravy
1/2 cup tomato juice
1/2 cup grated
    Cheddar cheese

Saute onion in butter in skillet until tender. Add ground beef. Cook until brown, stirring frequently; drain. Add seasonings and olives. Remove tamale wrappers. Cut into 1-inch slices. Add to skillet with chili gravy and tomato juice; mix well. Pour into 6 x 10-inch baking dish. Sprinkle with cheese. Bake at 350 degrees for 30 minutes. Serve over rice. Yield: 4 servings.

Louise Pochini
Preceptor Theta Psi, Stockton, California

Super Macaroni and Beef Bake

1 1/2 pounds
    ground beef
1 24-ounce jar
    spaghetti sauce
1 16-ounce carton
    cottage cheese
1/4 cup sour cream
1 8-ounce package
    cream cheese,
    softened
2 cups elbow
    macaroni, cooked
1/2 cup Parmesan cheese

Brown ground beef in skillet, stirring until crumbly; drain. Stir in spaghetti sauce. Cream cottage cheese, sour cream and cream cheese in mixer bowl until smooth. Layer macaroni, cheese mixture, sauce and Parmesan cheese in 9 x 13-inch baking dish. Chill, covered, overnight. Bake at 350 degrees for 1 hour.

Victoria Shepley
Xi Epsilon Mu, Harrow, Ontario, Canada

101

Main Dishes

Ground Beef-Macaroni Casserole

1 pound ground beef
1 7-ounce package
    macaroni, cooked
1 can tomato soup
1 can mushroom soup
1 2-ounce jar
    chopped pimento
1 green pepper, chopped
1 4-ounce package
    shredded Cheddar
    cheese
1 can French-fried
    onions

Brown ground beef in skillet, stirring until crumbly; drain. Add macaroni, soups, pimento and green pepper; mix well. Spoon half the ground beef mixture into 2-quart casserole. Layer 1/2 cup cheese, half the onions, remaining ground beef mixture and 1/2 cup cheese on top. Bake at 350 degrees for 30 minutes. Top with remaining onions. Bake for 5 minutes longer. Yield: 4 servings.

Eileen Bauderer
Laureate Alpha Mu, Mansfield, Ohio

Ground Beef and Spaghetti Casserole

2 pounds ground beef
1 green pepper, chopped
1 8-ounce bottle
    of catsup
1 large onion, chopped
Salt and pepper
    to taste
2 16-ounce cans
    spaghetti with
    cheese sauce

Brown ground beef in skillet, stirring until crumbly; drain. Add remaining ingredients; mix well. Pour into greased 9 x 13-inch baking dish. Bake at 350 degrees for 50 minutes. Yield: 8 servings.

Eleanor Hall
Preceptor Delta, Sulphur, Louisiana

Lynda's Lasagna

2 pounds
    ground beef
1 envelope dry onion
    soup mix
3 8-ounce cans
    tomato sauce
1/4 teaspoon
    garlic powder
1 8-ounce package
    lasagna noodles,
    cooked
1 8-ounce carton
    ricotta cheese
1 8-ounce package
    shredded
    mozzarella cheese

Brown ground beef in skillet, stirring until crumbly; drain. Combine soup mix, tomato sauce, garlic powder and 1 cup water in bowl; mix well. Add ground beef. Layer noodles, sauce, ricotta and mozzarella cheese alternately in casserole until all ingredients are used. Bake at 425 degrees for 25 minutes. Yield: 12 servings.

Lynda N. Keller
Xi Beta Nu, Des Moines, Iowa

Company's Coming Casserole

2 pounds ground beef
2 16-ounce cans
    tomatoes
2 8-ounce cans
    tomato sauce
1 tablespoon salt
1/2 teaspoon pepper
4 teaspoons sugar
1/4 teaspoon
    garlic powder
1 12-ounce package
    thin egg noodles
1 8-ounce package
    cream cheese
2 cups sour cream
12 green onions,
    chopped
2 cups grated
    Cheddar cheese

Combine first 7 ingredients in skillet. Cook for 15 minutes, stirring frequently. Cook noodles according to package directions; drain. Add cream cheese. Stir until cheese melts. Add sour cream and green onions; mix well. Spread noodles in greased 4-quart casserole. Spoon ground beef mixture over top. Sprinkle with cheese. Bake at 350 degrees for 40 minutes. Yield: 8-10 servings.

Pam Thompson
Xi Rho Zeta, Pasadena, Texas

Corned Beef-Noodle Casserole

1 8-ounce package
    noodles, cooked
1 12-ounce can
    corned beef,
    chopped
1 onion, chopped
1 can cream of
    chicken soup
1 soup can milk
1 8-ounce package
    Velveeta cheese,
    grated

Combine noodles, corned beef, onion, soup and milk in casserole; mix well. Sprinkle cheese on top. Bake at 350 degrees for 45 minutes or until bubbly.

Phyllis B. Painter
Preceptor Omega, Staunton, Virginia

Shelly's Reuben Casserole

1/2 cup mayonnaise
1/2 cup Thousand
    Island salad
    dressing
1 16-ounce can
    sauerkraut, drained
1 12-ounce can
    corned beef, sliced
2 cups shredded
    Swiss cheese
Pumpernickel
    bread crumbs

Combine mayonnaise and salad dressing in bowl; mix well. Layer sauerkraut, corned beef, cheese, mayonnaise mixture and bread crumbs in medium baking dish. Bake, covered, at 350 degrees for 45 minutes.

Shelly Magneson
Xi Beta Nu, Des Moines, Iowa

Spinach Fettucini; and Tomato and Basil Fettucini

Beef Burgundy for Two; Lemon Pilaf; and Chocolate Almond Mousse

Main Dishes

Swiss Hamlets

1 10-ounce
    package frozen
    broccoli spears
1/4 pound 4-inch square
    Swiss cheese slices
1/2 pound sliced ham

1 1-ounce package
    white sauce mix
1/4 cup sour cream
1 tablespoon
    prepared mustard
1/4 teaspoon dillweed

Cook broccoli spears using package directions until tender-crisp; drain. Place cheese on ham slices. Arrange broccoli spears on cheese with flowerets extending past edge on each side. Roll up tightly. Place in shallow baking dish. Prepare sauce mix using package directions. Stir in sour cream, mustard and dillweed. Pour over ham rolls. Bake at 350 degrees for 30 minutes. Yield: 6 servings.

Barbara Cavallo
Xi Beta Alpha, Neptune, New Jersey

Ham-Cheese-Broccoli Bake

1 1/2 10-ounce
    packages broccoli
    spears
10 thin slices ham
10 slices Swiss cheese

1 can cream of
    mushroom soup
1/2 soup can milk
1/2 cup toasted almonds

Cook broccoli using package directions for 3 minutes; drain. Place each ham slice on cheese slice. Roll each around broccoli spear; fasten with toothpicks. Place in buttered 9 x 11-inch baking pan. Blend soup and milk. Pour over rolls. Sprinkle almonds on top. Bake at 375 degrees for 45 minutes. Yield: 6-10 servings.

Jean Watson
Xi Alpha Psi, Wentworth, Wisconsin

Ham and Green Bean Rolls

2 cups biscuit mix
2/3 cup milk
1 tablespoon mustard
2 cups ground
    cooked ham
1/4 cup melted butter

1/4 cup flour
1/2 teaspoon salt
1/4 teaspoon pepper
2 cups milk
4 cups cooked
    green beans

Combine first 2 ingredients in bowl; mix well. Roll into 9 x 13-inch rectangle on floured surface. Spread with mustard. Sprinkle ham over dough. Roll as for jelly roll from long side. Cut into 8 slices. Place cut side down in 8-inch baking pan. Bake at 375 degrees for 25 minutes. Blend butter, flour and seasonings in saucepan. Stir in milk. Cook until thickened, stirring constantly. Add green beans. Spoon over ham rolls to serve. Yield: 4 servings.

Margaret Howard
Preceptor Laureate Nu, Lacey, Washington

Overnight Casserole

2 cups uncooked
    macaroni
1/4 pound Cheddar
    cheese, shredded
1/4 pound ground ham

2 cans cream of
    mushroom soup
1 onion, minced
4 hard-boiled
    eggs, chopped

Combine all ingredients in 2-quart casserole; mix well. Chill overnight. Bake at 350 degrees for 1 hour.
Yield: 4-6 servings.

Jackie Bergeron
Xi Mu Xi, Houston, Texas

Ham-Cheese-Potato Casserole

1/2 cup shredded
    sharp cheese
3/4 cup light cream
3 cups chopped
    cooked potatoes

2 to 3 cups chopped
    cooked ham
2 tablespoons chopped
    pimento (opt.)

Heat cheese and cream in saucepan until cheese melts, stirring constantly. Remove from heat. Stir in remaining ingredients. Pour into casserole. Bake, covered, at 350 degrees for 45 minutes. Yield: 6 servings.

Shirley Corder
Pi Chi, Corder, Missouri

Easy Pork Chops

1 package seasoned
    long grain and
    wild rice mix
1 16-ounce can
    Chinese vegetables,
    drained

1 can cream of
    mushroom soup
6 pork chops
Salt and pepper
    to taste

Combine rice, vegetables, soup and 1 1/2 cups water in bowl; mix well. Pour into 9 x 13-inch casserole. Arrange pork chops on top. Season with salt and pepper. Bake at 375 degrees for 1 hour. Yield: 6 servings.

Diane Nelms
Alpha Sigma, Mobile, Alabama

Main Dishes

Brunch Casserole

1 pound sausage,
  crumbled
1 8-ounce can
  refrigerator
  crescent
  dinner rolls
2 cups shredded
  mozzarella cheese
4 eggs, beaten
3/4 cup milk
1/4 teaspoon salt
1/8 teaspoon pepper

Brown sausage over medium heat in skillet, stirring occasionally; drain well. Line bottom of 9 x 13-inch baking dish with crescent roll dough; seal perforations. Layer sausage and cheese in prepared dish. Combine remaining ingredients in bowl; mix well. Pour over layers. Bake at 425 degrees for 15 minutes or until set. Cool for 5 minutes before cutting into squares. Yield: 6-8 servings.

Brenda Dailey
Xi Epsilon Epsilon, Norman, Oklahoma

Egg and Sausage Bake

12 to 16 ounces
  sausage
6 slices bread, cubed
1 cup Cheddar
  cheese, shredded
6 eggs, slightly beaten
1 teaspoon salt
1 teaspoon dry mustard
2 cups milk

Brown sausage in skillet, stirring until crumbly; drain. Combine with remaining ingredients in 9 x 13-inch casserole; mix well. Chill overnight. Bake at 350 degrees for 40 minutes. Yield: 12 servings.

Carolyn Reilly Conover
Epsilon Omicron, Kalamazoo, Michigan

Barbara's Sausage Casserole

1 1/2 pounds
  pork sausage
1 onion, chopped
1 green pepper, chopped
12 slices bread,
  crusts trimmed
8 ounces cheese,
  grated
4 eggs
2 1/4 cups milk
1 teaspoon salt

Brown sausage in skillet, stirring until crumbly; drain. Stir in onion and green pepper. Layer 6 bread slices, sausage, cheese and remaining bread in 9 x 13-inch baking pan. Pour mixture of eggs, milk and salt over layers. Chill overnight. Bake at 325 degrees for 1 hour or until brown.

Barbara Wilson
Preceptor Kappa, Corpus Christi, Texas

Baked Chicken Royal

1 package chicken-
  flavored Rice-A-Roni
1 can cream of
  chicken soup
1/2 cup sour cream
1/4 cup mayonnaise
1/2 teaspoon paprika
1/2 teaspoon
  curry powder
1 tablespoon
  parsley flakes
3 or 4 chicken breasts,
  cooked, boned

Prepare Rice-A-Roni using package directions. Place in greased 9 x 13-inch baking dish. Combine next 6 ingredients in bowl; mix well. Spread half the mixture over Rice-A-Roni. Top with chicken and remaining soup mixture. Sprinkle with additional paprika. Bake at 350 degrees for 30 minutes. Yield: 4-6 servings.
Note: May thin sauce with chicken broth if desired.

Jane Sinden
Eta Rho, Covington, Louisiana

Brenda's Chicken Casserole

5 large chicken breasts
Salt and pepper
1 stalk celery
1 can cream of
  chicken soup
1 16-ounce carton
  sour cream
1 1/2 sticks butter,
  melted
2 stacks butter
  crackers, crushed
1 1/2 tablespoons
  poppy seed

Cook chicken with salt, pepper and celery in water to cover in saucepan until tender. Drain chicken; debone and chop into bite-sized pieces. Place in 9 x 13-inch baking dish. Spread mixture of soup and sour cream over chicken. Combine remaining ingredients in bowl. Sprinkle over top. Bake at 350 degrees for 35 minutes or until bubbly. Serve with brown rice. Yield: 6-8 servings.

Brenda White
Delta Pi, Montgomery, Alabama

Curried Chicken Divan

2 10-ounce packages
  frozen broccoli
  spears
3 whole chicken
  breasts, cooked
1 can cream of
  chicken soup
1/3 cup evaporated
  milk
1/2 cup mayonnaise
1/2 cup shredded
  American cheese
1 teaspoon lemon juice
1/2 teaspoon
  curry powder
1 tablespoon
  butter, melted
1/2 cup bread crumbs

Cook broccoli using package directions; drain. Arrange in 2-quart casserole. Bone chicken; cut into quarters. Arrange over broccoli. Combine soup, evaporated milk, mayonnaise, cheese, lemon juice and curry powder in bowl; mix well. Pour over chicken. Sprinkle mixture of butter and bread crumbs over top. Bake at 350 degrees for 30 minutes. Yield: 6 servings.

Sue Burkholder
Xi Gamma, Burke, Virginia

Main Dishes

Chicken and Dressing Casserole

4 chicken breasts
1 small onion, chopped
2 or 3 stalks celery
1 can cream of
    mushroom soup
2 cups sour cream
1 1/2 cups chicken broth
1 8-ounce package
    herb-seasoned
    stuffing mix
1/4 cup melted butter
1/2 cup chicken broth

Cook chicken breasts with onion and celery in water to cover in saucepan until tender. Cool in broth. Bone and chop chicken. Place in greased 9 x 13-inch casserole. Pour mixture of soup, sour cream and 1 1/2 cups broth over chicken. Combine stuffing mix, butter and 1/2 cup broth in bowl. Sprinkle over casserole. Bake at 350 degrees for 30 minutes. Yield: 6 servings.

Chris Kebert
Laureate Beta Omicron, Harlingen, Texas

Chicken with Wild Rice Casserole

1 4 to 6-serving
    package wild rice
1 16-ounce package
    frozen chopped
    broccoli
3 chicken breasts,
    cooked, chopped
1 1/2 cups sliced
    mushrooms
1 cup sour cream
1 can cream of
    mushroom soup
1/2 cup sliced
    mushrooms

Cook wild rice and broccoli using package directions. Combine all ingredients except 1/2 cup mushrooms in casserole; mix well. Top with 1/2 cup mushrooms. Bake at 350 degrees for 20 to 30 minutes. Yield: 6 servings.

Carolyn Reilly Conover
Epsilon Omicron, Kalamazoo, Michigan

Linda's Chicken Casserole

4 or 5 pieces of chicken
1 can cream of
    celery soup
1 cup flour
1 stick margarine,
    melted
1 cup milk

Cook chicken in water to cover in saucepan until tender. Drain, reserving 2 cups broth. Bone chicken. Place chicken and reserved broth in 9 x 11-inch baking dish. Spread soup over top. Combine flour, margarine and milk in mixer bowl; mix well. Pour over casserole. Bake at 350 degrees until well browned. Yield: 6 servings.

Linda Pitman
Xi Alpha Lambda, Virginia Beach, Virginia

Drop-In Company Chicken Casserole

1 can cream of
    chicken soup
1 envelope dry onion
    soup mix
3/4 cup rice
2 1/2 teaspoons
    soy sauce
1 chicken, cut up

Combine first 4 ingredients and 2 soup cans water in bowl; mix well. Pour into greased 9 x 13-inch baking dish. Arrange chicken skin side down over top. Bake at 350 degrees for 2 hours. Yield: 6 servings.

Carole W. Thompson
Xi Alpha Kappa, Sidney, Nebraska

Susan's Chicken and Rice

1 fryer, cut up
1 can cream of
    celery soup
1 can cream of
    mushroom soup
1 envelope dry onion
    soup mix
1 cup rice
1 4-ounce can
    mushrooms (opt.)

Place chicken skin side up in 6-quart casserole. Mix remaining ingredients and 1 to 4 cups water in bowl. Pour over chicken. Bake, covered, at 350 degrees for 2 hours. Yield: 4-6 servings.

Susan Wilson
Preceptor Upsilon, Davisville, West Virginia

Crunchy Chicken

2 cups chopped celery
1 tablespoon
    chopped onion
3 to 4 tablespoons
    butter
1/4 cup flour
1/2 teaspoon salt
Dash of pepper
1 3/4 cups milk
2 to 3 cups chopped
    cooked chicken
1 cup grated cheese
1 6-ounce can
    water chestnuts
3 to 4 tablespoons
    melted butter
1/2 cup flour
1/4 teaspoon salt
1/2 cup toasted
    almonds
1/2 cup grated
    cheese

Saute celery and onion in 3 to 4 tablespoons butter in saucepan. Sift 1/4 cup flour, 1/2 teaspoon salt and pepper over vegetables; mix well. Stir in milk. Cook until thickened, stirring constantly. Add chicken, 1 cup cheese and water chestnuts; mix well. Pour into greased casserole. Combine remaining ingredients in bowl; mix well. Sprinkle over casserole. Bake at 400 degrees for 30 minutes or until bubbly.

Sue de Keyser
Xi Chi, Nanton, Alberta, Canada

Main Dishes

Barb's Chicken Casserole

2 10-ounce
   packages frozen
   chopped broccoli
2 cups chopped
   cooked chicken
2 cans cream of
   chicken soup

1 cup mayonnaise
1 teaspoon lemon juice
1 teaspoon curry powder
1/2 cup shredded
   Cheddar cheese
1/2 cup crushed
   seasoned croutons

Cook broccoli using package directions. Layer broccoli and chicken in shallow casserole. Combine soup, mayonnaise, lemon juice and curry powder in bowl; mix well. Pour over chicken. Sprinkle cheese and croutons over top. Bake at 350 degrees for 30 minutes. Yield: 6-8 servings.

Barbara Burton
Xi Eta Alpha, Naples, Florida

Kathleen's Chicken-Broccoli Casserole

2 10-ounce
   packages frozen
   broccoli, cooked
1 chicken,
   cooked, chopped
1/4 pound Velveeta
   cheese

1 can cream of
   chicken soup
1 cup sour cream
2 tablespoons
   Sherry (opt.)
Garlic salt to taste
Paprika to taste

Layer broccoli and chicken in 9 x 13-inch casserole. Combine remaining ingredients except paprika in saucepan. Heat until cheese melts, stirring frequently. Pour over chicken. Sprinkle with paprika. Bake at 350 degrees for 30 minutes or until bubbly. Yield: 6-8 servings.

Kathleen Montgomery
Eta Rho, Covington, Louisiana

Mary Kay's Chicken Salad Casserole

2 cups chopped
   cooked chicken
2 cups chopped celery
2 teaspoons
   grated onion
2 tablespoons
   lemon juice

2/3 cup toasted almonds
1 cup mayonnaise
1/2 teaspoon salt
1/2 cup grated
   Cheddar cheese
1 cup crushed
   potato chips

Combine first 7 ingredients in bowl; mix well. Layer chicken mixture, cheese and potato chips 1/2 at a time in greased 9 x 9-inch baking dish. Bake at 350 degrees for 25 to 30 minutes or until bubbly. Yield: 6 servings.

Mary Kay Simms
Preceptor Beta, Waukegan, Illinois

Susan's Hot Chicken Salad

3 cups chopped
   cooked chicken
3 cups finely
   chopped celery
2 tablespoons
   minced onion
1 1/2 cups slivered
   almonds

2 tablespoons
   lemon juice
1 1/2 cups mayonnaise
2 cups grated
   Cheddar cheese
2 cups crushed
   potato chips

Combine first 6 ingredients in bowl; mix well. Pour into greased 9 x 9-inch baking dish. Sprinkle with cheese and potato chips. Bake at 375 degrees for 10 minutes or until bubbly. Yield: 6 servings.

Susan Huchingson
Alpha Xi Nu, Spring, Texas

Holly's Hot Chicken Salad

2 cups chopped
   cooked chicken
2 cups minced celery
2 tablespoons
   minced onion
2 cups grated sharp
   Cheddar cheese
1 cup sliced almonds

2 cups herb-seasoned
   croutons
2 tablespoons
   lemon juice
1 cup mayonnaise
1 teaspoon salt
1 cup grated sharp
   Cheddar cheese

Combine all ingredients except 1 cup cheese in bowl; mix well. Pour into greased 9 x 13-inch baking dish. Top with remaining 1 cup cheese. Bake at 325 degrees for 30 to 40 minutes or until bubbly. Yield: 8-10 servings.

Holly J. Gillon
Alpha Beta, APO, New York

Scalloped Chicken

1 8-ounce package
   noodles
Chicken broth
1 chicken,
   cooked, chopped
1 can mushroom soup

1 8-ounce package
   cream cheese
1 small onion, chopped
Garlic to taste
Buttered bread crumbs

Cook noodles in chicken broth using package directions; drain. Add chicken, soup, cream cheese, 1 soup can broth, onion and garlic; mix well. Spoon into greased 9 x 13-inch baking dish. Top with crumbs. Bake at 350 degrees for 45 minutes. Yield: 12 servings.

Martha Thomas
Preceptor Theta, Wymore, Nebraska

Main Dishes

Chicken Enchilada Casserole

1 chicken bouillon cube
1 onion, chopped
1/2 stick margarine
2 to 3 cups chopped
    cooked chicken
2 4-ounce cans
    chopped green
    chilies, drained

2 cans cream of
    mushroom soup
1 12-count package
    soft tortillas
18 slices
    American cheese
1 8-ounce carton
    sour cream

Dissolve bouillon in 1 cup boiling water. Saute onion in margarine in skillet until tender. Add bouillon, chicken, chilies and soup; mix well. Cook until heated through. Tear tortillas into bite-sized pieces. Layer tortillas, chicken mixture and cheese 1/3 at a time, in buttered 11 x 14-inch baking dish. Top with sour cream. Bake at 350 degrees for 30 minutes.

Sherry Otis
Kappa Nu, Dallas, Texas

Mexicali Chicken

4 cups chopped
    cooked chicken
1 15-ounce can
    chili without beans
1 7-ounce can green
    chili salsa
1 3-ounce can
    pitted black
    olives, drained

1 bunch green
    onions, chopped
1 3-ounce package
    cream cheese,
    softened
1 cup shredded Monterey
    Jack cheese
1 cup shredded
    Cheddar cheese

Spread chicken in greased 9 x 13-inch baking dish. Combine chili, salsa, olives, green onions and cream cheese in bowl; mix well. Pour over chicken. Bake at 350 degrees for 20 minutes. Sprinkle Monterey Jack and Cheddar cheeses on top. Bake for 10 minutes longer. Yield: 6 servings.

Dorine Jones
Xi Upsilon Theta, Gustine, California

Chicken Tetrazzini

1/4 cup chopped celery
1 medium onion, chopped
1 green pepper, chopped
1/2 cup margarine
1 2 to 4-pound
    chicken, cooked,
    chopped
1 8-ounce package
    spaghetti, cooked
1 can cream of
    mushroom soup

1 8-ounce can
    chicken broth
1 4-ounce can chopped
    mushrooms, drained
1/2 cup chopped
    ripe olives
1 2-ounce jar
    chopped pimento
2 cups grated
    sharp cheese
Parmesan cheese

Saute celery, onion and green pepper in margarine in saucepan. Add remaining ingredients except Parmesan cheese; mix well. Spoon into greased 9 x 13-inch baking dish. Sprinkle with Parmesan cheese. Bake at 350 degrees for 35 to 45 minutes or until bubbly. Yield: 6-9 servings.

Dolores C. Sandusky
Preceptor Alpha Epsilon, Tucson, Arizona

Lee's Chicken Spaghetti

2 cups chopped
    cooked chicken
1 8-ounce package
    elbow spaghetti
2 cans cream of
    mushroom soup

2 cups milk
8 ounces sharp Cheddar
    cheese, cubed
4 hard-boiled
    eggs, chopped

Combine all ingredients in casserole; mix well. Chill overnight. Let stand at room temperature for 1 hour. Bake at 325 degrees for 1 1/2 hours. Yield: 8-10 servings.

Lee Downing
Preceptor Psi, Memphis, Tennessee

Chicken Lasagna

1 10-ounce
    package frozen
    chopped spinach
1/2 cup melted butter
1/2 cup flour
1/2 teaspoon each
    salt, basil
3 cups chicken broth
2 1/2 cups chopped
    cooked chicken

1 egg, slightly beaten
2 cups cottage cheese
8 ounces lasagna
    noodles, cooked
8 ounces mozzarella
    cheese, grated
1/2 cup Parmesan
    cheese

Thaw and drain spinach. Blend butter, flour and seasonings in saucepan. Stir in broth gradually. Bring to a boil, stirring constantly. Add chicken. Mix egg and cottage cheese in bowl. Spread 2 cups chicken in greased 9 x 13-inch baking dish. Layer noodles, cottage cheese, spinach, mozzarella and remaining chicken 1/2 at a time in prepared baking dish. Sprinkle Parmesan cheese over top. Bake at 375 degrees for 45 minutes. Let stand for 10 minutes before cutting into squares.

Nancy Ingman
Preceptor Iota Kappa, Corona del Mar, California

Main Dishes

Chicken Supper in-a-Dish

1 10-ounce package
   frozen carrots
   and peas
1 cup sliced celery
1/2 cup chopped onion
1/4 cup butter
2 cups chopped
   cooked chicken
1 cup sour cream

1/2 to 3/4 cup
   chicken broth
2 cups egg
   noodles, cooked
1 can cream of
   mushroom soup
1/2 teaspoon salt
1/4 teaspoon pepper

Cook carrots and peas using package directions. Saute celery and onion in butter in skillet. Combine all ingredients in buttered 2-quart casserole; mix well. Bake at 350 degrees for 30 minutes. Yield: 4-6 servings.

Mary L. Schuck
Xi Alpha Beta, Green River, Wyoming

Creamy Chicken Casserole

2 cups chopped
   cooked chicken
2 cups hot cooked rice
1 can cream of
   mushroom soup
3/4 cup mayonnaise

3 hard-boiled
   eggs, chopped
1/4 cup finely
   chopped onion
1/2 teaspoon salt
1 cup Grape Nuts

Combine chicken, rice, soup, mayonnaise, eggs, onion and salt in 2-quart casserole; mix well. Sprinkle Grape Nuts over top. Bake at 375 degrees for 45 minutes. Yield: 4-6 servings.

Mary Robertson
Gamma Omega, McCall, Idaho

Chicken and Cheese Casserole

2 cups chopped
   cooked chicken
1 cup chopped celery
1 8-ounce package
   cauliflower
2 cups cooked rice

1 cup chopped
   process cheese
1 cup sour cream
1/4 cup milk
1 envelope dry onion
   soup mix

Layer chicken, celery, cauliflower and rice in greased 2-quart casserole. Combine cheese, sour cream, milk and soup mix in saucepan. Heat until cheese melts, stirring constantly. Pour over layers; mix well. Bake at 350 degrees for 30 minutes or until bubbly. Yield: 6 servings.

Kathleen King
Delta Beta, Chippewa Falls, Wisconsin

Chicken Quickie

1 6-ounce can chicken
1 can chicken with
   rice soup
1 can cream of
   chicken soup
1 2-ounce jar
   chopped pimento,
   drained

1 4-ounce can
   mushrooms, drained
1 5-ounce can
   evaporated milk
1 3-ounce can chow
   mein noodles
Crushed potato chips

Combine chicken with next 6 ingredients in bowl; mix well. Spoon into greased baking dish. Bake at 350 degrees for 45 minutes. Sprinkle potato chips on top. Bake for 15 minutes longer. Serve with Dirty Rice (page 186). Yield: 4 servings.

Anita M. Wilson
Laureate Alpha Mu, Mansfield, Ohio

Chili Chicken

4 7-ounce cans
   chunky chicken
12 corn tortillas
1 can cream of
   mushroom soup
1 can cream of
   chicken soup

1/2 can chicken broth
1 can chili
   without beans
1 can green chili salsa
1 onion, chopped
8 ounces sharp Cheddar
   cheese, shredded

Place chicken in bottom of 9 x 13-inch baking dish. Cut tortillas into strips. Arrange over chicken. Combine soups, broth, chili, salsa and onion in bowl; mix well. Pour over tortillas. Sprinkle cheese over top. Bake, covered, at 350 degrees for 15 minutes. Bake, uncovered, for 30 minutes longer. Yield: 8-10 servings.

Eileen Veldman
Lambda Chi, Dayton, Ohio

Seven C's Casserole

2 7-ounce cans
   chunky chicken
1 4-ounce can
   mushrooms, drained
1 can cream of
   chicken soup
1 can cream of
   mushroom soup

1 small can
   evaporated milk
1 6-ounce can chow
   mein noodles
1 tablespoon finely
   chopped onion

Combine chicken, mushrooms, soups, evaporated milk, noodles and onion in bowl; mix well. Pour into greased 2-quart casserole. Bake at 350 degrees for 45 minutes or until golden brown. Yield: 6 servings.

Linda Jachino
Xi Kappa Iota, McHenry, Illinois

Main Dishes

Four-Can Casserole

1 7-ounce can
   boned chicken
1 can chicken
   noodle soup
1 can mushroom soup
1 3-ounce can chow
   mein noodles

Combine all ingredients in bowl; mix well. Pour into 8-inch baking dish. Bake at 350 degrees for 30 to 45 minutes.

Leslie Williams
Xi Alpha Rho, Danville, Kentucky

Turkey-Broccoli Casserole

2 10-ounce
   packages frozen
   broccoli, thawed
3 to 4 cups chopped
   cooked turkey
2 cans cream of
   chicken soup
1 tablespoon
   lemon juice
1 cup salad dressing
1/2 teaspoon
   curry powder
1/8 teaspoon thyme
1/2 cup bread crumbs
1/4 cup melted
   Cheddar cheese
2 tablespoons
   melted butter

Combine broccoli, turkey, soup, lemon juice, salad dressing, seasonings, bread crumbs, cheese and butter in order listed in bowl; mix well. Pour into 1 1/2-quart casserole. Bake at 350 degrees for 1 1/2 hours. Serve with garlic bread and Caesar salad.

Karen E. Bowe
Gamma Gamma, Kitchener, Ontario, Canada

Turkey Divan

4 10-ounce packages
   frozen broccoli
4 cups chopped
   cooked turkey
4 cans cream of
   mushroom soup
2 cups mayonnaise
1 teaspoon
   curry powder
2 teaspoons
   lemon juice
1 cup grated cheese
1 cup bread crumbs

Cook broccoli using package directions; drain. Place in greased 9 x 13-inch baking pan. Combine turkey, soup, mayonnaise and seasonings in bowl; mix well. Spoon over broccoli. Sprinkle cheese and crumbs over top. Bake at 350 degrees for 1 hour. Yield: 10-12 servings.

Melba Creager
Xi Alpha Zeta, Glenrock, Wyoming

Quick Turkey Casserole

2 cups chopped
   cooked turkey
1 cup peas
1 cup chopped celery
1 10-ounce can
   mushrooms, drained
1/2 cup (or more) gravy
1/2 onion, chopped
Salt and pepper
   to taste
Bread crumbs

Combine turkey, peas, celery, mushrooms, gravy, onion and seasonings in 2-quart casserole; mix well. Cover with bread crumbs. Bake at 425 degrees for 35 minutes.
Yield: 6 servings.

Ruth Mowat
Kappa, Souris, Manitoba, Canada

Turkey-Noodle Bake

1 1/2 cups milk
1 can cream of
   mushroom soup
3 eggs, beaten
3 ounces noodles,
   cooked
2 cups chopped
   cooked turkey
1 cup bread crumbs
1 cup shredded cheese
1/4 cup chopped
   green pepper
1/4 cup melted butter
2 tablespoons
   chopped pimento

Blend milk and soup in bowl. Stir in eggs. Add noodles, turkey, bread crumbs, cheese, green pepper, butter and pimento; mix well. Spoon into 7 x 12-inch baking dish. Bake at 350 degrees for 30 to 40 minutes. Yield: 6-8 servings.

Debbie Barnhill
Tau, Worland, Wyoming

Turkey and Wild Rice Casserole

1 medium onion, chopped
1/2 cup melted butter
1/3 cup flour
1/2 cup half and half
1 4-ounce can mushrooms
1 8-ounce can
   bamboo shoots
1 4-ounce can sliced
   water chestnuts
1 can cream of
   mushroom soup
2 to 3 cups chopped
   cooked turkey
1 package wild and
   long grain rice mix
1 can French-fried
   onion rings

Saute onion in butter in skillet. Stir in flour. Add half and half, undrained mushrooms, bamboo shoots, water chestnuts, soup, turkey and rice; mix well. Stir in seasonings from rice mix. Pour into 9 x 13-inch casserole. Sprinkle onion rings over top. Bake at 350 degrees for 1 hour. Yield: 6-8 servings.

Kathie Lane
Delta Omicron, Norfolk, Nebraska

Main Dishes

Basque Tuna Casserole

1 cup chopped onion
1 clove of garlic,
   minced
2 tablespoons olive oil
4 slices white
   bread, toasted
2 hard-boiled eggs
1/3 cup dry white wine
1/8 teaspoon hot
   pepper sauce

2 7-ounce cans
   oil-pack tuna,
   drained
1/4 cup chopped almonds
1/4 cup sliced pimento-
   stuffed olives
2 tablespoons
   chopped parsley
1/2 cup shredded
   Gruyere cheese

Saute onion and garlic in olive oil in skillet until tender. Combine bread, eggs, 1 cup water, wine and hot pepper sauce in blender container. Process on High for 1 minute or until smooth. Break tuna into chunks in medium bowl. Add bread mixture, sauteed vegetables, almonds, olives, parsley and half the cheese; mix well. Spoon into 1-quart baking dish. Sprinkle with remaining cheese. Bake at 350 degrees for 30 minutes or until heated through. Garnish with whole almonds and additional chopped parsley. Yield: 4 servings.

Photograph for this recipe on page 36.

Tuna-Broccoli Delight

1 6-ounce can tuna
1 10-ounce package
   frozen chopped
   broccoli, cooked
1 can mushroom soup

1 cup cooked rice
1 hard-boiled
   egg, chopped
2 tablespoons milk
American cheese slices

Combine all ingredients except cheese in large baking dish; mix well. Bake at 350 degrees for 20 minutes. Cover with cheese. Bake until cheese melts. Yield: 4 servings.

Vicky Weaver
Xi Kappa Omicron, Zanesville, Ohio

Tuna Confetti Casserole

1 8-ounce package
   macaroni, cooked
2 cups hot cooked peas
1 7-ounce can
   tuna, flaked

1 can cream of
   celery soup
1/2 cup milk
2 tablespoons
   chopped pimento

Combine all ingredients in bowl; toss lightly to mix. Spoon into greased 9 x 12-inch baking pan. Bake at 350 degrees for 25 minutes.

Betty Scholl Windle
Laureate Alpha Iota, Pinellas Park, Florida

Tuna-Noodle Casserole

1 8-ounce package
   egg noodles
2 7-ounce cans tuna
1/2 10-ounce package
   frozen mixed
   vegetables

1 can tomato soup
1/2 cup milk
1 tablespoon
   butter, melted
4 1-ounce slices
   cheese

Cook noodles using package directions; drain. Combine tuna, vegetables, soup, milk and butter in bowl; mix well. Add noodles; toss lightly to mix. Spoon into casserole. Bake, covered, at 350 degrees for 30 minutes. Bake, uncovered, for 30 minutes. Place cheese on top. Bake until cheese melts. Yield: 6 servings.

Julie Ryerson
Beta Iota, Clinton, Illinois

Off-the-Shelf Mandarin Casserole

1/4 cup chopped
   green onions
1 tablespoon (about)
   butter
1 cup sliced celery
1 can cream of
   mushroom soup

1 7-ounce can tuna
1/2 cup toasted cashews
2 cups chow
   mein noodles
1 8-ounce can
   mandarin oranges,
   drained

Saute green onions in butter in skillet. Add celery. Saute for several minutes. Add soup, tuna, cashews, half the noodles and 1/4 cup water; mix well. Spoon into 1-quart casserole. Sprinkle remaining noodles over top. Bake at 350 degrees for 15 minutes. Garnish with mandarin oranges. Yield: 4 servings.

Genevieve Van Epps
Preceptor Chi, Grand Ledge, Michigan

Fish Florentine

1 10-ounce
   package frozen
   spinach, thawed
3 ounces Cheddar
   cheese, shredded
3 or 4 fish fillets
Salt and pepper
   to taste

3 tablespoons
   margarine
3 tablespoons flour
3 tablespoons
   melted margarine
1 cup milk
Dash of white pepper

Squeeze excess moisture from spinach. Layer spinach, cheese and fish fillets in 9 x 9-inch baking dish. Sprinkle with salt and pepper. Dot with 3 tablespoons margarine. Bake, covered with foil, for 10 minutes. Blend flour and 3 tablespoons melted margarine in saucepan. Cook for 1 minute, stirring constantly. Add milk gradually. Cook until thickened, stirring constantly. Season with salt and white pepper. Pour half the sauce over fish. Bake for 10 to 15 minutes longer or until fish flakes easily. Serve with remaining sauce.

Kathleen Frischmann
Theta Iota, Fletcher, North Carolina

Main Dishes

Vera's Crab Meat Casserole

1 7-ounce can	Salt and pepper
crab meat	to taste
6 hard-boiled	1/4 cup chopped stuffed
eggs, mashed	green olives
1 cup mayonnaise	1 cup buttered soft
1/3 cup chopped onion	bread crumbs
3/4 cup milk	

Combine crab meat, eggs, mayonnaise, onion, milk and seasonings in bowl; mix well. Spoon into greased 1 1/2-quart casserole. Sprinkle olives and bread crumbs over top. Bake at 350 degrees for 20 minutes. Yield: 4 servings.

Vera Lally
Xi Zeta, Sparta, New Jersey

Rice-Crab Casserole

2 cups cooked rice	1 onion, minced
1 cup tomato juice	1/2 cup milk
1 7-ounce can	Salt to taste
crab meat	Dash of pepper
3/4 cup mayonnaise	Butter
1 4-ounce can	Bread crumbs
mushrooms	

Combine rice, juice, crab meat, mayonnaise, mushrooms, onion, milk and seasonings in bowl; mix well. Pour into 2-quart casserole. Dot with butter. Sprinkle bread crumbs over top. Bake at 350 degrees for 45 minutes. Yield: 6 servings.

Ruth Fischer
Preceptor Zeta Lambda, Santa Rosa, California

Corn and Oyster Casserole

2 7-ounce cans	1 egg
oysters, drained	2 tablespoons flour
2 20-ounce	Salt to taste
cans yellow	1 cup buttered
cream-style corn	bread crumbs

Place oysters in buttered 1-quart casserole. Combine corn, egg, flour and salt in bowl; mix well. Spread over oysters. Sprinkle with bread crumbs. Bake at 300 degrees for 1 hour. Yield: 6-8 servings.

Leora Dycus
Laureate Alpha Epsilon, Effingham, Illinois

Holly's Seafood Casserole

1 pound mushrooms,	2 7-ounce cans
sliced	crab meat
1 1/4 cups wild	1 1/2 cups mayonnaise
rice, cooked	1 teaspoon
1 cup chopped celery	Worcestershire sauce
1 onion, chopped	1 teaspoon curry powder
1 green pepper, chopped	Salt and pepper
2 7-ounce cans shrimp	to taste

Saute mushrooms in skillet. Combine with rice, vegetables, seafood, mayonnaise and seasonings in greased casserole. Bake, covered, at 350 degrees for 45 minutes. Yield: 8 servings.

Holly Loy
Delta Nu, Johnson City, Tennessee

Shrimp Casserole

6 slices bread,	1 cup mayonnaise
crusts trimmed	3 hard-boiled
1 1/2 to 2 pounds	eggs, chopped
cooked shrimp	2 teaspoons
2 cans cream of	Worcestershire sauce
mushroom soup	Salt and pepper
1 2-ounce jar	to taste
chopped pimento	Chopped almonds
1 clove of	Butter
garlic, grated	

Toast and crumble bread. Reserve a small amount for topping. Combine remaining crumbs, shrimp, soup, pimento, garlic, mayonnaise, eggs and seasonings in bowl; mix well. Spoon into greased 9 x 13-inch baking dish. Top with mixture of almonds and reserved crumbs. Dot with butter. Bake at 350 degrees for 20 minutes. Yield: 6-8 servings.

Emily McGinnis
Eta Rho, Covington, Louisiana

Elva's Egg Dish

2 cups grated	1 cup whipping cream
Velveeta cheese	1/2 teaspoon salt
1/4 cup butter	1/4 teaspoon pepper
2 teaspoons	12 eggs, beaten
prepared mustard	

Sprinkle cheese in greased 9 x 13-inch baking pan. Dot with butter. Combine mustard, cream and seasonings in bowl; mix well. Layer half the cream mixture, eggs and remaining cream mixture over cheese. Bake at 350 degrees for 40 minutes. Yield: 8 servings.

Julie Nelson
Alpha Pi, Maple Grove, Minnesota

Main Dishes

Savory Eggs

1 cup grated cheese
2 tablespoons butter
1 teaspoon
    prepared mustard
1/2 cup evaporated milk
1/2 teaspoon salt
1/4 teaspoon pepper
6 eggs, beaten

Sprinkle cheese in greased 8 x 8-inch baking dish. Dot with butter. Combine mustard, evaporated milk, salt and pepper in bowl; mix well. Layer half the evaporated milk mixture, eggs and remaining evaporated milk mixture over cheese. Bake at 350 degrees for 25 minutes or until knife inserted in center comes out clean. Cut into squares. Yield: 8 servings.

Mary Ann Hamm
Beta Omicron, Castle Rock, Colorado

Oven-Baked French Toast

French bread, sliced
    1 1/2 inches thick
8 eggs
1 teaspoon
    vanilla extract
3 cups milk
1 tablespoon sugar
1/2 teaspoon salt
Margarine, softened
Cinnamon

Arrange bread slices tightly in greased 9 x 13-inch baking dish. Combine eggs, vanilla, milk, sugar and salt in bowl; mix well. Pour over bread. Chill, tightly covered, overnight. Spread generously with margarine; sprinkle with cinnamon. Place in cold oven. Bake at 375 degrees for 45 minutes. Serve with confectioners' sugar and syrup. Yield: 8 servings.

Sally McFarland
Xi Nu, Gresham, Oregon

Best Cheese Enchiladas

1 28-ounce can
    enchilada sauce
1 medium onion,
    chopped
4 cups grated
    Cheddar cheese
1 4-ounce can sliced
    olives, drained
1 12-count
    package tortillas
2 cups grated Monterey
    Jack cheese

Spread 1 cup enchilada sauce in 9 x 13-inch baking dish. Combine onion, Cheddar cheese and half the olives in bowl. Place heaping 1/3 cup mixture on each tortilla; roll to enclose filling. Place seam side down in prepared dish. Pour remaining enchilada sauce over top. Sprinkle with Monterey Jack cheese and remaining olives. Bake, covered, at 350 degrees for 30 minutes. Yield: 6 servings.

Cyndy Talmant
Xi Alpha Mu, Sparks, Nevada

Mushroom Tetrazzini

1/2 pound mushrooms,
    thickly sliced
1 medium onion,
    chopped
6 tablespoons butter
3 tablespoons flour
1 1/2 teaspoons salt
Pinch of pepper
2 cups milk
1/4 cup Sherry
1 cup grated
    provolone cheese
1/2 cup chopped
    parsley
1 8-ounce package
    spaghetti, cooked
1/2 cup grated
    provolone cheese

Saute mushrooms and onion in butter in saucepan. Add flour, salt and pepper; mix well. Stir in milk and Sherry gradually. Add 1 cup cheese and parsley. Cook until thickened, stirring constantly. Place hot spaghetti in greased 2-quart baking dish. Pour sauce over top. Sprinkle with 1/2 cup cheese. Bake at 350 degrees for 10 minutes or until cheese melts. Yield: 8-12 servings.

Karen Perry
Pi Eta, Castalia, Ohio

Chiles Rellenos Casserole

2 7-ounce cans
    whole green chilies,
    rinsed, seeded
1 1/2 pounds Monterey
    Jack cheese, grated
4 eggs, slightly beaten
1/2 cup milk
1 teaspoon salt
1/2 teaspoon
    dry mustard
1/4 teaspoon pepper

Layer chilies and cheese 1/2 at a time in greased 7 x 11-inch casserole. Combine remaining ingredients in bowl; mix well. Pour over layers. Bake at 350 degrees for 30 minutes or until set. Cool for 5 minutes. Cut into squares. Yield: 8-12 servings.

Sonie Turner
Delta Delta Eta, Lake Isabella, California

Dilled Zucchini-Rice Bake

4 medium zucchini,
    sliced
2 cups cooked
    brown rice
1 16-ounce carton
    cottage cheese
1 medium onion, chopped
2 eggs, beaten
Salt and pepper
    to taste
1 tablespoon dillweed
Parmesan cheese

Cook zucchini in water to cover in saucepan for 5 minutes or until tender-crisp; drain. Combine rice, next 3 ingredients and seasonings in bowl; mix well. Layer zucchini and rice mixture 1/2 at a time in buttered 2-quart casserole. Top with Parmesan cheese. Bake at 350 degrees for 45 minutes or until browned and bubbly. Yield: 4-6 servings.

Mary Helen Pope
Beta Iota, McCall, Illinois

Creamed Chicken, recipe on page 117.

Breast of Chicken Cashew

8 chicken breasts, boned	3 tablespoons soy sauce
Salt and pepper to taste	2 teaspoons sugar
1/3 cup butter	1/2 teaspoon garlic powder
3 tablespoons chicken stock base	3 tablespoons Sherry
1 chicken bouillon cube	2 tablespoons cornstarch
	Cashews

Season chicken with salt and pepper. Brown lightly in butter in skillet. Place in 9 x 13-inch baking dish. Bake at 400 degrees for 25 minutes or until tender. Bring next 5 ingredients and 2 cups water to a boil in saucepan. Stir in mixture of Sherry and cornstarch. Cook until thickened, stirring constantly. Arrange chicken on serving plate. Pour sauce over top. Sprinkle with cashews. Serve with rice and mixed oriental vegetables. Yield: 8 servings.

Karen N. Kirscht
Alpha Pi, Maple Grove, Minnesota

Chicken Crescents

1 can cream of chicken soup	1 2-pound package chicken breasts, cooked, chopped
1 8-count can refrigerator crescent dinner rolls	1/2 cup grated Cheddar cheese

Mix soup with enough water to cover bottom of 8 x 8-inch baking pan. Separate crescent rolls. Place 1/4 cup chicken and 1 tablespoon cheese on each roll. Roll from wide end to enclose filling. Place seam side down in soup. Sprinkle with additional cheese. Bake, covered, at 375 degrees for 13 minutes or until brown. Yield: 8 servings.

Pam Thompson
Xi Rho Zeta, Pasadena, Texas

Chicken Piccata

1 egg	4 to 6 chicken breasts, skinned, boned
1 tablespoon lemon juice	1/4 cup margarine
1/4 cup flour	2 teaspoons instant chicken bouillon
1/8 teaspoon garlic powder	2 tablespoons lemon juice
1/8 teaspoon paprika	

Beat egg with 1 tablespoon lemon juice in bowl. Combine flour with garlic powder and paprika. Dip chicken in egg mixture; coat with seasoned flour. Brown in margarine in skillet. Dissolve bouillon in 1/2 cup boiling water. Stir in 2 tablespoons lemon juice. Pour over chicken. Simmer for 20 minutes. Yield: 4 servings.

Noreen Mehrtens
Preceptor Gamma Sigma, Sarasota, Florida

Main Dishes

Chicken Milanese

4 chicken breasts,
  skinned, boned
Salt and pepper
  to taste
Garlic salt to taste
2 tablespoons flour

1 egg, beaten
1/2 cup bread crumbs
2 tablespoons (about)
  margarine
2 tablespoons (about)
  shortening

Sprinkle chicken with salt, pepper, garlic salt and flour; shake to remove excess. Dip in egg; coat well with crumbs. Cook for 7 minutes on each side in mixture of margarine and shortening in skillet; drain. Yield: 4 servings.

Karen L. Larson
Alpha Eta, Williamsport, Pennsylvania

Georgia Chicken

2 chicken breasts,
  skinned, boned
1 egg, beaten
1/4 cup soy sauce

Seasoned bread crumbs
Oil for frying
1 16-ounce can
  sliced peaches

Cut chicken into bite-sized pieces. Dip in mixture of egg and soy sauce; coat with bread crumbs. Brown in 1 inch oil in skillet; drain. Place in 9 x 9-inch baking dish. Bake, covered, at 350 degrees for 30 minutes. Add peaches with juice. Bake, covered, for 15 minutes longer. Serve with rice pilaf.

Dana Lohman
Iota Chi, Manchester, Missouri

Paula's Chicken and Rice

1 1/2 pounds boned
  chicken breasts
3 stalks celery,
  chopped
1 medium onion,
  chopped
1 clove of garlic,
  chopped

2 tablespoons butter
1 pound mushrooms,
  sliced
1/4 teaspoon each salt
  and pepper
1/4 teaspoon oregano
2 tablespoons butter
2 cups cooked rice

Cut chicken into 1-inch pieces. Saute with celery, onion and garlic in 2 tablespoons butter in skillet for 5 minutes. Add mushrooms, seasonings and 2 tablespoons butter. Simmer, covered, for 30 minutes. Serve over rice. Yield: 4 servings.

Paula Pagliughi
Sigma, Bridgeton, New Jersey

Pineapple-Chicken Stir Fry

1/2 cup chicken broth
2 tablespoons
  white wine
1 tablespoon
  cider vinegar
2 tablespoons soy sauce
1 tablespoon sugar
Pinch each of ginger,
  red pepper
3/4 pound skinned
  boned chicken breasts
1 tablespoon oil

1 cup pineapple
  chunks
2 tablespoons
  pineapple juice
1/2 cup sliced
  water chestnuts
1/2 medium green
  pepper, chopped
1 10-ounce package
  frozen oriental
  vegetables
1 tablespoon cornstarch

Combine chicken broth with next 6 ingredients in bowl. Cut chicken into thin strips; place in bowl. Sprinkle with 2 table-spoons broth mixture. Let stand for 10 minutes. Stir-fry in hot oil in skillet. Add pineapple, juice, water chestnuts, green pepper and vegetables. Simmer, covered, for 2 minutes. Blend cornstarch into remaining broth mixture. Add to skillet. Cook for 1 minute or until thickened, stirring constantly. Serve over rice. Yield: 4 servings.

Jeanne Mills
Xi Alpha Nu, Kennewick, Washington

Quick Chicken Breasts

6 thin slices
  ham
6 boned chicken
  breasts

1 can cream of
  chicken soup
1/2 cup Durkee
  Famous Sauce

Place 1 slice ham on each chicken breast. Roll to enclose ham; secure with toothpick. Place in shallow baking dish. Spread with mixture of soup and Durkee Sauce. Bake, covered, at 350 degrees for 2 hours. Yield: 6 servings.

Phyllis McDuffie
Xi Omicron Gamma, Mesquite, Texas

Saucy Chicken

2 chicken breasts,
  skinned, boned
1/2 cup chopped onion
1/2 cup chopped
  green pepper
1 clove of
  garlic, minced
1 tablespoon oregano

1 4-ounce jar
  mushrooms
1 8-ounce can
  tomato sauce
1/4 cup white wine
1/2 tablespoon
  chopped parsley

Cut chicken into bite-sized pieces. Brown, covered, in a small amount of oil in skillet for 5 to 10 minutes. Remove and drain. Saute onion, green pepper and garlic in oil in skillet. Add chicken and remaining ingredients. Simmer, covered, for 15 to 20 minutes or until tender. Serve over spaghetti. Yield: 2 servings.

Sharon Mastrocco
Theta, Oklahoma City, Oklahoma

Main Dishes

Sweet and Sour Chicken Breasts

8 chicken breasts,
   skinned
1/2 teaspoon
   garlic salt
1/4 teaspoon pepper
2 cups julienne carrots
2 cups sliced
   green peppers
2 cups frozen peas
2 cups canned
   mushrooms
1/4 cup soy sauce
2 tablespoons
   cornstarch
1/3 cup vinegar

Place chicken and 1/2 cup water in 9 x 13-inch baking dish. Sprinkle with garlic salt and pepper. Bake at 350 degrees for 30 minutes. Cook carrots, green peppers, peas and mushrooms in 1 cup water in saucepan until tender. Combine soy sauce, cornstarch and 3 cups water in bowl. Stir into vegetables. Cook until thickened, stirring constantly. Stir in vinegar. Pour vegetables over chicken. Bake at 350 degrees for 30 minutes longer. Serve over rice. Yield: 8 servings.

Wanda Malin
Xi Xi, Great Falls, Montana

Chicken Adobo

1/4 cup soy sauce
1/4 cup vinegar
1 clove of garlic,
   chopped
Salt and pepper
   to taste
1 chicken, cut
   up, skinned

Combine soy sauce, vinegar, garlic, salt and pepper in bowl. Add chicken. Marinate for several hours. Pour into skillet. Simmer for 20 to 35 minutes or until tender, adding water as necessary to retain 1 inch liquid. Yield: 4-6 servings.

Norma Grace Bauer
Laureate Alpha Epsilon, Altamont, Illinois

Chicken and Dumplings Baked in Oven

1 chicken, cut up
3/4 cup flour
Salt and pepper
   to taste
3/4 cup chopped carrots
3/4 cup chopped celery
1 medium onion,
   chopped
1 can cream of
   chicken soup
1 recipe baking
   mix dumplings

Coat chicken with flour seasoned with salt and pepper. Brown on both sides in a small amount of oil in skillet; drain. Arrange in baking pan. Add vegetables and mixture of soup and 1 1/2 soup cans water. Bake, covered, at 350 degrees for 1 to 1 1/2 hours or until tender. Prepare dumplings using package directions. Drop by spoonfuls over chicken. Bake, covered, for 10 minutes. Bake, uncovered, for 10 minutes.

Carolyn A. Brenneis
Epsilon Nu, Blair, Nebraska

Chicken a l'Orange

1 chicken, cut up
2 tablespoons butter
1 teaspoon salt
1 tablespoon
   lemon juice
6 tablespoons
   orange marmalade
2/3 cup orange juice
2 tablespoons
   brown sugar
1 tablespoon
   cornstarch
Pinch of ginger

Brown chicken on both sides in butter in skillet. Sprinkle with salt. Add remaining ingredients. Bring to a boil; reduce heat. Simmer, covered, for 25 to 35 minutes or until tender. Yield: 6 servings.

Joan Stockman
Laureate Omega, Arvada, Colorado

Creamed Chicken

1 4-ounce can
   sliced mushrooms
1 chicken bouillon cube
1 tablespoon instant
   minced onion
3 tablespoons butter
3 tablespoons flour
1/2 teaspoon salt
Dash of pepper
1 large can
   evaporated milk
2 cups chopped
   cooked chicken
1 12-ounce package
   corn muffin mix
1 teaspoon paprika
2 tablespoons
   chopped chives

Drain mushrooms, reserving liquid. Add enough water to measure 1/2 cup. Heat liquid in saucepan; add bouillon. Saute mushrooms and minced onion in butter in skillet. Add flour, salt and pepper; blend well. Add mushroom liquid and evaporated milk. Cook over medium heat until thickened, stirring constantly. Add chicken. Heat to serving temperature, stirring occasionally. Prepare corn muffin mix according to package directions, adding paprika and chives. Spoon into well-buttered 4-cup ring mold. Bake at 400 degrees for 15 minutes. Invert and spoon chicken mixture into ring.

Photograph for this recipe on page 115.

Curried Chicken

6 frozen breaded
   chicken breast
   filets, thawed
1 stick butter
1 tablespoon
   curry powder
1 1/2 cups white wine
1 cup cream
3 cups chopped celery
2 large apples, chopped
2 cups minute rice,
   cooked

Cut chicken into bite-sized pieces. Brown in butter in skillet. Stir in curry powder. Add wine. Bring to a boil. Stir in cream. Sprinkle celery over chicken; reduce heat. Simmer, covered, for several minutes. Add apples. Simmer, covered, until apples are just tender. Place rice on serving platter. Spoon chicken over rice. Yield: 6-8 servings.

Mary Holcomb
Xi Epsilon Kappa, Rusk, Texas

Main Dishes

El Paso Chicken Legs

4 cups crushed
    corn chips
1 1/2 teaspoons
    chili powder
1/2 teaspoon
    onion powder

1/4 teaspoon
    garlic powder
6 to 8 chicken
    legs, skinned
1/4 cup mayonnaise

Combine corn chips with seasonings on waxed paper; mix well. Dry chicken legs with paper towels. Brush with mayonnaise; coat with crumb mixture. Arrange in greased 7 x 12-inch baking dish. Bake at 425 degrees for 45 minutes or until tender. Yield: 4 servings.

Elaine Sills
Preceptor Alpha Nu, El Paso, Texas

Hot Chinese Chicken Salad

8 chicken thighs, boned
1/4 cup cornstarch
1/4 cup corn oil
Garlic powder to taste
1/3 cup sliced
    water chestnuts
1 large tomato, chopped

1 4-ounce can
    sliced mushrooms
1 cup chopped
    green onions
1 cup sliced celery
1/4 cup soy sauce
2 cups shredded lettuce

Cut chicken into bite-sized pieces. Coat with cornstarch. Brown in corn oil in skillet. Sprinkle with garlic powder. Add water chestnuts, vegetables and soy sauce; mix well. Simmer, covered, for 5 minutes. Remove from heat. Add lettuce; toss lightly. Serve with rice or noodles. Yield: 4 servings.

Doris Beavers
Preceptor Gamma Mu, Lubbock, Texas

Impossible Chicken and Broccoli

1 1/2 cups chopped
    cooked chicken
1 10-ounce package
    frozen chopped
    broccoli, thawed
2 cups shredded
    Cheddar cheese
2/3 cup chopped onion

1 1/3 cups milk
3 eggs
3/4 cup buttermilk
    baking mix
3/4 teaspoon salt
1/4 teaspoon pepper
1 cup shredded
    Cheddar cheese

Combine chicken, broccoli, 2 cups cheese and onion in bowl. Spoon into greased 10-inch pie plate. Combine milk, eggs, baking mix and seasonings in blender container. Process on High for 15 seconds. Pour over chicken mixture. Bake at 400 degrees for 25 to 35 minutes or until knife inserted in center comes out clean. Sprinkle with 1 cup cheese. Bake for 1 to 2 minutes longer or until cheese melts. Let stand for 5 minutes before serving.

Quick Chicken and Mushrooms

3 slices bacon
1 to 1 1/2 pounds
    boned chicken
1 medium onion, sliced
1/2 pound mushrooms,
    quartered

2 tablespoons flour
1/2 cup chicken broth
1 cup red wine
1/2 teaspoon thyme
1 bay leaf

Fry bacon in skillet until crisp; remove and crumble. Cut chicken into bite-sized pieces. Brown in bacon drippings in skillet for 3 minutes. Add onion. Saute for 2 minutes. Add mushrooms. Saute for 1 minute. Sprinkle flour over all; mix gently. Add bacon and remaining ingredients. Bring to a boil. Cook for 2 minutes, stirring constantly; reduce heat. Simmer, covered, for 15 minutes. Remove bay leaf. Serve with rice or noodles. Yield: 4 servings.

Mary Wood
Preceptor Gamma Kappa, St. Louis, Missouri

Stir-Fried Chicken and Broccoli

8 chicken thighs, boned
1/4 teaspoon ginger
1/4 teaspoon pepper
1 bunch fresh broccoli
1 cup chopped scallions
2/3 cup chicken broth

1 teaspoon salt
1/2 teaspoon sugar
1 tablespoon
    cornstarch
1/4 cup chicken broth
1/4 cup Parmesan cheese

Cut chicken into bite-sized pieces. Sprinkle with ginger and pepper. Slice broccoli thinly crosswise. Stir-fry chicken in hot oil in wok for 3 minutes or until golden brown; push to side. Add broccoli and scallions. Stir-fry for 3 minutes. Add mixture of 2/3 cup broth, salt and sugar. Simmer, covered, for 2 minutes. Blend cornstarch with 1/4 cup broth. Stir into skillet. Cook for 1 minute, stirring constantly. Stir in Parmesan cheese. Serve over rice. Yield: 6 servings.

Adeline Smith
Iota Eta, Harvey, Louisiana

Gourmet Cornish Hen

1/4 cup chopped onion
1 clove of garlic,
    chopped
1/2 cup shredded
    zucchini
1/2 teaspoon tarragon

Pinch of salt
2 tablespoons
    Parmesan cheese
2 teaspoons lemon juice
1 22-ounce Cornish
    game hen

Saute onion and garlic in a small amount of oil in skillet. Add zucchini, tarragon and salt; cool. Stir in cheese and lemon juice. Cut hen through breast and remove keel bone. Stuff vegetable mixture carefully under skin. Place skin side up in shallow baking pan. Bake at 375 degrees for 45 minutes or until tender and brown. Yield: 2 servings.

Rosanna Fahl
Preceptor Alpha Epsilon, Oroville, California

Main Dishes

Barbecued Smoked Pork Chops, recipe on page 128.

Energy-Saving Pot Roast

1   5-pound rump roast
Salt and pepper
   to taste
Garlic cloves
1 onion, sliced
1 can beef consomme

Season roast with salt and pepper. Stud with garlic. Place in casserole with onion and consomme. Cover. Place in pre-heated 500-degree oven. Bake for 25 minutes. Turn oven off. Let stand in closed oven for 2 hours. Yield: 6-8 servings.

Mary Lou Aberasturi
Preceptor Zeta Psi, Marysville, California

Sherried Beef

1   2 to 3-pound
   beef roast
1 can cream of
   chicken soup
1 can cream of
   mushroom soup
1 soup can Sherry

Cut beef into cubes. Combine with remaining ingredients in casserole. Bake, covered, for 2 hours. Serve over noodles or rice.

Sandi S. Davison
Preceptor Gamma Upsilon, Kansas City, Missouri

Work Person's Roast

1 beef or pork roast
1 clove of garlic
1 can cream of
   mushroom soup
2 tablespoons
   Worcestershire sauce
1 envelope dry onion
   soup mix

Stud roast with garlic. Place on large sheet foil. Layer soup, Worcestershire sauce and dry onion soup mix over roast. Seal foil tightly, leaving air space above and around roast. Place in baking pan. Bake at 275 degrees for 3 hours.
Yield: 6-8 servings.

Susan Wilson
Preceptor Upsilon, Davisville, West Virginia

Beef Burgundy for Two

2 tenderloin steaks
2 slices bacon
2 tablespoons
   butter, melted
1/2 cup sliced
   mushrooms
1 envelope dry onion
   soup mix
1 tablespoon finely
   chopped parsley
1 1/2 teaspoons flour
1/4 cup dry red
   Burgundy
1 teaspoon lemon juice
1 teaspoon
   Worcestershire sauce

Wrap steaks with bacon; secure with string. Brown steaks in butter in skillet for 2 minutes on each side. Add mushrooms. Cook until mushrooms are tender. Add soup mix, parsley, flour blended with 1/2 cup water, Burgundy, lemon juice and Worcestershire sauce. Simmer for 8 minutes or until tender, turning steaks occasionally. Serve with hot cooked julienne-style vegetables.

Photograph for this recipe on page 104.

119

Creole Steak Strips

1 1/2 pounds boneless
    round steak
Salt and pepper
    to taste
1 onion, chopped
1 cup sliced celery
1 cup seasoned
    tomato juice
2 teaspoons
    Worcestershire sauce

1/8 teaspoon
    garlic powder
1 10-ounce package
    frozen okra
1 medium green
    pepper, chopped
1 2 1/2-ounce can
    sliced mushrooms,
    drained

Cut steak into 1/2 x 2-inch strips. Sprinkle with salt and pepper. Combine steak, onion, celery, tomato juice and seasonings in Crock-Pot. Cook on Low for 6 to 8 hours or until steak is tender. Add partially thawed okra, green pepper and mushrooms. Cook on High for 30 minutes or until okra is tender. Garnish with carrot curls. Serve over rice. Yield: 5-6 servings.

Nina Slaton
Preceptor Gamma Mu, Lubbock, Texas

Individual Beef Wellington

1 1 1/4-inch thick
    tenderloin steak
1 tablespoon margarine
1/4 cup sliced
    mushrooms

1/4 cup chopped onion
1 tablespoon red wine
1 frozen patty
    shell, thawed

Brown steak in margarine in skillet; remove steak. Add mushrooms and onion. Saute until tender. Stir in wine. Spoon onto steak. Roll out patty shell. Wrap around steak; seal edges. Place on rack in baking pan. Bake at 425 degrees for 15 minutes or until puffed and brown. Yield: 1 serving.

Norma Blum
Theta Iota, Hendersonville, North Carolina

Pepper Steak

1 1/2 pounds round
    steak, thinly sliced
1/4 cup soy sauce
1 clove of garlic
1 1/2 tablespoons
    ginger
1/4 cup oil

1 cup sliced onion
1 cup sliced
    red pepper
2 stalks celery,
    thinly sliced
1 tablespoon
    cornstarch

Combine steak, soy sauce, garlic and ginger in bowl. Saute in oil until brown. Simmer, covered, for 30 minutes. Add vegetables. Stir-fry over high heat for 10 minutes. Add mixture of cornstarch and 1 cup water. Cook until thickened, stirring constantly. Yield: 4 servings.

Louise Bland
Xi Psi Pi, Crystal Beach, Texas

Pepper Steak Caballero

1 1/2 pounds sirloin
1 tablespoon paprika
2 cloves of
    garlic, crushed
2 tablespoons butter
1 cup sliced green
    onions and tops
2 green peppers, cut
    into strips

2 large tomatoes,
    chopped
1 cup beef broth
2 tablespoons
    cornstarch
2 tablespoons
    soy sauce
3 cups hot
    cooked rice

Cut sirloin into 1/8-inch wide strips. Sprinkle with paprika. Let stand for several minutes. Brown steak with garlic in butter in skillet. Add green onions and green peppers. Cook until tender. Add tomatoes and broth. Simmer, covered, for 15 minutes. Blend cornstarch, soy sauce and 1/4 cup water in bowl. Stir into steak mixture. Cook until thickened, stirring constantly. Serve over rice. Yield: 6 servings.

Ann Jacek
Xi Beta Tau, Salamanca, New York

Green Pepper Steak

1 pound round steak,
    partially frozen
1/4 cup soy sauce
1 tablespoon oil

1 large green pepper,
    cut into strips
1 tablespoon
    cornstarch

Cut steak into 1 x 2-inch strips. Sprinkle with soy sauce. Brown on one side in oil in skillet. Add green pepper. Stir-fry until steak is browned. Add mixture of cornstarch and 1 cup water. Cook until thickened, stirring constantly. Serve over rice or noodles. Yield: 4 servings.

Sandra Freeman
Xi Gamma, Manchester, Connecticut

Beef Chop Suey

1 2-pound round steak
1 onion, cut into rings
1 stalk celery,
    sliced diagonally
1 green pepper,
    cut into strips

1/2 cup cornstarch
1 can bean sprouts
1/3 cup soy sauce
1 cup rice,
    cooked

Saute steak, onion, celery and green pepper in skillet until vegetables are tender. Add mixture of cornstarch and 1/2 cup water. Cook until thickened, stirring constantly. Add bean sprouts and soy sauce; mix well. Heat to serving temperature. Serve over rice.

Louise Bland
Xi Psi Pi, Crystal Beach, Texas

Main Dishes

Beef with Pea Pods and Mushrooms

1/2 pound lean sirloin, thinly sliced
1 tablespoon wine
2 tablespoons soy sauce
2 teaspoons cornstarch
2 tablespoons oil
1/2 cup sliced mushrooms
1 16-ounce package frozen pea pods
1 teaspoon salt

Cut sirloin into bite-sized pieces. Combine wine, soy sauce and cornstarch in bowl; mix well. Add sirloin. Marinate for 5 minutes. Heat oil in large skillet. Add sirloin and marinade. Stir-fry until cooked through. Add remaining ingredients. Stir-fry for 2 minutes longer. Serve with rice.
Yield: 4 servings.

Patricia McInerney
Xi Beta Zeta, Decatur, Alabama

Beef Strips and Pea Pods

1 pound flank steak
1 tablespoon cornstarch
1 tablespoon dry Sherry
1 teaspoon sugar
1/4 teaspoon MSG
1/8 teaspoon ginger
1/4 cup soy sauce
1 6-ounce package frozen pea pods
2 tablespoons peanut oil
1/4 teaspoon salt
2 tablespoons peanut oil

Cut steak cross grain into 1/4 x 2-inch slices. Combine with next 6 ingredients in bowl; mix well. Rinse pea pods; pat dry. Stir-fry pea pods in mixture of 2 tablespoons oil and salt in skillet for 1 minute. Remove pea pods. Add 2 tablespoons oil and steak mixture. Stir-fry until cooked through. Add pea pods. Heat to serving temperature. Yield: 4 servings.

Sharlet S. Wirzulis
Xi Gamma, Ellington, Connecticut

Round Steak with Green Beans

1 pound round steak, cut into bite-sized pieces
Salt and pepper to taste
3 to 4 tablespoons oil
1/2 onion, finely chopped
1 tablespoon minced garlic
1 28-ounce can tomatoes
2 16-ounce cans green beans

Season steak with salt and pepper. Brown in oil in skillet. Add onion and garlic. Stir-fry until onion is tender. Add tomatoes and beans. Simmer for 30 minutes, adding water if necessary.

Kimberly L. Birch
Eta Nu, Charles City, Iowa

Stir-Fry Beef and Vegetables

1/2 cup broccoli flowerets
1/4 cup sliced mushrooms
1 tablespoon corn oil
1/4 pound diagonally sliced beef
1/3 cup Easy Oriental Sauce Mix
4 cherry tomato halves

EASY ORIENTAL SAUCE MIX

1 1/2 tablespoons cornstarch
1 tablespoon brown sugar
1/2 teaspoon minced fresh ginger
1/4 teaspoon garlic powder
Dash of pepper
2 tablespoons soy sauce
1 tablespoon white vinegar
3/4 cup beef or chicken bouillon
2 tablespoons dry Sherry

Stir-fry broccoli and mushrooms in oil in skillet for 1 minute or until tender-crisp. Remove from skillet. Add beef; stir-fry for 1 to 2 minutes. Add broccoli mixture and sauce mix. Bring to a boil, stirring constantly. Boil for 1 minute. Stir in tomato halves; cook until heated through. Yield: 1 serving.
Note: May substitute 1 whole boned chicken breast cut into strips for beef, if desired.

Combine cornstarch, brown sugar, ginger, garlic powder and pepper in jar. Add soy sauce and vinegar. Cover and shake well. Add bouillon and Sherry. Store, covered, in refrigerator for 1 to 2 weeks. Shake before using. Yield: 1 cup.
Note: May freeze in 1/3-cup portions.

Photograph for this recipe on page 70.

Sharon's Beef Stroganoff

3 to 4 pounds sirloin steak
Flour
2 to 4 tablespoons butter
1 onion, thinly sliced
1 can beef consomme
1 teaspoon Worcestershire sauce
1 4-ounce can mushroom pieces

Cut steak into 1-inch strips; coat with flour. Brown in butter in skillet. Add onion, consomme, Worcestershire sauce, mushrooms and 1 consomme can water. Simmer for 1 hour. Serve over rice or noodles. Yield: 6 servings.

Sharon Bender
Gamma Gamma, Kitchener, Ontario, Canada

121

Main Dishes

Thirty-Minute Beef Stroganoff

1 pound round steak
1/2 onion, chopped
2 tablespoons butter

1 can tomato soup
1 cup sour cream

Cut steak into thin strips. Brown with onion in butter in skillet. Add soup and 1/2 soup can water. Cook for 20 minutes or until steak is tender. Stir in sour cream. Cook for 5 minutes longer. Do not boil. Serve over rice or noodles. Yield: 4 servings.

Janice L. Stewart
Xi Delta Phi, Chesapeake, Virginia

Quick Beef Stroganoff

1 pound round steak
1 tablespoon shortening
1 medium onion, chopped
1/2 teaspoon garlic salt

1 can cream of mushroom soup
1 cup sour cream
2 tablespoons catsup
2 teaspoons Worcestershire sauce

Cut steak into 1/4-inch strips. Brown in shortening in skillet. Add onion and garlic salt. Cook until tender-crisp. Add mixture of soup, sour cream, catsup and Worcestershire sauce. Cook until heated through. Serve over rice. Yield: 4 servings.

Bev Templeton
Delta Upsilon, Garner, Iowa

Wimpies

1 1/2 pounds ground beef
1 large onion, chopped
1 can tomato soup

1 tablespoon Worcestershire sauce
1 tablespoon brown sugar

Brown ground beef with onion in skillet; drain. Add soup, 1/2 soup can water, Worcestershire sauce and brown sugar; mix well. Bring to a boil. Simmer, covered, for 30 minutes, stirring occasionally. Serve on hamburger rolls or in pita-bread.

Doris Teufel
Xi Gamma Zeta, Pomona, New York

Corned Beef Sandwiches

1   12-ounce can corned beef, chopped
1 cup shredded longhorn cheese
1/2 cup chopped green olives

1/4 cup chopped green onions (opt.)
1/2 cup catsup
2 tablespoons Worcestershire sauce

Combine corned beef, cheese, olives and onions in bowl. Add catsup and Worcestershire sauce; mix lightly. Spoon onto small buns. Wrap in foil. Bake at 375 degrees for 15 minutes. Yield: 1 1/2 dozen.

Doris Patterson
Xi Eta Psi, Collinsville, Illinois

Porcupine Meatballs

1 can tomato soup
1 1/2 pounds ground beef
1/2 cup rice

1/2 cup chopped onion
Seasoned salt to taste
Pepper to taste

Combine soup and 1 soup can water in uncovered pressure cooker. Bring to a simmer. Combine remaining ingredients in bowl; mix well. Shape into 1-inch balls. Drop into hot soup. Process, covered, using manufacturer's directions at 15 pounds pressure for 15 minutes. Yield: 4 servings.

Margaret Bell
Theta, Oklahoma City, Oklahoma

Stove Top Beans and Meatballs

1 pound ground beef
1/2 cup evaporated milk
2/3 cup soft bread crumbs
1/8 teaspoon pepper
1 teaspoon salt
1 cup sliced onion

1 tablespoon shortening
1   16-ounce can baked beans
1 1/8 teaspoons salt
2 tablespoons catsup
1/4 teaspoon dry mustard

Combine first 5 ingredients in bowl; mix well. Shape into 16 meatballs. Brown with onion in shortening in skillet. Cook over low heat for 10 minutes. Add remaining ingredients. Cook, covered, until heated through. Yield: 4 servings.

Anne Lowe
Alpha Epsilon, Wrangell, Alaska

Working Girl's Meat Loaf

1 1/2 pounds ground beef
1 can onion soup

1 cup (or more) stuffing mix

Combine all ingredients in bowl; mix well. Shape into loaf in loaf pan. Bake at 350 degrees for 1 hour. Yield: 4-6 servings.

Betty Lou Fisher
Preceptor Alpha Gamma, Wichita, Kansas

Main Dishes

Minute-Saving Loaves

1   29-ounce can
       tomato sauce
2 teaspoons
       Worcestershire sauce
3 pounds ground beef
2 eggs

1 cup quick-cooking
       oats
1 cup minced onion
2 teaspoons salt
1/4 teaspoon pepper

Blend tomato sauce and Worcestershire sauce in bowl. Combine remaining ingredients in bowl; mix well. Add 1 cup tomato sauce mixture. Shape into 16 small oval loaves. Place in greased 9 x 13-inch baking dish. Bake at 450 degrees for 15 minutes; drain pan drippings. Pour remaining tomato sauce mixture over loaves. Bake for 10 minutes longer. Yield: 8 servings.

Mary Ann Baker
Beta Iota, Enid, Oklahoma

Nachos

1 pound ground beef
1 envelope taco
       seasoning mix
Tortilla chips
Grated cheese

Chopped lettuce
Chopped tomatoes
Chopped cucumbers
Sour cream (opt.)

Brown ground beef in skillet, stirring until crumbly; drain. Stir in taco seasoning mix and 3/4 cup water. Simmer for 10 to 15 minutes or to desired consistency. Layer tortilla chips, ground beef mixture, cheese, lettuce, tomatoes, cucumbers, additional cheese and dollop of sour cream on serving plate. Yield: 4 servings.

Janice L. Stewart
Xi Delta Phi, Chesapeake, Virginia

Taco Cups

1 pound ground beef
1   16-ounce can
       Manwich
1   10-count can
       refrigerator biscuits

Sour cream, grated
       cheese, chopped
       lettuce, chopped
       tomatoes, chopped
       onions (opt.)

Brown ground beef in skillet, stirring until crumbly. Add sauce; mix well. Simmer for several minutes. Roll out biscuits on floured surface. Shape to fit outside of greased muffin cups. Bake, using package directions. Spoon beef sauce into biscuit cups. Top with desired topping.

Suzanne Guerrant
Zeta Pi, Fulton, Missouri

Tangy Beef and Cheese Enchiladas

1 1/2 pounds
       ground beef
1   10-ounce can hot
       enchilada sauce
1   10-ounce can mild
       enchilada sauce
1   15-ounce can
       hot chili

1 large onion,
       finely chopped
4 cups grated
       Cheddar cheese
1   10-count package
       12-inch flour
       tortillas

Brown ground beef in skillet, stirring until crumbly; drain. Add enchilada sauces, chili and 3/4 cup water. Simmer for 10 minutes. Place onion and cheese on center of tortillas; roll to enclose filling. Place seam side down in greased 9 x 13-inch baking dish. Pour beef mixture over tortillas. Bake at 350 degrees for 25 minutes. Yield: 10 servings.

Billie K. Adams
Iota Eta, Marreno, Louisiana

Warsaw Hamburgers

1 1/2 pounds
       ground beef
1 can cream of
       celery soup
1/2 cup sour cream

1 can French-fried
       onions
2   8-count cans
       refrigerator crescent
       dinner rolls

Brown ground beef in skillet, stirring until crumbly; drain. Add soup, sour cream and onion rings; mix well. Separate rolls into triangles. Spoon ground beef mixture onto each roll. Pull corners up to enclose filling; seal edges. Place on baking sheet. Bake at 350 degrees until brown. Yield: 16 servings.

Dana Lohman
Iota Chi, Manchester, Missouri

Savory Beef Cakes

1 can Scotch broth soup
1 egg, beaten
1/2 cup quick-cooking
       oats
1/2 teaspoon salt
1 1/4 pounds
       ground beef

1 medium onion, sliced
       into rings
2 tablespoons oil
1/2 teaspoon
       instant beef
       bouillon

Mix soup, egg, oats and salt in bowl. Add ground beef; mix well. Shape into 12 patties. Brown with onion in oil in skillet for 7 minutes on each side. Remove to hot serving plate. Stir beef bouillon and 1/2 cup water into pan drippings. Bring to a boil, stirring to deglaze. Pour over patties. Yield: 12 servings.

Jessie L. Doome
Preceptor Omega, Staunton, Virginia

Main Dishes

Baked Burgers

1 pound ground beef
1/2 cup chopped
   green pepper
1/2 cup chopped onion
1/4 cup chopped celery
1/2 cup mayonnaise
Salt and pepper
   to taste

1 egg
3/4 cup bread crumbs
1/4 cup oil
3 slices cheese
1 can cream of
   mushroom soup
1/3 cup milk

Combine ground beef with next 6 ingredients in bowl; mix well. Shape into 6 patties. Beat egg with 1 tablespoon water in bowl. Dip patties in egg; coat with crumbs. Brown lightly on both sides in hot oil in skillet. Place in 9 x 9-inch baking dish. Cut each cheese slice into 2 triangles. Place triangle on each patty. Heat soup and milk in saucepan. Pour around patties. Bake at 350 degrees for 30 minutes. Yield: 6 servings.

Natalie N. Ruble
Laureate Kappa, Great Bend, Kansas

Skillet Lasagna

1 1/2 pounds
   ground beef
1/2 cup finely
   chopped onion
1 16-ounce carton
   cottage cheese
6 to 8 uncooked
   lasagna noodles
2 8-ounce cans
   tomato sauce
1 teaspoon basil

1 tablespoon
   parsley flakes
1 teaspoon
   garlic powder
1 teaspoon oregano
1/2 teaspoon
   celery flakes
1/4 teaspoon
   chili powder
2 cups shredded
   Cheddar cheese

Brown ground beef with onion in skillet, stirring frequently; drain. Spoon cottage cheese over ground beef. Arrange noodles across top. Combine tomato sauce, seasonings and 1 cup water in bowl. Pour over noodles. Simmer, covered, for 35 minutes or until noodles are tender. Top with cheese. Let stand for 5 minutes. Yield: 6 servings.

Angela Hersel
Beta Iota, McCall, Idaho

Skillet Spaghetti

1 pound ground beef
1 cup chopped onion
2 medium cloves of
   garlic, chopped
1 8-ounce can
   tomato sauce
1 6-ounce can
   tomato paste
1 16-ounce can
   tomato juice

1 tablespoon
   chili powder
1 teaspoon sugar
1 teaspoon oregano
2 teaspoons salt
Dash of pepper
1 8-ounce
   package spaghetti
Parmesan cheese

Brown ground beef, onion and garlic in skillet, stirring frequently. Add tomato sauce, paste, juice, seasonings and 1 1/2 cups water; mix well. Simmer, covered, for 30 minutes, stirring occasionally. Add spaghetti. Simmer, covered, for 30 minutes or until spaghetti is tender, stirring occasionally. Sprinkle with Parmesan cheese. Yield: 4-6 servings.

Marguerite Rinella
Laureate Delta, Louisville, Kentucky

Pan Spaghetti

1 pound ground beef
1 cup chopped onion
1 28-ounce can
   tomatoes
1/2 cup chopped
   green pepper
1 4-ounce can
   mushrooms,
   drained (opt.)

2 teaspoons
   chili powder
2 teaspoons salt
1 teaspoon sugar
1 7-ounce package
   thin spaghetti
1 cup shredded
   Cheddar cheese

Brown ground beef and onion in skillet, stirring frequently; drain. Add next 6 ingredients and 1/2 cup water; mix well. Break spaghetti into 3-inch pieces. Stir into beef mixture. Simmer, covered, for 25 to 30 minutes or until spaghetti is tender, stirring occasionally; add additional water if necessary for desired consistency. Sprinkle with cheese. Heat, covered, until cheese melts. Yield: 6-7 servings.

Mari Anne Isakson
Preceptor Epsilon, Duluth, Minnesota

Tamale Pie

1 1/2 pounds
   ground beef
1 medium onion, chopped
1 clove of garlic,
   chopped
1 can tamales
1 15-ounce can whole
   kernel corn

2 8-ounce cans
   tomato sauce
1 4-ounce can
   chopped olives
3 tablespoons
   cornmeal
Cheese slices

Brown ground beef, onion and garlic in skillet, stirring frequently; drain. Remove wrappers from tamales and mash. Add tamales, corn, tomato sauce and olives to ground beef; mix well. Bring to a boil. Sprinkle cornmeal over mixture; stir to mix well. Spoon into greased 9 x 13-inch baking dish. Bake at 350 degrees for 30 minutes. Arrange cheese slices over top. Bake for 15 minutes longer. Yield: 8 servings.

May H. Ruwe
Preceptor Xi, Seal Beach, California

Main Dishes

Bette's Hamburger Pie

1 pound ground beef
1 8-serving package
    instant mashed
    potatoes
1 egg
1 tablespoon instant
    minced onion
1/4 cup chili sauce
1 cup milk
1/2 teaspoon poultry
    seasoning
1 teaspoon salt
1/8 teaspoon pepper
1/2 cup shredded
    sharp Cheddar cheese

Combine ground beef, 1 1/3 cups dry instant mashed potatoes and next 7 ingredients in bowl; mix well. Press into 9-inch pie plate. Bake at 350 degrees for 35 minutes or until cooked through. Prepare remaining instant mashed potatoes using package directions for 4 servings. Spread over meat loaf. Top with cheese. Bake for 3 to 4 minutes longer or until cheese melts. Yield: 4-5 servings.

Bette L. Carraher
Preceptor Beta Upsilon, Ashtabula, Ohio

Beef and Potato Bake

4 cups frozen hashed
    brown potatoes,
    thawed
3 tablespoons oil
1/8 teaspoon pepper
1 pound ground beef
1 package brown
    gravy mix
1/2 teaspoon
    garlic salt
1 10-ounce package
    frozen mixed
    vegetables
1/2 cup shredded
    Cheddar cheese
1 can French-fried
    onions
1/2 cup shredded
    Cheddar cheese

Combine potatoes, oil and pepper in bowl; mix well. Press over bottom and sides of 9 x 13-inch baking dish to form shell. Bake at 400 degrees for 15 minutes. Brown ground beef in skillet, stirring until crumbly; drain. Add gravy mix, 1 cup water and garlic salt. Bring to a boil. Add mixed vegetables. Cook for 5 minutes. Stir in 1/2 cup cheese and half the onions. Pour into potato shell. Bake at 350 degrees for 15 minutes. Sprinkle 1/2 cup cheese and remaining onions over top. Bake for 5 minutes longer.

Lorraine Fenton
Xi Omicron, Milford, Massachusetts

Hamburger-Onion Pie

1/4 cup light cream
1 cup buttermilk
    baking mix
1 pound ground beef
1 large onion, chopped
1/2 teaspoon salt
1/2 teaspoon
    seasoned salt
1/4 teaspoon pepper
2 eggs, beaten
1 cup small curd
    cottage cheese
2 tablespoons
    buttermilk
    baking mix
Paprika

Combine cream and 1 cup baking mix in bowl; mix well. Knead gently on floured surface. Roll out and fit into 9-inch pie plate. Brown ground beef with onion and seasonings in skillet, stirring frequently. Spoon into pie shell. Combine eggs, cottage cheese and 2 tablespoons baking mix; mix well. Pour over ground beef. Sprinkle with paprika. Bake at 375 degrees for 30 minutes. Serve warm or cold. Yield: 6 servings.

Karol Atwell
Xi Gamma Eta, Melrose, Iowa

Peppy Mexican Crescent Pie

1 can refrigerator
    crescent dinner rolls
1 pound ground beef
2 cloves of garlic,
    crushed
1 tablespoon
    chili powder
Pinch of salt
2 medium tomatoes,
    thinly sliced
1/4 cup chopped
    green chilies
1 cup shredded
    Cheddar cheese
1/4 cup sliced
    ripe olives
1/4 cup finely
    chopped onion
1 cup sour cream
2/3 cup mayonnaise
1/2 cup shredded
    Cheddar cheese

Separate roll dough into triangles. Press into 9-inch pie plate to form crust, sealing edge. Brown ground beef and garlic with chili powder and salt in skillet, stirring until crumbly; remove garlic. Spoon into prepared crust. Arrange tomatoes in overlapping layer over ground beef. Sprinkle with chilies and 1 cup cheese. Combine olives, onion, sour cream and mayonnaise in bowl; mix well. Pour over pie. Top with 1/2 cup cheese. Bake at 375 degrees for 25 to 30 minutes or until crust is brown. Let stand for 5 minutes before serving. Yield: 6 servings.

Connie Sharp
Preceptor Upsilon, Omaha, Nebraska

French Bread Pizza

1 1/2 pounds
    ground beef
1 onion, chopped
1 4-ounce can
    mushrooms, drained
1 cup chopped olives
1 cup tomato sauce
1 teaspoon oregano
1/2 teaspoon
    garlic powder
1 pound Cheddar
    cheese, shredded
1 loaf French
    bread, split
1/2 pound mozzarella
    cheese, shredded

Brown ground beef and onion in skillet, stirring frequently; drain. Add next 6 ingredients; mix well. Spread on bread. Top with mozzarella cheese. Place on baking sheet. Bake at 350 degrees for 5 to 8 minutes or until cheese melts. Cut into serving pieces. Yield: 8-10 servings.

Murlynn Williams
Preceptor Lambda, McGill, Nebraska

125

Main Dishes

Upside-Down Pizza

1 1/2 pounds
    ground beef
1/4 cup chopped onion
1 envelope spaghetti
    sauce mix
1 16-ounce can
    tomato sauce

1/2 cup sour cream
2 cups grated
    mozzarella cheese
1 10-count can
    refrigerator biscuits
Melted butter
Parmesan cheese

Brown ground beef and onion in skillet, stirring frequently. Add spaghetti sauce mix and tomato sauce; mix well. Simmer for several minutes. Spoon into greased 9 x 13-inch baking dish. Top with sour cream and mozzarella cheese. Arrange biscuits over top. Brush with butter; sprinkle with Parmesan cheese. Bake at 375 degrees for 20 to 25 minutes or until biscuits are brown. Yield: 10 servings.

Mary Kopacek
Xi Alpha Epsilon, Britt, Iowa

Pizza Loaf

1 loaf French bread
3/4 pound
    ground beef
1 onion, chopped

1 16-ounce can
    pizza sauce
3/4 pound mozzarella
    cheese, grated

Split bread lengthwise to but not through side. Brown ground beef and onion in skillet, stirring frequently. Spread in loaf. Top with pizza sauce and cheese. Wrap loaf in foil. Bake at 300 degrees for 30 minutes. Yield: 4-6 servings.

Glenda C. Haas
Lambda Tau, Howard, Pennsylvania

Easy Beef Stroganoff

1 pound ground beef
1 can cream of
    mushroom soup

1/2 pint
    sour cream

Brown ground beef in skillet, stirring until crumbly. Add soup. Simmer for 3 or 4 minutes. Add sour cream. Simmer until heated through. Serve over rice, noodles or toast. Yield: 6 servings.

Sharon L. Coble
Epsilon Kappa, Playas, New Mexico

Susan's Hamburger Stroganoff

1 pound ground beef
1 medium onion,
    chopped
1/4 cup butter
2 tablespoons flour
1 teaspoon salt
1 teaspoon garlic salt
1/4 teaspoon pepper

1 8-ounce can sliced
    mushrooms, drained
1 can cream of
    chicken soup
1 cup sour cream
2 cups cooked
    egg noodles

Brown ground beef and onion in butter in skillet, stirring frequently. Add flour, salt, garlic salt, pepper and mushrooms; mix well. Cook for 5 minutes. Stir in soup. Simmer for 10 minutes. Stir in sour cream. Simmer until heated through. Serve over noodles.
Note: May be served over baked potatoes.

Susan Halfmann
Lamesa, Texas

Paulinda's Ground Beef Casserole

1 onion, chopped
1 clove of garlic
1 green pepper, chopped
1 tablespoon butter
1 to 1 1/2 pounds
    ground beef
Salt and pepper
    to taste

1 can golden
    mushroom soup
1 can tomato soup
1 6-ounce
    package macaroni,
    cooked
Cheese slices

Saute onion, garlic and green pepper in butter in skillet until tender. Add ground beef. Cook until browned, stirring frequently. Add seasonings, soups and macaroni. Place cheese on top.

Paulinda Proffitt
Xi Phi Upsilon, Granbury, Texas

Indian Corn

1 1/2 pounds
    ground beef
1 green pepper, chopped
1 large onion, chopped
3 stalks celery,
    chopped

1 29-ounce can
    tomatoes
1 16-ounce can Shoe
    Peg corn
Salt and pepper
    to taste

Brown ground beef in skillet, stirring until crumbly; drain. Add fresh vegetables, undrained tomatoes, corn with liquid and 2 cups water. Simmer until nearly dry. Stir in seasonings. Yield: 6 servings.

Anna Katherine Pierson
Laureate Delta, Louisville, Kentucky

Main Dishes

Quick Dish-for-One

1/4 pound ground beef
1 teaspoon oil
1 clove of
   garlic, minced
1 teaspoon
   minced onion
3 mushrooms, sliced

1/2 bunch spinach,
   chopped
Salt, pepper and
   nutmeg to taste
1 egg, beaten
Grated cheese
2 cherry tomatoes

Brown ground beef in oil in skillet, stirring until crumbly. Add garlic and onion. Cook until tender, stirring frequently. Add mushrooms, spinach and seasonings. Cook for several minutes. Add egg. Cook until egg is set, stirring constantly. Spoon onto serving plate. Sprinkle with cheese; serve with tomatoes. Yield: 1 serving.

Theda Mills
Preceptor Beta Lambda, Cottage Grove, Oregon

Zucchini-Beef Skillet

1 pound ground beef
3/4 cup chopped
   green pepper
1 cup chopped onion
1 clove of garlic,
   minced
2 large tomatoes,
   peeled, chopped

5 cups sliced zucchini
1 1/4 cups whole
   kernel corn
1/4 cup chopped parsley
1 teaspoon chili powder
1 1/2 teaspoons salt
1/4 teaspoon pepper

Brown ground beef, green pepper, onion and garlic in skillet, stirring frequently. Add remaining ingredients; mix well. Simmer, covered, for 10 to 15 minutes or until vegetables are tender. Yield: 6 servings.

Meryde G. English
Exemplar Xi Kappa, Winnemucca, Nevada

Chinese Hamburger

1 pound ground beef
2 tablespoons margarine
1 large onion, chopped
1 green pepper, chopped
1 cup chopped celery
1 5-ounce can
   water chestnuts
2 tablespoons soy sauce

1/4 cup Sherry
1 16-ounce can chop
   suey vegetables
1 can cream of
   mushroom soup
1/2 teaspoon
   garlic powder

Brown ground beef in margarine in skillet, stirring until crumbly. Add onion, green pepper and celery. Cook for 10 minutes, stirring frequently. Stir in remaining ingredients; mix well. Simmer for 15 minutes. Serve over rice or noodles. Yield: 6 servings.

Roseleen Corder
Psi Chi, Alma, Missouri

Loose Hamburgers

2 pounds ground beef
1 onion, chopped
1 12-ounce bottle of
   barbecue sauce

1/2 cup catsup
Juice of 1 lemon
Salt and pepper
   to taste

Brown ground beef and onion in skillet, stirring frequently. Add remaining ingredients; mix well. Simmer for 15 minutes. Serve over toasted buns. Yield: 6 servings.

Jolene Broussard
Preceptor Delta, Sulphur, Louisiana

Upside-Down Ham and Spinach Quiche

1 10-ounce package
   frozen chopped
   spinach, thawed
1 cup chopped ham
1 cup grated
   Swiss cheese
1/4 cup chopped onion

3/4 cup cracker meal
2 teaspoons
   baking powder
1/2 teaspoon salt
1/4 cup margarine
3 eggs
1 1/2 cups milk

Drain spinach. Layer spinach, ham, cheese and onion in 10-inch pie plate. Combine cracker meal, baking powder and salt in bowl. Cut in margarine until crumbly. Add eggs and milk; mix well. Pour into pie plate. Bake at 350 degrees for 30 minutes or until puffed and golden. Yield: 6 servings.

Dorothy Summers
Pi Chi, Alma, Missouri

Country-Style Ham and Noodles

1 1-pound 1/2-inch
   thick ham slice
1/3 cup chopped onion
2 tablespoons butter
1 can Franco-American
   mushroom gravy

2 tablespoons
   sour cream
1/2 teaspoon
   horseradish

Brown ham and onion in butter in skillet. Add gravy, sour cream and horseradish. Heat to serving temperature, stirring occasionally. Serve over noodles. Yield: 4 servings.

Photograph for this recipe on page 97.

Main Dishes

Quick Ham and Potatoes

4 medium potatoes,
   peeled, cubed
2 tablespoons butter

1 cup chicken broth
1 teaspoon minced onion
2 cups chopped cooked ham

Pat potatoes dry. Brown lightly in butter in skillet for 5 minutes, stirring frequently. Add broth, onion and ham; mix well. Simmer, covered, for 5 minutes. Cook, uncovered, until liquid is absorbed. Yield: 4-6 servings.

Dee McBride
Nu Delta, Burlington, Kansas

Chipped Ham Barbecue

1 pound chipped ham,
   chopped
1 cup catsup
1 medium onion, chopped
1/3 cup sugar

4 teaspoons mustard
1/8 teaspoon pepper
1/2 cup vinegar
4 teaspoons
   Worcestershire sauce

Combine ham, catsup, onion, sugar and seasonings in saucepan; mix well. Simmer for 30 minutes.

Alice Fae Jones
Laureate Xi, Fairmont, West Virginia

Barbecued Smoked Pork Chops

1/3 cup catsup
1 tablespoon
   brown sugar
1 tablespoon
   lemon juice
1 tablespoon butter

1/2 teaspoon
   Worcestershire sauce
1/8 teaspoon cloves
6 1-inch thick smoked
   pork loin chops

Combine catsup, 1/4 cup water, brown sugar, lemon juice, butter, Worcestershire sauce and cloves in saucepan. Bring to a boil, stirring constantly. Simmer for 15 minutes. Place pork chops on rack in roasting pan. Brush with barbecue sauce. Bake at 400 degrees for 30 minutes or until glazed.

Photograph for this recipe on page 119.

Orange Pork Chops

6 small pork chops
1/2 cup orange juice
1 teaspoon salt
1/4 teaspoon pepper

1/2 teaspoon
   dry mustard
1/4 cup packed
   brown sugar

Place pork chops in roasting pan. Combine juice, seasonings and brown sugar in bowl; mix well. Pour over chops. Bake at 350 degrees for 1 hour or until tender, basting occasionally.

Renee Nichols
Gamma Kappa, Cape Canaveral, Florida

Polynesian Pork

4 1-inch pork loin
   rib chops
1 tablespoon oil
1 14-ounce can
   pineapple
   chunks

1 tablespoon
   brown sugar
1 tablespoon soy sauce
1 teaspoon ginger
1 tablespoon cornstarch
1 green pepper, chopped

Brown pork chops in oil in skillet. Drain pineapple, reserving syrup. Combine reserved syrup with brown sugar, soy sauce and ginger. Pour over pork chops. Simmer, covered, for 45 minutes. Remove pork chops. Add mixture of cornstarch and 1 tablespoon water. Cook until thickened, stirring constantly. Add pork chops, pineapple and green pepper. Cook for 5 minutes. Serve with rice. Yield: 4 servings.

Sally Barber
Preceptor Gamma Theta, Ottawa, Ontario, Canada

Honey Pork Oriental

2 pounds pork
   shoulder steaks
2 tablespoons oil
1 envelope brown
   gravy mix
1/4 cup honey
3 tablespoons soy sauce
2 tablespoons red
   wine vinegar

1 teaspoon ginger
1/2 teaspoon
   garlic salt
4 carrots,
   thinly sliced
1 medium onion, cut
   into wedges
1 green pepper, cut
   into squares

Cut pork steaks into 1-inch pieces. Brown in oil in large skillet for 15 minutes, stirring frequently. Combine gravy mix, 3/4 cup water, honey, soy sauce, vinegar, ginger and garlic salt in bowl; mix well. Add to skillet. Cook, covered, for 20 minutes. Add carrots. Cook for 10 minutes. Add onion and green pepper. Cook for 5 to 10 minutes or until pork is tender. Yield: 4-5 servings.

Constance Cooper
Laureate Alpha Mu, Lexington, Ohio

Sweet and Sour Pork

3 or 4 pork steaks
Salt and pepper
   to taste
1 cup barbecue sauce

1/3 cup vinegar
1 green pepper
1 12-ounce jar
   pineapple preserves

Cut pork into bite-sized pieces. Brown with salt and pepper in skillet. Add mixture of barbecue sauce, vinegar and 1/2 cup water. Simmer for 45 minutes. Add green pepper and pineapple preserves. Simmer for 15 minutes longer. Serve over rice.

Marie Hunter

Main Dishes

Main Dish in Minutes

1 cup rice, cooked
1 tablespoon sweet
  pepper flakes
1 tablespoon
  onion flakes
3 tablespoons
  teriyaki sauce
1/4 teaspoon
  garlic powder
1 cup chopped
  cooked pork
2 tablespoons oil
1 package
  Japanese-style
  stir-fry
  vegetables
Teriyaki sauce

Cook rice using package directions, adding pepper flakes, onion flakes, teriyaki sauce and garlic powder to cooking water. Saute pork in oil in skillet until light brown. Add vegetables. Cook according to package directions, using teriyaki for water, for 4 minutes. Serve over rice.

Cynthia Kitchen
Preceptor Xi, Virginia Beach, Virginia

Barbecued Pork

1 pork
  roast
1 bottle of original
  recipe barbecue sauce

Cook roast in water to cover in Crock·Pot until tender. Drain, bone, trim and shred. Combine roast and barbecue sauce in Crock·Pot. Cook on Low for 30 minutes.
Note: May substitute beef for pork, if desired.

Barbara Saunders
Xi Beta Alpha, Huntsville, Alabama

Breakfast Pizza

1 pound sausage
1 package refrigerator
  crescent dinner rolls
1 cup frozen hashed
  brown potatoes
1 cup shredded
  Cheddar cheese
5 eggs
1/4 cup milk
1/2 teaspoon salt
1/8 teaspoon pepper
2 tablespoons
  Parmesan cheese

Brown sausage in skillet, stirring until crumbly; drain. Separate crescent rolls. Press over bottom and side of 12-inch pizza pan; seal perforations. Layer sausage, potatoes and Cheddar cheese over crust. Combine eggs, milk, salt and pepper in bowl; mix well. Pour over layers. Sprinkle with Parmesan cheese. Bake at 375 degrees for 25 minutes or until brown. Yield: 6-8 servings.

Linda Knutson
Xi Alpha Gamma, Polson, Montana

Meat Dish Pie

1 1/2 to 2 pounds
  sweet sausage
1 10-ounce package
  frozen chopped
  spinach
1 recipe 2-crust
  pie pastry
Prosciutto, chopped
2 cups ricotta
  cheese
1 1/2 cups grated
  mozzarella
  cheese

Brown sausage in skillet, stirring until crumbly. Cook spinach, using package directions; drain. Fit half the pastry into 9-inch pie plate. Layer sausage, spinach, prosciutto and cheeses in pie shell. Top with remaining pastry. Bake at 375 degrees for 35 minutes or until brown. Yield: 6-8 servings.

Laura R. Babcock
Preceptor, Athens, Pennsylvania

Jenni's Stromboli

1/4 pound sausage
1 loaf frozen bread
  dough, thawed
1 egg, separated
1/4 cup olive oil
1/4 teaspoon each
  oregano, mustard
  and garlic powder
1/4 teaspoon parsley
1/4 teaspoon each
  salt and pepper
1 4-ounce package
  sliced pepperoni
1 8-ounce package
  shredded
  mozzarella cheese
Chopped ham to taste

Brown sausage in skillet, stirring until crumbly; drain. Roll dough into 11 x 14-inch rectangle. Combine egg yolk, olive oil and seasonings in bowl; mix well. Brush over dough. Layer pepperoni, sausage, cheese and ham over top. Roll to enclose filling; seal tightly. Place seam side down on baking sheet. Brush with egg white. Sprinkle with additional parsley and oregano. Bake at 350 degrees for 20 minutes or until brown. Cut into slices.

Rose M. Bolen
Preceptor Gamma Upsilon, Kansas City, Missouri

Sausage Roll

1 loaf frozen
  bread dough
1 pound sausage
1 medium onion, chopped
1 small green
  pepper, chopped
1 4-ounce jar
  sliced mushrooms
1 8-ounce package
  sliced mozzarella
  cheese

Thaw dough and let rise using package directions. Roll into square on floured surface. Brown sausage with vegetables in skillet, stirring until crumbly; drain. Spread in center of dough. Top with cheese. Fold sides and ends in; seal edges. Place on baking sheet. Bake at 350 degrees for 45 minutes. Serve with salad. Yield: 4 servings..

Susan Thomason
Xi Alpha Rho, Danville, Kentucky

Main Dishes

Scotch Eggs

1 pound sausage
2 tablespoons parsley
1/2 teaspoon sage
1/2 teaspoon thyme
8 hard-boiled eggs
1/2 cup flour

Salt and pepper
   to taste
2 or 3 eggs, beaten
1 cup fine bread crumbs
Oil for deep frying

Combine sausage, parsley, sage and thyme in bowl; mix well. Divide into 8 portions. Mold each around egg, enclosing egg completely. Roll in mixture of flour, salt and pepper. Dip in beaten eggs then in bread crumbs to coat. Deep-fry for 10 minutes or until cooked through; drain. Serve hot or cold. Yield: 8 servings.

Jouett Smith
Epsilon Kappa, Hachita, New Mexico

Stuffed Zucchini

6 medium zucchini
1/2 pound Italian
   sausage
1/4 cup chopped onion
1 clove of garlic,
   crushed

1/3 cup Italian
   bread crumbs
1/4 cup grated
   Parmesan cheese
1/4 pound mozzarella
   cheese, shredded

Cut zucchini in half lengthwise. Cook in boiling salted water in large skillet for 10 minutes; drain. Scoop out and mash pulp, leaving 1/4-inch shells. Remove sausage casings; crumble sausage. Saute in skillet for 5 minutes. Add onion and garlic. Saute for 3 minutes. Stir in zucchini pulp and bread crumbs. Spoon into shells. Sprinkle with cheese. Place in baking pan. Bake at 350 degrees for 30 minutes. Yield: 6 servings.

Jeannie Cox
Preceptor Upsilon, Muncie, Indiana

Liver Dinner a la Doris

1 pound calves liver
1/4 cup flour
1/4 cup butter
1 medium onion, sliced
1 19-ounce can
   tomatoes
1 teaspoon sugar

1 teaspoon salt
1/8 teaspoon pepper
1 teaspoon
   Worcestershire sauce
1/4 teaspoon basil
1 1/2 cups grated
   cheese

Cut liver into thin strips. Coat with flour. Brown in butter in skillet over low heat. Add onion. Saute for several minutes. Add tomatoes and seasonings. Simmer, covered, for 15 minutes. Add cheese. Cook until melted, stirring constantly. Yield: 4-6 servings.

Doris Decker
Laureate Alpha Alpha, Kingston, Ontario, Canada

Fried Liver Strips

8 slices bacon
1 pound calves liver
1 bottle of French
   salad dressing

Flour
1 can French-fried
   onion rings

Fry bacon in skillet until crisp. Drain, reserving drippings. Cut liver into 1-inch strips. Dip in salad dressing; coat with flour. Brown in reserved bacon drippings. Garnish with bacon slices and onion rings.

Betty Rose Griffin
Xi Alpha Delta, Bedford, Indiana

Polynesian Wiki-Wiki

1 16-ounce can
   lunch meat
1 tablespoon cornstarch
1/3 cup pineapple juice
1 tablespoon vinegar
1/2 teaspoon
   Worcestershire sauce
1/4 teaspoon
   prepared mustard

1 teaspoon soy sauce
1 16-ounce can
   pineapple tidbits
1 tomato, chopped
1/2 green pepper,
   sliced
1/2 cup chopped celery
3 cups cooked rice

Chop lunch meat into 3/4-inch cubes. Brown lightly in skillet. Blend cornstarch, pineapple juice, vinegar, Worcestershire sauce, mustard, soy sauce and 1 cup water in bowl. Stir into skillet. Cook until thickened, stirring constantly. Add next 4 ingredients. Simmer for 5 minutes. Serve over rice. Yield: 4 servings.

Lela Green
Preceptor Chi, Tacoma, Washington

Stove Top Hot Dog Casserole

1 1/2 pounds hot dogs
1/4 pound sliced
   bacon, chopped
1 medium onion, chopped
1 16-ounce can whole
   kernel corn, drained

1 16-ounce can
   kidney beans,
   drained
Salt and pepper
   to taste

Slice hot dogs thinly. Saute with bacon and onion in skillet until bacon is crisp; drain. Add remaining ingredients. Cook over medium heat for 15 minutes. Serve over rice or corn bread. Yield: 6 servings.

Barbara Cormier
Preceptor Delta, Sulphur, Louisiana

Main Dishes

Meatless

Cheese-Egg Bake, recipe below.

Scrambled Breakfast

Assorted chopped
  meats, vegetables,
  cheese

2 eggs, beaten
1 tablespoon margarine

Add meat, vegetables and cheese as desired to eggs. Pour into margarine in skillet. Cook over low heat until set, stirring frequently. Yield: 1 serving.

Lorraine Brooks
Gamma Kappa, Cocoa, Florida

Cheese-Egg Bake

1/3 cup chopped onion
1 cup sliced fresh
  mushrooms
1/3 cup butter
1/4 cup flour
1 teaspoon salt
1 teaspoon
  dry mustard
1/8 teaspoon pepper
2 1/3 cups milk
1/2 cup shredded
  Cheddar cheese

1 10-ounce package
  frozen peas,
  cooked, drained
4 hard-boiled
  eggs, sliced
2 cups buttermilk
  biscuit mix
1/2 cup shredded
  Cheddar cheese
2/3 cup milk
1 cup shredded
  Cheddar cheese

Saute onion and mushrooms in butter in skillet. Add flour, salt, mustard and pepper; mix well. Stir in 2 1/3 cups milk gradually. Cook until thickened, stirring constantly. Add 1/2 cup cheese; stir until melted. Fold in peas and eggs. Pour into shallow 2-quart baking dish. Bake at 425 degrees for 10 minutes. Combine biscuit mix and 1/2 cup cheese in bowl. Stir in 2/3 cup milk. Pat into 9-inch circle on lightly floured surface; cut into 8 wedges. Top mushroom mixture with biscuit wedges. Bake for 10 minutes or until biscuits are brown. Sprinkle with 1 cup cheese. Bake for 1 minute longer. Yield: 6-8 servings.

Photograph for this recipe above.

Main Dishes

Hot Cottage Cheese Salad

2 8-ounce cartons cottage cheese	2 10-ounce packages frozen chopped spinach
1 stick margarine, sliced	Bread crumbs
6 eggs	8 ounces sliced American cheese
6 tablespoons flour	

Combine cottage cheese, margarine, eggs and flour in bowl; mix well. Stir in well-drained spinach. Spoon into greased 1 1/2-quart baking dish. Top with bread crumbs and cheese. Bake at 350 degrees for 1 1/4 hours. Yield: 8-12 servings.

Ruth E. Hughes
Laureate Alpha Mu, Mansfield, Ohio

Swiss Cheese Quiche

1 unbaked 9-inch pie shell	4 eggs
1 tablespoon butter, softened	1/2 teaspoon salt
2 cups cream	1 cup shredded Swiss cheese

Spread pie shell with butter. Combine cream, eggs and salt in bowl; mix with wire whisk until well blended. Stir in cheese. Pour into prepared pie shell. Bake at 425 degrees for 15 minutes. Reduce temperature to 325 degrees. Bake for 35 minutes or until knife inserted in center comes out clean. Yield: 4-6 servings.

Carol Banks
Xi Alpha Theta, Frankfort, Kentucky

Mushroom Crust Quiche

1/2 pound mushrooms, coarsely chopped	1 cup shredded Monterey Jack cheese
2 tablespoons butter	1/2 cup chopped green onions
1/2 cup fine dry bread crumbs	Garlic powder to taste
3 eggs, beaten	1/4 teaspoon salt
1 cup cottage cheese	

Saute mushrooms in butter in skillet for 10 minutes or until golden. Add bread crumbs; mix well. Press into greased 9-inch pie plate. Combine remaining ingredients in bowl; mix well. Pour into prepared pie plate. Bake at 350 degrees for 45 minutes. Cool for 10 minutes before serving. Yield: 6 servings.

Johnnie Templeton
Alpha Chi, Pope Air Force Base, North Carolina

Skillet Supper

1/2 cup chopped onion	1 teaspoon salt
1/2 cup chopped green pepper	1/2 teaspoon basil
2 tablespoons butter	1 medium tomato, chopped
8 eggs	4 slices crisp-fried bacon
1/4 cup milk	

Saute onion and green pepper in butter in skillet. Combine eggs, milk, salt and basil in bowl; mix well. Pour into skillet. Add tomato. Cook until eggs are set but moist, stirring frequently. Spoon into serving dish. Crumble bacon over top. Yield: 6 servings.

Margaret Scholtz
Preceptor Delta Mu, Lena, Illinois

Vegetarian Pasta

4 ounces tofu, crumbled	1/2 teaspoon basil
1/4 pound mushrooms, sliced	1/4 cup Parmesan cheese
1/2 cup chopped celery	1 8-ounce can tomato sauce
1 large onion, chopped	2 cups canned tomatoes and juice
1 clove of garlic, chopped	1/2 cup wine
2 tablespoons (about) butter	1 8-ounce package pasta
1 tablespoon chopped chives	2 tablespoons half and half
2 tablespoons chopped parsley	1/2 teaspoon basil
	1 tablespoon butter

Saute tofu, mushrooms, celery, onion and garlic in 2 tablespoons butter in skillet. Add next 7 ingredients; mix well. Simmer for 30 minutes. Cook pasta using package directions until just tender; drain. Add half and half, 1/2 teaspoon basil and 1 tablespoon butter; toss to coat well. Place on serving platter. Spoon sauce over top. Serve with additional Parmesan cheese. Yield: 6 servings.

Mary Foreman
Preceptor Alpha Alpha, Durango, Colorado

Main Dishes

Seafood

Shrimp Bourguignon, recipe on page 137.

Baked Fish

3 haddock fillets
1/2 cup milk
1/2 teaspoon salt
1/4 cup Parmesan cheese
3/4 cup seasoned crumbs
1/4 cup melted
   margarine
Paprika

Cut fish into serving pieces. Dip in mixture of milk and salt. Coat with mixture of Parmesan cheese and crumbs. Arrange in 8 x 8-inch baking dish. Drizzle with margarine; sprinkle with paprika. Bake at 525 degrees for 12 minutes or until fish flakes easily. Yield: 3-4 servings.

Gloria Hillegass
Xi Alpha Rho, Danville, Kentucky

Fish and Shrimp Parmesan

2 pounds white
   fish fillets
1/2 pound small
   cooked shrimp
2 tablespoons flour
3 tablespoons butter,
   melted
1/2 teaspoon salt
1 cup milk
1/4 cup Parmesan cheese

Layer fish and shrimp in buttered 2-quart baking dish. Blend flour into butter in saucepan. Cook until bubbly. Add salt and milk. Cook until thickened, stirring constantly. Spread over shrimp. Sprinkle with Parmesan cheese. Bake at 325 degrees for 20 to 25 minutes or until fish flakes easily. Yield: 4 servings.

Connie Bolle
Gamma Eta, Cleveland, Tennessee

Main Dishes

Crowned Fish Fillets

4 1/4-inch
thick mild
fish fillets

1/2 cup mayonnaise
2 egg whites,
stiffly beaten

Arrange fillets in baking dish. Fold mayonnaise into egg whites. Spread over fillets. Bake at 350 degrees for 5 minutes or until lightly browned and fish flakes easily. Place on warm serving platter; garnish with parsley and lemon slices. Yield: 4 servings.

Jane E. Shrader
Xi Alpha Tau, Williamsville, New York

Fillet of Sole with Dill Sauce

1 pound fillet of sole
Pam No-Stick
  Cooking Spray
1 medium carrot, cut
  into julienne strips
1 small zucchini, cut
  into julienne strips

2 green onions, cut
  into julienne strips
1/2 teaspoon salt
2 teaspoons cornstarch
1/4 cup sour cream
1/4 teaspoon dillweed

Cut fillets into serving pieces. Arrange sole in shallow baking dish sprayed with Pam. Bake at 400 degrees for 10 minutes or until fish flakes easily. Stir-fry vegetables with salt in large saucepan sprayed with Pam for 2 minutes. Add 1 cup water. Simmer, covered, for 5 minutes. Remove vegetables to bowl with slotted spoon. Blend cornstarch with 1 tablespoon water; stir into vegetable pan juices. Cook until thickened, stirring constantly; remove from heat. Stir in sour cream and dillweed. Spoon half the dill sauce into serving plate; arrange sole over sauce. Top with vegetables. Pour fish pan juices into remaining sauce in pan; blend well. Serve with sole. Yield: 4 servings.

Photograph for this recipe on page 1.

Herb-Baked Fish Fillets

1 package
  herb-seasoned
  stuffing mix
1 1/2 to 2 pounds
  fish fillets

1 stick margarine,
  melted
Juice of 1/2 lemon
1 lemon, cut
  into wedges

Process stuffing mix in blender container to make 1 cup fine crumbs. Dip each fillet in margarine; roll in crumbs to coat. Place in greased 9 x 9-inch baking dish. Stir lemon juice into remaining margarine. Pour carefully around but not on fish. Bake at 350 degrees for 30 minutes or until fish flakes easily. Serve with lemon wedges. Yield: 3-4 servings.

Eunice B. Toler
Preceptor Alpha, Lynchburg, Virginia

Newfoundland Cod au Gratin

2 pounds cod fillets
1/4 cup flour
1/2 teaspoon salt
1/2 teaspoon pepper

2 tablespoons
  melted butter
2 cups milk
1 cup shredded cheese

Arrange fillets in shallow baking dish. Blend flour and seasonings with butter in saucepan. Stir in milk gradually. Cook over low heat until thickened, stirring constantly. Add cheese; stir until melted. Pour over fillets. Bake at 350 degrees for 25 to 30 minutes or until fish flakes easily. Yield: 4 servings.

Beverly Lundrigan
Beta, Corner Brook, Newfoundland, Canada

Oven-Fried Fish

1 pound fish fillets
1/2 cup Italian
  salad dressing

1/2 cup bread
  crumbs

Marinate fillets in Italian dressing for 15 minutes, turning frequently. Roll in bread crumbs, coating well. Place on greased baking sheet. Bake at 450 degrees for 6 minutes; turn fillets over. Bake for 2 to 4 minutes longer or until fish flakes easily.

JoAnn J. Kresky
Preceptor Chi, Lansing, Michigan

Main Dishes

Linguine with Smoked Salmon Sauce

1/4 cup diagonally
   sliced green onions
1/4 cup olive oil
1 cup flaked
   smoked salmon
2 cups cream
Pepper to taste
1/4 cup olive oil

2 pounds fresh linguine
1/2 cup Parmesan cheese
2 tablespoons
   diagonally sliced
   green onions
2 tablespoons
   minced parsley

Saute 1/4 cup green onions in 1/4 cup olive oil in skillet for 1 minute. Add salmon, cream and pepper. Simmer until reduced by 1/3. Bring 4 quarts salted water with 2 tablespoons olive oil to a boil. Add linguine. Cook al dente; drain. Add remaining 2 tablespoons olive oil; toss to coat. Place on serving plates. Top with salmon sauce, Parmesan cheese, 2 tablespoons green onions and parsley. Yield: 6 servings.

Mary Helen Pope
Beta Iota, McCall, Idaho

Salmon Loaf

1 16-ounce can
   red salmon
1 cup soft
   bread crumbs
1/2 cup mashed potatoes
1 cup milk
1/4 cup melted butter
1 tablespoon
   chopped parsley

1/2 teaspoon salt
1/4 teaspoon paprika
1/4 teaspoon
   celery salt
1 recipe white sauce
Hard-boiled eggs,
   chopped
Cheese, grated (opt.)

Combine first 9 ingredients in bowl; mix well. Pour into buttered loaf pan. Bake at 350 degrees for 30 minutes. Let stand in pan for several minutes. Remove to serving plate. Combine remaining ingredients in saucepan. Heat to serving temperature. Spoon over Salmon Loaf. Yield: 6-8 servings.

Lillian Clausius
Laureate Alpha Epsilon, Effingham, Illinois

Salmon Patties

1 16-ounce can
   salmon
1 egg
1/3 cup minced onion
Dash of
   Worcestershire sauce

Dash of Tabasco
   sauce
1/2 cup flour
1 1/2 teaspoons
   baking powder

Drain salmon, reserving 2 tablespoons liquid. Combine salmon, egg, onion, Worcestershire and Tabasco sauces and flour; mix well. Blend baking powder with reserved salmon liquid. Add salmon mixture; mix well. Shape into small patties. Cook in skillet over medium heat until golden brown on both sides. Yield: 4 servings.

Billie Wisian
Preceptor Alpha Tau, Austin, Texas

Salmon Patty Casserole

1 16-ounce can
   salmon
Evaporated milk
1 onion, minced
2 eggs
3 cups bread crumbs
3/4 teaspoon
   minced parsley
1/4 teaspoon
   poultry seasoning

1/4 teaspoon salt
1 can cream of
   mushroom soup
1/2 cup evaporated
   milk
1/8 teaspoon
   curry powder
1/2 teaspoon
   paprika

Drain salmon, reserving liquid. Add enough evaporated milk to reserved liquid to measure 1/2 cup. Combine salmon, milk mixture and next 6 ingredients in bowl; mix well. Shape into large patties. Place in 7 x 11-inch baking dish. Blend soup, 1/2 cup evaporated milk, curry powder and paprika in bowl. Pour over patties. Bake at 350 degrees for 45 minutes.

Jean Restad
Nu Gamma, Crescent City, California

Salmon Souffle

2 eggs, separated
4 ounces salmon
2 slices bread,
   crumbled
1 to 2 tablespoons
   grated onion

1/4 cup milk
1 tablespoon lemon juice
1/2 teaspoon salt
1 tablespoon oil
Paprika

Beat egg whites in bowl until stiff. Combine egg yolks, salmon and next 6 ingredients in bowl; mix well. Fold in egg whites gently. Spoon into greased 1-quart casserole. Sprinkle with paprika. Bake at 300 degrees for 1 hour or until puffed and lightly browned Yield: 2 servings.

Ruth Epright
Alpha Iota, Parkside, Pennsylvania

Main Dishes

Tuna and Rice

1/4 cup chopped onion
1/4 cup chopped celery
3 tablespoons
    butter, melted
1 7-ounce can
    tuna, drained
2 cups cooked rice
1/4 cup chopped
    parsley
Salt and paprika
    to taste

Saute onion and celery in 3 tablespoons butter in skillet until tender. Stir in remaining ingredients. Cook until heated through, stirring constantly. Yield: 4 servings.

Carol Harris
Alpha Lambda, Salisbury, North Carolina

Tuna Loaf with White Sauce

1 12-ounce can
    tuna, drained
2 cups soft
    bread crumbs
1/2 cup milk
1 egg, well beaten
2 tablespoons
    minced onion
2 tablespoons
    chopped parsley
2 tablespoons
    melted margarine
2 tablespoons
    lemon juice
Pinch of cayenne
    pepper
2 tablespoons
    melted butter
2 tablespoons flour
Pepper and salt
    to taste
Paprika to taste
1 cup milk

Combine tuna with next 8 ingredients; mix well. Spoon into greased loaf pan. Bake at 350 degrees for 40 minutes. Blend butter, flour, pepper, salt and paprika in saucepan. Stir in 1 cup milk gradually. Cook until thickened, stirring constantly. Remove tuna loaf to serving plate. Pour sauce over top. Yield: 8 servings.

Wanda Malin
Xi Xi, Great Falls, Montana

Spaghetti with White Clam Sauce

2 7-ounce cans
    minced clams
2 large cloves of
    garlic, minced
1/3 cup olive oil
1/4 cup butter
2 tablespoons
    minced parsley
1 1/2 teaspoons salt
1 8-ounce package
    spaghetti, cooked
Parmesan cheese

Drain clams, reserving 3/4 cup liquid. Saute garlic in olive oil and butter in skillet for 5 minutes; remove from heat Stir in reserved clam liquid, parsley and salt. Bring to a boil. Simmer for 20 minutes. Add clams. Simmer for 5 minutes or until heated through. Toss spaghetti with Parmesan cheese. Place on serving plates. Spoon clam sauce over top. Garnish with lemon wedges. Yield: 4 servings.

Leilani Thomas
Xi Zeta Zeta, Colby, Kansas

Deep-Dish Crab Quiche

1 cup shredded
    Swiss cheese
1/2 cup Parmesan cheese
3 tablespoons flour
1 1/2 cups
    whipping cream
5 eggs
1/4 teaspoon salt
1/8 teaspoon pepper
1 5-ounce can
    crab meat
1 10-ounce package
    frozen spinach,
    thawed
1 unbaked deep-dish
    pie shell

Mix cheeses and flour in small bowl. Combine whipping cream, eggs, salt and pepper in bowl. Stir in crab meat, cheese mixture and well-drained spinach; mix well. Pour into pie shell. Place on preheated baking sheet. Bake at 425 degrees for 15 minutes. Reduce temperature to 350 degrees. Bake for 30 minutes. Let stand for 15 minutes before serving. Yield: 6 servings.

Anita R. Yates
Alpha Eta, Green River, Wyoming

Crab Cakes

1 egg, beaten
1 cup soft
    bread crumbs
3 tablespoons
    minced onion
2 tablespoons
    minced celery
3 tablespoons minced
    green pepper
3 tablespoons butter
1 pound crab meat
1 tablespoon
    chopped parsley
1 teaspoon
    Worcestershire sauce
1/4 cup (about)
    mayonnaise
1 teaspoon dry mustard
1/2 teaspoon salt
Dash of Tabasco sauce

Mix egg and bread crumbs in small bowl. Saute onion, celery and green pepper in butter in skillet. Add bread crumbs and remaining ingredients; mix well. Chill for 1 hour. Shape into small cakes. Fry in a small amount of shortening for about 5 minutes on each side; drain. Serve with Newburg sauce or lemon wedges. Yield: 8 servings.

Betty Scholl Windle
Laureate Alpha Iota, Pinellas Park, Florida

Main Dishes

Barbara's Crab Quiche

1 2/3 cup crab meat
3 ounces Swiss
   cheese, grated
5 ounces Cheddar
   cheese, grated
1/3 cup chopped
   green onions

1/2 cup mayonnaise
1 tablespoon flour
1/2 cup milk
2 eggs, beaten
1 unbaked 9-inch
   pie shell

Combine crab meat, cheeses and next 5 ingredients in bowl; mix well. Pour into pie shell. Bake at 350 degrees for 40 to 45 minutes or until set. Yield: 6 servings.

Barbara Hill
Delta Pi, Montgomery, Alabama

Seafood Newburg

1/4 cup melted butter
1/4 cup flour
1/2 teaspoon salt
1/4 teaspoon pepper

2 cups milk
2 egg yolks, beaten
2 cups chopped lobster
1 tablespoon Sherry

Blend butter, flour and seasonings in saucepan. Cook over low heat until smooth and bubbly, stirring constantly; remove from heat. Stir in milk gradually. Cook until thickened, stirring constantly. Stir a small amount of hot sauce into egg yolks; stir egg yolks into hot sauce. Fold in lobster and Sherry. Serve in pastry cups or on toast or noodles. Yield: 4-6 servings.
Note: May substitute shrimp or crab for lobster and lemon juice for Sherry.

Laraine Hopper
Nu Gamma, Crescent City, California

Shrimp Bourguignon

8 small mushrooms
4 slices bacon, chopped
1/4 cup butter
1 pound shrimp, cleaned
1 cup canned small
   white onions, drained
1/2 teaspoon salt

2 tablespoons
   chopped parsley
1/8 teaspoon pepper
2 cups Burgundy
1 tablespoon butter,
   softened
2 teaspoons flour

Remove and slice mushroom stems. Cook bacon in 1/4 cup butter in skillet until brown. Remove bacon; add shrimp. Saute until lightly browned; remove shirmp. Add onions and mushrooms and stems. Saute until browned. Add bacon, salt, parsley, pepper and Burgundy. Simmer for 15 minutes. Blend 1 tablespoon butter with flour; stir into skillet. Add shrimp. Simmer for 5 minutes. Serve over hot noodles. Yield: 4 servings.

Photograph for this recipe on page 133.

Shrimp in Beer

1 12-ounce can beer
1 small onion, chopped
Juice of 1/4 lemon
1/2 teaspoon
   Worcestershire sauce
1/2 teaspoon oregano

1/4 cup chopped
   celery leaves
1 bay leaf
1 1/2 teaspoons salt
1 pound unpeeled shrimp

Combine all ingredients except shrimp in saucepan; mix well. Add shrimp. Bring to a boil; reduce heat. Simmer for 5 to 10 minutes or until shrimp are cooked through, turning once. Serve shrimp with melted butter. Yield: 4 servings.

Teri Fleming
Delta Iota Epsilon, Santa Maria, California

Shrimp over Rice

1 can cream of
   mushroom soup
1/2 cup milk
1 cup grated
   Cheddar cheese

1 pound cleaned shrimp
1 cup sliced mushrooms
Pepper to taste
2 cups hot cooked rice

Combine soup, milk and cheese in saucepan. Cook until cheese melts, stirring frequently. Add shrimp, mushrooms and pepper. Cook over medium heat for 5 minutes or until heated through. Serve over hot rice. Yield: 4 servings.

Carol Spadafora
Preceptor Xi, Virginia Beach, Virginia

Shrimp Scampi

1 tablespoon
   melted butter
1 tablespoon olive oil
2 teaspoons
   lemon juice
2 tablespoons
   minced parsley

2 green onions,
   minced
1 large clove of
   garlic, minced
1/2 teaspoon salt
1 1/4 pounds large
   peeled shrimp

Combine all ingredients except shrimp in broiler pan; mix well. Add shrimp, turning to coat well. Arrange in single layer in pan. Broil for 5 to 8 minutes or until pink and curled, turning once. Place shrimp in serving dish. Spoon pan drippings over top. Garnish with lemon wedges. Yield: 4 servings.

Marilyn Borras
Xi Epsilon Alpha, Stafford, Virginia

Main Dishes

Ham Chowder, recipe on page 140.

Karen's Ground Beef Soup

2 pounds ground beef
4 bay leaves
10 bouillon cubes
3 large onions, chopped
1/2 cup rice
1/4 cup barley
2 16-ounce cans
   mixed vegetables
4 cups canned
   tomatoes

Brown ground beef in skillet. Add bay leaves, bouillon cubes and 12 cups water. Bring to a boil; remove bay leaves. Combine with remaining ingredients in Crock·Pot. Cook for 6 to 8 hours. Yield: 6 servings.

Karen L. Larson
Alpha Eta, Williamsport, Pennsylvania

Homemade Vegetable Soup

3 pounds ground beef
1 48-ounce can
   tomato juice
1 envelope dry onion
   soup mix
1 20-ounce package
   frozen vegetable
   soup mix
1 small head cabbage,
   shredded (opt.)
1 cup barley (opt.)
1 tablespoon
   sugar (opt.)
Salt and pepper
   to taste

Brown ground beef in heavy stockpot; drain. Add remaining ingredients. Cook for 15 to 30 minutes or until tender. Freezes well. Yield: 4 quarts.

Mary Louise Graham
Xi Zeta Lambda, Titusville, Florida

Joyce's Cheese Soup

1 pound ground beef
3 medium potatoes,
   peeled, cubed
3 carrots, sliced
1 medium onion, chopped
3 stalks celery, sliced
Several sprigs of
   parsley (opt.)
1 16-ounce can whole
   kernel corn, drained
1/2 teaspoon
   lemon pepper
6 drops of
   Tabasco sauce
1 16-ounce jar
   Cheez Whiz

Brown ground beef in skillet, stirring until crumbly; drain. Combine all vegetables except corn in saucepan; add enough water or chicken broth to cover. Cook until tender. Add ground beef and remaining ingredients; mix well. Simmer for 10 minutes, stirring frequently. Yield: 6 servings.

Lavedia J. Huggins
Chi Theta, Henderson, Texas

Main Dishes

Taco Beef Soup

1/2 pound ground beef
1/4 cup chopped onion
1 16-ounce can
  stewed tomatoes
1 8-ounce can
  kidney beans
1 8-ounce can
  tomato sauce
2 tablespoons taco
  seasoning mix
1 small avocado,
  chopped
Cheese, shredded
Corn chips
Sour cream

Brown ground beef with onion in skillet, stirring until crumbly; drain. Add tomatoes, beans, tomato sauce, seasoning mix and 1 1/2 cups water. Simmer, covered, for 15 minutes. Serve with bowls of avocado, cheese, corn chips and sour cream for garnishing individual servings to taste. Yield: 6 servings.

Joann Kikel
Xi Gamma Epsilon, Corvallis, Oregon

Mrs. Bowman's Chicken-Corn-Noodle Soup

1 can cream of
  chicken soup
1/2 cup noodles
1/2 cup frozen corn

Blend soup and 2 soup cans water in saucepan. Bring to a boil over medium heat. Add noodles and corn. Cook until noodles are tender. Yield: 4 servings.

Kandee Graham
Preceptor Beta Kappa, Hershey, Pennsylvania

Clam Chowder

1 can cream of
  potato soup
1 can cream of
  onion soup
1 soup can milk
1 10-ounce can
  minced clams

Blend soups and milk in saucepan. Add clams and juice. Heat to serving temperature, stirring frequently. Serve with crusty bread. Yield: 4-6 servings.

Rose Stafford
Preceptor Gamma, Medford, Massachusetts

Cod Chowder

3 pounds salt pork,
  chopped
3 potatoes, peeled,
  sliced
2 large onions,
  chopped
2 pounds fresh cod
  fillets, cubed
Salt and pepper
  to taste
1 cup evaporated milk

Brown salt pork in skillet. Add potatoes. Cook until brown. Add onions. Cook for 2 minutes, stirring constantly. Add 3 cups water. Arrange cod over top; add seasonings. Simmer for 15 minutes. Add milk just before serving. Yield: 6 servings.

Beverley Lundrigan
Beta, Corner Brook, Newfoundland, Canada

Maine-ly Fish Chowder

1 onion, chopped
1 tablespoon margarine
2 or 3 potatoes,
  chopped
1 16-ounce can
  cream-style corn
1 16-ounce can whole
  kernel corn
1 7-ounce can shrimp
1 can cream of
  shrimp soup
1/2 green pepper,
  chopped
1 large can
  evaporated milk
Salt, pepper and
  Worcestershire
  sauce to taste

Saute onion in margarine in skillet until tender. Add potatoes and enough water to just cover. Cook until tender. Combine potato mixture and remaining ingredients in Crock·Pot. Cook on Low for 4 to 5 hours. Yield: 6-8 servings.

Marilyn Kimball
Beta Alpha, Bridgton, Maine

Elizabeth's Ham Chowder

4 large carrots,
  chopped
4 stalks celery,
  chopped
4 large potatoes,
  peeled, chopped
1 small onion, chopped
2 tablespoons butter
2 to 3 cups
  chopped ham
2 1/2 cups milk
Salt and pepper
  to taste
3/4 to 1 cup instant
  potato flakes

Cook vegetables in water to cover in large saucepan for 20 minutes or until tender. Add remaining ingredients except potato flakes. Simmer for 10 to 20 minutes. Add enough potato flakes to make of desired consistency; mix well. Yield: 6 servings.

Elizabeth Phillips
Gamma Omega, McCall, Idaho

Main Dishes

Ham Chowder

2 1/2 cups chopped
    cooked ham
1 cup chopped onion
2 cups sliced potatoes
2/3 cup sliced carrots

1 tablespoon butter
1 envelope buttermilk
    farm-style salad
    dressing mix
2 cups milk

Saute ham, onion, potatoes and carrots in butter in large skillet for 6 minutes or until vegetables are tender. Add 2 cups water. Simmer, covered, for 15 minutes. Combine salad dressing mix and milk in bowl; mix well. Stir into ham and vegetables. Simmer, covered, for 5 minutes. Ladle into soup bowls. Garnish with chopped parsley. Yield: 6 servings.

Photograph for this recipe on page 138.

Nine-Bean Soup

1 pound each dried red
    kidney beans, navy
    beans, split peas,
    black-eyed peas,
    pinto beans, Great
    Northern beans, black
    beans, barley pearls
    and lentils
2 cups chopped ham

1 large onion, chopped
3 cloves of garlic,
    thinly sliced
1 16-ounce can
    tomatoes, mashed
1 can Ro-Tel
Salt and pepper
    to taste

Combine all dried ingredients in large container; mix well. Remove 2 cups mixture. Store remaining mixture in airtight container for future use. Soak 2 cups beans in water to cover overnight. Drain and rinse. Combine beans, 8 cups water, ham, onion and garlic in stockpot. Cook for 1 1/2 hours or until tender. Add tomatoes and Ro-Tel. Simmer for 30 minutes. Season to taste.

Mary Delle Hudson
Alpha Sigma, Mobile, Alabama

Kielbasa Soup

1 pound kielbasa,
    sliced 1/2-inch thick
2 cups sliced
    frozen carrots
1/4 teaspoon
    caraway seed

2 cups cream of
    celery soup
1/2 head cabbage,
    finely shredded

Brown kielbasa in heavy saucepan. Add remaining ingredients and 2 soup cans water; mix well. Simmer for 10 minutes or until cabbage is tender. Yield: 4-6 servings.

Mary Gamble
Xi Beta Alpha, Huntsville, Alabama

Portuguese Soup

2 pounds smoked
    sausage, sliced
1 onion, chopped
3 cloves of garlic,
    chopped
3 tablespoons margarine
1 cup catsup

1 16-ounce can
    pinto beans
6 small potatoes,
    chopped
1/2 head cabbage,
    grated
2 cans consomme

Brown sausage in skillet. Saute onion and garlic in margarine in skillet. Combine with remaining ingredients and 2 consomme cans water in Crock-Pot on Low until potatoes are tender. Yield: 6 servings.

Doris Beavers
Preceptor Gamma Mu, Lubbock, Texas

Beer Stew

5 pounds stew beef
22 ounces beer
2 packages dry onion
    soup mix

1 bay leaf
1 clove of garlic,
    minced

Brown stew beef in Dutch oven. Add remaining ingredients; mix well. Bake at 250 degrees for 8 hours. Do not peek. Serve with hot cooked wide noodles. Yield: 6 servings.

Robin Bull
Gamma Omega, McCall, Idaho

Sweet and Sour Beef Stew

1 pound stew beef
1 onion, chopped
2 carrots
1/4 pound mushrooms,
    sliced
1 8-ounce can
    tomato sauce

1/4 cup vinegar
1/4 cup packed
    brown sugar
1 tablespoon
    Worcestershire sauce
1 tablespoon cornstarch

Brown stew beef in skillet. Add remaining ingredients except cornstarch. Simmer, covered, until beef is tender. Add cornstarch dissolved in 1/4 cup water. Cook until thickened, stirring constantly. Serve over steamed rice.

Bev Delucry
Delta Kappa, Mississauga, Ontario, Canada

Main Dishes

Beef for Crock•Pot

2 pounds stew beef
1 envelope dry onion
   soup mix
1 can cream of
   mushroom soup
1/2 cup red wine
1 can sliced water
   chestnuts, drained
1 4-ounce jar
   mushroom pieces,
   drained

Combine all ingredients in Crock•Pot; mix well. Cook on Low for 8 to 12 hours or until beef is tender. Serve over rice or noodles. Yield: 4 servings.

Sandra Stokes
Xi Alpha, Louisville, Kentucky

Easy Beef Stew

2 pounds stew beef
2 large packages
   stew-cut frozen
   mixed vegetables
4 cups tomato juice
1 28-ounce can
   tomatoes
3 tablespoons tapioca
1 teaspoon salt
1/2 teaspoon pepper

Combine all ingredients and 2 cups water in 5-quart baking pan. Bake, covered, at 300 degrees for 4 hours.

Martha Creed
Preceptor Laureate Eta, Cairo, Missouri

Tummy Beef

2 pounds stew beef
1 can cream of
   mushroom soup
1 can onion soup
1 can cream of
   chicken soup
1 4-ounce can
   mushroom pieces

Combine all ingredients and 1/2 soup can water in casserole. Bake, covered, at 325 degrees for 3 1/2 hours or until tender. Serve over noodles, rice or mashed potatoes. Yield: 6 servings.
Note: May cook in Crock•Pot on High for 5 hours.

Judy Smallstey
Preceptor Beta Zeta, Mansfield, Ohio

Chili

1 1/2 pounds
   ground beef
1 large onion, chopped
1/2 green pepper,
   chopped
1 16-ounce can
   tomatoes
1 8-ounce can
   tomato sauce
Chili powder and salt
   to taste
1 8-ounce can pork
   and beans

Brown ground beef with onion and green pepper in large skillet. Add tomatoes, tomato sauce and seasonings. Simmer for several minutes. Add beans. Heat to serving temperature. Serve with corn bread. Yield: 6 servings.

Theresa A. Wise
Beta, Abqaiq, Saudi Arabia

Quick Stew

1 pound ground
   chuck
1 small onion,
   chopped
1 can chunky
   vegetable soup
1/2 teaspoon
   garlic salt

Brown ground chuck and onion in 1 1/2-quart saucepan, stirring frequently; drain. Add soup and garlic salt; mix well. Heat to serving temperature. Yield: 4 servings.

Patricia Paynter
Laureate Alpha Gamma, Miami, Florida

Schwalbe Stew

1 pound ground beef
2 medium potatoes,
   cubed
1 medium onion,
   chopped
1 20-ounce can
   tomatoes
Salt and pepper
   to taste

Brown ground beef in skillet, stirring until crumbly; drain. Brown potatoes in a small amount of oil in skillet. Combine all ingredients in large saucepan. Add enough water to cover; mix well. Cook, covered, over low heat until potatoes are tender. Serve with salad and corn bread or biscuits.

Minta Schwalbe Ross
Alpha Mu Zeta, Del Rio, Texas

Corned Beef-Vegetable Stew

1 46-ounce can
   tomato juice
1 16-ounce can
   English peas
1 16-ounce can
   cream-style corn
1 12-ounce can corned
   beef, chopped
Salt and pepper
   to taste
1/2 to 1 cup
   elbow macaroni

Combine first 5 ingredients and 1 cup water in saucepan. Simmer for 20 minutes. Add macaroni. Simmer for 8 minutes or until macaroni is tender, stirring occasionally. Yield: 8-10 servings.

Jane Koehn
Laureate Alpha Zeta, Jacksonville, Florida

Sauces

Vowel's Hot Sauce

2 16-ounce cans
   tomatoes
1/4 onion, chopped
Jalapeno peppers
   to taste
2 tablespoons crushed
   red pepper
Dash of cayenne
   pepper

Combine all ingredients in blender container. Process at high speed for several seconds. Use as taco sauce, dip or topping as desired.

Linda Vowel
Gamma Gamma, Blackwell, Oklahoma

Fruit Sauce for Ham

1 16-ounce can
   pineapple chunks,
   drained
1 16-ounce can pears,
   drained
1 16-ounce can
   peaches, drained
1 22-ounce can cherry
   pie filling

Combine all ingredients in bowl; mix well. Pour into baking dish. Bake at 300 degrees until bubbly. Serve with baked ham, ham loaf or ham balls.

Garlene Knight
Preceptor Beta Epsilon, Cedar Rapids, Iowa

Barbecue Sauce

1 26-ounce bottle of
   barbecue sauce
1 18-ounce bottle
   of catsup
1 6-ounce bottle of
   A-1 sauce
1 6-ounce bottle of
   Heinz 57 sauce
4 teaspoons
   Worcestershire sauce
1 tablespoon vinegar
1 tablespoon
   lemon juice
Tabasco sauce to taste
1 tablespoon mustard
2 teaspoons liquid
   smoke
1/2 cup packed
   brown sugar
1 small onion, chopped
1 teaspoon garlic
   powder

Combine all ingredients in saucepan; mix well. Cook for 10 minutes, stirring frequently. Store in covered container in refrigerator. Use as needed.

Jo Ann J. Kresky
Preceptor Chi, Lansing, Michigan

Cranberry-Burgundy Sauce

1 16-ounce can
   cranberry sauce
1 cup packed
   brown sugar
1/2 cup Burgundy
2 teaspoons
   prepared mustard

Combine all ingredients in saucepan. Simmer until brown sugar is dissolved, stirring constantly. Baste ham or chicken while cooking. Pass remaining sauce.

Marjorie K. Lessman
Xi Alpha Kappa, Dalton, Nebraska

No-Cook Pizza Sauce

1 29-ounce can
   tomato puree
1 15-ounce can
   tomato sauce
3/4 cup oil
2 tablespoons
   grated cheese
1 tablespoon sugar
1 tablespoon parsley
   flakes
1 tablespoon oregano
1 teaspoon garlic salt
1 teaspoon salt
1/2 teaspoon pepper

Combine all ingredients in 1-quart jar. Shake to mix well. Store in refrigerator for 1 month or less. Use as desired. Yield: 1 1/2 quarts.

Darlene Borger
Sigma Iota, Lake Jackson, Texas

Microwave Magic

CocoRibe Fruit Bake, Made-in-Minutes Pork Chops, recipes on pages 148 and 153.

Microwave Magic

Marinated Chicken Wings

1/4 cup Dijon mustard
3 tablespoons honey
2 tablespoons dry
white wine
1/2 teaspoon salt
1/4 teaspoon
browning sauce (opt.)

1 clove of garlic,
minced
12 chicken wings,
cut apart
2 cups herb-seasoned
stuffing mix, crushed

Combine first 6 ingredients in bowl; mix well. Add chicken. Marinate, tightly covered, for 2 hours to overnight. Drain chicken, reserving marinade; dip chicken in stuffing mix to coat. Arrange half the chicken around edge of 12-inch plate. Microwave on High for 8 minutes, turning plate once. Repeat with remaining chicken. Blend 2 tablespoons water with reserved marinade. Cover with SARAN WRAP™, turning back edge to vent. Microwave on High for 3 minutes. Serve with chicken.

Photograph for this recipe on page 2.

Wrapped Chicken Livers

1/2 cup Sherry
1 1/2 teaspoons
dry mustard
1/4 teaspoon hot
pepper sauce

1/2 teaspoon salt
10 chicken livers,
cut into halves
10 slices bacon, halved

Combine first 4 ingredients in bowl; mix well. Add chicken livers. Cover tightly with SARAN WRAP™. Marinate for 2 to 3 hours, stirring occasionally. Drain. Microwave bacon between double paper towels on High for 2 minutes. Wrap each liver with 1 piece of bacon; secure with toothpick. Arrange half the appetizers around edge of plate. Microwave on High for 3 minutes. Repeat with remaining appetizers.

Photograph for this recipe on page 2.

Crab Supremes

1 7-ounce can
crab meat
1/2 cup minced celery
4 teaspoons sweet
pickle relish

2 green onions, sliced
2 teaspoons prepared
mustard
1/2 cup mayonnaise
16 toast rounds

Combine crab meat with next 5 ingredients in bowl; mix well. Spread mixture on toast rounds. Place 8 at a time on paper towel-lined glass plate. Microwave, loosely covered, on Medium-High for 30 seconds or until hot. Yield: 16 servings.

Kate Williams
Xi Epsilon Sigma, Oscoda, Michigan

Paul's Favorite Bean Dip

1 15-ounce can
refried beans
3 to 4 tablespoons
sour cream

2 tablespoons chopped
green chilies
1 1/2 cups shredded
Cheddar cheese

Combine beans, sour cream and chilies in 1-quart glass dish. Add half the cheese; mix well. Microwave on Medium-High for 4 minutes or until bubbly. Sprinkle remaining cheese on top. Microwave for 1 minute or until cheese melts. Serve with nacho-flavored tortilla chips.

Gail E. Frics
Preceptor Upsilon, Omaha, Nebraska

Mary's Mock Oyster Dip

1/4 cup margarine
1 small onion, minced
1 4-ounce can
chopped mushrooms,
drained
1 can cream of
mushroom soup

8 ounces Velveeta
cheese, chopped
1 10-ounce
package frozen
chopped broccoli,
cooked

Place margarine in 2-quart glass bowl. Microwave on High for 1 minute or until melted. Add onion. Microwave for 1 1/2 to 2 minutes or until tender. Stir in mushrooms and soup; mix well. Microwave for 2 minutes. Add cheese. Microwave for 2 minutes longer or until cheese melts; mix well. Stir in broccoli. Place in chafing dish. Serve with tortilla chips.

Lorraine Brooks
Gamma Kappa, Cocoa, Florida

Shrimp Dip

1 can cream of
shrimp soup
1 can cream of
mushroom soup
2 6-ounce rolls
garlic cheese, sliced

2 6-ounce cans small
shrimp, drained
1 4-ounce jar
chopped mushrooms,
drained

Combine soups in glass bowl; blend well. Microwave on High for 2 to 3 minutes or until heated through, stirring several times. Add cheese. Microwave on Medium-High for 3 to 6 minutes or until cheese melts, stirring frequently. Stir in shrimp and mushrooms. Place in chafing dish. Serve with tortilla chips.

Mary Eve Summers
Xi Beta Rho, Norman, Oklahoma

Microwave Magic

Date Appetizers

12 pitted
    dates

4 slices bacon,
    cut into thirds

Wrap each date with 1/3 slice bacon; secure with toothpick. Arrange on glass plate. Microwave on High for 3 minutes or until bacon is crisp. Serve warm.

Juanita Carlsen
Laureate Xi, North Bend, Oregon

Marvelous Mushrooms

1 pound mushrooms
2 slices French
    bread, crumbled
1 hard-boiled egg,
    chopped

1 cup grated Monterey
    Jack cheese
1 large clove of garlic
1/2 teaspoon Tabasco
    sauce

Clean and stem mushrooms; discard stems and arrange caps on glass plate. Combine crumbs and remaining ingredients in blender container. Process until smooth. Spoon into mushroom caps. Place on glass plate. Microwave, covered, on High for 5 to 6 minutes, turning plate once. Let stand for 2 minutes before serving. Yield: 6-8 servings.

Cyndy Talmant
Xi Alpha Mu, Sparks, Nevada

Mexicali Nachos

1 8-ounce package
    cream cheese,
    softened
1 16-ounce can chili
    without beans
1 4-ounce can
    chopped green chilies

1 small green
    pepper, chopped
1 small onion,
    minced
1 cup shredded
    Cheddar cheese

Spread cream cheese in 8 x 8-inch glass dish. Layer remaining ingredients in order listed on top. Microwave on High for 5 minutes or until cheese melts. Serve warm with tortilla chips.

Luan Montag
Iota Phi, West Bend, Iowa

Mini Pizzas

4 English muffins
1 8-ounce can
    tomato sauce
1/2 teaspoon oregano
1 cup shredded
    mozzarella cheese

Mushrooms, olives,
    chopped green pepper,
    chopped onion,
    browned ground beef
    or Italian sausage,
    pepperoni (opt.)

Split muffins and toast. Spread with mixture of tomato sauce and oregano. Sprinkle with mozzarella cheese. Top with 1 or more remaining ingredients. Place on paper plate. Microwave 4 at a time on High for 1 minute or until cheese melts. Yield: 8 servings.

Lillian Hibbard
Xi Zeta Theta, Rural Waverly, Missouri

Shrimp and Cheese Canapes

1/4 pound frozen shrimp
1 cup shredded
    Swiss cheese
1/2 cup fresh
    bread crumbs
1/3 cup mayonnaise

1 teaspoon
    lemon juice
1/4 teaspoon salt
1/8 teaspoon thyme
20 slices party
    rye bread

Microwave 1/2 cup water in 2-cup glass measure on High until boiling. Add shrimp. Cover with SARAN WRAP™, turning back edge to vent. Microwave for 1 1/2 minutes. Let stand for 3 minutes. Drain and chop. Combine shrimp, cheese and next 5 ingredients in bowl; mix well. Spoon onto bread slices. Microwave 10 at a time on plate on Medium-High for 1 minute or until heated through, turning dish once.

Photograph for this recipe on page 2.

Spanish Rolls

1 cup chopped
    green chilies
6 green onions, chopped
1 cup chopped
    ripe olives
1/4 cup olive oil
1/2 8-ounce can
    tomato sauce
1 tablespoon hot
    sauce (opt.)

1 1/2 pounds Velveeta
    cheese, cubed,
    softened
1 pound ground
    round, crumbled
1 clove of garlic,
    chopped
36 small sourdough
    French rolls

Combine first 7 ingredients in bowl; mix well. Let stand for several minutes. Place beef and garlic in 2-quart glass dish. Microwave on High for 4 to 6 minutes or until beef is no longer pink; drain. Add to cheese mixture; mix well. Slice one end from each roll; scoop out centers. Stuff with beef mixture; replace ends. Wrap each in waxed paper. Microwave on Medium until heated through. Yield: 3 dozen.

Nancy Ingman
Preceptor Iota Kappa, Corona del Mar, California

Boston Brown Bread

1 cup buttermilk
1/2 cup molasses
1/2 cup raisins
1/2 teaspoon
baking powder
1/2 teaspoon soda

1/2 teaspoon salt
1/2 cup whole
wheat flour
1/4 cup flour
1/2 cup yellow
cornmeal

Combine buttermilk and molasses in bowl; mix well. Add raisins, baking powder, soda and salt; mix well. Add flour and cornmeal. Stir until moistened. Pour into well-greased 4-cup glass measure. Cover loosely with plastic wrap; secure with rubber band. Microwave on Medium for 8 1/2 to 9 1/2 minutes or just until set. Let stand, uncovered, for 10 minutes. Remove from measure. Let stand for 5 minutes before slicing.

Jane E. Cooley
Xi Beta Mu, Lynnwood, Washington

Desserts

Apple Brown Betty

6 medium apples,
peeled, sliced
1/4 cup honey
2 tablespoons
lemon juice
1/4 teaspoon cinnamon

1 cup oats
1/4 cup packed
brown sugar
1/2 teaspoon cinnamon
2 tablespoons butter

Arrange apples in lightly greased 1 1/2-quart glass baking dish. Drizzle with mixture of honey, lemon juice and 1/4 teaspoon cinnamon. Microwave, covered, on High for 5 minutes. Turn apples over. Combine remaining ingredients in bowl; mix well. Sprinkle over apples. Microwave, covered, on High for 5 minutes. Serve with ice cream. Yield: 8 servings.

Colleen Jensen
Beta Alpha, Kelvington, Saskatchewan, Canada

Apple Crisp

4 cups sliced apples
1/2 cup oats
1/4 cup flour
1/4 cup packed
brown sugar

1/4 cup butter
1 teaspoon lemon juice
1/2 teaspoon cinnamon
1/8 teaspoon nutmeg

Place apples in 8 x 8-inch glass baking dish. Combine remaining ingredients in bowl; mix well. Sprinkle over apples. Microwave, covered, on High for 8 to 10 minuttes or until apples are tender. Serve warm or cool. Yield: 4 servings.

Rosalie Goff
Xi Alpha Zeta, Glenrock Wyoming

Cherry-Chocolate Bundt Cake

1 2-layer package
chocolate pudding-
recipe cake mix
1 20-ounce can
cherry pie filling

3 eggs, beaten
1 teaspoon
almond extract
1 16-ounce can
chocolate frosting

Combine first 4 ingredients in mixer bowl; beat until well blended. Pour into greased microwave bundt pan. Microwave on High for 12 to 13 minutes or until cake tests done. Let stand, covered, for 20 to 30 minutes. Invert on serving plate. Remove top from frosting can. Microwave on High for 1 minute. Drizzle over cake.

Elizabeth S. Fields
Preceptor Omega, Staunton, Virginia

Orange Blossom Cake

1/4 cup melted butter
3/4 cup orange
marmalade
1/2 cup shredded
coconut

1 2-layer
package yellow
cake mix
3 eggs

Grease microwave bundt pan; sprinkle with sugar. Combine butter, marmalade and coconut in glass measure. Spread evenly in prepared pan. Beat cake mix, eggs and 1 cup water at high speed for 2 minutes. Pour into prepared pan. Microwave on Medium for 9 to 11 minutes; turn pan. Microwave on High for 4 to 5 1/2 minutes or until cake tests done. Cool upright in pan for 10 minutes. Invert on wire rack to cool.

Pat Koziar
Xi Kappa Gamma, Dayton, Ohio

Rocky Road Fudge

1 12-ounce package
chocolate chips
1 cup peanut butter

1 stick butter
3 cups miniature
marshmallows

Combine chocolate chips, peanut butter and butter in 9 x 9-inch glass dish. Microwave on High for 1 to 2 minutes or until melted; mix well. Stir in marshmallows; cool. Cut into squares.

Jeanne Flude
Xi Sigma, Regina, Saskatchewan, Canada

Microwave Magic

Choc-Co-Peanut Fudge

1 6-ounce package
   chocolate chips
1 6-ounce package
   butterscotch chips
1/2 cup chunky
   peanut butter

1 14-ounce can
   sweetened condensed
   milk
1/2 cup flaked coconut
1/2 cup chopped walnuts

Combine chocolate chips and butterscotch chips in glass bowl. Microwave on Medium-High for 2 1/2 minutes or until melted; mix well. Blend in peanut butter and condensed milk. Microwave on Medium-High for 1 1/2 minutes. Stir in coconut and walnuts. Pour into buttered 8 x 12-inch dish. Cool before cutting.

Barbara Cavallo
Xi Beta Alpha, Neptune New Jersey

Fabulous Fudge

1 6-ounce package
   chocolate chips
1 6-ounce package
   butterscotch
   chips

1 can chocolate
   frosting
1/2 cup chopped nuts
1 1/2 cups miniature
   marshmallows

Combine chocolate chips and butterscotch chips in glass bowl. Microwave on High for 1 to 2 minutes or until melted; mix well. Blend in frosting. Fold in nuts and marshmallows. Pour into greased 9 x 9-inch dish. Chill for 1 hour before cutting.

Mary Lou Szymanski
Xi Pi Psi, Eagle Lake, Texas

Pamela's Fudge

1/2 cup cocoa
1 16-ounce package
   confectioners' sugar
1/4 cup milk

1 stick butter
1 teaspoon
   vanilla extract
1/2 cup chopped nuts

Blend cocoa and confectioners' sugar in glass bowl. Pour milk over top; dot with butter. Do not stir. Microwave on High for 2 minutes. Add vanilla and nuts; mix well. Pour into buttered 8 x 8-inch dish. Chill for 1 hour before cutting. Yield: 4-5 dozen.

Pamela Maheras
Alpha Pi, Maple Grove, Minnesota

Caramel Snappers

144 pecan halves
36 light caramels

1/2 cup semisweet
   chocolate chips

Arrange pecans flat side down in groups of 4 on buttered glass plate. Place 1 caramel on each pecan cluster. Microwave on High for 1 minute or until caramels soften, turning plate once. Flatten caramels with buttered spatula. Cool slightly; remove to waxed paper. Microwave chocolate chips in small glass bowl on High for 1 minute. Spread over caramels. Yield: 3 dozen.

Mary Scherbarth
Xi Alpha Theta, Fairbury, Nebraska

Chocolate Caramels

1 1/4 cups flour
1/2 teaspoon salt
1/4 cup sugar
1/2 cup butter
2/3 cup packed
   brown sugar
2 tablespoons
   corn syrup

1/2 cup margarine
3/4 cup sweetened
   condensed milk
1/2 teaspoon
   vanilla extract
4 1-ounce squares
   semisweet chocolate

Combine flour, salt, sugar and butter in bowl; mix well. Press into 8 x 8-inch glass baking dish. Microwave on High for 3 minutes. Combine next 4 ingredients in glass bowl. Microwave on High until mixture boils. Microwave for 4 to 5 minutes, stirring once. Stir in vanilla. Beat until smooth. Pour over prepared crust. Chill in refrigerator. Place chocolate in small glass dish. Microwave on Medium for 1 minute or until melted. Spread over chilled layer. Cut into 1-inch squares.

Jill Buckingham
Rho, Bedford, Nova-Scotia, Canada

Peanut Brittle

1 cup sugar
1/2 cup light
   corn syrup
1/8 teaspoon salt
1 1/2 cups roasted
   peanuts

1 tablespoon
   butter
1 teaspoon
   vanilla extract
1 teaspoon soda

Combine sugar, corn syrup and salt in 2-quart glass bowl. Microwave on High for 5 minutes. Stir in peanuts. Microwave for 5 minutes or until lightly browned, stirring after 2 and 4 minutes. Add remaining ingredients; mix until foamy. Spread 1/4 inch thick on buttered baking sheet; cool. Break into bite-sized pieces. Yield: 1 pound.

Erika Lapham
Xi Epsilon Kappa, Ligonier, Indiana

Microwave Magic

Linda's Caramel Corn

1/2 cup butter
1 cup packed
  brown sugar
1/4 cup light
  corn syrup
1/4 teaspoon salt
1/2 teaspoon soda
4 quarts popped
  popcorn

Combine butter, brown sugar, corn syrup and salt in 4-cup glass measure. Microwave on High for 2 to 3 minutes or until mixture boils. Microwave for 2 minutes longer. Stir in soda. Pour over popcorn in microwave popcorn popping bag; shake to coat well. Microwave on High for 3 1/2 minutes, shaking after 1 1/2 minutes, 2 1/2 minutes and 3 1/4 minutes. Spread on greased baking sheets. Break into pieces when cool. Store in airtight container.

Linda Shively
Zeta Zeta, Lafayette, Indiana

Pralines

1 1/2 cups packed
  brown sugar
2/3 cup half and half
2 tablespoons margarine
1/8 teaspoon salt
2 cups chopped pecans

Combine all ingredients in 2-quart glass dish; mix well. Microwave on High for 18 minutes, stirring after 6 minutes, 11 minutes and 15 minutes. Stir well. Let stand for 1 minute. Beat for 3 to 5 minutes or until thickened. Drop by spoonfuls onto waxed paper; cool. Yield: 3-4 dozen.

Pat Howell
Xi Pi Epsilon, Big Spring, Texas

Easy Fruit Cobbler

1 20-ounce can
   pie filling
1 1-layer package
   yellow cake mix
1 teaspoon cinnamon
1/2 cup chopped walnuts
1/4 cup melted butter

Pour pie filling into 9 x 9-inch glass baking dish. Combine remaining ingredients in bowl; mix well. Spread over pie filling. Microwave, covered, on High for 9 to 10 minutes. Microwave, uncovered, for 3 to 4 minutes longer. Yield: 6 servings.

Dianne Wilson
Zeta Epsilon, Orangeville, Ontario, Canada

CocoRibe Fruit Bake

3 large pears,
  peeled, sliced
1/2 cup chopped
  dried apricots
1/2 cup CocoRibe
  coconut rum
3 tablespoons
  brown sugar
2 tablespoons flour
1/4 teaspoon cinnamon
2 tablespoons butter
2 cups chopped pecans
1/2 cup whipping cream
1 tablespoon CocoRibe
  coconut rum

Combine pears, apricots and 1/2 cup coconut rum in 9-inch glass pie plate. Let stand for 30 minutes, stirring occasionally. Combine brown sugar, flour and cinnamon in small bowl; cut in butter until crumbly. Stir in pecans. Sprinkle over fruit. Microwave on High for 3 minutes. Whip cream with 1 tablespoon coconut rum. Serve fruit warm or cold with whipped cream. Yield: 4-6 servings.

Photograph for this recipe on page 143.

Almond Bark Cookies

2 pounds almond bark
1 cup chunky
  peanut butter
2 cups dry-roasted
  peanuts
2 cups miniature
  marshmallows
3 cups crisp
  rice cereal

Place almond bark in glass bowl. Microwave on Medium-Low for 4 to 8 minutes or until melted. Stir in remaining ingredients; mix well. Drop by teaspoonfuls onto waxed paper; cool. Yield: 5-6 dozen.

Jeannette Brown
Xi Alpha Beta, Council Bluffs, Iowa

Brownies

2 eggs
1 cup sugar
1/2 teaspoon salt
1 teaspoon
  vanilla extract
1/2 cup melted butter
3/4 cup flour
1/2 cup cocoa
1 cup chopped nuts

Combine first 4 ingredients in mixer bowl. Beat at medium speed for 1 minute. Beat in butter until well blended. Mix in flour and cocoa at low speed. Stir in nuts. Spoon into greased 8 x 8-inch glass baking dish. Microwave on High for 6 to 7 minutes or until Brownies test done, turning dish every 2 minutes. Cool. Cut into squares. Yield: 2 dozen.

Fern Ryan
Rawlins, Wyoming

Microwave Magic

Strawberry Pie

1 cup sugar
3 tablespoons cornstarch
2 tablespoons light corn syrup
Pinch of salt
3 tablespoons strawberry gelatin
Several drops of red food coloring
1 quart strawberries
1 baked pie shell

Combine first 4 ingredients and 1 cup water in glass bowl. Microwave on High for 4 1/2 minutes or until clear and thickened. Stir in gelatin and food coloring. Fold in strawberries. Pour into pie shell. Chill in refrigerator. Top with whipped topping. Yield: 6-8 servings.

Gloria Sumpter
Xi Iota Mu, Webb City, Missouri

Strawberry-Rhubarb Souffle

4 cups sliced rhubarb
3/4 cup sugar
1 envelope unflavored gelatin
3 egg whites
1/4 cup sugar
1 pint strawberries, coarsely chopped
1 cup whipping cream, whipped

Combine rhubarb and 3/4 cup sugar in 2-quart casserole. Cover tightly with SARAN WRAP™, turning back edge to vent. Microwave on High for 8 to 10 minutes or until rhubarb is tender, stirring once. Chill, covered, in refrigerator. Soften gelatin in 1/4 cup cold water. Microwave on High for 1 minute or until gelatin is dissolved, stirring once. Cool to room temperature. Beat egg whites until soft peaks form. Add 1/4 cup sugar gradually, beating until stiff. Add gelatin gradually, beating constantly at medium speed. Mix strawberries with 1 cup chilled rhubarb mixture. Fold in egg whites and half the whipped cream gently. Spoon remaining rhubarb mixture into 4-cup souffle dish with 2-inch collar. Spoon strawberry mixture over top; smooth top. Chill for 4 hours or until set. Spoon remaining whipped cream on top. Garnish with whole strawberries. Spoon fluffy souffle onto dessert plates; top with rhubarb sauce from bottom of souffle dish.

Photograph for this recipe on cover.

Yogurt Pudding

1 cup yogurt
1/2 cup sugar
2 eggs
1/4 cup flour
1 teaspoon vanilla extract
1 teaspoon almond extract

Combine all ingredients in bowl; mix well. Spoon into 4 glass custard cups. Microwave on Medium-High for 4 minutes or until set. Chill in refrigerator. Serve with mandarin oranges. Yield: 4 servings.

Jill Buckingham
Rho, Bedford, Nova Scotia, Canada

Main Dishes

Chicken and Asparagus Casserole

1 1/2 pounds chicken breasts
1 10-ounce package frozen cut asparagus
1 3-ounce package sliced almonds
2 eggs, beaten
1 16-ounce carton ricotta cheese
1 2-ounce jar chopped pimento
1 cup chopped ham
3 cups cooked rice
3/4 cup milk
1 tablespoon instant chicken bouillon
1 teaspoon dried onion flakes
1/4 teaspoon pepper
1/4 cup Parmesan cheese
1/4 teaspoon paprika

Arrange chicken skin side up in shallow glass baking dish. Microwave, loosely covered, on High for 9 to 10 minutes or until tender, turning dish once. Drain, reserving pan juices. Bone and chop chicken; set aside. Microwave asparagus in package on High for 2 to 2 1/2 minutes or until partially thawed. Combine chicken, asparagus, reserved juices, 1/2 cup almonds and next 9 ingredients in bowl; mix well. Spoon into 8 x 12-inch glass baking dish. Mix remaining almonds, Parmesan cheese and paprika in bowl. Sprinkle over casserole. Microwave on High for 11 to 13 minutes or to 150 degrees on microwave meat thermometer, turning dish twice. Yield: 8-12 servings.

Linda Todd
Xi Alpha Beta, Coldwater, Michigan

Microwave Magic

Cheesy Chicken

4 chicken breasts,
  skinned
1/4 cup melted butter

3 cups crushed
  cheese crackers

Brush chicken with butter. Coat with cracker crumbs. Arrange in shallow glass baking dish. Microwave, covered, on High for 12 to 15 minutes or until tender, turning dish once. Let stand, covered, for 2 to 3 minutes. Yield: 4 servings.

Janielle Riley
Xi Zeta Epsilon, Westfield, Indiana

Wanda's Chicken Casserole

1/2 cup chopped onion
1 cup sliced celery
2 tablespoons butter
2 cans cream of
  chicken soup
10 drops of Tabasco sauce

3 cups chopped
  cooked chicken
1/2 cup chopped
  cashews
1 cup chow mein noodles

Saute onion, celery and butter in skillet. Add soup, Tabasco sauce and chicken; mix well. Simmer for 5 minutes. Pour into 2-quart glass casserole. Sprinkle with cashews and noodles. Microwave on High for 2 minutes or until heated through. Yield: 6 servings.

Wanda Arnold
Xi Alpha Delta, Louisville, Tennessee

Chicken Cordon Bleu

8 chicken breasts,
  boned
Salt to taste
8 thin slices
  boiled ham
8 thin slices
  Swiss cheese

1/2 cup melted
  butter
1/2 cup bread
  crumbs
1/3 cup sesame
  seed
Paprika

Pound chicken breasts with meat mallet until thin. Season with salt. Place ham slice and cheese slice on each chicken breast. Roll to enclose filling; secure with toothpicks. Dip chicken in butter; coat with mixture of bread crumbs and sesame seed. Arrange in shallow glass baking dish. Drizzle with remaining butter; sprinkle with paprika. Microwave on High for 12 to 15 minutes or until tender, rearranging chicken and turning dish once. Let stand for 5 minutes. Yield: 8 servings.

Judy C. Lansford
Gamma Eta, Cleveland, Tennessee

Chicken Divan

2 10-ounce packages
  frozen broccoli
  spears, cooked
4 chicken breasts,
  cooked, chopped
1 can cream of
  chicken soup
1 to 2 tablespoons
  milk

1/2 cup sour cream
Garlic salt to taste
3 tablespoons
  margarine
1/2 cup slivered
  almonds
1 cup grated
  sharp cheese

Place broccoli in 2-quart glass baking dish. Arrange chicken over broccoli. Combine soup, milk, sour cream and garlic salt in bowl; mix well. Pour over chicken. Dot with margarine. Sprinkle with almonds and cheese. Microwave on High for 15 minutes. Yield: 4-6 servings.

Juanita Jameson
Xi Iota, Garden City, Kansas

Chicken and Yellow Rice

2 packages yellow
  Rice-A-Roni
1 10-ounce package
  frozen peas,
  thawed (opt.)

6 chicken
  breasts
3 tablespoons
  butter

Prepare Rice-A-Roni according to package directions, using 3 3/4 cups water. Stir in peas. Spoon into 2-quart glass baking dish. Arrange chicken on top. Dot with butter. Microwave on High for 25 minutes or until chicken is tender. Yield: 6 servings.

Connie Hurlebaus
Xi Zeta Phi, Orlando, Florida

Chicken Breasts with Tarragon Sauce

3/4 cup chicken stock
3/4 cup dry white wine
1 1/2 pounds chicken
  breast filets,
  skinned
3 egg yolks, beaten
2 tablespoons
  cornstarch

1 cup whipping cream
1 tablespoon tarragon
2 teaspoons salt
1/4 teaspoon
  white pepper
1/4 teaspoon
  celery salt
1 cup green peas

Combine chicken stock and wine in 2-quart glass baking dish. Microwave on High for 4 minutes or until mixture boils. Add chicken. Microwave for 2 minutes or until tender; remove chicken. Mix egg yolks, cornstarch and whipping cream in bowl. Stir 1/4 cup hot stock into egg mixture; stir egg yolk mixture into hot stock. Add seasonings. Microwave on High for 5 minutes, stirring 4 times. Fold in peas and chicken. Serve with buttered noodles. Yield: 4-6 servings.

Jane Gabel
Xi Mu Eta, Houston, Texas

Microwave Magic

Simple Chicken Potpie

2 cups chopped
    cooked chicken
1 can cream of
    chicken soup
1 10-ounce package
    frozen mixed
    vegetables, thawed

1/2 cup milk
1/8 teaspoon pepper
Dash of Worcestershire
    sauce
2 cups crumbled
    leftover stuffing

Combine first 6 ingredients in 2-quart glass baking dish; mix well. Microwave, tightly covered, on Medium-High for 8 to 10 minutes or until heated through, stirring once. Sprinkle stuffing over top. Microwave for 4 to 5 minutes longer. Let stand for 7 minutes before serving. Yield: 4 servings.
Note: May substitute seasoned croutons for stuffing.

Jane E. Cooley
Xi Beta Mu, Lynnwood, Washington

Dawn's Pasty

1 1/2 pounds round
    steak, cut into
    bite-sized pieces
5 large potatoes,
    chopped
2 large onions, chopped

Salt and pepper
    to taste
1/4 cup butter
1 10-count can
    refrigerator biscuits

Combine steak, vegetables and seasonings in shallow glass baking dish. Dot with butter. Add 1/2 cup water. Microwave, covered, on High for 12 minutes or until tender. Roll biscuits into rectangle on floured surface. Place on casserole; seal edges. Bake at 450 degrees for 6 minutes or until brown. Yield: 8 servings.

Dawn Moudy
Beta Iota, McCall, Idaho

Oriental Steak Fingers

3 pounds strip steak
1/3 cup soy sauce
1/3 cup
    Worcestershire sauce

2 tablespoons minced
    garlic
1 1/2 tablespoons
    beer

Cut steak into 1-inch strips. Arrange in 8 x 12-inch glass baking dish. Pour soy sauce over strips. Marinate for 5 minutes. Pour mixture of Worcestershire sauce, garlic and beer over strips. Marinate, covered, for 5 minutes. Microwave on Medium for 10 minutes; turn strips over. Microwave on High for 4 to 5 minutes or until tender. Yield: 4 servings.

Pamela Majoras
Omicron Pi, Vermilion, Ohio

Roast Beef Casserole

2 cups chopped
    roast beef
2 carrots, chopped
2 potatoes, chopped
1 4-ounce can
    mushrooms, drained

1 onion, chopped
1/2 cup roast beef
    drippings
1/4 cup white wine
1 tablespoon
    Worcestershire sauce

Combine all ingredients in 2-quart glass baking dish; mix well. Microwave, covered, on High for 15 minutes or until vegetables are tender, stirring after 10 minutes. Yield: 4 servings.

Dottie Cote
Preceptor Beta, Honolulu, Hawaii

Crunchy Taco Bake

1 pound ground
    beef, crumbled
2 tablespoons dried
    onion flakes
1/2 teaspoon salt
1 15-ounce can
    chili beans
1 8-ounce can
    tomato sauce

1 6-ounce can
    tomato paste
1 1/2 teaspoons
    chili powder
3 cups coarsely
    crushed corn chips
1 cup shredded
    Cheddar cheese

Combine ground beef and onion flakes in 2-quart glass baking dish. Microwave on High for 4 to 6 minutes or until beef is no longer pink, stirring once. Add next 5 ingredients; mix well. Microwave on High for 6 to 8 minutes or until heated through. Sprinkle 2 cups crushed chips in 8 x 8-inch glass dish. Layer ground beef mixture, remaining chips and cheese in dish. Microwave on High for 2 to 4 minutes or until cheese melts. Yield: 4 servings.

Erika Lapham
Xi Epsilon Kappa, Ligonier, Indiana

Hamburger Stroganoff

1 pound ground beef
1 can cream of
    mushroom soup
1 4-ounce can sliced
    mushrooms, drained
1/2 cup sliced
    green onions

1/4 cup catsup
1/2 teaspoon
    dry mustard
1/2 teaspoon salt
1 cup sour cream
2 tablespoons dry
    white wine (opt.)

Crumble ground beef into 2-quart glass baking dish. Microwave, covered, on High for 4 to 5 minutes or until no longer pink, stirring once. Add next 6 ingredients; mix well. Microwave, covered, on High for 4 to 6 minutes or until heated through, stirring once. Stir in sour cream and wine. Microwave for 1 to 2 minutes or until bubbly, stirring once. Serve over rice or noodles. Yield: 4 servings.

Jean Zeller
Laureate Theta, New Albany, Indiana

Microwave Magic

Susan's Mexican Casserole

2 pounds ground beef, crumbled	1 8-ounce can taco sauce
1 medium onion, chopped	1 can cream of mushroom soup
1 4-ounce can chopped green chilies (opt.)	1 12-count package corn tortillas
1 10-ounce can enchilada sauce	9 slices American cheese
	Parmesan cheese

Brown ground beef and onion in skillet, stirring until crumbly; drain. Add chilies, sauces and soup; mix well. Alternate tortillas, ground beef and cheese slices in greased 3-quart casserole until all ingredients are used. Top with Parmesan cheese. Microwave, covered, on High for 12 to 15 minutes or until bubbly. Let stand for 5 minutes. Yield: 4-6 servings.

Susan Jones
Zeta Omega, Leavenworth, Kansas

Kathy's Lasagna

1/2 pound ground beef, crumbled	1 egg, beaten
1 32-ounce jar spaghetti sauce	1/2 teaspoon pepper
	6 uncooked lasagna noodles
1 16-ounce carton ricotta cheese	1 pound mozzarella cheese, grated

Microwave ground beef in glass baking dish on High for 3 to 5 minutes or until no longer pink; drain. Add spaghetti sauce and 1/2 cup water; mix well. Combine ricotta cheese, egg and pepper in bowl; mix well. Spoon 1/3 of the sauce into 8 x 12-inch glass baking dish. Layer half the noodles, half the ricotta mixture and 1/3 of the mozzarella cheese over sauce. Repeat layers. Top with remaining sauce and mozzarella cheese. Microwave on High for 8 minutes. Microwave on Medium for 30 minutes. Let stand for several minutes. Yield: 8 servings.

Kathy Harris
Lambda Chi, Dayton, Ohio

Easy Lasagna Roll-Ups

1 cup cottage cheese	4 lasagna noodles, cooked
1 cup shredded mozzarella cheese	2 cups spaghetti sauce
	Parmesan cheese

Combine cottage cheese and mozzarella cheese in bowl; mix well. Place 1/2 cup mixture on each noodle. Roll to enclose filling. Place seam side down in 8 x 8-inch glass baking dish. Pour spaghetti sauce over top. Microwave on High for 5 minutes or until heated through, turning dish once. Sprinkle with Parmesan cheese. Yield: 4 servings.

Karen Perry
Pi Eta, Castalia, Ohio

Best Ever Meat Loaf

1 1/2 pounds ground beef	1/8 teaspoon dried garlic flakes (opt.)
1 8-ounce can tomato sauce	1/4 teaspoon pepper
1 egg, beaten	1/3 cup catsup
1 cup oats	2 tablespoons brown sugar
1 tablespoon dried onion flakes	3/4 teaspoon dry mustard
3/4 teaspoon salt	

Combine ground beef with next 7 ingredients in bowl; mix well. Shape into loaf; place in glass loaf pan. Microwave on High for 6 to 8 minutes or to 150 degrees on microwave meat thermometer. Mix catsup, brown sugar and dry mustard in small bowl. Pour over meat loaf. Microwave for 2 to 4 minutes or to 160 degrees. Yield: 6 servings.

Diane Neuberger
Delta Upsilon, Garner, Iowa

Macho Meat Loaf

1 1/2 pounds ground chuck	1/8 teaspoon pepper
1 envelope dry onion soup mix	1/8 teaspoon garlic salt
1 egg, beaten	1 to 2 8-ounce cans tomato sauce
1/2 cup cracker meal	1 2-ounce can sliced mushrooms, drained
1/2 teaspoon salt	

Combine ground chuck with next 6 ingredients in bowl; mix well. Place in microwave ring dish or shape into circle in glass baking dish. Microwave, loosely covered, on Medium-High for 12 to 13 minutes; drain. Top with tomato sauce and mushrooms. Microwave for 2 to 3 minutes longer. Let stand, covered, for 3 to 5 minutes. Yield: 6 servings.

Diana Allen
Preceptor Alpha Zeta, Grand Prairie, Texas

Microwave Magic

Cheesy Meat Loaf

1 pound ground sirloin
1 cup soft
   bread crumbs
1 egg, beaten
1/4 cup chopped onion

2 tablespoons
   Parmesan cheese
1 teaspoon salt
1/2 teaspoon basil
1/4 teaspoon pepper

Combine all ingredients and 1/4 cup water in bowl; mix well. Shape into meat loaf in lightly greased 1 1/2-quart glass baking dish. Microwave on High for 12 minutes, turning dish occasionally. Let stand for 2 minutes before slicing. Yield: 4 servings.

Patti Geistfeld
Delta Beta Beta, Eureka, California

Juanita's Meat Loaf

1 1/2 pounds ground
   beef
1 egg, beaten
1/2 cup bread crumbs
Salt and pepper
   to taste
1/2 cup chopped onion
3/4 cup chopped
   mushrooms

1/4 cup chopped celery
1 cup bread crumbs
3/4 teaspoon
   poultry seasoning
3 tablespoons
   margarine, melted
1 16-ounce can
   beef gravy

Combine ground beef, egg, 1/2 cup bread crumbs and salt and pepper in bowl; mix well. Pat into rectangle on foil. Combine remaining ingredients except gravy in bowl; mix well. Spread over ground beef mixture. Roll as for jelly roll from long side. Shape into circle in microwave ring dish; seal ends. Microwave on High for 6 minutes. Microwave on Medium for 8 to 15 minutes or until cooked through. Let stand for several minutes. Invert on serving plate. Pour warm gravy over top. Yield: 4-6 servings.

Juanita Carlsen
Laureate Xi, North Bend, Oregon

Clarice's Pork Chops

4 pork chops
Salt and pepper
   to taste

Flour
1 can cream of
   mushroom soup

Season pork chops with salt and pepper. Coat with flour. Brown in a small amount of oil in skillet; drain. Place in shallow glass baking dish. Add mixture of soup and 1 1/2 soup cans water. Microwave on Medium for 12 minutes or until tender, stirring once. Yield: 4 servings.

Clarice Williams
Xi Alpha Rho, Danville, Kentucky

Made-In-Minutes Pork Chops

4 1/2-inch thick
   pork chops
1 5-ounce can
   juice-pack sliced
   pineapple
1/3 cup CocoRibe
   coconut rum
1 tablespoon
   Dijon mustard

1 tablespoon soy sauce
1 clove of garlic,
   minced
1 teaspoon chopped
   fresh ginger
Browning and
   seasoning sauce
1 1/2 teaspoons
   cornstarch

Arrange pork chops in single layer in 9-inch glass pie plate. Drain pineapple, reserving juice. Combine coconut rum, 2 tablespoons reserved pineapple juice, mustard, soy sauce, garlic and ginger in bowl; mix well. Pour over chops. Let stand at room temperature for 1 hour. Remove chops from marinade; brush both sides with browning and seasoning sauce. Return to marinade; cover with plastic wrap. Microwave on High for 3 1/2 minutes. Turn chops over. Place pineapple slice on each chop. Microwave, covered, for 4 minutes longer. Remove chops and pineapple to a serving platter. Combine cornstarch and 2 tablespoons reserved pineapple juice; stir into juices in pie plate. Microwave on High for 1 1/2 minutes or until thickened, stirring once. Spoon sauce over chops. Yield: 4 servings.

Photograph for this recipe on page 143.

Kate's Sweet and Sour Pork

2 pounds lean
   boneless pork
1 16-ounce can
   pineapple chunks
4 medium carrots,
   thinly sliced
1/4 cup oil
1 medium onion, sliced
2 green peppers,
   sliced

1/4 cup cornstarch
1/2 cup soy sauce
1/2 cup packed
   brown sugar
1/4 cup wine vinegar
1 tablespoon
   Worcestershire sauce
1/4 teaspoon hot
   pepper sauce
1/2 teaspoon pepper

Cut pork into 3/4-inch cubes. Drain pineapple, reserving 1/2 cup syrup. Combine carrots and oil in 3-quart glass casserole. Microwave, covered, on High for 4 minutes. Add onion, green peppers and pork; mix well. Microwave, covered, for 5 minutes. Blend cornstarch and reserved pineapple syrup in bowl. Add remaining ingredients; mix well. Add to pork with pineapple chunks; mix well. Cook, covered, for 10 minutes or until sauce is thickened and pork is tender. Serve over rice or chow mein noodles. Yield: 8 servings.

Kate Williams
Xi Epsilon Sigma, Oscoda, Michigan

Microwave Magic

Barb Boos' Sweet and Sour Pork

1 1/2 pounds lean pork
    roast, cubed
2 tablespoons
    cornstarch
3 tablespoons soy sauce
1/4 cup white vinegar
1 20-ounce can
    pineapple chunks

1 teaspoon salt
1/4 cup packed
    brown sugar
1/4 teaspoon ginger
1 small onion,
    thinly sliced
1 medium green pepper,
    cut in strips

Coat pork with cornstarch. Combine with remaining ingredients except green pepper in 2-quart glass baking dish. Microwave, covered, on High for 25 minutes. Stir in green pepper. Microwave for 5 minutes or until pork is tender. Let stand for 5 minutes. Serve with rice. Yield: 6-8 servings.

Barb Boos
Theta Rho, New Hampton, Iowa

Beer-Cheese Soup

1/4 cup butter
1/2 cup flour
2 tablespoons dried
    onion flakes
1 cup milk

1 13-ounce can
    evaporated milk
1 16-ounce jar
    Cheez Whiz
1 12-ounce can beer

Place butter in 3-quart glass bowl. Microwave on High for 30 seconds or until melted. Stir in flour and onion flakes. Add milk and evaporated milk 1/3 at a time, mixing well after each addition. Microwave for 5 to 7 minutes or until thickened, stirring every minute. Add cheese spread. Stir until melted and smooth. Add beer; mix well. Microwave for 1 to 2 minutes to serving temperature. Yield: 6 servings.

Cheryl Shields
Eta Iota, Oklahoma City, Oklahoma

Cheese and Onion Quiche

1 unbaked 9-inch
    pie shell
4 slices bacon
1 tablespoon butter
1 small onion,
    thinly sliced
1 cup shredded
    Swiss cheese

3 eggs
1 cup light cream
1 tablespoon flour
1/4 teaspoon
    dry mustard
1/2 teaspoon salt
1/8 teaspoon white
    pepper

Prick pie shell at 1/2-inch intervals. Microwave on High for 6 minutes or until crisp. Place bacon on paper towel-lined glass plate. Microwave on High for 4 minutes or until crisp; crumble. Place butter and onion in glass bowl. Microwave on High for 4 minutes or until tender. Spread bacon, onion and cheese in pie shell. Combine remaining ingredients in 4-cup glass measure. Microwave on High for 2 minutes or until slightly thickened, stirring twice. Pour into pie shell. Microwave on High for 10 minutes or until set, turning dish once. Garnish with paprika. Let stand for 5 minutes before serving. Yield: 6 servings.

Rosalie Goff
Xi Alpha Zeta, Glenrock, Wyoming

Cheese Omelet

2 eggs
1 slice cheese,
    crumbled

2 tablespoons milk
Salt and pepper
    to taste

Beat eggs well in glass bowl. Add remaining ingredients; mix well. Microwave on High for 1 1/2 minutes, stirring and turning bowl once. Yield: 1 serving.

Lorna Davis
Laureate Pi, Grand Junction, Colorado

Baked Curried Fish

1 cup sliced celery
2 medium onions,
    thinly sliced
1 teaspoon
    curry powder

1 tablespoon butter
1/4 cup skim milk
1 1/2 to 2 pounds fish
    fillets, cut into
    serving pieces

Place celery, onions, curry powder and butter in 7 x 12-inch glass baking dish. Microwave, covered, for 3 minutes or until vegetables are tender. Stir in milk. Add fish; spoon sauce over top. Microwave, covered, on High for 7 to 10 minutes or until fish flakes easily. Yield: 6 servings.

Laura R. Babcock
Exemplar Preceptor, Athens, Pennsylvania

M-M-M-Good Fish

2 to 3 pounds fish
    fillets
1 cup melted butter
5 tablespoons
    lemon juice
4 teaspoons
    garlic powder

1 tablespoon chopped
    parsley
Salt and pepper
    to taste
1 1/2 cups crushed
    club crackers
2 teaspoons paprika

Place fish in 9-inch glass baking dish. Combine butter, lemon juice, garlic powder, parsley, salt and pepper in bowl. Pour over fish. Sprinkle with cracker crumbs and paprika. Microwave on High for 5 minutes. Microwave on Medium for 10 minutes or until fish flakes easily. Yield: 4-5 servings.

Mary Scherbarth
Xi Alpha Theta, Fairbury, Nebraska

Microwave Magic

Quick Hawaiian Fish Fillets

1 8-ounce can
    crushed pineapple,
    drained
1/2 cup teriyaki sauce
1/4 cup butter

1/4 cup slivered
    almonds
1 pound white fish
    fillets

Combine pineapple and teriyaki sauce. Let stand for several minutes. Place butter and almonds in 8 x 8-inch glass baking dish. Microwave on High for 5 minutes or until almonds are golden, stirring once. Remove almonds with slotted spoon; set aside. Place fish in dish, turning to coat with butter. Microwave, tightly covered, on High for 5 minutes or until fish flakes easily. Add pineapple mixture. Microwave, covered, for 2 minutes. Sprinkle with almonds. Yield: 4 servings.

Button Ruzicka
Xi Delta Sigma, Corpus Christi, Texas

Creamed Tuna

1 12-ounce can
    water-pack tuna
1/2 cup milk

2 cans cream of
    mushroom soup

Combine all ingredients in 2-quart glass baking dish; mix well. Microwave, covered, on High for 5 to 8 minutes or until heated through, stirring and turning dish several times. Serve over rice or toast. Yield: 6 servings.

Patti Geistfeld
Delta Beta Beta, Eureka, California

Hot Bean Salad

6 slices bacon
Vinegar
1 tablespoon cornstarch
1/4 cup sugar
1 16-ounce can wax
    beans, drained

1 16-ounce can green
    beans, drained
1 16-ounce can
    kidney beans, drained
1 medium onion,
    sliced into rings

Microwave bacon in glass baking dish on High for 5 minutes or until crisp. Drain and crumble bacon, reserving drippings. Add enough vinegar to drippings to measure 1/2 cup. Blend with cornstarch and sugar in 2-quart glass baking dish. Microwave on High for 3 minutes or until thickened, stirring twice. Stir in beans and onion. Sprinkle bacon over top. Microwave on High for 4 to 5 minutes or until heated through. Yield: 8-10 servings.

Joyce Horvath
Xi Iota Gamma, Wellington, Ohio

Fruit Salad

1 16-ounce can
    sliced peaches
1 16-ounce can
    pineapple chunks
1 11-ounce can
    mandarin oranges

1 3-ounce package
    vanilla pudding and
    pie filling mix
1 3-ounce package
    tapioca pudding mix

Drain fruits, reserving juices. Add enough water to juices to measure 3 cups. Combine with pudding mixes in glass bowl; mix well. Microwave on High for 6 minutes or until mixture is thick and clear; stir. Microwave for 3 minutes longer; cool. Stir in fruit. Chill in refrigerator.

Linda Nelson
Theta Rho, New Hampton, Iowa

Vegetables

Broccoli Casserole

2 10-ounce packages
    frozen chopped
    broccoli
1 medium onion,
    chopped
1/4 cup margarine

1/2 cup milk
1 cup minute rice
1 8-ounce jar
    Cheez Whiz
1 can cream of
    mushroom soup

Microwave broccoli using package directions for 7 minutes; drain. Place onion and margarine in glass dish. Microwave on High for 2 minutes. Stir in broccoli, 1/4 cup water and remaining ingredients; mix well. Microwave on High for 15 minutes. Yield: 6 servings.

Linda Kaufmann
Nu Gamma, Crescent City, California

Green Rice Casserole

1 10-ounce package
    frozen chopped
    broccoli, cooked
1/2 cup cooked rice
1 can celery soup

1/2 8-ounce jar
    Cheez Whiz
1/2 cup chopped celery
1/2 cup chopped onion
1/4 cup butter

Combine broccoli, rice, soup and Cheez Whiz in glass baking dish. Brown celery and onion in butter in skillet. Add to rice mixture; mix well. Microwave on Medium-High for 30 minutes or until heated through.

Sandi S. Davison
Preceptor Gamma Upsilon, Kansas City, Missouri

155

Microwave Magic

Mushrooms and Rice

1   10-ounce can
       beef consomme
1 can onion soup
1/2 stick margarine

1 cup rice
1 to 2   4-ounce cans
       mushrooms, drained

Combine consomme, soup and margarine in 1 1/2-quart glass dish. Microwave on High for 4 minutes or until bubbly. Stir in rice and mushrooms. Microwave, covered, on Medium-Low for 28 minutes. Let stand for 5 minutes. Yield: 8-10 servings.

Mary Ellen Snook
Preceptor Pi, Conway, South Carolina

Mexican Potatoes

6 medium potatoes,
       peeled, sliced
1/2 cup chopped onion
1/2 teaspoon
       garlic salt
1 teaspoon instant
       beef bouillon

1 teaspoon salt
2 cups grated
       Cheddar cheese
1   4-ounce can
       chopped green
       chilies, drained

Combine potatoes, onion, garlic salt, bouillon, salt and 1 cup water in saucepan. Simmer for 10 to 12 minutes or until tender; drain. Layer half the potatoes, half the cheese and half the chilies in shallow 2-quart glass dish. Repeat layers. Microwave on Medium for 4 to 5 minutes or until cheese melts. Yield: 6 servings.

Mary Ann Hamm
Beta Omicron, Castle Rock, Colorado

Parmesan Potatoes

4 potatoes,
       peeled, sliced
Salt and pepper
       to taste

3 tablespoons butter,
       melted
1/4 cup Parmesan
       cheese

Place potatoes and 2 tablespoons water in 9-inch glass dish. Microwave, covered, on High for 6 minutes or until tender; drain. Add remaining ingredients; mix well. Bake at 350 degrees for 30 minutes or until crisp. Yield: 3 servings.

Anna Pocras
Laureate Epsilon, Las Vegas, Nevada

Scalloped Potatoes

3 tablespoons butter
2 tablespoons flour
1 teaspoon salt
1/4 teaspoon pepper
3 cups milk

3 or 4 medium potatoes,
       peeled, sliced
1/2 onion, chopped
Grated cheese

Microwave butter in glass bowl on High for 30 seconds or until melted. Blend in flour and seasonings. Add milk gradually. Microwave on High for 8 to 10 minutes or until thickened, stirring every 3 minutes. Layer half the potatoes, half the onion and half the white sauce in greased 3-quart glass dish. Repeat layers. Microwave, covered, on High for 15 to 19 minutes or until potatoes are tender, stirring after 10 minutes. Sprinkle with cheese. Let stand, covered, for 5 minutes.

Vickie Waltrip
Xi Pi, Pittsburg, Kansas

Sweet Potato Pudding

2 pounds sweet
       potatoes, peeled,
       grated
1/2 cup sugar
1 cup dark corn syrup
3 eggs, well beaten

1/2 cup butter,
       softened
Grated rind of
       1/2 orange
1 teaspoon salt

Combine all ingredients in greased glass baking dish. Microwave on High for 30 minutes, stirring every 10 minutes. Let stand until set. Yield: 8 servings.
Note: May serve with whipped cream for dessert.

Jane Gabel
Xi Mu Eta, Houston, Texas

Zucchini-Mushroom Quiche

3 cups cooked rice
2 eggs
1 cup grated
       mozzarella cheese
1 tablespoon butter
1 cup chopped onion
1 cup chopped
       zucchini

1   4-ounce can sliced
       mushrooms, drained
1   8-ounce package
       cream cheese,
       softened
1/4 cup milk
1/2 teaspoon salt
1 egg

Combine rice, 2 eggs and mozzarella cheese in bowl; mix well. Press into buttered 12-inch shallow round glass baking dish. Microwave on High for 6 minutes, turning dish every 2 minutes. Remove from oven. Melt 1 tablespoon butter in shallow 2-quart glass baking dish on High for 1 minute. Add onion, zucchini and mushrooms. Microwave, covered, for 3 minutes or until vegetables are tender-crisp. Combine cream cheese, milk, salt and 1 egg in bowl; beat until smooth. Stir into vegetables. Pour evenly over rice crust. Microwave on High for 7 minutes or until set, turning dish every 2 minutes.

Linda Rostenberg
Omega, Kansas City, Missouri

Vegetable Pasta Salad, recipe on page 171.

Salads

Apple Salad

2 apples, chopped
1 banana, sliced
12 red grapes, seeded
2 stalks celery,
   chopped
1/2 cup salad dressing
1/4 cup milk
1/2 head lettuce,
   chopped

Combine first 4 ingredients in bowl. Mix salad dressing and milk in small bowl. Add to fruit mixture; mix lightly. Add lettuce; mix lightly. Yield: 8 servings.

Helen Daws
Preceptor Delta Mu, Lena, Illinois

Apricot-Buttermilk Salad

1 20-ounce can
   juice-pack
   crushed pineapple
2 3-ounce packages
   apricot gelatin
2 cups buttermilk
1 8-ounce carton
   whipped topping
1/2 cup chopped pecans

Combine pineapple and gelatin in saucepan; mix well. Bring to a boil; cool. Add remaining ingredients; mix well. Pour into 8 x 12-inch serving dish. Chill until firm. Yield: 20 servings.

Jenny Hungerbuhler
Epsilon Zeta, Corbin, Kentucky

Fruit-Yogurt Frozen Salad

1 16-ounce can
   apricots, drained
1/2 cup (scant) sugar
1/2 cup chopped pecans
2 8-ounce cartons
   peach yogurt

Chop apricots. Combine apricots, sugar, pecans and yogurt in bowl; mix well. Fill lined muffin cups 3/4 full. Freeze until firm. Remove liners. Arrange on chilled serving tray. Yield: 12 servings.

Phyllis McBee
Laureate Lambda, Wichita, Kansas

Champagne Salad

1 cup green grapes
1 cup purple grapes
1 pint strawberries
1 large peach,
   peeled, chopped
1 large pear,
   peeled, chopped
1 cup fresh
   pineapple chunks
Sliced kiwifruit,
   oranges, bananas,
   mangos or
   cherries (opt.)
2 tablespoons sugar
1/3 cup Brandy
1 bottle of
   Champagne

Combine grapes, strawberries, peach, pear, pineapple and remaining fruit in bowl. Sprinkle with sugar. Add Brandy. Marinate in refrigerator for several hours. Fill tall glasses 1/3 full with fruit. Add Champagne. Serve with iced tea spoons.

Cheryl Hassett
Alpha Gamma, Lara, Victoria, Australia

Super Simple Cherry Salad

1 can cherry
   pie filling
1 8-ounce carton
   sour cream
1 16-ounce can fruit
   cocktail, drained
2 cups miniature
   marshmallows

Combine pie filling and sour cream in bowl; mix well. Add fruit cocktail and marshmallows; mix well. Spoon into serving dish. Yield: 12-15 servings.

Diana L. Stewart
Xi Alpha Omega, Oelwein, Iowa

Frozen Cherry Salad

1 20-ounce can
   crushed pineapple
1 15-ounce can
   sweetened
   condensed milk
1 cup chopped pecans
1 can cherry
   pie filling
1 16-ounce carton
   whipped topping

Partially drain pineapple. Combine all ingredients in bowl in order listed, mixing well after each addition. Spoon into 9 x 13-inch dish. Freeze until firm. Cut into squares. Yield: 12 servings.

Joan Fairchild
Alpha Sigma, Mobile, Alabama

Leora's Cranberry Salad

1 3-ounce package
   gelatin
1/2 cup orange juice
1 11-ounce can
   mandarin oranges,
   drained
1/3 cup chopped nuts
1 16-ounce can whole
   cranberry sauce
1 3-ounce package
   cream cheese,
   softened
2 tablespoons
   mayonnaise

Dissolve gelatin in 1 cup boiling water in bowl. Add orange juice. Chill until partially set. Add oranges, nuts and cranberry sauce. Pour half the gelatin mixture into 1 1/2-quart mold. Chill until firm. Blend cream cheese and mayonnaise in bowl. Spread over congealed layer. Add remaining gelatin. Chill until firm. Unmold on serving plate. Yield: 8 servings.

Leora Dycus
Laureate Alpha Epsilon, Effingham, Illinois

Salads

Holiday Fruit Salad

1   12-ounce carton
    whipped topping
1   8-ounce carton
    sour cream
1   3-ounce package
    cherry gelatin

1 can cherry
    pie filling
1/2 cup coconut
2 cups miniature
    marshmallows
1 can mandarin oranges

Combine first 3 ingredients in mixer bowl. Beat at medium speed until well blended. Fold in pie filling, coconut, marshmallows and oranges. Spoon into serving dish. Chill in refrigerator. Yield: 6-8 servings.

Kari Pearson
Xi Alpha Iota, West Yellowstone, Montana

Christmas Cranberry Mold

2   3-ounce packages
    strawberry gelatin
1   16-ounce package
    cranberries

1/2 cup sugar
1   20-ounce can
    crushed pineapple

Prepare gelatin using package directions. Grind cranberries. Add to gelatin with sugar and pineapple; mix well. Pour into large mold. Chill until firm. Unmold on serving plate. Yield: 12 servings.

Caralyn VanHorn
Xi Gamma Omega, Star Route, Pennsylvania

Annabeth's Cranberry Salad

1   16-ounce can
    cranberry sauce
3 tablespoons
    lemon juice
1/4 cup mayonnaise

1/4 cup confectioners'
    sugar
1/2 cup whipping
    cream, whipped
Nuts, chopped

Combine cranberry sauce and lemon juice in bowl; mix well. Pour into 9 x 9-inch dish. Fold mayonnaise and sugar into whipped cream. Spread over cranberry mixture. Sprinkle nuts on top. Freeze until firm. Cut into squares.

Annabeth Lockhart
Xi Gamma Eta, Steamboat Springs, Colorado

Cranberry-Mallow Salad

2 cups cranberries,
    ground
4 cups miniature
    marshmallows
1/2 cup sugar

1 apple, chopped
1/2 cup chopped nuts
1 cup whipping
    cream, whipped

Combine cranberries, marshmallows and sugar in bowl; mix well. Chill overnight. Add apple and nuts; mix well. Fold in whipped cream. Chill in refrigerator. Yield: 10-12 servings.

Barbara Nelson
Zeta Delta, Greeley, Colorado

Mom's Cranberry Salad

1   12-ounce package
    cranberries
3/4 cup chopped nuts
4 apples, chopped
1 cup sugar

1 ounce Drambuie
1 1/3 cups chopped
    celery
1 cup miniature
    marshmallows

Chop cranberries. Combine all ingredients in serving bowl; mix well. Chill in refrigerator.

Patricia Thorpe
Nu Gamma, Crescent City, California

Holiday Gelatin Salad

1   3-ounce package
    lime gelatin
1 cup hot applesauce
1/2 cup chopped celery
1 cup 7-Up

1   3-ounce package
    cherry gelatin
1 cup hot cranberry
    sauce
1 cup 7-Up

Dissolve lime gelatin in hot applesauce. Cool. Add celery and 1 cup 7-Up; mix well. Pour into 9 x 12-inch dish. Chill until firm. Dissolve cherry gelatin in hot cranberry sauce. Add 1 cup 7-Up; mix well. Pour over congealed layer. Chill until firm. Yield: 10-12 servings.

Signe E. Wallis
Pi, Portland, Oregon

Cookie Salad

1 cup buttermilk
1 small package
    vanilla instant
    pudding mix
3/4   16-ounce package
    fudge stripe
    cookies
1   16-ounce carton
    whipped topping

1   16-ounce can
    fruit cocktail
1   15-ounce can
    pineapple
    tidbits
1   11-ounce can
    mandarin
    oranges

Combine buttermilk and pudding mix in bowl; mix well. Crush cookies. Add whipped topping and 2/3 of the cookies to pudding mixture. Add fruit; mix well. Spoon into serving bowl. Sprinkle with remaining cookies. Yield: 6-12 servings.

Mardele Toth
Xi Tau, Havre, Montana

Salads

Gelatin Delight

1 small package gelatin
1 4-ounce package
  shredded mild
  Cheddar cheese

1 3-ounce package
  chopped walnuts
1 8-ounce carton
  whipped topping

Prepare gelatin in bowl using package directions. Chill until partially set. Stir in remaining ingredients. Spoon into mold. Chill until set. Unmold on serving plate. Yield: 6-10 servings.

Bette Fritz
Xi Sigma, Houston, Texas

Norma's Fruit Salad

1 28-ounce can
  pineapple chunks
1 4-ounce jar
  maraschino cherries
1 8-ounce can
  mandarin oranges

1 3-ounce package
  vanilla instant
  pudding mix
3 or 4 bananas,
  sliced

Drain fruit, reserving juice. Combine pudding mix and reserved juice in bowl; mix well. Add pineapple, cherries and oranges; mix well. Chill in refrigerator. Fold in bananas. Spoon into serving dish. Yield: 6-8 servings.

Norma Blum
Theta Iota, Hendersonville, North Carolina

Fruit Surprise

1 3-ounce package
  gelatin
1 to 1 1/2 cups liquid
1 8-ounce carton
  yogurt

1 16-ounce can
  fruit or 2
  bananas, sliced
1/2 cup chopped
  pecans

Dissolve gelatin in boiling liquid in bowl. Add yogurt, fruit and pecans; mix well. Pour into mold. Chill until firm. Unmold onto serving plate. Yield: 6 servings.

Carolyn Cole
Theta Iota, Fletcher, North Carolina

Diana's Frozen Fruit Salad

1 15-ounce can
  sweetened
  condensed milk
1/4 cup lemon juice
1 8-ounce package
  cream cheese,
  softened

1 16-ounce can
  crushed pineapple,
  drained
1 20-ounce can fruit
  cocktail, drained
1 8-ounce carton
  whipped topping

Combine condensed milk and lemon juice in bowl; mix well. Add cream cheese; mix well. Stir in pineapple and fruit cocktail. Fold in whipped topping. Pour into shallow dish. Freeze until firm. Yield: 6-8 servings.

Diana A. Burge
Xi Beta Alpha, Niles, Michigan

Betty Petty's Fruit Salad

2 apples, chopped
1 orange, sectioned
1 cup grapes
1/2 cup raisins
1 grapefruit, sectioned

1/2 cup mayonnaise
1/4 cup honey
1 tablespoon
  lemon juice
1 teaspoon celery seed

Combine fruit in serving bowl. Mix mayonnaise, honey, lemon juice and celery seed in small bowl. Serve over fruit.

Betty Petty
Preceptor Beta Epsilon, Wetmore, Colorado

Happy Day Salad

1 small package vanilla
  instant pudding mix
1 28-ounce can
  fruit cocktail,
  drained

1 cup coconut
2 cups miniature
  marshmallows
2 bananas, sliced
1 cup whipped topping

Prepare pudding mix using package directions. Add remaining ingredients; mix well. Chill in refrigerator. Yield: 6-8 servings.

Carol Figueroa
Alpha Nu, APO New York

Molded Salad

1 3-ounce package
  lemon gelatin
1 3-ounce package
  lime gelatin
2 cups crushed
  pineapple
2 tablespoons
  lemon juice

3/4 cup milk
2 teaspoons
  horseradish
1/2 cup chopped nuts
1/2 cup mayonnaise
8 ounces dry curd
  cottage cheese

Dissolve gelatins in 2 cups boiling water in bowl. Add remaining ingredients; mix well. Pour into ring mold. Chill until firm. Unmold on lettuce-lined plate. Yield: 10-12 servings.

Mary Ellen Snook
Preceptor Pi, Conway, South Carolina

Salads

Orange Stuff

1 8-ounce carton
    whipped topping
1 small package
    sugar-free
    orange gelatin

1 16-ounce carton
    cottage cheese
1 12-ounce can
    mandarin oranges,
    drained

Mix whipped topping and gelatin in serving bowl. Fold in cottage cheese and oranges. Yield: 4-6 servings.

Shirley Moore
Preceptor Tau, Norwalk, Ohio

Pear and Grape Salad

4 ripe pears,
    peeled
1/2 pound black
    seedless grapes

1 cup cream
    cheese, softened
2 tablespoons French
    salad dressing

Cut pears and grapes in half. Remove cores from pears. Blend cream cheese and French dressing in bowl. Place pears cut side down on lettuce-lined salad plates. Spread with cream cheese. Press grape halves into cream cheese to resemble bunch of grapes. Yield: 4 servings.

Jane E. Cooley
Xi Beta Mu, Lynnwood, Washington

Darn Good Salad

1 3-ounce package
    lemon gelatin
1 3-ounce package
    cream cheese,
    softened
12 large marshmallows
1 cup shredded carrots

1 cup crushed
    pineapple, drained
1 cup coconut
1/4 teaspoon salt
1 cup whipping
    cream, whipped
1 cup nuts

Dissolve gelatin in 2 cups boiling water in bowl. Add cream cheese and marshmallows. Stir until marshmallows are dissolved. Cool. Fold in remaining ingredients. Pour into mold. Chill until firm. Unmold on serving plate.
Note: May add layer of red gelatin to mold after first layer is congealed.

Thelma Knipmeyer
Alma, Missouri

Lemon-Pineapple Delight

1 3-ounce package
    lemon gelatin
1 pint vanilla
    ice cream

1 8-ounce can
    crushed
    pineapple

Dissolve gelatin in 1 cup boiling water in bowl. Add ice cream; mix until melted. Stir in pineapple. Pour into mold. Chill until set. Unmold on serving plate. Yield: 4-6 servings.

Judith M. Weaver
Omega, Staunton, Virginia

Pineapple-Lemon-Lime Salad

1 3-ounce package
    lemon gelatin
1 3-ounce package
    lime gelatin
1 8-ounce can
    crushed pineapple

2 teaspoons prepared
    horseradish
1 3-ounce package
    cream cheese,
    softened

Rinse 8-cup ring mold with cold water; place in freezer. Dissolve gelatins in 2 cups very hot water. Add enough very cold water to pineapple to measure 2 cups. Combine gelatin, pineapple, horseradish and chopped cream cheese in blender container. Process until smooth. Pour into prepared ring mold. Chill for 2 hours. Unmold on serving plate. Yield: 8 servings.
Note: Delightful with ham.

Kathryn M. Fenn
Preceptor Nu, Lena, Illinois

Mary's Pistachio Salad

1 28-ounce can
    crushed pineapple
1 small package
    pistachio instant
    pudding mix

1 c. miniature
    marshmallows
1 12-ounce carton
    whipped topping

Combine pineapple and juice, pudding mix and marshmallows in bowl; mix well. Fold in whipped topping. Spread in 9 x 13-inch dish. Chill until serving time.
Yield: 10-12 servings.

Mary Beatty
Preceptor Laureate Nu, Olympia, Washington

Always-Available Frozen Fruit Salad

2 cups sour cream
2 teaspoons
    lemon juice
3/4 cup sugar
1/8 teaspoon salt
1 banana, chopped

1 8-ounce can
    crushed pineapple,
    drained
1/4 cup chopped
    maraschino cherries
1/4 cup chopped pecans

Combine first 4 ingredients in bowl; mix well. Fold in fruit and pecans. Spoon into lined muffin cups. Freeze until firm. Store in freezer bags. Thaw in refrigerator for 1 hour before serving. Yield: 12 servings.

Betty Bower
Preceptor Delta, Pompano Beach, Florida

Salads

Snow Salad

1 10-ounce package
   miniature
   marshmallows
1 16-ounce carton
   small curd
   cottage cheese

1 8-ounce carton
   whipped topping
1 28-ounce can
   crushed pineapple
1/4 cup mayonnaise

Combine all ingredients in serving bowl; mix well. Chill for 24 hours.

Margaret Truttmann
Xi Gamma Sigma, Elma, Washington

Raspberry Gelatin Salad

1 6-ounce package
   raspberry
   gelatin
1 8-ounce package
   cream cheese,
   softened

2 tablespoons
  mayonnaise
1/2 cup chopped nuts
1 10-ounce
   package frozen
   raspberries, thawed

Prepare gelatin using package directions. Pour into round mold. Chill until thick. Combine cream cheese, mayonnaise and nuts in bowl; mix well. Shape into balls. Drain raspberries; pat dry. Add cream cheese balls and raspberries alternately to gelatin. Chill until firm. Unmold on serving plate.

Karen Bauer
Beta Tau, Stevensville, Montana

Seven-Up Salad

1 6-ounce package
   lemon gelatin
2 cups 7-Up
1 20-ounce can
   crushed pineapple
2 bananas, sliced
1 cup miniature
  marshmallows
1/4 cup sugar

2 tablespoons flour
1 cup pineapple juice
1 egg, beaten
2 tablespoons butter
1 8-ounce carton
   whipped topping
A small amount of
  grated longhorn
  cheese

Dissolve gelatin in 2 cups boiling water in bowl. Add 7-Up. Stir in pineapple, bananas and marshmallows. Pour into 9 x 13-inch dish. Chill until firm. Combine sugar and flour in saucepan. Stir in juice and egg. Cook until thickened, stirring constantly. Stir in butter. Cool. Fold in whipped topping. Spread over congealed layer. Sprinkle with cheese. Chill overnight. Cut into squares.

Kim L. Tapscott
Preceptor Beta Mu, Telford, Pennsylvania

Strawberries and Cream Dream Salad

1 3-ounce package
   strawberry gelatin
1 12-ounce
   can pineapple
   chunks

1 12-ounce carton
   cottage cheese
1 8-ounce carton
   whipped topping
Fresh strawberries

Combine dry gelatin with next 3 ingredients in serving bowl; mix well. Top with fresh strawberries.

Barbara Matzinger
Preceptor Delta Eta, Arlington, Texas

Strawberry Satin Salad

1 8-ounce carton
   whipped topping
1 20-ounce can
   crushed pineapple,
   drained

1 can strawberry
  pie filling
1 15-ounce can
   sweetened
   condensed milk

Combine all ingredients in bowl; mix well. Spoon into serving bowl. Chill in refrigerator.

Karla Albert
Zeta Pi, Fulton, Missouri

Pink Cloud

2 10-ounce
   packages frozen
   strawberries
1 cup vanilla
  ice cream

1 8-ounce package
   cream cheese,
   softened
1 8-ounce carton
   whipped topping

Thaw and drain strawberries. Soften ice cream. Mix strawberries and ice cream in bowl. Add cream cheese and whipped topping; mix well. Spoon into lined muffin cups. Freeze until firm. Remove liners. Place on lettuce-lined salad plates. Thaw for 5 minutes before serving. Yield: 6 servings.

Kathy Dorich
Xi Zeta Epsilon, Noblesville, Indiana

Salads

Barbara's Pretzel Salad

2 cups crushed pretzels
3 tablespoons sugar
3/4 cup melted margarine
1 8-ounce package cream cheese, softened
1 cup sugar
4 teaspoons drained crushed pineapple
1 8-ounce carton whipped topping
1 6-ounce package strawberry gelatin
2 10-ounce packages frozen strawberries

Mix pretzels, 3 tablespoons sugar and margarine in bowl. Press into 9 x 13-inch baking dish. Bake at 400 degrees for 12 minutes; cool. Combine cream cheese, 1 cup sugar and pineapple in bowl; mix well. Fold in whipped topping. Spread over crust. Dissolve gelatin in 2 cups boiling water; stir in strawberries. Chill until partially set. Pour over cream cheese layer. Chill until firm. Yield: 6 servings.

Barbara Lyons
Xi Gamma, Lewiston, Maine

Watergate Salad

1 16-ounce can crushed pineapple
1 small package pistachio instant pudding mix
1 8-ounce can mandarin oranges, drained (opt.)
2 cups miniature marshmallows
1/2 cup chopped nuts
1/2 cup shredded coconut
6 ounces whipped topping

Drain pineapple, reserving juice. Combine juice and pudding mix in bowl; mix well. Add pineapple, oranges, marshmallows, nuts and coconut; mix well. Fold in whipped topping. Spoon into serving bowl. Yield: 10 servings.

Lorna Davis
Laureate Pi, Grand Junction, Colorado

Deviled Eggs

6 hard-boiled eggs
1/4 cup sandwich spread
1/4 teaspoon salt
Paprika

Cut eggs in half lengthwise; separate yolks from whites. Mash yolks in small bowl. Add sandwich spread and salt; mix well. Spoon into whites. Sprinkle with paprika. Yield: 6 servings.

Patti Geistfeld
Delta Beta Beta, Eureka, California

Chicken Brunch Salad

1 cup chopped cooked chicken
1/2 cup chopped celery
1 8-ounce can cut green beans, drained
1 8-ounce can pineapple chunks, drained
1/2 cup macaroni, cooked
1/4 cup sour cream
1/4 cup mayonnaise
1/4 teaspoon allspice
1 tablespoon lemon juice
1/4 cup toasted slivered almonds (opt.)

Combine chicken, celery, beans and pineapple in bowl. Add cooled macaroni; mix well. Blend sour cream, mayonnaise, allspice and lemon juice in bowl. Fold into chicken mixture. Spoon into lettuce-lined salad bowl. Sprinkle almonds on top. Chill until serving time. Yield: 4 servings.

Robbie Parsley
Laureate Xi, Scottsdale, Arizona

Oriental Chicken-Cabbage Salad

1 medium head cabbage, chopped
3 or 4 green onions, chopped
1/2 green pepper, chopped
4 teaspoons sesame seed
1/4 cup slivered almonds
2 cups chopped cooked chicken
1/4 cup vinegar
3/4 cup oil
1 tablespoon sugar
1/2 teaspoon salt
3/4 teaspoon MSG (opt.)
1 tablespoon soy sauce
1/2 teaspoon white pepper
1 package uncooked Ramen noodles, crushed

Layer first 6 ingredients in order listed in serving bowl. Combine vinegar, oil, sugar, salt, MSG, soy sauce and pepper in bowl; mix well. Pour over salad; toss lightly to coat. Chill for 1 hour. Add noodles just before serving; toss gently. Yield: 10-12 servings.

Leslie Peacock
Xi Upsilon Rho, Oxnard, California

Salads

Chicken and Rice Salad

1 6-ounce package
   rice, cooked,
   chilled
2 cups chopped
   cooked chicken
1 cup seedless
   grape halves
1 cup sliced celery
3/4 cup chopped nuts

2 tablespoons finely
   chopped onion
1/2 teaspoon salt
3/4 cup mayonnaise
1/4 cup lemon juice
Orange slices
Lemon slices
1/2 cup seedless grapes

Combine rice, chicken, grape halves, celery, nuts, onion, salt, mayonnaise and lemon juice in bowl; mix well. Arrange orange and lemon slices around top edge of lettuce-lined serving bowl. Spoon chicken mixture into center. Place 1/2 cup grapes in center. Chill for several hours. Yield: 6 servings.

Helen Heath
Preceptor Upsilon, Muncie, Indiana

Mexican Chef Salad

1 pound ground beef
1 15-ounce can
   kidney beans, drained
1/4 teaspoon salt
1 head lettuce
4 tomatoes
1 onion, chopped

4 ounces grated cheese
1 8-ounce bottle of
   Italian salad
   dressing
1 7 1/2-ounce bag
   corn chips, crushed

Brown ground beef in skillet, stirring until crumbly; drain. Add beans and salt. Simmer for 10 minutes. Cool. Combine lettuce, tomatoes, onion, cheese and salad dressing in large salad bowl. Add ground beef mixture; toss lightly. Add corn chips just before serving; toss lightly. Yield: 8 servings.

Ann Doucet
Xi Rho Zeta, Deer Park, Texas

Easy Mexican Salad

1 pound ground beef
1 package taco
   seasoning mix
1 8-ounce package
   cream cheese,
   softened
1 can bean dip
1 bottle of taco sauce

Lettuce, chopped
Tomatoes, chopped
Cheese, grated
Black olives,
   chopped (opt.)
Onions, chopped (opt.)
Avocado, chopped (opt.)

Brown ground beef in skillet, stirring until crumbly; drain. Add seasoning mix; mix well. Spread cream cheese in serving dish. Layer bean dip, taco sauce, ground beef, lettuce, tomatoes and cheese over cream cheese. Sprinkle olives, onions and avocado over layers.

Carol Cummins
Alpha Omega Phi, New Boston, Texas

Taco Salad

1 1/2 pounds ground
   chuck
1/3 cup French salad
   dressing
1 small onion, chopped
1/2 teaspoon salt
1/4 teaspoon pepper
1/2 teaspoon oregano
1/2 head lettuce
2 radishes, sliced
2 tomatoes, chopped
1 8-ounce can
   whole kernel corn

1 can garbanzo
   beans, drained
2/3 cup French
   salad dressing
1 8-ounce package
   corn chips
1 avocado, chopped
4 ounces Cheddar
   cheese, shredded
12 ripe olives,
   sliced
1 cup sour cream

Brown ground chuck in skillet, stirring until crumbly; drain. Stir in 1/3 cup salad dressing, onion and seasonings. Simmer for 5 minutes. Combine next 5 vegetables and remaining salad dressing in large bowl; toss lightly. Layer corn chips, ground chuck mixture and vegetable mixture in serving bowl. Top with avocado, cheese, olives and sour cream.
Yield: 6 servings.

Ella Kernodle
Laureate Upsilon, Kansas City, Missouri

Summer Salad

1 box Jiffy corn
   bread mix
4 green onions, chopped
1 green pepper, chopped
1 tomato, chopped
3 or 4 radishes
2 tablespoons mustard

1/4 cup creamy
   cucumber salad
   dressing
1/2 teaspoon each
   salt and pepper
1/4 cup mayonnaise

Prepare corn bread using package directions. Cool and crumble. Combine all ingredients in serving bowl; mix well. Chill in refrigerator.

Natalie N. Ruble
Kappa Laureate, Great Bend, Kansas

Salads

Texas Corn Bread Salad

1 recipe corn
    bread, crumbled
1 large onion,
    finely chopped

1 pound bacon,
    crisp-fried
1 cup mayonnaise
1 tomato, chopped

Combine corn bread and onion in bowl. Crumble bacon. Add to corn bread. Stir in mayonnaise. Chill overnight. Add tomato before serving; mix well. Yield: 8-10 servings.

Leslie Peacock
Xi Upsilon Rho, Oxnard, California

Green and White Salad

3 bunches fresh spinach
2 cups cooked pasta
1 cup sliced mushrooms
1 cup red wine vinegar

1/2 cup oil
1/2 teaspoon salt
1/2 teaspoon pepper

Wash spinach; tear into pieces. Combine with pasta and mushrooms in serving bowl. Mix remaining ingredients in covered jar; shake vigorously. Pour over salad. Yield: 4-6 servings.

Pamela Majoras
Omicron Pi, Vermilion, Ohio

Italian Garden Salad

2 cups cooked rotini
2 cups fresh broccoli
    flowerets
2 cups chopped tomato
3/4 cup grated carrots

2 cups sliced mushrooms
2 cups ripe olives
1 bottle of Italian
    salad dressing

Combine rotini, vegetables and olives in large serving bowl; mix well. Pour salad dressing over salad. Marinate in refrigerator for 24 hours. Yield: 20 servings.

Karen Perry
Pi Eta, Castalia, Ohio

Macaroni Salad

2 cups cooked macaroni
1 cup chopped celery
1/3 cup chopped
    green pepper
6 green onions, sliced
1 2-ounce jar
    chopped pimento

3/4 cup mayonnaise
2 tablespoons cider
    vinegar
1 tablespoon sugar
Seasoned salt and
    pepper to taste

Combine all ingredients in bowl; mix well. Chill for 2 hours or longer. Serve on lettuce-lined plate. Yield: 6-8 servings.

Mrs. Charles McMichael
Alpha Omega Phi, New Boston, Texas

No-Wilt Salad

1 16-ounce package
    frozen broccoli and
    baby carrots with
    water chestnuts
3 cups cooked
    spiral macaroni
1 cup sliced mushrooms

3/4 cup chopped
    sweet red pepper
2/3 cup Italian
    salad dressing
Pepper to taste
4 slices crisp-fried
    bacon, crumbled

Thaw vegetables in strainer under cold running water; drain. Combine with macaroni, mushrooms, red pepper, salad dressing and pepper to taste in serving bowl; mix well. Sprinkle bacon over top. Chill, covered, in refrigerator. Yield: 6-8 servings.

Joyce Lusk
Delta Eta Iota, Chico, California

Screwy Rotini Salad

1 16-ounce package
    rotini
1 cup oil
1 jar Salad Supreme
    seasoning
1 cup (about) vinegar

2 green peppers,
    chopped
2 tomatoes, chopped
1 large onion, grated
1 4-ounce container
    Parmesan cheese

Cook rotini using package directions for 10 minutes. Combine oil and seasoning in 2-cup measure. Add enough vinegar to measure 2 cups. Combine rotini, vegetables, cheese and dressing in bowl; mix well. Chill in refrigerator, stirring occasionally. Spoon into lettuce-lined serving bowl. Yield: 12 servings.

Betty F. Ramsey
Omega Preceptor, Staunton, Virginia

Rice and Pea Patio Salad

1 10-ounce package
    frozen peas
1/2 teaspoon salt
1 1/3 cups instant rice
1 tablespoon
    minced onion

3/4 cup mayonnaise
1/2 cup chopped
    dill pickles
Lemon juice to
    taste (opt.)

Bring peas, salt and 1 1/2 cups water to a boil in covered saucepan. Remove from heat. Stir in rice and onion; cover. Let stand for 15 minutes. Cool. Stir in mayonnaise, pickles and lemon juice. Chill in refrigerator. Yield: 6-8 servings.

Jouett Smith
Epsilon Kappa, Hachita, New Mexico

Salads

Curried Rice and Egg Salad

2 7-ounce packages frozen rice with peas and mushrooms	1 cup chopped cooked meat
2 to 3 teaspoons curry powder	1/2 cup mayonnaise
4 hard-boiled eggs, chopped	1/2 cup sour cream
	2 tablespoons minced parsley

Prepare rice using package directions. Add curry powder; mix well. Cool. Add remaining ingredients; toss lightly. Chill, covered, for several hours. Serve in tomato or avocado shells. Yield: 6 servings.

Debby Didawick
Theta Nu, Winchester, Virginia

Crab Louis

1/2 head lettuce, separated	3 hard-boiled eggs, mashed
1 6-ounce can claw crab meat, drained, mashed	1/2 cup mayonnaise
	Chili sauce to taste
	6 or 8 ripe olives

Arrange lettuce on small serving plate. Spread crab meat and eggs on lettuce. Combine mayonnaise and chili sauce in bowl; mix well. Spoon over crab. Garnish with olives.

Vivian Jean Brown
Preceptor Laureate Alpha Upsilon, San Antonio, Texas

Mock Crab Salad

1/2 head lettuce, torn	1 cup imitation crab meat
1 cup bean sprouts	1 cup cubed Cheddar cheese
2 cups shredded carrots	2 avocados, sliced
1/2 cup shredded red cabbage	
1/2 cup sunflower seed	

Layer lettuce, bean sprouts, carrots and cabbage in salad bowl. Add remaining ingredients just before serving. Serve with lemon wedges. Yield: 6 servings.

Angela Hersel
Beta Iota, McCall, Idaho

Jo Ella's Crab Salad

1 large loaf bread, crusts trimmed	1 large onion, chopped
Butter, softened	2 cans shrimp, drained
4 hard-boiled eggs, chopped	1 can crab, drained
	1 cup chopped celery
	3 cups mayonnaise

Spread bread slices with butter; cube. Combine bread, eggs and onion in bowl; toss to mix. Let stand, covered, overnight. Add remaining ingredients; mix well. Spoon into serving bowl. Garnish with cherry tomatoes, lettuce and cucumber flowers. Yield: 20 servings.

Jo Ella Bollar
Gamma Omega, McCall, Idaho

Quick-Set Salmon Mousse

1 15-ounce can red salmon	3/4 teaspoon salt
2 tablespoons wine vinegar	1/4 teaspoon cayenne pepper
2 envelopes unflavored gelatin	1/2 cup yogurt
1 small onion, cut into quarters	1/4 cup sour cream
1/2 cup mayonnaise	1/4 cup chopped green pepper
1 cup yogurt	1/2 teaspoon salt
1/4 cup chopped fresh dillweed	1 small cucumber, seeded, chopped

Drain salmon, reserving juice. Combine reserved juice, vinegar, gelatin and 1/2 cup boiling water in blender container. Process for 40 seconds. Add onion, mayonnaise, 1 cup yogurt, dillweed, 3/4 teaspoon salt, cayenne pepper and salmon. Process for 30 seconds or until smooth. Pour into shallow 4-cup mold. Chill in freezer for 20 to 30 minutes or in refrigerator for 2 hours or until firm. Combine remaining ingredients in bowl; mix well. Unmold salmon on serving plate. Serve with cucumber dressing.

Beverly Conway
Preceptor Epsilon Epsilon, Hollandale, Florida

Pawpaw Salmon Salad

4 medium potatoes, peeled	1/4 cup sliced ripe olives
2 ripe tomatoes	1/4 cup sliced stuffed green olives
1 16-ounce can salmon	1/4 cup Italian salad dressing
4 hard-boiled eggs, sliced	1/4 cup mayonnaise
1/2 cup chopped celery	1/4 cup chopped parsley
1/2 cup chopped green onions	

Cut potatoes and tomatoes into wedges. Cook potatoes in water to cover in saucepan until tender; drain. Drain salmon, reserving 1/4 cup liquid Mound salmon in center of large serving platter. Arrange potatoes around salmon. Place eggs and tomatoes on potatoes. Combine celery, onions, olives, salad dressing and salmon liquid in bowl; mix well. Spoon over salmon and vegetables. Top with mayonnaise. Sprinkle with parsley.

Mary Ann O'Sullivan
International Honorary Member, Gretna, Louisiana

Salads

Special Shrimp Salad

1 can tomato soup
1 1/2 ounces cream
   cheese
1/2 cup chopped
   green onions
1/2 cup finely
   chopped celery

1 cup mayonnaise
1 envelope
   unflavored gelatin
2 6-ounce cans
   shrimp, drained,
   chopped

Bring soup to a boil in saucepan. Add cream cheese. Stir until smooth. Remove from heat. Add remaining ingredients. Pour into small mold. Chill until firm. Unmold on lettuce-lined serving plate.

Note: May substitute cream of mushroom soup for tomato and crab meat for shrimp.

Elaine Rowett
Preceptor Pi, Sturgis, South Dakota

Lynn's Tuna Salad

1 8-ounce package
   elbow macaroni,
   cooked
1 10-ounce
   package frozen
   peas, thawed

1 12-ounce can
   tuna, drained
Mayonnaise to taste
Onion, minced
Pepper to taste
Parsley to taste

Combine cooled macaroni, peas and tuna in serving bowl; mix well. Add remaining ingredients; mix well.

Lynn Pikey
Preceptor Nu, Kodiak, Alaska

Tuna Shoestring Salad

1 6-ounce can
   tuna, drained
1 cup shredded carrots
1 cup chopped celery

1/4 cup minced onion
3/4 to 1 cup mayonnaise
1 4-ounce can
   shoestring potatoes

Combine first 5 ingredients in bowl; toss to mix. Add potatoes just before serving; toss lightly.

Betty Paul
Preceptor Theta Psi, Stockton, California

Creamy Tuna Twist

1 cup mayonnaise
2 tablespoons
   cider vinegar
Dash of pepper
4 ounces macaroni
   twists, cooked
1 cup sliced celery

1 7-ounce can tuna,
   drained, flaked
1/2 cup chopped
   red onion
1 tablespoon
   dried dillweed

Combine first 3 ingredients in bowl; mix well. Add macaroni, celery, tuna, onion and dillweed; toss to mix. Spoon into lettuce-lined serving bowl. Chill, covered, in refrigerator. Garnish with radish roses and cucumber slices.

Helen Schoenrock
Preceptor Epsilon, Fairbury, Nebraska

Tooie's Easy Salad

2 8-ounce cans
   quartered artichoke
   hearts
2 8-ounce cans
   mushroom pieces

1 8-ounce bottle
   of zesty
   Italian
   dressing

Drain vegetables; pat dry with paper towel. Combine with salad dressing in serving bowl; mix well. Chill for several hours to several days. Yield: 4-6 servings.

Evelyn Carmier
International Honorary Member, New Orleans, Louisiana

Spicy Avocado Salad

1 large ripe avocado
1 large firm tomato
1 medium onion

Pepper and garlic
   salt to taste

Chop avocado, tomato and onion; place in serving bowl. Sprinkle with seasonings; mix well. Chill until serving time. Salad will make its own dressing. Yield: 4 servings.

Carol Sassin
Xi Psi Beta, Beeville, Texas

Sweet and Sour Beans

2 medium onions,
   thinly sliced
1 16-ounce can green
   beans, drained
1 16-ounce can kidney
   beans, drained

1 16-ounce can
   yellow wax
   beans, drained
1 cup vinegar
1 cup sugar
1/3 cup oil

Combine onions and beans in bowl; toss lightly. Combine vinegar, sugar and oil in saucepan. Bring to a boil, stirring until sugar dissolves. Pour over bean mixture. Chill overnight in refrigerator. Spoon into serving bowl. Yield: 6 servings.

Lynda N. Keller
Xi Beta Nu, Des Moines, Iowa

Salads

Three-Bean Salad

1 16-ounce can red kidney beans	1/4 cup vinegar
1 16-ounce can white kidney beans	1/2 cup oil
1 16-ounce can cut green beans	1/4 teaspoon sugar
1 medium onion, sliced into rings	1/2 teaspoon salt
	Pinch of thyme, basil and garlic powder

Drain beans; combine with onion rings in serving bowl. Mix remaining ingredients in small bowl. Pour over vegetables; toss to mix. Chill, covered, for several hours to overnight. Yield: 8 servings.

Frances C. Lorenz
Laureate Chi, Pottsville, Pennsylvania

Virginia's Bean Salad

1 16-ounce can green beans	1/2 cup chopped green pepper
1 16-ounce can yellow beans	1/2 cup chopped celery
1 16-ounce can kidney beans	1/2 cup vinegar
1 16-ounce can garbanzo beans	1/2 cup sugar
1/2 cup chopped onion	1/2 cup oil
	Salt and pepper to taste

Drain all beans. Rinse and drain kidney beans and garbanzo beans. Combine beans and chopped vegetables in large bowl. Combine vinegar, sugar and oil in saucepan. Bring to a boil, stirring until sugar dissolves. Pour over vegetables. Add salt and pepper. Let stand at room temperature for 2 hours. Chill until serving time. Spoon into serving bowl.

Virginia Lucisano
Xi Beta Rho, Norman, Oklahoma

Beet Mold

1 3-ounce package lemon gelatin	1 teaspoon Worcestershire sauce
1 cup beet juice	1/2 teaspoon salt
1 8-ounce can diced beets	1 teaspoon vinegar
	1 teaspoon sugar

Dissolve gelatin in boiling beet juice. Add 1 cup cold water and remaining ingredients. Chill until set. Serve on lettuce-lined plates; garnish with mayonnaise.

Margene Betts
Laureate Rho, Norristown, Pennsylvania

Easy Beet Salad

1 jar sliced pickled beets, drained	1 Bermuda onion, sliced into rings
1/2 cup sour cream	Romaine lettuce

Combine beets, sour cream and onion in bowl; toss lightly. Chill until serving time. Spoon onto romaine lettuce-lined plates. Yield: 4 servings.

Sandy Wagner
Xi Alpha Rho, Danville, Kentucky

Broccoli Salad

1 bunch broccoli	1/2 cup sour cream
2 small tomatoes, finely chopped	1/2 cup mayonnaise
3 green onions, finely chopped	1 tablespoon lemon juice
	Salt and pepper to taste

Cut broccoli into bite-sized pieces. Combine with tomatoes and green onions in serving bowl. Add sour cream, mayonnaise, lemon juice, salt and pepper; mix gently. Chill until serving time. Yield: 6 servings.

Carol Figueroa
Alpha Nu, APO New York

Dorothy's Broccoli Salad

2 small bunches broccoli	1/2 pound bacon, crisp-fried, crumbled
1/2 large red sweet onion	1 cup salad dressing
	1/4 cup vinegar
	1/4 cup sugar

Chop broccoli and onion finely. Combine broccoli, onion and bacon in serving bowl 10 minutes before serving. Blend salad dressing, vinegar and sugar in small bowl. Pour over broccoli; toss lightly. Yield: 10 servings.

Dorothy Shaw
Preceptor Delta Mu, Lena, Illinois

Estelle's Broccoli Salad

2 bunches broccoli	1 cup mayonnaise
1 small onion, minced	1/3 cup sugar
1/2 to 1 cup raisins	1 tablespoon vinegar
1/2 cup bacon bits	

Chop broccoli, peeling stem if necessary. Combine with onion, raisins and bacon bits in serving bowl. Blend mayonnaise, sugar and vinegar in small bowl; pour over broccoli mixture. Do not stir. Chill for several hours to overnight. Mix just before serving. Yield: 8-10 servings.

Estelle D. Seachrist
Preceptor Alpha Kappa, Fishersville, Virginia

Salads

Rita's Broccoli Salad

1 bunch broccoli
  flowerets
4 scallions

2 medium tomatoes
1/2 cup sour cream
1/2 cup mayonnaise

Chop vegetables; combine in serving bowl. Add sour cream and mayonnaise; toss lightly.

Rita Kelly
Alpha Kappa Upsilon, The Colony, Texas

Broccoli Sunshine Salad

2 bunches broccoli
1/2 cup raisins
1/2 cup sunflower seed
1/2 cup chopped
  green onions
1/2 cup alfalfa
  sprouts

8 slices crisp-fried
  bacon, crumbled
1/2 cup mayonnaise
2 tablespoons vinegar
2 tablespoons sugar
1/4 cup milk

Cut flowerets from broccoli; discard stems. Combine broccoli, raisins, sunflower seed, green onions, alfalfa sprouts and bacon in serving bowl; toss lightly. Blend mayonnaise, vinegar, sugar and milk in small bowl. Pour over vegetables. Chill, covered, for 2 hours to overnight. Yield: 6-8 servings.

Kathie Lane
Delta Omicron, Norfolk, Nebraska

Carole's Carrot Salad

4 16-ounce cans
  carrots, drained
1 large green
  pepper, chopped
1 can tomato soup
1 cup sugar

3/4 cup vinegar
3/4 cup oil
1 teaspoon dry mustard
1 teaspoon salt
1/8 teaspoon pepper

Combine carrots, green pepper, soup, sugar, vinegar, oil, mustard, salt and pepper in serving bowl; mix well. Chill until serving time. Yield: 10 servings.

Carole A. Wachtel
Delta Pi, Montgomery, Alabama

Cauliflower and Broccoli Salad

1 cup mayonnaise
1 tablespoon sugar
1 tablespoon vinegar
1 teaspoon salt
1/2 teaspoon pepper

1 head cauliflower,
  broken into flowerets
4 cups broccoli
  flowerets
1 cup chopped onion

Combine mayonnaise and next 4 ingredients in large bowl; blend well. Add vegetables; toss lightly to coat. Serve immediately or store, covered, in refrigerator for 2 days or less. Yield: 10 cups.

Marlene McDougall
Beta Theta, Goderich, Ontario, Canada

Salad Bowl Romano

1/2 head cauliflower
1/2 bunch broccoli
1/4 pound bacon, crisp-
  fried, crumbled
1/3 cup chopped onion

1 carrot, thinly sliced
1 cup salad dressing
1/4 cup sugar
1/4 cup Romano cheese

Break cauliflower and broccoli into flowerets. Combine with bacon, onion and carrot in serving bowl. Blend salad dressing, sugar and cheese in small bowl. Chill vegetables and dressing until serving time. Toss vegetables with dressing just before serving. Yield: 6-8 servings.

Colleen Abar
Laureate Delta, Grand Forks, North Dakota

Cauliflower Delight

1 head cauliflower
2 stalks celery,
  chopped
1 medium green
  pepper, chopped
1 2-ounce jar
  pimento, drained
3/4 cup sliced
  stuffed olives

8 ounces Cheddar
  cheese, cubed
1 8-ounce bottle
  of Caesar
  salad dressing
1 cup sour cream
3 tablespoons
  olive juice

Break cauliflower into flowerets. Combine with celery, green pepper, pimento, olives and cheese in serving bowl. Blend salad dressing, sour cream and olive juice in bowl. Pour over cauliflower mixture; mix well. Chill for several hours to overnight. Yield: 8-10 servings.

Sharon C. Johnson
Preceptor Alpha Zeta, Arlington, Texas

Barbara's Cauliflower Salad

1 head cauliflower
1 green pepper
4 stalks celery
1 pound Cheddar
  cheese, diced

1 medium jar
  green olives
1/2 cup sour cream
1/2 cup salad dressing
Dash of paprika

Separate cauliflower into flowerets; chop green pepper and celery. Combine vegetables with cheese and olives in serving bowl. Add mixture of remaining ingredients; mix well. Chill until serving time.

Barbara Gribben
Preceptor Beta Epsilon, Florence, Colorado

Salads

Cauliflower Salad

1 large head
　cauliflower
1 large green pepper
2 tablespoons
　finely chopped
　onion
8 slices crisp-fried
　bacon, crumbled
1 cup shredded
　Cheddar cheese
1 cup mayonnaise
2 tablespoons sugar

Coarsely chop cauliflower and green pepper. Combine with onion, bacon and cheese in serving bowl. Add mayonnaise and sugar; mix well. Chill for 3 hours to overnight. Yield: 8 servings.

Janielle Riley
Xi Zeta Epsilon, Westfield, Indiana

Shoe Peg Corn Salad

1　16-ounce can
　Shoe Peg corn
1　16-ounce can
　green beans
1　16-ounce can
　early peas
1 cup chopped celery
1 cup chopped
　green onions
1/2 cup sugar
1 cup oil
1/4 cup white vinegar
Salt and pepper
　to taste

Drain canned vegetables. Combine with celery and green onions in serving bowl. Mix sugar, oil, vinegar, salt and pepper in small bowl. Pour over vegetables; toss lightly. Marinate in refrigerator overnight. Yield: 8-10 servings.

Nina Slaton
Preceptor Gamma Mu, Lubbock, Texas

Greek Salad

1 small head romaine
　lettuce, torn
1 small head green
　leaf lettuce, torn
2 medium cucumbers,
　thinly sliced
1 medium red onion,
　thinly sliced
3 medium tomatoes,
　chopped
1 1/2 cups crumbled
　feta cheese
1/3 cup lemon juice
1 clove of garlic,
　crushed
1 tablespoon oregano
2/3 cup olive oil
2 tablespoons
　minced parsley

Combine vegetables and feta cheese in salad bowl; toss lightly. Combine lemon juice, garlic and oregano in blender container. Add olive oil in fine stream, processing constantly at low speed. Pour over salad; toss lightly. Sprinkle with parsley. Yield: 6 servings.

Mary Helen Pope
Beta Iota, McCall, Idaho

Hominy Salad

2 cans hominy, drained
1/4 cup chopped celery
1/4 cup chopped
　green pepper
1/4 cup shredded
　carrots
1/4 cup chopped
　green onions
1/2 cup sour cream
1/4 cup mayonnaise
2 tablespoons vinegar
1 tablespoon mustard

Combine hominy and vegetables in serving bowl. Blend sour cream, mayonnaise, vinegar and mustard in small bowl. Add to hominy mixture; mix well. Chill overnight. Yield: 8 servings.

Prexy Pegram
Preceptor Eta Beta, Boerne, Texas

Wilted Lettuce Salad

4 slices bacon,
　chopped
3 eggs, beaten
1/4 cup cider vinegar
2 teaspoons sugar
1/4 teaspoon salt
1/8 teaspoon pepper
1/2 teaspoon dried
　dillweed (opt.)
4 cups shredded
　leaf lettuce
1/3 cup chopped
　green onions

Fry bacon in 10-inch skillet. Beat eggs with vinegar, sugar, salt, pepper and dillweed. Add to skillet. Cook for several minutes until heated through, stirring constantly; remove from heat. Add lettuce and green onions. Toss until wilted. Spoon into serving dish. Serve immediately. Yield: 4 servings. Note: May substitute shredded cabbage for lettuce and add 5 stalks chopped celery and 1/2 teaspoon celery seed.

Norma Grace Bauer
Laureate Alpha Epsilon, Altamont, Illinois

Egg and Lettuce Salad

1 small head
　lettuce, torn
3 hard-boiled
　eggs, chopped
1/2 cup mayonnaise
1 tablespoon sugar
1 tablespoon mustard
Salt and pepper
　to taste
Chopped onion (opt.)

Mix lettuce and eggs in salad bowl. Blend mayonnaise with remaining ingredients in small bowl. Add enough dressing to lettuce to moisten; mix well.

Carol Weis
Xi Alpha Beta, Council Bluffs, Iowa

Salads

Mushroom Salad

1 pound fresh
mushrooms, sliced
8 ounces Swiss
cheese, diced
2 bunches green
onions, thinly sliced

1/2 cup oil
1/4 cup red wine
vinegar
1 tablespoon
all-purpose Greek
seasoning

Combine mushrooms, cheese and green onions in serving bowl. Add mixture of oil, vinegar and seasoning; mix well. Chill until serving time. Yield: 8 servings.

Barbara Morrison
Nu Gamma, Crescent City, California

Hearts of Palm Salad

2 tablespoons vinegar
1/2 teaspoon Italian
seasonings
1 clove of garlic
1/4 teaspoon pepper
1/3 cup oil
1 tablespoon
mustard

1   14-ounce can
hearts of
palm, drained
6 cups assorted greens
1 medium tomato,
cut into wedges
1   6-ounce can crab
meat, drained

Combine first 6 ingredients in small bowl; mix well. Let stand for 1 hour. Cut hearts of palm into bite-sized pieces. Combine with greens in salad bowl. Pour dressing over greens. Arrange tomato and crab meat over top. Yield: 6 servings.

Pam Moore
Xi, Honolulu, Hawaii

Vegetable-Pasta Salad

1 small head
cauliflower, broken
into flowerets
1/2 pound fresh green
beans, cut
into pieces
2/3 cup oil
1/4 cup freshly
squeezed lemon juice
1 clove of garlic,
minced

1 teaspoon sugar
1 teaspoon basil
3/4 teaspoon salt
1/4 teaspoon pepper
1 small red onion,
thinly sliced
1 cup cherry
tomatoes
2 cups cooked
pasta

Steam cauliflower and green beans in 1 inch boiling water in saucepan for 8 minutes or until tender-crisp. Drain. Cool to room temperature. Combine oil, 2 tablespoons water and next 6 ingredients in covered jar; shake vigorously. Combine cauliflower, beans, onion, cherry tomatoes and pasta in serving bowl. Add dressing; toss lightly. Chill, covered, for several hours. Yield: 6 servings.

Photograph for this recipe on page 157.

Spinach Salad

1/2 package spinach
1/2 head lettuce,
chopped
5 hard-boiled eggs,
chopped
6 to 8 slices
crisp-fried
bacon, crumbled
1 cup frozen peas,
cooked

1 tablespoon sugar
2 or 3 green
onions, chopped
1 1/4 cups sour
cream
1 1/4 cups
mayonnaise
1/2 cup shredded
Cheddar cheese

Layer spinach, lettuce, eggs, bacon, peas, sugar and green onions in order listed in 9 x 13-inch glass dish. Pour mixture of sour cream and mayonnaise over layers. Top with cheese. Chill overnight. Yield: 12 servings.

Mary Jane Black
Kappa Kappa, Newcastle, Ontario, Canada

Crazy Pea Salad

1 head lettuce, torn
2 stalks celery,
chopped
1 green pepper, chopped
1 cucumber, chopped
1 bunch green
onions, chopped

1   10-ounce package
frozen peas
1 1/2 cups mayonnaise
6 slices crisp-fried
bacon, crumbled
1 cup shredded
Cheddar cheese

Alternate layers of lettuce, celery, green pepper, cucumber and green onions in 2-quart dish, sprinkling each layer with peas. Do not thaw peas. Spread mayonnaise over vegetables, sealing to edge. Sprinkle bacon and cheese over top. Chill overnight.

Adrianna Salinas
Epsilon Nu, Moses Lake, Washington

Salads

Pea Salad Delight

1   16-ounce can
      tiny peas
2 cups shredded sharp
      Cheddar cheese

1/2 cup chopped
      green onions
1/4 cup pickle relish
1/3 cup mayonnaise

Combine all ingredients in serving bowl; mix lightly. Chill for 1 hour to 3 days. Yield: 8-12 servings.

Velma G. Sherwood
Xi Delta Phi, Blue Springs, Missouri

Marinated Tomato Salad

2 cups chopped tomatoes
1/2 cup sliced
      pimento-stuffed
      olives

1/4 cup sliced
      green onions
1/3 cup French dressing
1 avocado, sliced

Combine tomatoes, olives, green onions and salad dressing in bowl. Chill, covered, for 1 to 2 hours. Spoon onto lettuce-lined plates. Arrange avocado slices on top. Yield: 4 servings.

Helen Heath
Preceptor Upsilon, Muncie, Indiana

Tomatoes Rose

4 large tomatoes
1/2 cup Rose wine
1/3 cup oil
3 tablespoons wine
      vinegar
1/4 cup finely
      chopped celery

1/4 cup thinly
      sliced green
      onions
1 envelope
      Italian salad
      dressing mix

Slice tomatoes thinly; arrange in shallow dish. Combine remaining ingredients in covered jar; shake vigorously. Pour over tomatoes. Chill, covered, for several hours. Arrange tomato slices on serving platter; garnish with celery leaves. Serve with dressing. Yield: 6 servings.

JoAnn J. Kresky
Preceptor Chi, Lansing, Michigan

Green Vegetable Medley

1   16-ounce can
      French-style
      green beans
1   16-ounce can
      tiny peas
1   16-ounce can
      Chinese vegetables
1 can water
      chestnuts, thinly
      sliced

1 small jar chopped
      pimento (opt.)
1 1/2 cups thinly
      sliced celery
3 medium onions,
      thinly sliced
1 cup sugar
3/4 cup vinegar
1 teaspoon salt
Pepper to taste

Drain canned vegetables. Combine all ingredients in serving bowl; mix well. Chill, covered, overnight to several weeks Yield: 8 servings.

Mrs. Rea Thomas
Xi Upsilon Omega, Forney, Texas

Marinated Vegetables

1 can French-style
      green beans
1 can Shoe Peg corn
1 can tiny sweet peas
1 small jar chopped
      pimento
1 bunch green onions
1 cup chopped celery

1 green pepper
1/2 head cauliflower
1 cup vinegar
3/4 cup sugar
1/2 cup oil
Salt and pepper
      to taste

Drain canned vegetables; chop fresh vegetables. Combine all vegetables in serving bowl. Bring vinegar and remaining ingredients to a boil in saucepan; cool. Pour over vegetables. Marinate salad in refrigerator for several days.

Juanita Long
Laureate Alpha Lambda, Gladewater, Texas

Swedish Marinated Salad

1   16-ounce can
      French-style
      green beans
1   16-ounce can whole
      kernel corn
1   16-ounce can
      English peas
1 cup chopped celery
1 medium onion,
      thinly sliced
1 cup sliced
      cooked carrots

1/2 cup sliced
      green pepper
1 jar chopped
      pimento
1/2 cup sugar
3/4 cup white
      vinegar
1/3 cup oil
1 teaspoon salt
1/8 teaspoon
      pepper

Drain canned vegetables. Combine all vegetables in large serving bowl. Mix sugar, vinegar, oil, salt and pepper in small bowl; mix well. Pour over vegetables; mix well. Chill for several hours to several weeks. Yield: 2 1/2 quarts.
Note: May add other vegetables of choice such as garbanzos and mushrooms.

Vivian Jean Brown
Preceptor Laureate Alpha Upsilon, San Antonio, Texas

Vegetables & Side Dishes

Stir-Fried Celery with Broccoli, recipe on page 178.

Vegetables

Artichoke Casserole

1/4 cup finely
   chopped onion
1/2 stick margarine
1 can artichoke
   hearts, drained

1 16-ounce can
   Italian tomatoes
1/2 teaspoon basil
Salt and pepper
   to taste

Saute onion in margarine in skillet until tender. Cut artichokes in quarters. Drain tomatoes, reserving half the juice; chop tomatoes. Combine onion, artichokes, tomatoes, reserved juice and seasonings in casserole; mix well. Bake at 325 degrees for 20 minutes.

Cathy Petrung
Delta Pi, Montgomery, Alabama

Asparagus Casserole

24 soda crackers,
   crushed
2 cans cut asparagus
1 can cream of
   mushroom soup

4 hard-boiled eggs,
   chopped
Salt and pepper
   to taste
1 stick butter, melted

Sprinkle 1/3 of the cracker crumbs in buttered 2-quart casserole. Drain asparagus, reserving 1 cup liquid. Mix reserved liquid and soup in bowl. Stir in asparagus, eggs and seasonings. Spoon into prepared casserole. Drizzle butter over top. Sprinkle with remaining crumbs. Bake at 350 degrees for 30 minutes. Yield: 8-10 servings.

Edith Durbin
Laureate Alpha Epsilon, Effingham, Illinois

Fay's Green Bean Casserole

1 16-ounce can
   green beans,
   drained
1 3-ounce can
   French-fried onions
1 can cream of
   mushroom soup

1 3-ounce can
   mushrooms
2 tablespoons chopped
   toasted almonds
1/2 cup shredded
   Cheddar cheese

Alternate layers of beans and onions in greased 2-quart casserole. Combine soup, mushrooms with liquid and almonds in bowl. Pour over layers. Top with cheese. Bake at 375 degrees for 30 minutes. Yield: 6 servings.

Fay Voove
Xi Zeta Omega, Glendale, California

Green Bean Casserole

2 medium onions,
   chopped
1 stick butter
3 20-ounce cans
   French-style
   green beans
1 tablespoon caraway
   seed
Salt and pepper
   to taste

1 tablespoon Accent
1 can cream of
   mushroom soup
4 slices crisp-fried
   bacon, crumbled
1 cup grated cheese
Butter crackers,
   crumbled
Butter

Saute onions in 1 stick butter in saucepan. Add beans and seasonings; mix well. Simmer for 1 hour. Drain, reserving 1/4 cup liquid. Combine reserved liquid with soup, bacon and cheese in bowl. Stir in beans. Spoon into greased 2-quart casserole. Sprinkle cracker crumbs over top. Dot with additional butter. Bake at 350 degrees for 30 minutes. Yield: 8 servings.

Ann Doucet
Xi Rho Zeta, Deer Park, Texas

Italian Green Beans

1 2-pound package
   frozen green beans
1/4 cup bacon bits

1 cup Italian
   salad dressing

Cook green beans using package directions; drain. Stir in bacon bits and salad dressing; toss to coat well. Spoon into serving dish. Yield: 6 servings.

Kathleen J. Shafer
Theta Epsilon, Julesburg, Colorado

Baked Beans

1/2 pound ground beef
1/2 pound bacon,
   chopped
1/2 onion, chopped
1 16-ounce can
   baked beans
1 16-ounce can
   kidney beans

1 16-ounce can
   lima beans
1/2 cup packed
   brown sugar
1/2 cup catsup
1 teaspoon vinegar
1 teaspoon mustard

Brown ground beef, bacon and onion in skillet, stirring frequently; drain. Add remaining ingredients; mix well. Pour into greased casserole. Bake at 350 degrees for 1 1/2 hours. Note: May cook in Crock·Pot on High for 2 1/2 hours.

Marlene Morse
Alpha Sigma, Devil's Lake, North Dakota

Vegetables

Easy Baked Beans

1 16-ounce can pork
   and beans in
   tomato sauce
1 small onion, chopped
1 green pepper,
   chopped

Catsup and tomato
   sauce to taste
1 teaspoon mustard
1 teaspoon
   chili powder
2 slices bacon

Combine beans with all ingredients except bacon in bowl; mix well. Pour into greased 2-quart casserole. Top with bacon. Bake at 350 degrees for 30 to 40 minutes or until bubbly. Yield: 4-6 servings.

Renee Nichols
Gamma Kappa, Cape Canaveral, Florida

Five-Bean Casserole

1/2 pound bacon,
   chopped
2 medium onions,
   chopped
1 green pepper, chopped
1/2 cup packed
   brown sugar
1/2 cup vinegar
1 teaspoon each salt,
   garlic salt,
   turmeric and
   dry mustard

1 16-ounce can
   kidney beans
1 16-ounce can
   lima beans
1 16-ounce can
   butter beans
1 16-ounce can
   pinto beans
1 16-ounce
   can Morton
   House beans

Brown bacon, onions and green pepper in skillet. Stir in brown sugar, vinegar and seasonings. Simmer for 20 minutes. Add beans; mix well. Pour into greased 3-quart casserole. Bake at 350 degrees for 1 hour or until bubbly.
Yield: 20 servings.
Note: Flavor improves if casserole is reheated on second day.

Frankie Henson
Xi Lambda Xi, Clarendon, Texas

Nippy Beets

3 tablespoons melted
   butter
2 tablespoons prepared
   mustard
1 tablespoon honey

1 teaspoon
   Worcestershire sauce
Salt to taste
2 cups hot drained
   beets

Blend butter, mustard, honey, Worcestershire sauce and salt in saucepan. Cook until just heated through. Add beets, stirring to glaze well. Pour into serving dish. Yield: 4 servings.

JoAnn J. Kresky
Preceptor Chi, Lansing, Michigan

Bonnie's Broccoli Casserole

2 10-ounce
   packages frozen
   chopped broccoli
1/2 cup sour
   cream

1 cup cream of
   mushroom soup
1/2 cup shredded
   cheese
Slivered almonds

Layer ingredients in order given in greased 2-quart casserole. Bake at 325 degrees for 25 minutes.

Bonnie Webster
Preceptor Alpha, Fairbanks, Alaska

Broccoli and Corn Bake

1 10-ounce package
   frozen chopped
   broccoli, thawed
1 14-ounce can
   cream-style corn
1/4 cup cracker crumbs
1 egg, beaten
2 tablespoons
   melted butter

1 tablespoon finely
   chopped onion
1/2 teaspoon salt
Dash of pepper
1/4 cup cracker
   crumbs
2 tablespoons
   melted butter

Combine broccoli, corn and next 6 ingredients in bowl; mix well. Pour into greased 1 1/2-quart casserole. Mix 1/4 cup cracker crumbs with 2 tablespoons melted butter. Sprinkle over casserole. Bake, covered, at 350 degrees for 30 minutes. Bake, uncovered, for 15 minutes longer. Yield: 6 servings.

Charlotte Woolfrey
Sigma, Lewisporte, Newfoundland, Canada

Broccoli Dish

1 2-pound package
   frozen broccoli
2 eggs, beaten
1 cup mayonnaise

1 cup grated
   Cheddar cheese
Bread crumbs

Cook broccoli using package directions; drain. Stir in mixture of eggs and mayonnaise. Pour into greased casserole. Top with cheese and bread crumbs. Bake at 350 degrees for 30 minutes.

Marilyn Borras
Xi Epsilon Alpha, Stafford, Virginia

Vegetables

Broccoli Puff

2 10-ounce packages frozen chopped broccoli	2 eggs
	1/2 teaspoon salt
	1 cup shredded
1 cup baking mix	Cheddar cheese
1 cup milk	

Cook broccoli according to package directions; drain. Combine baking mix, milk, eggs and salt in mixer bowl. Beat until smooth. Stir in broccoli and cheese. Spoon into buttered 1 1/2-quart casserole. Bake at 325 degrees for 1 hour or until knife inserted between center and edge comes out clean. Yield: 6 servings.

Maryann Cotterill
Theta Iota, Hendersonville, North Carolina

Broccoli Supreme

2 10-ounce packages frozen chopped broccoli	2 eggs, beaten
	1 cup grated
	Cheddar cheese
1 can cream of mushroom soup	Salt and pepper to taste
1 cup mayonnaise	Cracker crumbs
1 small onion, finely chopped	Butter

Cook broccoli in saucepan according to package directions; drain well. Combine soup, mayonnaise, onion, eggs, cheese and seasonings in bowl; mix well. Fold in broccoli. Spoon into greased 9 x 13-inch baking dish. Top with cracker crumbs. Dot with butter. Bake at 400 degrees for 20 minutes. Yield: 10-12 servings.

Judith Woods
Xi Pi, Clovis, California

Jerry's Rice and Broccoli Casserole

1 2-pound package frozen broccoli, thawed	1 can cream of mushroom soup
	2 cups minute rice
1 small jar Cheez Whiz	1/2 cup butter, melted

Combine all ingredients and 1 cup water in bowl; mix well. Pour into greased 9 x 13-inch baking dish. Bake at 350 degrees for 45 minutes. Yield: 8 servings.

Jerry Heubach
Alpha Sigma, Mobile, Alabama

Mary's Broccoli Puff

1 pound fresh broccoli, trimmed	1/4 cup mayonnaise
	1 egg, beaten
1 can cream of mushroom soup	1 1/4 cups dry bread crumbs
1/2 cup shredded Cheddar cheese	1 tablespoon melted butter
1/4 cup milk	

Cook broccoli in water in saucepan for 5 minutes; drain. Arrange in greased 9 x 13-inch baking dish. Combine soup, cheese, milk, mayonnaise and egg in bowl; mix well. Pour over broccoli. Top with mixture of bread crumbs and butter. Bake at 350 degrees for 45 minutes or until bubbly.

Mary Allen
Xi Gamma Rho, Columbus, Georgia

Nutty Broccoli Casserole

4 10-ounce packages frozen broccoli	1 cup chopped pecans
	1 cup sliced water chestnuts
2 sticks margarine, melted	1 cup (about) bread crumbs
1 envelope dry onion soup mix	

Arrange thawed broccoli in greased 9 x 13-inch baking dish. Combine margarine, soup mix, pecans and water chestnuts in bowl. Spread over broccoli. Top with bread crumbs. Bake at 300 degrees for 1 hour. Yield: 8-10 servings.

Betty Lou Fisher
Preceptor Alpha Gamma, Wichita, Kansas

Pat's Broccoli Casserole

1 10-ounce package frozen chopped broccoli, thawed	1 can cream of chicken soup
	1 8-ounce jar Cheez Whiz with jalapeno peppers
1/2 cup finely chopped onion (opt.)	1 stick butter, melted
1 cup minute rice	
1 can cream of mushroom soup	

Combine all ingredients in bowl; mix well. Spoon into greased 2-quart casserole. Bake at 350 degrees for 45 minutes to 1 hour or until bubbly and brown. Yield: 8 servings.

Pat Buturla
Alpha Nu, Baton Rouge, Louisiana

Vegetables

Quick Broccoli Casserole

2 10-ounce packages
    frozen broccoli,
    cooked
1 medium onion,
    chopped
2 eggs, well beaten
3/4 cup mayonnaise

1 can cream of
    mushroom soup
1/4 cup margarine,
    softened
1 cup grated
    sharp cheese
1/2 cup croutons (opt.)

Combine all ingredients except croutons in bowl; mix well. Spoon into greased 2-quart casserole. Top with croutons. Bake at 350 degrees for 30 minutes. Yield: 8-10 servings.

Marilyn A. Christensen
Eta Alpha, Quincy, California

Rice and Broccoli Casserole

1 1/2 cups minute rice
1 10-ounce package
    frozen chopped
    broccoli, cooked
1/2 cup chopped celery

1 small onion,
    chopped
1 can cream of
    chicken soup

Cook rice according to package directions. Add remaining ingredients; mix well. Pour into greased 2-quart casserole. Bake at 350 degrees for 1 hour. Yield: 6-8 servings.

Carolyn A. Brenneis
Epsilon Nu, Blair, Nebraska

Ritzy Broccoli

2 10-ounce packages
    frozen chopped
    broccoli
2 eggs, beaten
1 cup grated cheese

1 can cream of
    mushroom soup
1/2 cup mayonnaise
Ritz crackers, crumbled

Cook broccoli in salted water in saucepan for 5 minutes; drain. Arrange in greased 6 x 10-inch casserole. Spread with mixture of eggs, cheese, soup and mayonnaise. Top with cracker crumbs. Bake at 350 degrees for 30 to 35 minutes or until bubbly. Yield: 6-8 servings.

Nancy Edwards
Preceptor Laureate Alpha, Agawam, Massachusetts

Cabbage Casserole

1 head cabbage,
    shredded
Salt and red pepper
    to taste
1 can cream of
    mushroom soup

1/2 stick butter,
    sliced
1 onion, chopped
8 ounces cheese,
    grated
1/2 cup bread crumbs

Cook cabbage in water in saucepan until tender; drain. Arrange in greased 10 x 10-inch casserole. Layer seasonings, soup, butter, onion and cheese over cabbage. Mix gently. Top with bread crumbs. Bake at 350 degrees for 45 minutes. Yield: 6-8 servings.

Ellen Boudreaux
Theta Eta, Erath, Louisiana

Cabbage Mallum

2 to 3 teaspoons
    minced onion
2 teaspoons garlic
    flakes
3 to 4 tablespoons
    margarine
2 small heads cabbage,
    finely shredded

1 1/2 teaspoons salt
2 cups shredded
    coconut
1/4 teaspoon turmeric
1 teaspoon pepper
3/4 teaspoon crushed
    mustard seed

Saute onion and garlic flakes in margarine in skillet. Add cabbage and salt. Saute until cabbage is tender, stirring frequently. Combine remaining ingredients in bowl. Stir into cabbage. Cook until heated through. Spoon into serving dish. Yield: 6 servings.

Beverly Oldaker
Co-Laureate Alpha Delta, Pueblo, Colorado

Orange-Ginger Carrots

1 pound carrots
1 tablespoon sugar
1/4 teaspoon salt
1 teaspoon cornstarch

1/4 teaspoon ginger
1/4 cup orange juice
1 tablespoon butter

Peel carrots; slice diagonally 1 inch thick. Cook in 1 inch lightly salted water in saucepan for 10 to 15 minutes or until tender-crisp; drain. Combine sugar, salt, cornstarch, ginger and orange juice in small bowl. Pour over carrots. Cook over low heat for 3 minutes or until thickened, stirring constantly. Add butter, stirring to coat well. Spoon into serving dish. Yield: 4 servings.

Margaret M. Olmsted
Laureate Xi, Coldwater, Michigan

Vegetables

Orange-Glazed Carrots

1 1/2 pounds carrots,
    peeled, sliced
1/4 cup butter

1 cup maple syrup
1 orange, sliced

Cook carrots in salted water to cover in saucepan until tender; drain. Add remaining ingredients. Bring to a boil; reduce heat. Simmer for 15 minutes. Spoon into serving dish. Yield: 6 servings.

Norma Dagas
Xi Tau, Lafayette, Louisiana

Stella's Marinated Carrots

2 packages carrots,
    peeled
1 medium onion,
    finely chopped
1 green pepper,
    finely chopped

1 can tomato soup
6 tablespoons oil
2/3 cup sugar
1/3 cup wine vinegar
2 teaspoons
    Worcestershire sauce

Cook carrots in water in saucepan until tender; drain. Slice diagonally 1/4 inch thick. Combine remaining ingredients in bowl; mix well. Add 5 cups carrots; mix well. Chill, covered, overnight to 2 days. Spoon into serving bowl. Yield: 8-10 servings.

Stella I. Furr
Xi Psi, Douglas, Arizona

Cauliflower in-a-Hurry

1 head cauliflower
Milk
Mayonnaise

Grated Cheddar cheese
Paprika
Bacon bits

Cook cauliflower in mixture of half milk, half water and salt to taste in saucepan; drain. Place cauliflower in baking dish. Spread with mayonnaise. Sprinkle with cheese, paprika and bacon bits. Broil for 10 minutes or until browned. Yield: 4 servings.

Carol Sassin
Xi Psi Beta, Beeville, Texas

Fried Cauliflower

1 head cauliflower
2 eggs, beaten
1 1/2 cups fine
    bread crumbs

1/2 cup grated
    Romano cheese
Olive oil

Break cauliflower into flowerets. Cook in salted water in saucepan until tender-crisp; drain and pat dry. Dip in egg, then in mixture of bread crumbs and cheese. Fry in small amount of olive oil in skillet until golden brown on all sides. Arrange on serving plate. Yield: 4-6 servings.

Gail Duchamp
Alpha Epsilon, Lafayette, Louisiana

Celery and Water Chestnut Casserole

2 cups thinly
    sliced celery
1 cup sliced
    water chestnuts
1 can cream of
    chicken soup

1 stick butter, melted
1 4-ounce package
    butter crackers,
    crushed
1 2-ounce package
    sliced almonds

Cook celery in salted water in saucepan for 7 minutes or until tender-crisp. Add water chestnuts and soup; mix well. Pour into greased casserole. Top with mixture of remaining ingredients. Bake at 350 degrees for 30 minutes.

Lois Mansfield
Laureate Alpha Epsilon, Effingham, Illinois

Stir-Fried Celery with Broccoli

1 bunch broccoli
1 clove of garlic,
    crushed
1/4 cup oil
6 cups diagonally
    sliced celery

1 large onion, cut
    into rings
3 tablespoons
    soy sauce
3/4 teaspoon ginger
1/8 teaspoon pepper

Cut broccoli into flowerets; cut stems into 1/2-inch slices. Stir-fry garlic in hot oil in wok for 30 seconds. Add celery and broccoli. Stir-fry for 3 minutes. Add onion, soy sauce, ginger and pepper. Stir-fry for 2 to 3 minutes or until vegetables are tender-crisp. Yield: 4-6 servings.

Photograph for this recipe on page 173.

Celery Casserole

4 cups sliced celery
1 can water
    chestnuts, chopped
1 can cream of
    chicken soup
2 tablespoons
    chopped pimento

3/4 cup soft bread
    crumbs
1 2-ounce package
    sliced almonds
2 tablespoons
    margarine

Cook celery in water to cover in saucepan until tender-crisp; drain. Stir in water chestnuts, soup and pimento; mix well. Pour into greased casserole. Brown bread crumbs and almonds in margarine in skillet. Sprinkle over casserole. Bake at 350 degrees for 35 minutes.

Sheila Krook
Beta Iota, Rawlins, Wyoming

Vegetables

Corn Stuffing Balls

1 16-ounce can
   cream-style corn
1 package herb-seasoned
   stuffing mix
1 small onion, chopped
1/2 cup chopped celery

2 eggs, lightly beaten
1 teaspoon poultry
   seasoning
1/8 teaspoon pepper
1/4 cup melted
   margarine

Combine all ingredients except margarine in bowl. Add 1/4 cup water; mix well. Shape into 7 or 8 balls. Place in Crock-Pot. Drizzle with margarine. Cook on Low for 3 to 4 hours. Yield: 7-8 servings.

Jane O'Mara
Nu Delta, Burlington, Kansas

Creole Corn

2 slices bacon
1 large onion, sliced
1 medium green
   pepper, chopped
1 small bay leaf

1 16-ounce can
   tomatoes
2 cups fresh corn
1/4 teaspoon salt
1/8 teaspoon pepper

Fry bacon in skillet until crisp; remove bacon and crumble. Saute onion and green pepper in bacon drippings until tender-crisp. Add bay leaf and tomatoes. Simmer for 10 minutes. Stir in corn. Simmer for 10 minutes; discard bay leaf. Add bacon and seasonings. Heat until bubbly.
Yield: 6-8 servings.

Sally A. Luman
Pi Beta, Aurora, Illinois

Missouri Corn Pudding

1 box Jiffy corn
   bread mix
1 16-ounce can
   whole kernel corn
1 16-ounce can
   cream-style corn

1 cup sour cream
1 cup grated
   Cheddar cheese
2 eggs
1 stick butter, melted
Grated Cheddar cheese

Combine first 7 ingredients in bowl; mix well. Pour into greased 2-quart casserole. Bake at 350 degrees for 35 to 45 minutes or until browned and set. Sprinkle with cheese.
Yield: 10-12 servings.

Button Ruzicka
Xi Delta Sigma, Corpus Christi, Texas

Scalloped Corn

1 16-ounce can
   cream-style corn
1 16-ounce can whole
   kernel corn, drained

1 cup sour cream
2 eggs, beaten
1 stick margarine

Combine all ingredients except margarine in bowl; mix well. Pour into greased rectangular 2-quart baking dish. Dot with margarine. Bake at 375 degrees for 45 minutes or until brown. Yield: 8-12 servings.

Reve' Beattie
Alpha Omega Omicron, Azle, Texas

Mom's Cucumbers

1/2 cup sugar
1/3 cup (about) vinegar
1/4 teaspoon each
   salt and pepper

2 to 3 medium
   cucumbers, peeled,
   thinly sliced

Combine sugar, vinegar, seasonings and 1/3 cup water in bowl; mix well. Add cucumbers. Chill for several hours to overnight.

Gillian McDaniel
Laureate Alpha Omicron, Victoria, Texas

Easy-Licious Eggplant Parmesan

2 medium eggplant
1 cup flour
1/2 cup oil
1 16-ounce jar
   spaghetti sauce

1/2 cup Parmesan
   cheese
1 cup shredded
   mozzarella cheese

Peel eggplant and slice 1/2 inch thick. Coat with flour. Brown on both sides in hot oil in skillet; drain. Place a small amount of sauce in 9 x 13-inch baking dish. Layer eggplant, remaining sauce, Parmesan and mozzarella cheeses in dish. Bake at 375 degrees for 10 to 15 minutes or until cheese is lightly browned. Yield: 9 servings.

Jeanne Mills
Xi Alpha Nu, Kennewick, Washington

Eggplant Casserole

1 eggplant, peeled,
   chopped
2 to 3 cups
   stuffing mix

1 can cream of
   mushroom soup
Grated Monterey
   Jack cheese

Cook eggplant in lightly salted water in saucepan for 5 minutes; drain. Add stuffing mix and soup; mix well. Pour into buttered 2-quart casserole. Top with cheese. Bake at 350 degrees for 30 minutes. Yield: 4 servings.

Kimberly L. Birch
Eta Nu, Charles City, Iowa

Vegetables

Okra Italiano

1 10-ounce package
   frozen okra
1 29-ounce can
   Italian tomatoes
2 green peppers,
   chopped

1 large onion, sliced
1 bay leaf
1/2 teaspoon basil
Garlic powder to taste
Pinch of oregano
Croutons

Combine all ingredients except croutons in saucepan. Simmer for 15 to 20 minutes or until onion and peppers are tender-crisp, stirring frequently. Remove bay leaf. Spoon into serving dish; sprinkle with croutons. Yield: 6 servings.

Nancy Watson
Xi Gamma, El Cajon, California

Chinese Peas

1 10-ounce package
   frozen peas, cooked
1 16-ounce can
   Chinese vegetables,
   drained

1 can cream of
   celery soup
1 can chow mein
   noodles

Combine peas, Chinese vegetables and soup in bowl; mix well. Spoon into greased 9 x 9-inch casserole. Top with chow mein noodles. Bake at 350 degrees until bubbly and brown. Yield: 6 servings.

Marilynne Rohr
Xi Kappa Theta, Morrow, Ohio

Cheesy Potatoes

1 16-ounce package
   frozen O'Brien
   potatoes, thawed
1 can cream of
   chicken soup
1/2 medium onion,
   chopped

1/2 cup sour cream
1 5-ounce package
   grated sharp
   Cheddar cheese
1/2 teaspoon
   seasoned salt
Chopped parsley

Combine all ingredients except parsley in bowl; mix well. Spoon into greased 8 x 8-inch baking dish. Sprinkle with parsley. Bake at 350 degrees for 1 1/2 hours, stirring occasionally. Garnish with additional cheese and parsley. Yield: 4-6 servings.

Ruth Q. Larsen
Laureate Gamma Chi, Colorado Springs, Colorado

Creamy Tuna Potato Topper

2 tablespoons butter,
   melted
3 tablespoons flour
2 1/2 cups milk
1/2 teaspoon dry
   mustard
1/4 teaspoon hot
   pepper sauce

2 7-ounce cans tuna,
   drained, flaked
1/4 cup chopped
   pitted ripe olives
1/4 cup chopped pimento
4 Idaho potatoes,
   baked

Combine butter and flour in saucepan; mix well. Cook over medium heat for 3 minutes, stirring constantly. Remove from heat. Stir in milk gradually. Cook until thickened, stirring constantly. Add mustard and hot pepper sauce. Fold in tuna, olives and pimento. Spoon sauce over potatoes. Yield: 4 servings.

Photograph for this recipe on page 35.

Crispy Cheese Potatoes

6 cups thinly sliced
   potatoes
1 teaspoon salt
2 teaspoons melted
   butter

1 4-ounce package
   grated Cheddar
   cheese
1 1/2 cups bread
   crumbs

Season potatoes with salt; toss lightly. Arrange in greased 9 x 13-inch baking dish. Drizzle with butter. Sprinkle with cheese and bread crumbs. Bake at 450 degrees for 20 minutes or until tender. Yield: 6-8 servings.

Margaret Scholtz
Preceptor Delta Mu, Lena, Illinois

Glorious Mashed Potatoes

3 large baking
   potatoes, peeled,
   sliced 1/4 inch
   thick
1/4 cup milk
2 tablespoons butter,
   softened
1/4 cup sour cream

1 3-ounce package
   cream cheese with
   chives, softened
1/2 teaspoon salt
1/8 teaspoon pepper
1 teaspoon chopped
   chives (opt.)

Cook potatoes, loosely covered, in water to cover in saucepan for 15 minutes or until tender; drain. Mash with milk. Add remaining ingredients except chives; mix well. Spoon into serving dish. Sprinkle with chives. Yield: 4 servings.
Note: May hold, covered with foil, in 250-degree oven for 30 minutes. Shape leftovers into patties and brown for 5 minutes on each side in hot oil.

Margaret M. Olmsted
Laureate Xi, Coldwater, Michigan

Vegetables

Mashed Potato Casserole

2 pounds potatoes,
    peeled, chopped
1/2 cup milk
1/4 cup margarine
1/4 cup chopped
    green pepper
1 tablespoon chopped
    chives

1 3-ounce package
    cream cheese,
    chopped
1/2 cup sour cream
1 teaspoon each salt,
    onion salt
Dash of pepper

Cook potatoes in water to cover in saucepan until tender; drain. Mash with milk and margarine. Beat in remaining ingredients. Spoon into greased 1 1/2-quart casserole. Bake, covered, at 350 degrees for 40 minutes or until heated through. Garnish with parsley and paprika. Yield: 6 servings.

Victoria Shepley
Xi Epsilon Mu, Harrow, Ontario, Canada

Potato Souffle

1 8-serving package
    instant mashed
    potatoes
2 3-ounce packages
    cream cheese,
    softened

1 egg, beaten
2 tablespoons finely
    chopped onion
2 tablespoons chopped
    parsley

Prepare potatoes in saucepan according to package directions, omitting butter. Beat in remaining ingredients. Spoon into well-buttered casserole. Bake at 400 degrees for 30 minutes. Yield: 8 servings.

Virginia B. Hall
Xi Alpha Tau, Kenmore, New York

Potato Swirls

2 teaspoons salt
6 tablespoons butter
1 2/3 cups sour cream

3 1/2 cups instant
    potato flakes

Bring 3 1/2 cups water, salt and butter to a boil in saucepan. Stir in sour cream and potatoes; mix until smooth. Spoon into pastry bag with star tip. Pipe into swirls 2 inches apart on greased baking sheet. Chill for 30 minutes or longer. Bake at 350 degrees for 25 minutes. Yield: 8 servings.
Note: May drop by tablespoonfuls onto baking sheet.

Lela Green
Preceptor Chi, Tacoma, Washington

Party Potato Casserole

1 32-ounce package
    frozen hashed
    brown potatoes
1 can cream of
    celery soup
1/4 to 1/2 cup chopped
    onion
1 8-ounce carton
    sour cream

2 cups grated
    Cheddar cheese
1/2 cup melted
    margarine
1 teaspoon salt
1/4 teaspoon pepper
1 cup cornflake crumbs
1/4 cup melted
    margarine

Spread potatoes in greased shallow 2-quart baking dish. Combine soup, onion, sour cream, cheese, 1/2 cup margarine and seasonings in bowl; mix well. Spread over potatoes. Top with mixture of cornflake crumbs and 1/4 cup margarine. Bake at 350 degrees for 1 hour. Yield: 8-10 servings.

Marjorie Anderson Dakin
Laureate Xi, Spokane, Washington

Helen's Potato Casserole

1 2-pound package
    frozen hashed brown
    potatoes, thawed
1 can cream of
    potato soup
1 can cream of
    celery soup

1 cup milk
1 cup sour cream
Salt and pepper
    to taste
2 cups grated Cheddar
    cheese (opt.)

Combine all ingredients except cheese in bowl; mix lightly. Spoon into greased 9 x 13-inch baking dish. Bake, covered with foil, for 1 hour. Sprinkle cheese over top. Bake for 30 minutes longer. Yield: 12 servings.

Helen Still
Mu Alpha, Smithville, Missouri

Supreme Scalloped Potatoes

1 2-pound package
    frozen southern-style
    hashed brown potatoes
1/2 to 1 cup chopped
    onion
1 can cream of
    chicken soup

2 cups sour cream
1 stick margarine,
    melted
1 cup shredded
    sharp cheese
1 cup cornflakes

Combine all ingredients except cornflakes in bowl; mix well. Spoon into greased 9 x 13-inch baking dish. Sprinkle with cornflakes. Bake at 350 degrees for 40 to 50 minutes or until bubbly and brown. Yield: 12-15 servings.
Note: May freeze unbaked casserole, adding cornflakes at cooking time.

Reva J. Falk
Preceptor Theta, Tucson, Arizona

Vegetables

Ratatouille Topping

1 small eggplant, cut
    into 1-inch cubes
1 medium red onion,
    chopped
3 cloves of garlic,
    minced
1 large green pepper,
    coarsely chopped
1 medium red pepper,
    coarsely chopped

2 large tomatoes,
    coarsely chopped
1 cup cooked cut
    green beans
1 zucchini, cut into
    1-inch strips
1 cup sliced mushrooms
4 Idaho potatoes,
    baked

Saute eggplant in large skillet over medium heat. Add onion and garlic. Saute for 1 minute. Add peppers. Cook for 1 minute longer. Add tomatoes and 1/2 cup water. Simmer for 3 minutes. Add green beans, zucchini and mushrooms. Cook until heated through. Spoon topping over potatoes. Yield: 4 servings.

Photograph for this recipe on page 35.

Sausage Special

1 pound sweet Italian
    sausages, peeled,
    sliced
1 large red pepper,
    sliced
1 large green pepper,
    sliced
1 medium onion, diced
1 tablespoon (or more)
    curry powder

2 tablespoons Dijon
    mustard
1 1/2 cups dry
    white wine
1/2 pound mushrooms,
    sliced
1 cup sour cream
4 Idaho potatoes,
    baked

Saute sausages in medium skillet until lightly browned. Add peppers and onion. Cook for 5 minutes. Stir in curry powder and mustard. Cook for 5 minutes longer. Add wine. Cook until slightly thickened. Stir in mushrooms and sour cream. Heat to serving temperature. Spoon sauce over potatoes. Yield: 4 servings.

Photograph for this recipe on page 35.

Swiss-Scalloped Potatoes

2 tablespoons
    melted butter
2 tablespoons flour
1 teaspoon salt
1 cup milk
1 cup sour cream
1 cup shredded
    Swiss cheese
1 tablespoon dillweed

1/2 cup sliced
    green onions
4 large potatoes,
    cooked, sliced
1/2 cup shredded
    Swiss cheese
1/2 cup bread crumbs
1/4 cup melted butter

Blend 2 tablespoons butter, flour and salt in saucepan. Stir in milk. Cook until thickened, stirring constantly. Simmer for 2 minutes longer, stirring constantly; remove from heat. Stir in sour cream. Combine 1 cup cheese, dillweed and green onions in small bowl. Arrange 1/2 of the potatoes in greased 9 x 13-inch baking dish. Layer half the cheese mixture, half the sour cream mixture and half the remaining potatoes over first layer. Repeat layers. Sprinkle with mixture of remaining 3 ingredients. Bake at 350 degrees for 30 minutes. Yield: 10 servings.

Jeanette E. Jacobson
Preceptor Xi, Long Beach, California

Quick Cream of Potato Soup

3 cups finely
    chopped potatoes
1 small onion,
    finely chopped

2 beef bouillon cubes
2 cups milk
Salt and pepper
    to taste

Combine potatoes, onion, bouillon cubes and 1 1/2 cups boiling water in saucepan. Cook, covered, for 15 minutes or until potatoes are tender. Mash partially with fork. Stir in remaining ingredients. Heat just to a simmer. Yield: 4 servings.

Pearl Clarke
Preceptor Beta Lambda, Grand Rapids, Michigan

Creamed Spinach

2 10-ounce packages
    frozen chopped
    spinach

1/3 cup sour cream
1/2 teaspoon nutmeg

Cook spinach in saucepan using package directions; drain. Stir in sour cream; mix well. Spoon into serving dish. Sprinkle with nutmeg. Yield: 6-8 servings.

Lila Warrell
Preceptor Upsilon, Muncie, Indiana

Spinach-Artichoke Casserole

1 16-ounce can
    artichoke hearts
1 8-ounce package
    cream cheese
1 stick butter

2 10-ounce packages
    frozen chopped
    spinach, thawed
Bread crumbs

Drain artichoke hearts and cut into quarters. Arrange in greased 9 x 9-inch baking dish. Melt cream cheese and butter in saucepan. Stir in well-drained spinach. Spread over artichokes. Top with bread crumbs. Bake at 350 degrees for 20 minutes or until bubbly. Yield: 4-6 servings.

Marian Swain
Xi Delta Alpha, North Fort Myers, Florida

Vegetables

Spinach Fettucini

4 cups torn fresh
    spinach
1 cup fresh parsley
3/4 cup grated
    Parmesan cheese
1/2 cup walnuts
1/2 cup olive oil

1 clove of garlic
1/2 teaspoon salt
1/4 teaspoon pepper
1 12-ounce package
    fettucini, cooked
Parmesan cheese (opt.)

Combine spinach, parsley, 3/4 cup Parmesan cheese, walnuts, olive oil, garlic, salt and pepper in blender container. Process until smooth. Combine with hot fettucini in large serving dish. Toss until fettucini is coated. Garnish with additional Parmesan cheese. Yield: 4-6 servings.

Photograph for this recipe on page 103.

Jan's Spinach Soup

6 cups chicken broth
1 can cream of
    celery soup
3/4 soup can milk
1 tablespoon dried
    onion
1/2 teaspoon pepper

2 tablespoons
    parsley flakes
2 cups minute rice
1 10-ounce package
    frozen chopped
    spinach, thawed

Bring broth, soup, milk, onion, pepper and parsley flakes to a boil in saucepan. Add rice and spinach. Simmer, covered, for 5 minutes or until rice is tender. Yield: 8-10 servings.
Note: May substitute 1 1/2 cups cooked rice for minute rice.

Jan Abraham
Xi Delta Sigma, Los Gatos, California

Squash Casserole

1/2 green pepper,
    chopped
1 medium onion, chopped
1/2 stick margarine
2 cans squash, drained
1 can cream of
    mushroom soup

2 eggs, beaten
Salt and pepper
    to taste
Seasoned bread crumbs
2 tablespoons
    margarine

Saute green pepper and onion in margarine in skillet. Combine with squash and soup in bowl; mix well. Stir in eggs and seasonings. Pour into greased casserole. Sprinkle with bread crumbs. Dot with margarine. Bake at 350 degrees for 30 minutes. Yield: 4-6 servings.

Mariann Taylor
Delta Kappa, Ellisville, Mississippi

Squash Dressing

1/2 stick margarine,
    melted
1 package corn
    bread mix, prepared
1 can cream of
    celery soup

4 medium yellow
    squash, sliced,
    cooked
1 large onion, chopped
Salt to taste

Mix margarine and crumbled corn bread in bowl. Stir in soup, squash, onion and salt. Pour into greased 9 x 13-inch baking dish. Bake at 350 degrees until golden brown.
Yield: 10 servings.

Dorothy Gilley
Alpha Omega Omicron, Azle, Texas

Squash Puffs

1 cup mashed cooked
    yellow squash
1 egg, beaten
1/3 cup flour
1/3 cup cornmeal

1 teaspoon
    baking powder
1/2 teaspoon salt
1 medium onion, grated
Oil for frying

Combine squash and egg in bowl; mix well. Stir in mixture of flour, cornmeal, baking powder and salt. Add onion; mix well. Drop by tablespoonfuls into hot oil in skillet. Cook until golden brown.

Elizabeth Walden
Laureate Eta, Warner Robins, Georgia

Sweet Potatoes Deluxe

1 17-ounce can sweet
    potatoes, drained
3 tablespoons honey
1/2 teaspoon salt
1 teaspoon cinnamon

3 tablespoons butter,
    melted
Miniature marshmallows
1/2 cup chopped pecans

Beat sweet potatoes in mixer bowl until light. Add honey, salt, cinnamon and butter; mix well. Spread half the mixture in greased 8-inch square baking dish. Top with marshmallows. Sprinkle with pecans. Spoon remaining sweet potato mixture over top. Cover with marshmallows. Bake, covered, at 375 degrees for 15 minutes. Bake, uncovered, for 5 to 10 minutes longer or until marshmallows are golden. Yield: 6 servings.

Phyllis A. Wallace
Xi Tau Phi, Canyon Lake, Texas

Vegetables

Sweet Potato Casserole

3 medium sweet
 potatoes, cooked,
 mashed
1/2 cup margarine
1 cup sugar
2 eggs, beaten
1/2 cup milk

1 teaspoon vanilla
 extract
1 cup packed
 brown sugar
1/2 cup flour
1/3 cup margarine,
 softened

Combine hot sweet potatoes and 1/2 cup margarine in bowl; stir until margarine is melted. Stir in sugar, eggs, milk and vanilla. Spoon into greased casserole. Mix brown sugar and flour in bowl. Cut in 1/3 cup margarine until crumbly. Sprinkle over sweet potato mixture. Bake at 350 degrees for 25 minutes or until firm. Yield: 12 servings.

Buena Snellgrove
Xi Alpha Psi, New Brockton, Alabama

Tomato and Basil Fettucini

1/4 cup chopped onion
1 clove of garlic,
 minced
1/4 cup olive oil
1 28-ounce can
 peeled tomatoes
1 teaspoon salt

1/2 teaspoon pepper
6 fresh basil
 leaves, chopped
1 12-ounce package
 fettucini, cooked
Parmesan cheese (opt.)

Saute onion and garlic in oil in medium skillet until onion is tender. Do not brown. Chop tomatoes into small pieces; reserve liquid. Add tomatoes, tomato liquid, salt, pepper and basil to skillet. Bring to a boil over medium heat; reduce heat. Simmer for 15 minutes, stirring occasionally. Combine hot fettucini with tomato-basil sauce in large serving dish. Toss until coated. Garnish with Parmesan cheese.
Yield: 4-6 servings.

Photograph for this recipe on page 103.

Cheesy Tomato Soup

2 packages Hickory
 Farms tomato
 soup mix

1/2 cup chopped
 Cheddar cheese

Bring soup mix and 5 cups water to a boil in saucepan; reduce heat. Add cheese. Simmer until heated through, stirring frequently. Yield: 4 servings.

Kathy Berndtson
Xi, Honolulu, Hawaii

Baked Zucchini with Cheese

3 medium zucchini
1/2 teaspoon salt
1/4 teaspoon paprika

1/2 cup shredded
 mozzarella cheese
1/8 teaspoon paprika

Slice zucchini 1/2 inch thick. Place in 8-inch square baking dish. Sprinkle with salt and paprika; toss gently. Bake at 350 degrees for 30 minutes or until tender, stirring occasionally. Sprinkle with cheese and paprika. Bake for 2 minutes longer or until cheese melts. Yield: 4 servings.

Fay Voove
Xi Zeta Omega, Glendale, California

Zucchini Skillet Dish

1 green pepper, chopped
1 onion, chopped
1 tablespoon oil
3 tomatoes, chopped

1 zucchini, cut into
 1-inch pieces
Italian spices
 to taste

Saute green pepper and onion in oil in skillet. Stir in remaining ingredients. Cook, covered, over low heat for 15 minutes. Cook, uncovered, until zucchini is tender.

Elizabeth E. Heltzel
Xi Delta Upsilon, Warren, Ohio

Stuff

1 head cabbage,
 chopped
6 carrots, sliced
1 can peas
1 can whole kernel corn

1 head cauliflower,
 chopped
1 large onion, sliced
4 to 6 slices
 American cheese

Layer vegetables in skillet in order listed. Arrange cheese over top. Simmer over medium heat until vegetables are tender and cheese is melted. Yield: 10 servings.
Note: Add 1/4 cup water if necessary.

Judy Williams
Xi Zeta Epsilon, Noblesville, Indiana

Vegetable Hot Dish

1 4-ounce can
 mushrooms, drained
1 8-ounce can green
 beans, drained
1 16-ounce can
 whole tomatoes

3 or 4 slices
 bacon,
 chopped
1 medium onion,
 chopped

Combine mushrooms, green beans and tomatoes in saucepan. Simmer for 15 minutes. Fry bacon with onion in skillet. Pour over vegetables in serving dish. Yield: 4-5 servings.

Irene Elter
Preceptor Beta, Mandan, North Dakota

Side Dishes

Creamed Medley

1 package frozen
    sliced carrots
1 package frozen
    cauliflower
1 package frozen
    green peas
1 can cream of
    chicken soup

1/4 cup chopped parsley
1 tablespoon instant
    minced onion
1/2 teaspoon salt
1 cup shredded
    sharp Cheddar
    cheese

Place vegetables in large bowl. Let stand until partially thawed. Combine soup, parsley, onion and salt in bowl; mix well. Stir in vegetables. Pour into 1 1/2-quart casserole. Bake at 400 degrees for 35 minutes. Stir gently. Sprinkle cheese over top. Bake for several minutes longer or until cheese melts.

JoAnn J. Kresky
Preceptor Chi, Lansing, Michigan

Mixed Vegetable Casserole

1 20-ounce package
    frozen mixed
    vegetables
Cream
1/3 cup melted butter
1/4 cup (heaping) flour
Pinch each of
    nutmeg, thyme

1 1/2 teaspoons salt
1 cup grated
    sharp cheese
2 tablespoons
    white wine
Bread cubes
3 to 6 tablespoons
    butter, melted

Pour 1 1/4 cups hot water over vegetables in bowl. Let stand for 5 minutes; drain, reserving liquid. Mix liquid with enough cream to measure 2 cups. Combine 1/3 cup butter and flour in saucepan. Stir in cream mixture and seasonings. Cook until mixture begins to thicken, stirring constantly. Stir in cheese. Cook until thickened, stirring constantly. Mix in wine. Pour over vegetables in 9 x 11-inch baking pan. Cover with bread cubes. Drizzle with 3 to 6 tablespoons butter. Bake at 350 degrees for 30 to 45 minutes or until hot and bubbly. Yield: 12 servings.

Reva J. Falk
Preceptor Theta, Tucson, Arizona

Side Dishes

Chili Pie

1 16-ounce can chili
    without beans
1 8-ounce package
    corn chips

1 small onion, chopped
1/2 pound American
    cheese, grated

Layer half the chili, corn chips, onion and remaining chili in greased 1 1/2-quart casserole. Sprinkle cheese over top. Bake at 350 degrees for 30 minutes.

Blanche Bourge
Preceptor Delta, Sulphur, Louisiana

Aggie's Corn Bread Dressing

1 recipe corn bread,
    baked
6 biscuits
3 tablespoons
    chopped onion
1 1/2 cups chopped
    celery
1 egg, beaten

1/3 cup melted butter
1 teaspoon salt
1/4 teaspoon pepper
1/4 teaspoon
    poultry seasoning
Sage to taste
Broth

Crumble corn bread and biscuits in large bowl. Add onion, celery, egg, butter and seasonings; mix well. Stir in enough broth to moisten. Spoon into casserole. Bake at 350 degrees for 40 to 45 minutes or until brown. Yield: 6-8 servings.

Sarah M. Singleton
Xi Omega, Bowling Green, Kentucky

Creamy Stuffed Eggs

12 hard-boiled eggs
1 3-ounce package
    cream cheese,
    softened
3 tablespoons
    mayonnaise

1/2 teaspoon prepared
    mustard
1/4 teaspoon instant
    chicken bouillon
12 pimento-stuffed
    olives, cut in half

Slice eggs in half lengthwise. Mash egg yolks in bowl. Mix in cream cheese, mayonnaise, mustard and bouillon. Fill egg whites with yolk mixture. Top each with olive half. Yield: 12 servings.

Ann H. Westland
Brunswick, Missouri

Side Dishes

Cajun Cheese Grits

1 1/2 cups grits
1 1/2 tablespoons
  seasoned salt
3/4 cup margarine
3/4 pound Velveeta
  cheese, grated

1/2 teaspoon
  garlic powder
3 eggs, beaten
2 or 3 jalapeno
  peppers, finely
  chopped

Stir grits into 6 cups boiling salted water. Cook until water is absorbed, stirring frequently. Stir in remaining ingredients. Pour into greased casserole. Bake at 350 degrees for 30 to 35 minutes or until set. Yield: 15 servings.

Margareta J. Miles
Alpha Omega Omicron, Azle, Texas

Fettucini Alfredo

1 pint heavy cream
1 stick margarine
2 eggs, beaten
1/2 cup grated
  Italian cheese

1/2 cup parsley
Pinch of garlic powder
1 16-ounce package
  fettucini, cooked

Combine heavy cream and margarine in saucepan. Cook over low heat until margarine is melted. Do not boil. Stir a small amount of hot cream into eggs. Stir eggs, cheese, parsley and garlic powder into hot cream. Pour sauce over hot fettucini in serving dish; toss lightly.

Ida Damesimo
Xi Beta, Fayetteville, New York

Vermont Macaroni and Cheese Supreme

1/2 green pepper,
  chopped
1 medium onion,
  chopped
3 to 4 tablespoons
  butter
2 tablespoons flour
1 3/4 cups milk
Salt and pepper
  to taste

10 ounces extra
  sharp Cheddar
  cheese, grated
1 egg, beaten
2 cups macaroni,
  cooked
2 slices bread,
  crumbled
2 tablespoons butter,
  melted

Saute green pepper and onion in butter in skillet. Stir in flour, milk, salt and pepper. Add cheese. Cook until cheese melts, stirring constantly. Stir in egg. Combine with macaroni in 2-quart casserole. Sprinkle with bread crumbs. Drizzle melted butter over top. Bake at 350 degrees until brown. Yield: 6 servings.

Jane T. White
Xi Alpha, Colchester, Vermont

Homemade Macaroni and Cheese

2 tablespoons butter
2 tablespoons flour
2 cups milk
1/2 pound Cheddar
  cheese, grated

2 cups macaroni,
  cooked
1/2 pound Cheddar
  cheese, sliced

Blend butter and flour in saucepan. Add milk gradually, stirring constantly. Cook until thickened, stirring constantly. Stir in grated cheese. Combine with macaroni in casserole. Arrange sliced cheese on top. Bake at 350 degrees for about 15 minutes or until cheese is melted.

Krista Mikesell
Eta Alpha, Quincy, California

Scalloped Pineapple

2 tablespoons flour
1 20-ounce can
  crushed pineapple

3 eggs
1 cup sugar

Stir flour into pineapple and juice in bowl. Beat eggs with sugar in mixer bowl until thick. Add to pineapple; mix well. Spoon into greased 2-quart casserole. Bake at 350 degrees for 1 hour. Serve with ham.

Diann Androw
Laureate Alpha Mu, Mansfield, Ohio

Carol's Pineapple Scallop

1 cup melted
  margarine
2 cups sugar
3 eggs

4 cups bread cubes
1 29-ounce can
  crushed pineapple
1/4 cup milk

Combine margarine, sugar and eggs in baking dish; mix well. Top with bread cubes, pineapple and milk. Bake at 325 degrees for 1 hour.

Carol Glaeser
Preceptor Gamma Upsilon, Gladstone, Missouri

Anita's Dirty Rice

1 can onion soup
1 small can
  mushroom pieces
1 cup minute rice

Salt and pepper
  to taste
1 stick margarine,
  melted

Combine soup, mushrooms, rice, seasonings and margarine in bowl; mix gently. Pour into 1-quart casserole. Bake, covered, at 350 degrees for 1 hour. Yield: 4 servings.

Anita M. Wilson
Laureate Alpha Mu, Mansfield, Ohio

Side Dishes

Brown Rice

1 1/2 cups rice
1 stick margarine
2 cans beef consomme

1 clove of garlic,
finely chopped

Brown rice lightly in margarine in heavy skillet, stirring occasionally. Pour into casserole. Add consomme and garlic; mix gently. Bake, covered, at 350 degrees for 1 hour, stirring occasionally. Yield: 6-8 servings.

Wanda E. Dudley
Preceptor Pi, Albuquerque, New Mexico

Onion Rice

1 cup rice
1 envelope dry
onion soup mix

1 tablespoon butter,
melted

Combine rice and soup mix in bowl. Pour into casserole. Stir in butter and 2 1/2 cups boiling water. Bake at 425 degrees for about 25 minutes or until water is absorbed.

Marty Courville
Preceptor Pi, Reno, Nevada

Rice Pilaf

1 medium onion, chopped
1 clove of garlic,
minced
1 stick margarine
1 cup brown rice

1 teaspoon salt
1/2 teaspoon oregano
1 can beef consomme
1 4-ounce can
mushrooms

Saute onion and garlic in margarine in skillet. Add rice. Cook until lightly browned, stirring frequently. Spoon into 2-quart casserole. Stir in remaining ingredients and 1 consomme can water. Bake at 350 degrees for 1 1/2 hours. Yield: 6 servings.

Ireene C. Fournier
Preceptor Theta Beta, Dallas, Texas

Estelle's Rice Pilaf

1 4-ounce can
mushrooms
1 stick margarine,
melted
1 cup rice
1 can consomme
Pinch of salt

Pepper to taste
2 tablespoons
onion flakes
1 tablespoon
parsley flakes
2 tablespoons
Worcestershire sauce

Drain mushrooms, reserving liquid. Combine margarine, mushrooms, rice and consomme in 1-quart casserole. Combine reserved mushroom liquid with enough water to fill consomme can. Pour into casserole; stir gently. Sprinkle remaining ingredients over top. Bake, covered, at 350 degrees for 1 hour.

Estelle D. Seachrist
Preceptor Alpha Kappa, Fishersville, Virginia

Lemon Pilaf

1/3 cup sliced celery
1/3 cup sliced green
onions and tops
2 teaspoons butter
1 cup rice, cooked

1 teaspoon grated
lemon rind
1/4 teaspoon salt
Dash of pepper

Saute celery and green onions in butter in skillet over medium heat until tender. Do not brown. Stir in remaining ingredients. Cook over low heat until heated through.

Photograph for this recipe on page 104.

Special Rice Pilaf

1 cup rice
1/4 cup slivered
almonds
1/4 cup butter
1/8 to 1/4 teaspoon
saffron
1 teaspoon salt

1 1/2 cups chicken
broth
1/2 cup dry Sherry
Chopped green pepper
Chopped green onion
Sliced mushrooms

Brown rice and almonds in butter in skillet. Cook until butter is absorbed. Add seasonings and liquids; mix well. Pour into greased baking dish. Bake, covered, at 325 degrees for 1 hour. Add 1/4 cup additional broth if necessary. Stir in vegetables. Bake for 15 minutes longer.

Tinka Piper
Xi, Honolulu, Hawaii

Quicky Rice Casserole

1 can cream of
mushroom soup
1/2 stick butter,
melted

1 can beef broth
1 cup rice
1 4-ounce can
mushrooms

Combine soup, butter and broth in bowl; mix well. Stir in rice and mushrooms. Pour into 2-quart casserole. Bake at 350 degrees for 1 1/2 hours, stirring once. Yield: 8 servings.

Debbie Olmstead
Psi, Jerome, Idaho

Index
of Contributors

Index

Index

Index

PHOTOGRAPHY CREDITS

The Dow Chemical Company, makers of SARAN WRAP^TM brand plastic film; General Foods; Idaho Potatoes; Spanish Green Olive Commission; Pam No-Stick Cooking Spray; Argo and Kingsford's Cornstarch; San Giorgio Skinner Company; The Rice Council; California Avocado Advisory Board; The McIlhenney Company; Olive Administrative Committee; Processed Apples Institute, Inc.; American Spice Trade Association; National Dairy Council; Northwest Cherry Growers; Sunkist Growers, Inc.; The Quaker Oats Company; United Fresh Fruit and Vegetable Association; The Nestle Company; Hershey Foods Corporation; California Strawberry Advisory Board; Campbell Soup Company; Pickle Packers International, Inc.; Evaporated Milk Association; National Live Stock and Meat Board; International Shrimp Council; General Foods; Coco Ribe; and Florida Celery Commission.

Index

Index

Index

Index

Index

Index

Index

Beta Sigma Phi Cookbooks

available from *Favorite Recipes Press* are chock-full of mouth-watering, home-tested recipes that earn you the best compliment of all..."More Please!"

Every cookbook includes:

- 128 to 232 pages
- 300 to 500 delicious family-pleasing recipes
- color and black-and-white photos
- lie-flat binding
- wipe-clean color covers
- easy-to-read format
- comprehensive index

To place your order, call our **toll free** number
1-800-251-1520
(In Tennessee call collect **1-615-790-4256**) or clip and mail the convenient form below.

☐ **YES.** Please send me the cookbooks I've checked below. I understand that if I'm not completely delighted I may return any book within 30 days for a full refund.

BETA SIGMA PHI COOKBOOKS	Item #	Qty.	Retail Price	Total
The Cook Quick Cookbook	65889		$12.95	
All-Occasion Casseroles Cookbook With Menus	28029		4.50	
Desserts and Party Foods Cookbook	25275		4.50	
The Golden Anniversary Cookbook	13706		5.95	
The Dining Room	13595		5.95	
Recipes From The World of Beta Sigma Phi	13692		5.95	
Dieting to Stay Healthy	13684		5.95	
Gourmet Cookbook	13617		5.95	
Party Book	13668		5.95	
Save & Win	13676		5.95	
Bicentennial Heritage Recipes	13560		5.95	
Shipping and Handling	36579	1	$ .95	$ .95
TOTAL AMOUNT				

☐ Payment Enclosed.
☐ Please Charge My: ☐ Visa ☐ MasterCard
  Account Number _____
  Signature _____

Name _____

Chapter Name _____

Chapter Number _____

Address _____

City _____ State _____ Zip _____

Daytime Phone (___)_____

No COD orders, please.

Call our **toll free** number for return information.

Prices subject to change without notice.

Books offered subject to availability.

Please allow 30 days for delivery.

Mail completed order form to:

Favorite Recipes Press

P. O. Box 1408
Nashville Tennessee 37202